REED'S MATHEMATICS
FOR ENGINEERS

REED'S MATHEMATICS FOR ENGINEERS

WILLIAM EMBLETON OBE
CEng, FIMarE, MIMechE
Extra First Class Engineers' Certificate

Revised by
LESLIE JACKSON
BSc, MA, CEng, FIMarE, FRINA
Extra First Class Engineers' Certificate

ADLARD COLES NAUTICAL
London

Published by Adlard Coles Nautical
an imprint of A & C Black Publishers Ltd
37 Soho Square, London W1D 3QZ
www.adlardcoles.com

First edition published by Thomas Reed Publications 1961
Reprinted 1965
Second edition 1969
Third edition 1973
Fourth edition 1976
Reprinted 1979
Fifth edition 1980
Sixth edition 1988
Reprinted 1991
Seventh edition 1997
Reprinted by Adlard Coles Nautical 2003

ISBN 0-7136-6837-7

A CIP catalogue record for this book is available from the British Library.

A & C Black uses paper produced with elemental chlorine-free pulp,
harvested from managed sustainable forests

Printed and bound in Great Britain

Note: While all reasonable care has been taken in the publication of this
book, the publisher takes no responsibility for the use of the methods or
products described in the book.

PREFACE

This book covers the syllabus in Mathematics for the Marine Engineer Officer Certificates of Competency in the Merchant Navy. The examinations are administered by the Scottish Vocational Education Council (SCOTVEC) on behalf of the Department of Transport (DTp). It will also be an invaluable aid to all students on Business and Technology Education Council (BTEC), SCOTVEC and City and Guilds of London Institute (CGLI) courses up to Certificate/Diploma level together with their related National, and Scottish, Vocational Qualifications (NVQ, etc).

Basic principles are dealt with, commencing at a fairly elementary stage. Each chapter has fully worked examples interwoven into the text, test examples are set at the end of each chapter, and finally there are some typical examination questions included. Non-programmable calculators may be used.

The author has gone beyond the normal practice of merely supplying bare answers to the test examples and examination questions by providing fully worked step by step solutions leading to the final answers.

This latest revision is a major update in the subject to take the material for study into the twenty-first century.

CONTENTS

CHAPTER   1–ARITHMETIC
Powers and roots. Surds. Ratio and proportion.
Method of unity. Variation. Percentage.
Constituent parts. Averages. Logarithms;
common, to different bases, natural (Naperian). ...   1–21

CHAPTER   2–ALGEBRA
Addition and subtraction, collection of terms,
powers and roots, multiplication and division.
Removal of brackets. Factorisation. Lowest
Common Multiple. Fractions. Remainder and
Factor theorems. Binomial theorem.   23–44

CHAPTER   3–SIMPLE EQUATIONS
Problems involving simple equations.
Transposition and evaluation of formulae.
Logarithmic equations.   45–58

CHAPTER   4–SIMULTANEOUS LINEAR EQUATIONS
Various methods of solving. Examples involving
two or three unknowns.   59–67

CHAPTER   5–QUADRATIC AND CUBIC EQUATIONS
Solutions by factorisation, completing the square,
and formula. Equations reducible to quadratics.
Simultaneous quadratics. Problems involving
quadratic equations. Cubic equations.   69–86

CHAPTER   6–GRAPHS
Plotting. Determining equation to straight line
graph. Graphical solution of simultaneous linear
and quadratic equations. Determination of laws.
Curve sketching.   87–107

CHAPTER   7–TRIGONOMETRY AND GEOMETRY
Measurement of angles. Trigonometric ratios.
Complementary and supplementary angles.
Theorem of Pythagoras. Identities. Reading
ratios. Angles greater than 90°. Graphical
representation. Latitude and longitude. Compass
bearings. Geometrical construction of triangles.
Some important geometrical facts. Crossed

chords. Cyclic triangles and quadrilaterals.
Circumscribed and inscribed circles. Similar
triangles. Congruent triangles.   109–142

CHAPTER   8–SOLUTION OF TRIANGLES
Ratios for right angled triangles. Triangles other
than right angled. Sine rule and cosine rule.
Areas of triangles. Equilateral and isosceles
triangles. Circumscribed and inscribed circles.
Compound and double angles.   143–164

CHAPTER   9–MENSURATION OF AREAS
Parallelogram, Rhombus. Trapezium. Triangles.
Polygons. Circle, sector and segment. Ellipse.
Surface areas of cylinder, sphere, cone and
frustum. Theorem of Pappus. Similar figures.
Irregular figures, Simpson's and mid-ordinate
rules.   165–189

CHAPTER   10–MENSURATION OF VOLUMES AND MASSES
Volume, mass, density and specific gravity.
Volumes of prisms, pyramids, frustums and the
sphere. Segment of a sphere. Theorem of Pappus
applied to volumes. Force, weight and centre of
gravity (mass). Applications. Similar solids.
Simpson's rule applied to volumes. Flow of liquid
through pipes and valves. First moments for
centre of gravity.   191–225

CHAPTER   11–DIFFERENTIAL CALCULUS
Gradient, zero gradient, gradient of a curve.
Differential coefficient, second differential
coefficient. Distance, velocity and acceleration.
Maxima and minima. Differential coefficient of
$\sin x$, $\cos x$, $\ln x$, e^x. Functional notation.   227–252

CHAPTER   12–INTEGRAL CALCULUS
Integration, constant of integration. Integration
of $\sin x$, $\cos x$, $1/x$, e^x. Area by integration.
Definite integral integration as a summation.
Volume of solid of revolution. Distance and
velocity by integration.   253–271

RULES AND FORMULAE
Selection of rules and formulae from the
Chapters.   273–278

CONTENTS

SOLUTIONS TO TEST EXAMPLES   279–399

A SELECTION OF EXAMINATION QUESTIONS   401–417

SOLUTIONS TO EXAMINATION QUESTIONS   419–491

INDEX   493–495

ARITHMETIC

POWERS

An index is a short method of expressing a quantity multiplied by itself a number of times, thus,

4×4 is written 4^2, this is the 'second power' of 4 commonly called the 'square' of 4.

$x \times x \times x$ is written x^3, this is the 'third power' of x commonly called the 'cube' of x.

$10 \times 10 \times 10 \times 10 \times 10 \times 10$ is written 10^6, and so on.

TO MULTIPLY POWERS OF THE SAME QUANTITY, add their indices, thus,

$$2^3 \times 2^4$$
$$\text{written right out} = 2 \times 2 \times 2 \times 2 \times 2 \times 2 \times 2$$
$$= 2^7$$

The same result is obtained by adding the indices 3 and 4.

$$2^3 \times 2^4$$
$$= 2^{3+4}$$
$$= 2^7$$

TO DIVIDE POWERS OF THE SAME QUANTITY, subtract their indices, thus,

$$3^5 \div 3^2$$
$$= \frac{3 \times 3 \times 3 \times 3 \times 3}{3 \times 3}$$
$$= 3 \times 3 \times 3$$
$$= 3^3$$

The same result is obtained by subtracting the indices,

$$3^5 \div 3^2$$
$$= 3^{5-2}$$
$$= 3^3$$

NEGATIVE INDICES

Consider the example $5^2 \div 5^6$

written right out

$$= \frac{5 \times 5}{5 \times 5 \times 5 \times 5 \times 5 \times 5}$$

$$= \frac{1}{5^4}$$

or, subtracting the indices,

$$5^{2-6}$$

$$= 5^{-4}$$

Hence a quantity with a negative index, in this case 5^{-4}, is equal to the reciprocal of that quantity with a positive index, that is,

$$5^{-4} = \frac{1}{5^4}$$

Similarly,

$$x^{-2} = \frac{1}{x^2}$$

$$10^{-3} = \frac{1}{10^3}$$

Likewise,

$$\frac{1}{x^{-3}} = x^3$$

$$\frac{1}{10^{-9}} = 10^9$$

POWER OF UNITY. Any quantity to a power of unity is the quantity itself, thus,

$$3^3 \div 3^2 = 3^{3-2} = 3^1$$

$$3^1 = 3$$

ZERO POWER. Any quantity to a power of zero is equal to unity, thus,

$$2^3 \div 2^3 = 2^{3-3} = 2^0$$

$$2^0 = 1$$

similarly, $x^2 \div x^2 = x^{2-2} = x^0$

$$x^0 = 1$$

TO RAISE A POWERED QUANTITY TO A FURTHER POWER, multiply their indices, thus,

$$(2^2)^3$$

written right out $\quad = 2^2 \times 2^2 \times 2^2$

$$= 2 \times 2 \times 2 \times 2 \times 2 \times 2$$

$$= 2^6$$

therefore $\quad\quad (2^2)^3$

$$= 2^{2 \times 3}$$

$$= 2^6$$

ROOTS

A root is the opposite of a power and the root symbol is $\sqrt{}$.

$^2\sqrt{}$ represents the 'square root' of a quantity and means that it is required to find the number which, when squared, will be equal to that quantity.

Thus, $^2\sqrt{25} = 5$ because 5^2 is 25.

$^3\sqrt{}$ represents the 'cube root' of a quantity, this means that it is required to find the number whose cube is equal to that quantity.

Thus, $^3\sqrt{27} = 3$ because $3^3 = 27$.

Similarly, $\quad\quad\quad\quad\quad\quad {}^4\sqrt{16} = 2$

$$^5\sqrt{243} = 3$$

The square root of a quantity is usually written without any figure indicating the root, thus the square root of 64 is usually written $\sqrt{64}$ instead of $^2\sqrt{64}$. The value of any other root must of course be clearly stated.

Another method of indicating a root of a quantity is by expressing it as a power equal to the reciprocal of the root, for example,

the square root of 49 may be written,

$\sqrt{49}$ or $49^{\frac{1}{2}}$, which is 7;

the cube root of 27 may be written,

$^3\sqrt{27}$ or $27^{\frac{1}{3}}$, which is 3;

the fourth root of x may be written,

$^4\sqrt{x}$ or $x^{\frac{1}{4}}$

The square of the cube root of 64 may be written,
$(^3\sqrt{64})^2$ or $64^{\frac{2}{3}}$, which is 16.

The root of a minus quantity is inadmissible.

POWERS AND ROOTS OF VULGAR FRACTIONS

The power or root of a vulgar fraction is equal to the power or root of the numerator divided by the power or root of the denominator.

$$\left(\frac{6}{2}\right)^2 = 3^2 = 9$$

or $$\frac{6^2}{2^2} = \frac{36}{4} = 9$$

$$\sqrt{\frac{64}{4}} = \sqrt{16} = 4$$

or $$\frac{\sqrt{64}}{\sqrt{4}} = \frac{8}{2} = 4$$

The advantage of applying the above rule will be seen in the following examples,

$$\left(\frac{3}{8}\right)^2 = \frac{3^2}{8^2} = \frac{9}{64}$$

$$\left(1\tfrac{1}{2}\right)^2 = \left(\frac{3}{2}\right)^2 = \frac{3^2}{2^2} = \frac{9}{4} = 2\tfrac{1}{4}$$

$$^3\sqrt{\frac{125}{27}} = \frac{^3\sqrt{125}}{^3\sqrt{27}} = \frac{5}{3} = 1\tfrac{2}{3}$$

SURDS

A root which does not work out exactly is termed a surd, such as:

$$\sqrt{2} = 1{\cdot}41421\ldots \text{etc.}$$

$$= 1{\cdot}414 \quad \text{to nearest four figures.}$$

Similarly, $\sqrt{3}$, $\sqrt{5}$, $\sqrt{6}$, are all surds.

It will be found very useful if, at least, the values of $\sqrt{2}$ and $\sqrt{3}$ to the nearest four figures, were committed to memory. Many useful manipulations can be performed easily and quickly when solving or simplifying expressions which include these quantities as factors,

Memorise:

$$\sqrt{2} = 1\cdot414$$
$$\sqrt{3} = 1\cdot732$$

Example:

$$\sqrt{18} = \sqrt{2} \times \sqrt{9}$$
$$= 1\cdot414 \times 3$$
$$= 4\cdot242 \quad \text{Ans.}$$

Example:

$$\frac{2 \times \sqrt{2}}{\sqrt{6}}$$

$$= \frac{2 \times \sqrt{2}}{\sqrt{2} \times \sqrt{3}} \quad \sqrt{2} \text{ cancels top and bottom}$$

$$= \frac{2}{\sqrt{3}} \quad \text{now multiply top and bottom by } \sqrt{3}$$

$$= \frac{2 \times \sqrt{3}}{\sqrt{3} \times \sqrt{3}} \quad \text{on the bottom line } \sqrt{3} \times \sqrt{3} = 3$$

$$= \frac{2 \times \sqrt{3}}{3}$$

$$= \frac{2 \times 1\cdot732}{3}$$

$$= \frac{3\cdot464}{3}$$

$$= 1\cdot155 \quad \text{(to nearest four figures)} \quad \text{Ans.}$$

RATIO

A ratio is a comparison of the magnitude of one quantity with another quantity of the same kind; it expresses the relationship of one to the other and therefore may be stated in fractional form. Being a means of comparison it is often convenient to express a ratio in terms of unity. The ratio sign is the colon:

Thus, if the lengths of two bars are 250 mm and 2 m respectively, the ratio of one to the other may be expressed,

    250 : 2000   (note both quantities must be expressed in the
or,   1 : 8   same units in this case both in mm)

or, the former is $\frac{1}{8}$ of the length of the latter.

Example. The mass of a solid shaft 300 mm diameter is 1200 kg. Another shaft is hollow, 300 mm outside diameter and 150 mm bore and of the same length as the solid shaft. If the mass of the hollow shaft is 900 kg, express the ratio of the mass of the hollow shaft to that of the solid shaft.

Ratio of masses, hollow : solid

900 : 1200

3 : 4

$\frac{3}{4}$: 1.   Ans.

PROPORTION

Proportion is an equation of ratios, that is, it expresses that the ratio of one pair of quantities is equal to the ratio of another pair. The proportion sign is the double colon : : but the equal sign may be used. For example, the ratio of 5 to 10 is equal to the ratio of 20 to 40, and this may be expressed,

5 : 10 :: 20 : 40

or,   5 : 10 = 20 : 40

or, $\dfrac{5}{10} = \dfrac{20}{40}$

It can also be seen that the two inside terms multiplied together is equal to the two outside terms multiplied together, thus,

$$10 \times 20 = 5 \times 40$$

this is sometimes expressed in the manner *the product of the means is equal to the product of the extremes*, and is a useful method to find that missing term when one of the terms is unknown.

Example. A pump takes 55 min to deliver 4400 l of water. Under similar conditions, how long would it take to deliver 6000 l?

Let x = time (in min) to deliver 6000 l,

Ratio of times taken :: Ratio of quantities delivered.

$$55 : x :: 4400 : 6000$$
$$x \times 4400 = 55 \times 6000$$
$$x = \frac{55 \times 6000}{4400}$$
$$x = 75 \text{ min} \quad \text{Ans.}$$

Example.   The ratio of the areas of two circles is equal to the ratio of the squares of their diameters. The diameter of one circle is 20 mm and its area is 314 mm^2, another circle is 30 mm diameter, find its area.

Let x represent the area of the second circle,

$$\text{Ratio of areas :: Ratio of diameters}^2$$
$$314 : x :: 20^2 : 30^2$$
$$314 : x :: 400 : 900$$
$$x \times 400 = 314 \times 900$$
$$x = \frac{314 \times 900}{400} = \frac{314 \times 9}{4}$$
$$x = 706 \cdot 5 \text{ mm}^2 \quad \text{Ans.}$$

INVERSE PROPORTION.   The above examples are cases of *direct* proportion because, in the pump question for instance, an *increase* in time of running results in an *increase* in quantity of water delivered, thus, the quantity of water delivered *varies directly* as the time. There are however, many cases where the increase in one quantity causes a *decrease* in another, this is *inverse* proportion where one quantity is stated to *vary inversely* as the other. Suppose one pump could empty a tank in 20 min then two similar pumps drawing from this tank could empty it in half the time, i.e., 10 min, or three pumps would do the work in one-third of the time. Here the *greater* the number of pumps, the *less* the time taken; the time *varies inversely* as the number of pumps. In setting down such a problem by the proportion method, one of the pairs of ratios must be reversed.

METHOD OF UNITY

It is often more convenient to apply the method of unity to proportion problems, especially when dealing with compound proportion in which there are more than two pairs of quantities. The following examples demonstrate working by this method.

Example.   If 8 men can erect 2 engines in 18 d, how long would it take 12 men, working at the same rate, to erect 5 similar engines?

Time for 8 men to erect 2 engines $= 18$ d

Time for 1 man to erect 2 engines $= 18 \times 8$ d

Time for 1 man to erect 1 engine $= \dfrac{18 \times 8}{2}$

Time for 12 men to erect 1 engine $= \dfrac{18 \times 8}{2 \times 12}$

Time for 12 men to erect 5 engines $= \dfrac{18 \times 8 \times 5}{2 \times 12}$

$= 30$ d   Ans.

Example.   A general service pump can pump out a tank in 10 h and the ballast pump can pump out the same tank in 5 h. If both pumps are working together, how long will it take to empty the tank?

Quantity pumped by G.S. pump in 10 h $=$ whole tank

Quantity pumped by G.S. pump in 1 h $= \frac{1}{10}$ of tank

Quantity pumped by ballast pump in 5 h $=$ whole tank

Quantity pumped by ballast pump in 1 h $= \frac{1}{5}$ of tank

Quantity pumped in 1 h by both pumps working together

$= \frac{1}{10} + \frac{1}{5}$ of the tank

$= \frac{3}{10}$ of the tank

$\therefore$ Time to empty $= \frac{10}{3}$ h

$= 3\frac{1}{3}$ h   Ans.

VARIATION

Variation is a further step in ratio and proportion. As previously explained, when an increase of one quantity depends upon the increase of another, one is said to *vary directly* as the other; when an increase in one quantity depends upon the decrease of another, one is said to *vary inversely* as the other. The variation sign is α, thus, if the cost of casting a propeller varies as its mass, this may be written:

$$\text{cost} \propto \text{mass}$$

and, if the time to travel a certain distance varies inversely as the speed, this may be written:

$$\text{time} \propto \frac{1}{\text{speed}}$$

Taking a simple numerical example on the first case: The cost of a propeller of 2 t mass is £800, the cost of another propeller of 3 t mass is £1200,

1st propeller, $\quad \dfrac{\text{cost}}{\text{mass}} = \dfrac{800}{2} = £400/t$

2nd propeller, $\quad \dfrac{\text{cost}}{\text{mass}} = \dfrac{1200}{3} = £400/t$

hence, $\quad \dfrac{\text{cost}}{\text{mass}} = \text{a constant amount}$

therefore, $\quad \dfrac{\text{cost}_1}{\text{mass}_1} = \dfrac{\text{cost}_2}{\text{mass}_2}$

For the second case take the example: A train travels a certain distance in 5 h when travelling at an average speed of 60 km/h; another train takes 4 h over the same journey travelling at an average speed of 75 km/h.

1st train, speed × time = 5 × 60 = 300 km

2nd train, speed × time = 4 × 75 = 300 km

hence, $\quad$ speed × time = a constant (distance)

therefore, speed$_1$ × time$_1$ = speed$_2$ × time$_2$

Summing up, (i) when one quantity varies directly as another, their *quotient* is constant; (ii) when one quantity varies inversely as another, their *product* is constant.

Example.   Within a certain range, the power of an engine varies directly as the mass/h of fuel burned. An engine uses 180 kg/h of fuel when the power developed is 800 kW, what will be the fuel consumption when the power is 900 kW?

$$\text{fuel/h} \propto \text{power}$$

$$\therefore \frac{\text{fuel/h}}{\text{power}} = \text{a constant}$$

$$\therefore \frac{\text{fuel}_1}{\text{power}_1} = \frac{\text{fuel}_2}{\text{power}_2}$$

$$\frac{180}{800} = \frac{\text{fuel}_2}{900}$$

$$\therefore \text{fuel}_2 = \frac{180 \times 900}{800}$$

$$= 202 \cdot 5 \text{ kg/h} \quad \text{Ans.}$$

Example.   If a gas is maintained at the same temperature its pressure varies inversely as its volume. 6 m³ of gas at atmospheric pressure is compressed until its pressure is four times as much, the temperature remaining unaltered, find the volume of the compressed gas.

$$\text{pressure} \propto \frac{1}{\text{volume}}$$

$$\text{pressure} \times \text{volume} = \text{a constant}$$

$$\therefore p_1 \times V_1 = p_2 \times V_2$$

$$1 \times 6 = 4 \times V_2$$

$$V_2 = \frac{1 \times 6}{4}$$

$$V_2 = 1 \cdot 5 \text{ m}^3 \quad \text{Ans.}$$

Example.   The resistance of a conducting wire varies directly as its length and inversely as its cross-sectional area. A wire 100 m long and 1 mm^2 cross-sectional area has a resistance of 2 Ω, what would be the resistance of a wire of similar material 250 m long and 0·5 mm^2 cross-sectional area?

$$\text{resistance} \propto \text{length}$$

also, $$\text{resistance} \propto \frac{1}{\text{area}}$$

$$\therefore \quad \frac{\text{resistance} \times \text{area}}{\text{length}} = \text{a constant}$$

$$\frac{R_1 \times A_1}{l_1} = \frac{R_2 \times A_2}{l_2}$$

$$\frac{2 \times 1}{100} = \frac{R_2 \times 0.5}{250}$$

$$R_2 = \frac{2 \times 1 \times 250}{0.5 \times 100}$$

$$R_2 = 10 \ \Omega \quad \text{Ans.}$$

PERCENTAGE

Percentage is another method of expressing a ratio in fractional form, using 100 as the denominator, and substituting the denominator of 100 with the percentage symbol %.

Thus, the ratio of 4 to 25

can be written $\dfrac{4}{25}$ in fractional form

which is equal to $\dfrac{16}{100}$ on a denominator of 100

and written 16% in percentage form.

Since a fraction is part of unity, and a percentage is part of one hundred, a fraction is converted into a percentage by multiplying the fraction by 100. Conversely, a percentage is converted into a fraction by dividing by 100. Thus:

$$\tfrac{1}{2} = 50\%$$

$$\tfrac{1}{3} = 33\tfrac{1}{3}\%$$

$$\tfrac{3}{8} = 37\tfrac{1}{2}\%$$

To express percentage increase or percentage decrease:

$$\% \text{ increase} = \frac{\text{total increase}}{\text{original amount}} \times 100$$

$$\% \text{ decrease} = \frac{\text{total decrease}}{\text{original amount}} \times 100$$

Example. (i) A spring of original length 80 mm, is stretched to a length of 100 mm, what is the percentage increase in length?
(ii) Another spring of original length 100 mm, is compressed to a length of 80 mm, what is the percentage decrease in length?

(i)   actual increase = 20 mm

$$\% \text{ increase} = \frac{20}{80} \times 100$$

$$= 25 \quad \text{Ans. (i)}$$

(ii) actual decrease = 20 mm

$$\% \text{ decrease} = \frac{20}{100} \times 100$$

$$= 20 \quad \text{Ans. (ii)}$$

Example.   The ratio of the mass of engine A to engine B is 5 to 3. Find (i) by what percentage is A heavier than B, (ii) by what percentage B is lighter than A.

$$\text{Difference} = 5 - 3 = 2$$

(i) % increase of A over B $= \dfrac{2}{3} \times 100 = 66\tfrac{2}{3}$

∴ A is $66\tfrac{2}{3}$% heavier than B   Ans. (i)

(ii) % decrease of B over A $= \dfrac{2}{5} \times 100 = 40$

∴ B is 40% lighter than A   Ans. (ii)

CONSTITUENT PARTS

The parts which constitute a whole, such as the quantities of metals mixed together to form an alloy, may be expressed in the form of ratios, fractions or percentages, and it is often convenient to convert one form into another when solving problems. Consider a brass consisting of two parts copper and one part zinc, in every 3 g of brass there will be 2 g of copper and 1 g of zinc, therefore two-thirds (i.e. $66\frac{2}{3}\%$) of the total mass of the brass is copper and the remaining one-third (i.e. $33\frac{1}{3}\%$) is zinc. Hence to convert ratio of parts into fractional amounts, add the ratios together to produce a common denominator, and then each ratio forms its own respective numerator. The fractions are multiplied by 100 to convert them into percentages.

Example. A fusible metal is composed of 5 parts bismuth, 3 parts lead and 2 parts tin. Express this ratio as fractional quantities and percentages, and find the mass of each element required to produce 1·5 kg of fusible metal.

Ratio, bismuth : lead : tin $= 5 : 3 : 2$

Sum of ratios $= 5 + 3 + 2 = 10$

$\therefore$ mass of bismuth $= \frac{5}{10} = \frac{1}{2} = 50\%$ of total mass ⎫

mass of lead $= \frac{3}{10} = 30\%$ of total mass ⎬ Ans

mass of tin $= \frac{2}{10} = \frac{1}{5} = 20\%$ of total mass ⎭

To produce 1·5 kg $= 1500$ g of metal:

mass of bismuth $= \frac{1}{2} \times 1500 = 750$ g ⎫

mass of lead $= \frac{3}{10} \times 1500 = 450$ g ⎬ Ans

mass of tin $= \frac{1}{5} \times 1500 = 300$ g ⎭

mass of fusible metal $=$ sum $= 1500$ g.

Example. In a certain two-cylinder engine, the power developed in No. 1 cylinder is 20% more than the power developed in No. 2 cylinder. What percentage of the total power of the engine is developed in each cylinder?

Ratio of powers, No.1 : No. 2

$= 120 : 100$

$= 1\cdot2 : 1$

Sum of ratios $= 1\cdot2 + 1 = 2\cdot2$

∴ percentage of total power developed in No. 1 cylinder

$$= \frac{1 \cdot 2}{2 \cdot 2} \times 100 = 54 \cdot 55 \quad \text{Ans.}$$

∴ percentage of total power developed in No. 2 cylinder

$$= \frac{1}{2 \cdot 2} \times 100 = 45 \cdot 45 \quad \text{Ans.}$$

Example.   Of the total heat in the fuel burned in the cylinders of a diesel engine, 40% is converted into indicated power, 30% is carried away by the cooling water, 2% is lost by radiation, and the remainder is carried away in the exhaust gases. (i) What percentage of the total heat of the fuel does the heat in the exhaust gases represent? (ii) If 80% of the indicated power is usefully imparted to the crankshaft as brake power and the remainder lost in friction, what percentage of the total heat of the fuel does the brake power represent? (iii) If 40% of the heat in the exhaust gases is recovered in an exhaust gas boiler and the remainder carried away up the stack, what percentage of the total heat in the fuel is recovered in the boiler?

The full amount of heat in the fuel is represented by 100%.

Heat converted to ip = 40%

Heat carried away in cooling water = 30%

Radiation loss = 2%
___

total = 72%

Remainder = 100 − 72 = 28

∴ Exhaust gases carry away 28% of the total heat   Ans. (i)

$$\text{bp} = 80\% \text{ of } 40\%$$
$$= \frac{8}{10} \text{ of } 40\%$$
$$= 32\%$$

Heat equivalent of bp = 32%   Ans. (ii)

(Friction loss represents $40 - 32 = 8\%$ of the total heat)

Recovery in boiler $= 40\%$ of 28%

$$= \frac{4}{10} \text{ of } 28\%$$

$$= 11 \cdot 2\% \quad \text{Ans. (iii)}$$

(Heat carried away up the stack $= 28 - 11 \cdot 2 = 16 \cdot 8\%$)

A 'heat-balance' diagram can now be drawn to illustrate the distribution of the heat in the fuel:

Fig. 1

AVERAGES

The average (or *mean*) value of a group of collected quantities is obtained by dividing the total of the quantities by the number of quantities in the group.

Example. The distances covered by a ship on four successive days were 320, 300, 310 and 330 naut. miles respectively. Find the average day's run.

$$\text{Average day's run} = \frac{\text{total distance}}{\text{total number of days}}$$

$$= \frac{320 + 300 + 310 + 330}{4}$$

$$= \frac{1260}{4}$$

$$= 315 \text{ naut. miles.} \quad \text{Ans.}$$

Example. A ship travels a distance of 15 naut. miles up-river against the current, in 72 min, and then 15 naut. miles down-river with the current, in 50 min.

Find   (i) the average speed up-river;

(ii) the average speed down-river;

(iii) the average speed over the double journey.

$$\text{Speed} = \frac{\text{distance}}{\text{time}}$$

$$\text{Speed up-river} = 15 \text{ naut. miles} \div \frac{72}{60} \text{ h}$$

$$= \frac{15 \times 60}{72}$$

$$= 12\tfrac{1}{2} \text{ naut. miles/h}$$

$$= 12\tfrac{1}{2} \text{ knot} \quad \text{Ans. (i)}$$

$$\text{Speed down-river} = 15 \text{ naut. miles} \div \frac{50}{60} \text{ h}$$

$$= \frac{15 \times 60}{50}$$

$$= 18 \text{ naut. miles/h}$$

$$= 18 \text{ knot} \quad \text{Ans. (ii)}$$

Average speed over the double journey

$$= \frac{\text{total distance}}{\text{total time}}$$

$$= 30 \text{ naut. miles} \div \frac{122}{60} \text{ h}$$

$$= \frac{30 \times 60}{122}$$

$$= 14 \cdot 75 \text{ knot} \quad \text{Ans. (iii)}$$

The above example illustrates speed being obtained by dividing distance by time. Units of speed are usually expressed in km/h, or m/s.

Speeds of ships and aircraft are usually measured in knots (naut. miles/h). One international nautical mile is equal to 1·852 km.

It is important to note how essential it it to divide one total by another total to obtain an average. In the last example, total distance was divided by total time to obtain the average speed over the double journey, it would be wrong to take the average of the average speeds up and down river.

LOGARITHMS

Calculators have replaced logarithms (and slide rules) for numerical calculations. However there are cases where logarithms still apply in mathematics and in technological applications (see examples in later chapters).

The logarithm (log) of a number to a given base is the power to which the base must be raised to be equal to that number.

$2^3 = 8$, in this case, 3 is the logarithm of 8 to the base of 2, and would be written $\log_2 8 = 3$. $x^n = N$, this represents n as the logarithm of N to the base of x, and would be written $\log_x N = n$.

The whole number part of the logarithm is called the *characteristic* and can be positive or negative; the decimal part is called the *mantissa* and is positive. Values can be read off a table of logarithms. Antilogarithm tables (if used) are the reverse to log tables and can be used to read off the number corresponding to the given logarithm. Log and antilog values are directly obtainable by the use of a suitable scientific calculator.

The rules for using logarithms are the same as those for other indices, hence,

(i) to multiply numbers, add their logarithms,

$$\log(x \times y) = \log x + \log y$$

(ii) to divide numbers, subtract their logarithms,

$$\log(x \div y) = \log x - \log y$$

(iii) to raise a number to a power, multiply the logarithm of the number by the power,

$$\log(x^m) = (\log x) \times m$$

(iv) to extract a root of a number, divide the logarithm of the number by the root,

$$\log \sqrt[m]{x} = (\log x) \div m$$

the resultant, in each case, is the logarithm of the answer.

COMMON LOGARITHMS (lg)

Are logs to base 10.

e.g. lg of 5 to base 10 is $0 \cdot 6990$ because $10^{0 \cdot 6990} = 5$

lg of $400 \cdot 0 = 1 \cdot 6021$

lg of $0 \cdot 006 = \bar{3} \cdot 7782$ (bar three, $\bar{3}$, is -3)

also lg of $0 \cdot 006 = -2 \cdot 2218$ (as a minus number)

RELATION BETWEEN LOGARITHMS TO DIFFERENT BASES

As previously explained, the logarithm (log) of a number to a given base is the power to which the base must be raised to be equal to that number.

Then, if x is the log of N to the base a then, $a^x = N$

and, if y is the log of N to the base b then, $b^y = N$.

Hence,

$$a^x = b^y$$

$$b = a^{x/y}$$

$$\frac{x}{y} = \log_a b$$

$$y = \frac{x}{\log_a b}$$

$$\log_b N = \frac{\log_a N}{\log_a b}$$

Example.   Find the log of 8 to base 2 using common logs.

$$\log_2 8 = \frac{\lg 8}{\lg 2} = \frac{0 \cdot 9030}{0 \cdot 3010} = 3   \text{Ans.}$$

this is obviously correct because $2^3 = 8$.

NATURAL (NAPERIAN) LOGARITHMS (ln)

Are logs to base 2·718 i.e. exponential, e or ε, sometimes called hyperbolic logs. From previous:

$$\log_b N = \frac{\log_a N}{\log_a b}$$

$$\ln N = \frac{\lg N}{\lg 2\cdot718}$$

$$= \frac{\lg N}{0\cdot4343} \quad \text{or } 2\cdot303 \times \lg N$$

Values (log and antilog) for numbers 1 to 10 if read directly from the main table include the characteristic (only shown in the first column, under the zero heading) with complementary tables (2) to allow greater or less numbers to be evaluated (i.e. $\ln 10^n$ and $\ln 10^{-n}$). The following illustrative examples are solved using tables. They could also be evaluated directly using a scientific calculator:

(i) $N = 7\cdot754$ $\quad \ln N = 2\cdot0482$

(ii) $\ln N = 1\cdot0794$ $\quad N = 2\cdot943$

(iii) $N = 4189 = 4\cdot189 \times 10^3$

$$\ln N = 1\cdot4325 + 6\cdot9078$$

$$= 8\cdot3403$$

(iv) $N = 0\cdot2418 = 2\cdot418 \times 10^{-1}$

$$\ln N = 0\cdot8829 + \bar{3}\cdot6974$$

$$= \bar{2}\cdot5803 \quad \text{(i.e. } -1\cdot4197\text{)}$$

(v) $\ln N = 8\cdot4304$

Look for next figure below, i.e. 6·9078 for 10^3

$8\cdot4304 - 6\cdot9078 = 1\cdot5226$ which reads 4·584

$$N = 4\cdot584 \times 10^3$$

$$= 4584$$

(vi) $\ln N = \bar{4}\cdot7177$ $\quad$ (i.e. $-3\cdot2823$)

Look for next figure below, i.e. $\bar{5}\cdot3948$ for 10^{-2}

$\bar{4}\cdot7177 - \bar{5}\cdot3948 = 1\cdot3229$ which reads 3·754

$$N = 3\cdot754 \times 10^{-2}$$

$$= 0\cdot03754$$

Note. Use of a calculator simplifies the work in that the bar quantity is not used because the minus number can be entered into directly.

TEST EXAMPLES 1

1. Find the value of $\dfrac{10^{\frac{3}{2}} \times 10^4 \times 10^{\frac{3}{4}}}{10^3 \times 10^{\frac{1}{4}} \times 10^2}$

2. Evaluate $\dfrac{4^2 \times 4^{\frac{2}{3}} \times 4^{-2}}{4^{\frac{1}{2}} \times 4^{\frac{1}{6}}}$

3. Find the value of $\dfrac{8^{-2}}{8^{-5}}$

4. Evaluate $\dfrac{(3^{\frac{2}{5}})^{\frac{5}{3}} \times \sqrt{3} \times 3}{3^{-\frac{4}{3}} \times 3^3}$

5. Find the value of $(1\frac{2}{3})^2 + \sqrt{\dfrac{4}{81}} + \sqrt{200}$

6. Evaluate $\dfrac{(2^2)^3 \times \sqrt{3} \times 27^{\frac{2}{3}} \times \sqrt{12}}{\sqrt[4]{81} \times 4^{\frac{3}{2}}}$

7. The ratio of the volumes of two spheres is equal to the ratio of the cubes of their diameters; the volume of one sphere is 24·25 cm³, find the volume of another sphere whose diameter is twice as much.

8. A pump can empty a tank in 12 h, another pump can empty the same tank in 4 h, and another can empty this tank in 9 h. If all three pumps are set working together on this tank, how long would it take to empty it?

9. The strength of a beam varies directly as its breadth, directly as the square of its depth, and inversely as its length. A beam is 5 m long, 40 mm broad, and 100 mm deep; find the breadth of another beam of similar material, 3 m long and 80 mm deep, to have equal strength.

10. A piece of mild steel 50 mm long between gauge points and 80 mm² cross-sectional area, was tested in a tensile testing machine

and broke when the gauge length was 62·5 mm and cross- sectional area 48 mm². Find the percentage elongation and the percentage reduction in cross-sectional area.

11. In a certain three cylinder engine, the power developed in No. 1 cylinder is 15% more than in No. 3, and 5% less power is developed in No. 2 than in No. 3. What percentage of the total engine power is developed in each cylinder? Give the answers to the nearest one-tenth %.

12. A leaded yellow brass is composed of 71% copper, 1% tin, 3% lead and the remainder zinc. Find the mass required of each constituent, to make 500 kg of this alloy.

13. The heights of an indicator diagram measured at regular intervals along its length are as follows: 27, 39, 47, 51, 48, 32, 20, 11, 8, 5 mm respectively. Find the mean height of the diagram in mm.

14. 200 t of oil were bought at one port at £60/t and 600 t of oil at another port at £70/t. What was the average cost of oil/t?

15. Evaluate, $\ln \dfrac{850}{492} + \dfrac{840}{850} + 0.6 \ln \dfrac{1160}{850}$

16. Find a multiplier to convert logs to base 10 into logs to base 2, and use this to find the log to base 2 of 1·5.

17. Evaluate $0.06326^{-0.25}$
    (a) using common logs,
    (b) using natural (Naperian) logs.

18. Find the value of k in the following expression, using natural logs only,

$$k = 2.55 \times \sqrt{\dfrac{0.08234}{0.36 \times 10.2}}$$

CHAPTER 2

ALGEBRA

Algebra is a convenient system of short-hand arithmetic using letters of the alphabet to represent certain articles, quantities or hidden numbers. For instance if, in a box containing 25 bolts, 34 nuts and 47 washers, add 15 bolts and 18 washers and take away 14 nuts, there would then be in the box 40 bolts, 20 nuts and 65 washers. This could be set down in the following manner:

$$25b + 34n + 47w$$
$$\text{add} \quad 15b - 14n + 18w$$

$$\text{result} \quad 40b + 20n + 65w$$

If the sign of the first term of an expression is positive it is usually omitted as in the above example. Similarly for any single term, thus $5x$ means $+5x$.

The number which multiplies a term is called a coefficient. In the above example, the result line shows $+40$ as the coefficient of b, $+20$ as the coefficient of n, and $+65$ as the coefficient of w.

An algebraic expression is a collection of terms. One term may be a single quantity or a group of quantities multiplied (or divided) together, terms are separated from each other by plus or minus signs. When a term consists of quantities multiplied together, it is usual to omit the multiplication signs, $x \times y \times z$ is written xyz.

In the expression $2x^2y + 4xy + 6xy^2$ there are three terms,

$$2 \times x^2 \times y$$
$$4 \times x \times y$$
$$\text{and} \quad 6 \times x \times y^2$$

An algebraic expression which consists of two terms is called a *binomial* expression, and one consisting of three terms is called a *trinomial* expression.

ADDITION

Set the expressions down with similar terms under each other, re-arranging the terms if necessary (they can be written in any order), then add the numbers of each column separately in the usual way.

Example.   Add together $2a + 7b + 3c$ and $6c + 5a - 2b$.

$$2a + 7b + 3c$$
$$\text{add} \quad 5a - 2b + 6c$$
$$\overline{\hspace{3cm}}$$
$$7a + 5b + 9c \quad \text{Ans.}$$

Example.   Add together $3x - 5y + 6z$ and $4x + 2y - 8z$.

$$3x - 5y + 6z$$
$$\text{add} \quad 4x + 2y - 8z$$
$$\overline{\hspace{3cm}}$$
$$7x - 3y - 2z \quad \text{Ans.}$$

SUBTRACTION

To subtract numbers or algebraic terms, change the sign of the term to be subtracted and then add.

Examples.
   (i) From $8x$ take away $5x$

$$\text{written} \quad 8x - 5x$$
$$= 3x \quad \text{Ans. (i)}$$

   (ii) From $8x$ take away $-5x$

$$\text{written} \quad 8x - (-5x)$$
$$= 8x + 5x$$
$$= 13x \quad \text{Ans. (ii)}$$

   (iii) From $-8x$ take away $5x$

$$\text{written} \quad -8x - 5x$$
$$= -13x \quad \text{Ans. (iii)}$$

(iv) From $-8x$ take away $-5x$

$$\text{written} \quad -8x - (-5x)$$
$$= -8x + 5x$$
$$= -3x \quad \text{Ans. (iv)}$$

Example.

Subtract $\quad 6c - 3b + 4a - 7d \quad$ from $\quad 5b + 3d + 2a - 9c$

For expressions consisting of a number of terms, set down as shown below with like terms under each other; to subtract, change the signs of the subtracting expression mentally, add and write down the results.

From $2a + 5b - 9c + 3d$
Subtract $4a - 3b + 6c - 7d$
$$\overline{ -2a + 8b - 15c + 10d \quad \text{Ans.}}$$

COLLECTION OF TERMS

An expression may contain a number of similar terms, the first process in solving an algebraic problem is to simplify such an expression by collecting like terms together and writing down the expression in its simplest form.

Example.

Simplify $\quad 2x + 5y + 4x - 3z - 2y - z - x$
Re-arranging, $\quad 2x + 4x - x + 5y - 2y - 3z - z$
Collecting like terms, $\quad 5x + 3y - 4z \quad \text{Ans.}$

POWERS AND ROOTS

The same rules apply with regard to powers and roots as for ordinary numbers, therefore when observing the following examples, refer if necessary to the explanations given in Chapter 1.

Examples.

$$x \times x = x^2$$
$$2a \times a \times 4a = 8a^3$$
$$x^2 \times x^3 = x^{2+3} = x^5$$
$$x^5 \div x^2 = x^{5-2} = x^3$$
$$x^2 \div x^5 = x^{2-5} = x^{-3} = \frac{1}{x^3}$$
$$a^3 \div a^7 = a^{3-7} = a^{-4} = \frac{1}{a^4}$$
$$(x^2)^3 = x^{2\times3} = x^6$$

$\sqrt{x}$ may be written $x^{\frac{1}{2}}$

$(\sqrt[3]{x})^2$ may be written $x^{\frac{2}{3}}$

$$x^3 \div x^2 = x^{3-2} = x^1 = x$$
$$x^2 \div x^2 = x^{2-2} = x^0 = 1$$

MULTIPLICATION AND DIVISION

When algebraic quantities are to be multiplied together, the multiplication sign may be omitted, thus,

$x \times y$ may be written xy

$2 \times a \times b$ may be written $2ab$

$(3x + y) \times (x - 4y)$ may be written $(3x + y)(x - 4y)$

When one quantity is to be divided by another, such as x divided by y, it may be written in any of the following forms:

$$x \div y \quad \text{or} \quad \frac{x}{y} \quad \text{or} \quad x/y$$

The signs are very important, the above are ordinary positive values but care must be taken when any of the terms are negative. The rule is: *like signs multiplied or divided give a positive answer, unlike signs multiplied or divided give a negative answer.*

Examples.

$$+2x \quad \text{multiplied by} \quad +4x \quad \text{equals} \quad +8x^2$$
$$+2x \quad \text{multiplied by} \quad -4x \quad \text{equals} \quad -8x^2$$
$$-2x \quad \text{multiplied by} \quad +4x \quad \text{equals} \quad -8x^2$$
$$-2x \quad \text{multiplied by} \quad -4x \quad \text{equals} \quad +8x^2$$
$$+8x^2 \quad \text{divided by} \quad +2x \quad \text{equals} \quad +4x$$
$$-8x^2 \quad \text{divided by} \quad +2x \quad \text{equals} \quad -4x$$
$$-8x^2 \quad \text{divided by} \quad -2x \quad \text{equals} \quad +4x$$
$$+8x^2 \quad \text{divided by} \quad -2x \quad \text{equals} \quad -4x$$

Example.

$$\text{Multiply} \quad (2x + 3y) \quad \text{by} \quad (3x - 2y)$$

Procedure:

(i) set down in long multiplication style;

(ii) multiply $2x + 3y$ by one term of the multiplier, say $3x$;

(iii) Multiply $2x + 3y$ by the other term, $-2y$, putting like terms under each other;

(iv) collect terms by addition.

$$
\begin{array}{l}
2x \ + 3y \\
3x \ - 2y \\
\hline
6x^2 + 9xy \\
\quad\ \ - 4xy - 6y^2 \\
\hline
6x^2 + 5xy - 6y^2 \quad \text{Ans.}
\end{array}
$$

When the two expressions to be multiplied together each have only two terms, the multiplication can quite easily be done mentally. In the above example,

$$(2x + 3y)(3x - 2y) = 6x^2 + 5xy - 6y^2$$

Note that the first term of the answer is the product of the first terms of the two expressions, i.e., $2x \times 3x = 6x^2$; the last term of the answer is the product of the last terms, i.e., $3y \times -2y = -6y^2$; the middle term of the answer is the sum of the product of the 'means' and the product of the 'extremes', i.e., $3y \times 3x$ plus $2x \times -2y = 9xy - 4xy = +5xy$.

Now check the following:

$$(x + 4)(x + 5) = x^2 + 9x + 20$$
$$(4x + 3)(2x - 1) = 8x^2 + 2x - 3$$
$$(2x - 5y)(x + 3y) = 2x^2 + xy - 15y^2$$
$$(3x - 4y)(5x - 6y) = 15x^2 - 38xy + 24y^2$$
$$(a + b)(a + b) = a^2 + 2ab + b^2$$
$$(a - b)(a - b) = a^2 - 2ab + b^2$$
$$(a + b)(a - b) = a^2 - b^2$$
$$(a^2 + b^2)(a^2 - b^2) = a^4 - b^4$$

Example.   Multiply $4x + 3y - 2z$ by $x - 2y$

$$
\begin{array}{l}
4x \ + 3y \ - 2z \\
\qquad\quad x \ - 2y \\
\hline
4x^2 + 3xy - 2xz \\
\quad\ - 8xy \qquad\quad - 6y^2 + 4yz \\
\hline
4x^2 - 5xy - 2xz - 6y^2 + 4yz \quad \text{Ans.}
\end{array}
$$

Example.   Divide $6x^3 - x^2 - 14x + 8$ by $3x - 2$

Procedure:
    (i) set down in long division style;
    (ii) see how many times the first term of the divisor goes into the first term of the dividend and write this down as the first term of the answer: thus, $3x$ into $6x^3$ goes $2x^2$ times;
    (iii) multiply the divisor by $2x^2$ and set down under the dividend, like terms under each other;
    (iv) subtract, this gives $3x^2$;
    (v) bring down the next term of the dividend (i.e., $-14x$);

(vi) repeat the operations as from (ii);

$$3x - 2)\overline{6x^3 - x^2 - 14x + 8}(2x^2 + x - 4 \quad \text{Ans.}$$
$$\underline{6x^3 - 4x^2}$$
$$3x^2 - 14x$$
$$\underline{3x^2 - 2x}$$
$$-12x + 8$$
$$\underline{-12x + 8}$$

Example. Divide $2x^2 + 5x - 7$ by $x + 4$

$$x + 4)\overline{2x^2 + 5x - 7}(2x - 3$$
$$\underline{2x^2 + 8x}$$
$$-3x - 7$$
$$\underline{-3x - 12}$$
$$+ 5 \quad \text{remainder}$$

(i) Proceed as in the previous example by setting down as long division (see above).

(ii) The first term of the divisor, x, into the first term of the dividend, $2x^2$, goes $2x$ times, write this as the first term of the answer.

(iii) Multiply the divisor by $2x$, which gives $2x^2 + 8x$ and set this down under the dividend.

(iv) Subtract to get $-3x$.

(v) Bring down the next term of the dividend, that is -7, to give $-3x - 7$.

(vi) Repeat procedure as from (ii), i.e., x into $-3x$ goes -3 times, put -3 into the answer. Multiply the divisor by -3 to get $-3x - 12$ and set this down. Subtract, and this leaves $+5$. There is now nothing more to bring down from the dividend and x will not go into $+5$, hence this is left over and written as a remainder:

$$(2x^2 + 5x - 7) \div (x + 4) = (2x - 3) \text{ remainder} + 5 \quad \text{Ans.}$$
$$\text{or} \qquad 2x^2 + 5x - 7 = (x + 4)(2x - 3) + 5$$

EFFECT OF ZERO IN MULTIPLICATION AND DIVISION

When any quantity is multiplied by zero, the result is zero.

Examples. $3 \times 0 = 0$

$$a \times b \times c \times 0 = 0$$

$$(x + y) \times 0 = 0$$

When zero is divided by any quantity, the result is zero.

Examples. $0 \div 4 = 0$

$$\frac{0}{a + b} = 0$$

$$0/(x^2 - y^2) = 0$$

When any quantity is divided by zero, the result is infinity.

Examples. $5 \div 0 = \infty$

$$\frac{2x + 3y}{0} = \infty$$

When an expression works out to be zero divided by zero, the result is indefinite, that is, it can have any value and indicates that the problem requires to be solved by a different method.

Examples.   Solve $\dfrac{a^2 - b^2}{a - b}$ when $a = 3$, and $b = 3$

One method, $\dfrac{3^2 - 3^2}{3 - 3}$

$$= \frac{0}{0}$$

Other method, $\dfrac{a^2 - b^2}{a - b}$

$$= \frac{(a + b)(a - b)}{a - b} \quad (a - b) \quad \text{cancels}$$

$$= a + b$$

$$= 3 + 3$$

$$= 6 \quad \text{Ans.}$$

REMOVAL OF BRACKETS

A quantity immediately in front (or behind) a bracket indicates that every term inside the bracket must be multiplied by that quantity on removing the brackets. Care must be taken with regard to the signs, if the multiplier is positive, the signs of the terms in the brackets will remain the same, if the multiplier is negative all the signs of the terms will be changed. If the bracket is preceded by a sign only, e.g., $+$ or $-$, it indicates that the multiplier is unity.

Examples.
$$2(x^2 + 3x - 5)$$
$$= 2x^2 + 6x - 10 \quad \text{Ans.}$$

$$- 3(2a^2 - 7ab + 3b^2)$$
$$= - 6a^2 + 21ab - 9b^2 \quad \text{Ans.}$$

$$4(2x - y) - 2x(x + 3y) - (3x + 4y)$$
$$= 8x - 4y - 2x^2 - 6xy - 3x - 4y$$
$$= - 2x^2 + 8x - 3x - 6xy - 4y - 4y$$
$$= - 2x^2 + 5x - 6xy - 8y \quad \text{Ans.}$$

BRACKETS CONTAINED WITHIN BRACKETS

The common sets of brackets are,

$\quad$ ($\qquad$) $\quad$ small, used as inner brackets,

$\quad$ { $\qquad$ } $\quad$ intermediate brackets,

$\quad$ [$\qquad$] $\quad$ square, used as outer brackets.

When simplifying expressions composed of bracketed quantities within other brackets, it is usual to remove the inner brackets first, then the intermediate brackets, and finally the outer brackets.

Example.
$$y(1 + 3x) + [3x(x - y) - \{-2(x - 1) + 3x^2\} - y]$$
$$= y + 3xy + [3x^2 - 3xy - \{-2x + 2 + 3x^2\} - y]$$
$$= y + 3xy + [3x^2 - 3xy + 2x - 2 - 3x^2 - y]$$
$$= y + 3xy + 3x^2 - 3xy + 2x - 2 - 3x^2 - y$$
$$= 3x^2 - 3x^2 + 3xy - 3xy + 2x + y - y - 2$$
$$= 2x - 2 \quad \text{Ans.}$$

FACTORISATION

Factorising is the reverse of multiplying, that is, it is the process of finding the numbers or quantities which, when multiplied together, will constitute the expression given to be factorised. Generally, expressions to be factorised fall into one or more of four types: (i) those made up of terms with common multipliers, (ii) difference between two squares, (iii) perfect squares, and (iv) those whose factors have to be found by trial and error.

(i) Factorising expressions which contain common multipliers. If every term contains a common factor, divide throughout by this factor and express the factor as a multiplier to the resultant terms enclosed in a bracket, thus,

$$2 \times 3 + 2 \times 4 - 2 \times 5$$
$$= 2(3 + 4 - 5)$$

This is the reverse process to removal of brackets.

Examples.
$$3x + 2xy - xz$$
$$= x(3 + 2y - z) \quad \text{Ans.}$$
$$\frac{2a^2}{b} - \frac{2a}{3b} + \frac{4ac^2}{b}$$
$$= \frac{2a}{b}(a - \tfrac{1}{3} + 2c^2) \quad \text{Ans.}$$

(ii) Factorising expressions which are the difference between two squares. Examine first the following cases and note the similarity of the factors and the results of the multiplications:

$$(x + 3)(x - 3) = x^2 - 9$$
$$(x + 1)(x - 1) = x^2 - 1$$
$$(x + y)(x - y) = x^2 - y^2$$
$$(2a + 3b)(2a - 3b) = 4a^2 - 9b^2$$

Hence if the *sum* of two terms is multiplied by the *difference* between those two terms, the result is the difference between the squares of the two terms. Therefore any expession which consists of the difference between two squares can be readily factorised.

Factors of $\qquad a^2 - b^2 = (a+b)(a-b)$

Factors of $\qquad y^2 - 16 = (y+4)(y-4)$

Factors of $\qquad 16D^2 - 25d^2 = (4D+5d)(4D-5d)$

(iii) Factorising expressions which are perfect squares. Firstly, check the following and note the form of the result in each case.

$$(x+3)^2 = (x+3)(x+3) \quad = x^2 + 6x + 9$$
$$(x-5)^2 = (x-5)(x-5) \quad = x^2 - 10x + 25$$
$$(x-4y)^2 = (x-4y)(x-4y) = x^2 - 8xy + 16y^2$$

The above are simple cases where the coefficients of x^2 is unity, such expressions can be easily recognised as perfect squares because, in each case, the third term is equal to the square of half the coefficient of x. Note that,

$+\ 9 \qquad$ is the square of half of $\quad +\ 6$

$+25 \qquad$ is the square of half of $\quad -\ 10$

$+16y^2 \quad$ is the square of half of $\quad -\ 8y$

Examples. $\qquad \sqrt{(a^2 + 4a + 4)} = a + 2 \quad$ Ans.

$\qquad\qquad \sqrt{(x^2 - 12x + 36)} = x - 6 \quad$ Ans.

Now check and examine the following slightly more difficult cases.

$$\sqrt{(9x^2 + 24x + 16)} = 3x + 4 \quad \text{Ans.}$$
because, $\qquad (3x+4)(3x+4) = 9x^2 + 24x + 16$

$$\sqrt{(16x^2 - 48x + 36)} = 4x - 6 \quad \text{Ans.}$$
because, $\qquad (4x-6)(4x-6) = 16x^2 - 48x + 36$

$$\sqrt{(25x^2 + 70xy + 49y^2)} = 5x + 7y \quad \text{Ans.}$$
because, $\qquad (5x+7y)(5x+7y) = 25x^2 + 70xy + 49y^2$

Expressions which are perfect squares can therefore be recognised at once and their square root becomes obvious. Note particularly the effect of the minus sign.

(iv) Factorising by trial and error.

Check the following and the form of the expressions:

$$(x + 2)(x + 3) = x^2 + 5x + 6$$
$$(2x + 5)(3x - 4) = 6x^2 + 7x - 20$$
$$(3x + 2y)(4x - 5y) = 12x^2 - 7xy - 10y^2$$

Note that the first term of the expression is the product of the first terms of the factors, the last term of the expression is the product of the last terms of the factors, the middle term of the expression is the sum of the product of the mean terms and the product of the extremes.

Example.   Factorise $x^2 + 5x + 6$

The factors of x^2 are x and x

The factors of $+6$ can be $+6$ and $+1$

or -6 and -1

or $+2$ and $+3$

or -2 and -3

Although any of these pairs *multiplied* together will give the third term, i.e., $+6$, only one of the pairs *added* together will give the coefficient of the middle term, i.e., $+2$ added to $+3$ is $+5$, hence the factors of

$$x^2 + 5x + 6 = (x + 2)(x + 3)   \text{Ans.}$$

Example.   Factorise $6x^2 + 7x - 20$

The factors of $6x^2$ can be $6x$ and x

or $2x$ and $3x$

The factors of -20 can be $+20$ and -1

or -20 and $+1$

or $+10$ and -2

or -10 and $+2$

or $+ 5$ and -4

or $- 5$ and $+4$

Now try combining the pairs of factors of $6x^2$ with the pairs of factors of -20 until it is seen that the combination which will produce the correct middle term is $(2x + 5)$ and $(3x - 4)$ hence, the factors of

$$6x^2 + 7x - 20 = (2x + 5)(3x - 4) \quad \text{Ans.}$$

After a little practice, with an eye on the middle term, obvious misfits can quickly be eliminated and the correct factors spotted without much trouble.

LOWEST COMMON MULTIPLE

As in arithmetic, the L.C.M. of a group of algebraic terms is the lowest quantity into which each of the terms will divide.

For example, the L.C.M. of $4x^2y$, $6xy^2$, $2xyz$ and x^2z^2 is $12x^2y^2z^2$.

FRACTIONS

To add and subtract algebraic fractions, bring them all to a common denominator by finding the L.C.M. of the given denominators of the fractions, then add and subtract, like terms being combined together. The procedure is demonstrated in the following example.

$$\text{Simplify} \quad \frac{3x + 1}{2x} - \frac{x + 2}{3x} - \frac{2x - 3}{6x}$$

The L.C.M. of the denominators is $6x$.

First fraction: $6x \div 2x = 3$, thus the denominator of $2x$ is to be multiplied by 3 to make it $6x$, therefore the numerator must also be multiplied by 3.

Second fraction: $6x \div 3x = 2$, the denominator of $3x$ is to be multiplied by 2, therefore the numerator must also be multiplied by 2.

Third fraction: the denominator is already $6x$ therefore the numerator also remains unchanged.

$$\frac{3x+1}{2x} - \frac{x+2}{3x} - \frac{2x-3}{6x}$$

$$= \frac{3(3x+1)}{6x} - \frac{2(x+2)}{6x} - \frac{(2x-3)}{6x}$$

usually written $\dfrac{3(3x+1) - 2(x+2) - (2x-3)}{6x}$

$$= \frac{9x+3-2x-4-2x+3}{6x}$$

$$= \frac{5x+2}{6x} \quad \text{Ans.}$$

Note that the given expression contained no brackets, the reason being that division lines of fractions act as a double purpose, to indicate that the numerator is divided by the denominator but also to indicate that everything above (or below) the line is one complete term, thus

$$\frac{3x+1}{2x} \quad \text{could be written} \quad \frac{(3x+1)}{2x}$$

However, when proceeding with the simplification of the expression, it is necessary to insert the brackets before multiplying out to ensure that all the quantities constituting the term are so affected.

The final answer could be written $\quad \dfrac{(5x+2)}{6x} \quad \text{or} \quad \dfrac{5x+2}{6x}$

EVALUATION

Evaluation is the process of substituting the numerical values of the algebraic symbols and working out the value of the whole expression.

The substitution of the algebraic symbols by their numerical values may be done in the original expression to be evaluated, or, the expression may be simplified first and numerical values substituted later, whichever is the more convenient.

The usual rules of arithmetic apply, i.e., quantities enclosed in brackets should be solved first, and multiplication and division must be performed before addition and subtraction.

Example.   Evaluate $3xy + x^2 - 4y$

when $x = 2$, and $y = 3$

$$3xy + x^2 - 4y$$
$$= 3 \times 2 \times 3 + 2^2 - 4 \times 3$$
$$= 18 + 4 - 12$$
$$= 10 \quad \text{Ans.}$$

Example.   Evaluate $3a^2 - 3b^2 - 4c^2$
when $a = 4$, $b = -2$, and $c = 3$

$$3a^2 - 3b^2 - 4c^2$$
$$= 3 \times 4^2 - 3 \times (-2)^2 - 4 \times 3^2$$
$$= 3 \times 16 - 3 \times 4 - 4 \times 9$$
$$= 48 - 12 - 36$$
$$= 0 \quad \text{Ans.}$$

Example.   Evaluate $(a + b)^2 - (c + d) + x^3 - y$
when $a = 3$, $b = 4$, $c = 5$, $d = 6$, $x = -2$, $y = -3$

$$(a + b)^2 - (c + d) + x^3 - y$$
$$= (3 + 4)^2 - (5 + 6) + (-2)^3 - (-3)$$
$$= (7)^2 - (11) + (-8) - (-3)$$
$$= 49 - 11 - 8 + 3$$
$$= 33 \quad \text{Ans.}$$

Example.   Evaluate $\dfrac{3x + 2y}{z} + \dfrac{x - z}{y} - \dfrac{2y + z}{x}$

when $x = 4$, $y = 3$, $z = -2$

$$\frac{3x + 2y}{z} + \frac{x - z}{y} - \frac{2y + z}{x}$$

$$= \frac{3 \times 4 + 2 \times 3}{-2} + \frac{4 - (-2)}{3} - \frac{2 \times 3 + (-2)}{4}$$

$$= \frac{12 + 6}{-2} + \frac{4 + 2}{3} - \frac{6 - 2}{4}$$

$$= \frac{18}{-2} + \frac{6}{3} - \frac{4}{4}$$

$$= -9 + 2 - 1$$

$$= -8 \quad \text{Ans.}$$

REMAINDER AND FACTOR THEOREMS

The *remainder theorem* states that if a polynomial in x is divided by $x - a$, the remainder is equal to the result obtained when a is substituted for x in the polynomial.

A *polynomial* is an expression consisting of a number of terms, each term being a multiple of an integral power of a quantity such as x. The *degree* of the polynomial signifies the highest power.

For example: $3x^2 - 4x + 2$ is a polynomial of the second degree in x; $4y^3 + 2y^2 + 3y - 5$ is a polynomial of the third degree in y, and so on.

A *function* of a quantity is an expression which depends upon that quantity. For example: $2x^3 + 3x^2 - 2x - 5$ is a function of x and denoted by $f(x)$; $2a^3 + 3a^2 - 2a - 5$ is a function of a and denoted by $f(a)$; $2(2)^3 + 3(2)^2 - 2(2) - 5$ is a function of 2 and denoted by $f(2)$.

Hence, using the above notations, and R for the remainder, the remainder theorem may be written:

$$R = f(a) \quad \text{when} \quad f(x) \div (x - a)$$

Note that if $f(a) = 0$, the remainder is zero, which means that $x - a$ is then a factor of $f(x)$. This is the *factor theorem*.

Example. Find the remainder when $2x^3 - 3x^2 - 3x + 5$ is divided by $x - 2$.

$$\text{Let } x - a = x - 2$$
$$\text{then } a = +2$$
$$f(x) = 2x^3 - 3x^2 - 3x + 5$$
$$R = f(a) = 2(2)^3 - 3(2)^2 - 3(2) + 5$$
$$= 16 - 12 - 6 + 5$$
$$= 3 \quad \text{Ans.}$$

Example. Find the value of y in the expression $x^2 - 5x + y$ if $(x - 7)$ is a factor.

If $(x - a)$ is a factor of $f(x)$, the remainder is zero, and $f(a) = 0$

$$\text{Let } x - a = x - 7$$
$$\text{then } a = +7$$
$$x - 7 \text{ is a factor, } \therefore f(+7) = 0$$
$$f(x) = x^2 - 5x + y$$
$$f(+7) = (7)^2 - 5(7) + y$$
$$0 = 49 - 35 + y$$
$$y = -14 \quad \text{Ans.}$$

Example. Find the values of b and c if $x^3 + bx^2 + cx - 6$ is divisible by $(x + 1)(x - 2)$ with no remainder.

$$\text{Let } x - a = x + 1$$
$$\text{then } a = -1$$
$$x + 1 \text{ is a factor, } \therefore f(-1) = 0$$
$$f(x) = x^3 + bx^2 + cx - 6$$
$$f(-1) = (-1)^3 + b(-1)^2 + c(-1) - 6$$
$$0 = -1 + b - c - 6$$
$$c = b - 7 \quad \ldots \quad \ldots \quad \ldots \quad \ldots \text{ (i)}$$

$$\text{Let } x - a = x - 2$$
$$\text{then } a = +2$$

$x - 2$ is a factor, $\therefore f(+2) = 0$

$$f(x) = x^3 + bx^2 + cx - 6$$
$$f(+2) = (2)^3 + b(2)^2 + c(2) - 6$$
$$0 = 8 + 4b + 2c - 6$$
$$2c = 6 - 8 - 4b$$
$$c = -1 - 2b \qquad \ldots \qquad \ldots \qquad \ldots \quad \text{(ii)}$$

From (i) and (ii):

$$b - 7 = -1 - 2b$$
$$3b = 6$$
$$b = 2$$

From (i):

$$c = 2 - 7 = -5$$

Values of b and c are, 2 and -5 Ans.

Example.   Find the constants b and c if, when $x^3 + 2x^2 + bx + c$ is divided by $(x + 3)$ there is no remainder, and when divided by $(x + 2)$ the remainder is 11.

Using Factor theorem:

$$\text{Let } x - a = x + 3$$
$$\text{then } a = -3$$

$x + 3$ is a factor, hence $f(-3) = 0$

$$f(x) = x^3 + 2x^2 + bx + c$$
$$f(-3) = (-3)^3 + 2(-3)^2 + b(-3) + c$$
$$0 = -27 + 18 - 3b + c$$
$$c = 3b + 9 \qquad \ldots \qquad \ldots \qquad \ldots \quad \text{(i)}$$

Using Remainder theorem:

$$\text{Let } x - a = x + 2$$
$$\text{then } a = -2$$
$$f(x) = x^3 + 2x^2 + bx + c$$
$$R = f(a) = (-2)^3 + 2(-2)^2 + b(-2) + c$$
$$11 = -8 + 8 - 2b + c$$
$$c = 2b + 11 \quad \ldots \quad \ldots \quad \ldots \quad \text{(ii)}$$

From (i) and (ii),

$$3b + 9 = 2b + 11$$
$$b = 2$$

Substituting value of b into (i),

$$c = 3 \times 2 + 9 = 15$$

Constants are 2 and 15   Ans.

BINOMIAL THEOREM

Is used in approximation and error calculations. It can be shown, by induction, that:

$$(a + x)^n = a^n + na^{n-1}x^1 + \frac{n(n-1)}{2 \times 1} a^{n-2}x^2$$
$$+ \frac{n(n-1)(n-2)}{3 \times 2 \times 1} a^{n-3}x^3 + \text{etc.}$$

which is more readily applied as:

$$(1 + x)^n = 1 + nx + \frac{n(n-1)}{2 \times 1}x^2 + \frac{n(n-1)(n-2)}{3 \times 2 \times 1}x^3 + \text{etc.}$$

and is true for all values of n provided $-1 < x < 1$ i.e., x is numerically less than one.

Example.   Evaluate $\sqrt[3]{998}$, correct to five places of decimals.

$$(998)^{\frac{1}{3}} = (1000 - 2)^{\frac{1}{3}} = 10(1 - 0 \cdot 002)^{\frac{1}{3}}$$

$$(998)^{\frac{1}{3}} = 10\left\{1 + \tfrac{1}{3}(-0 \cdot 002) + \frac{\tfrac{1}{3}(\tfrac{1}{3} - 1)}{2 \times 1}(-0 \cdot 002)^2\right.$$

$$\left. + \frac{\tfrac{1}{3}(\tfrac{1}{3} - 1)(\tfrac{1}{3} - 2)}{3 \times 2 \times 1}(-0 \cdot 002)^3\right\}$$

$$= 10(1 - \tfrac{1}{3} \times 0 \cdot 002 - \tfrac{1}{9} \times 0 \cdot 000004)$$

$$= 9 \cdot 99333 \quad \text{Ans.}$$

TEST EXAMPLES 2

1. (i) Add together $3x + 4y - 5z$ and $-2x - 5y + 4z$
    (ii) Add together $2a^2b - ab + 3ab^2$ and $5ab^2 - a^2b + ab$
    (iii) Subtract $2x + 5y - 3z$ from $5x - 4z + 3y$
    (iv) Subtract $-4c - 5b - a$ from $3a + 6c - 2b$

2. Simplify the following expressions by collecting terms,
    (i) $5x - 3z - 4x - 2y + 4y + 2z - y$
    (ii) $2 \cdot 5a + c - 1 \cdot 2a + 2 \cdot 5b - 3c + b + 1 \cdot 7a$
    (iii) $b^2 - 3ab^2 + 2a^2b - 4a^2 - 2b^2 + 5a^2 - 2ab^2$

3. Simplify the following,
    (i) $\dfrac{x \times x^3 \times x^5}{x^2 \times x^4}$
    (ii) $x^5 \times x^{-3} \times x^{-2}$
    (iii) $\sqrt{x} \times x^{\frac{1}{2}} \times x^{\frac{1}{3}}$
    (iv) $\sqrt[2]{(x^4y^2)}$
    (v) $(x^2)^3 \times \sqrt[3]{x^{\frac{1}{2}}} \times x^{-5}$

4. (i) Multiply $(x + 2y)$ by $(2x + y)$
    (ii) Multiply $(2x + y)$ by $(3x - 2y)$
    (iii) Multiply $(3x - 4y)$ by $(2x - 3y)$

5. Work out the following:
    (i) $(a + b)^2$

(ii) $(a - b)^2$
(iii) $(a + b)^3$
(iv) $(a - b)^3$

6. (i) Divide $(8a^2 - 8ab - 6b^2)$ by $(2a - 3b)$
    (ii) Divide $(9x^3 - 9x^2y - 10xy^2 + 8y^3)$ by $(3x - 4y)$
    (iii) Divide $(x^3 - y^3)$ by $(x - y)$

7. Simplify the following by removing brackets and collecting terms:
    (i) $(a + b) + (c - d) - (a - b) - (c + d) + (a - b)$
    (ii) $2\{a - 3(a + 2) + 4(2a - 1) + 5\}$
    (iii) $2x - [2x - \{2x - (2x - 2) - 2\} - 2] - 2$

8. Factorise the following expressions:
    (i) $3b^2 - 6b + 9$
    (ii) $pv + pvx$
    (iii) $ax^3 - 2bx^2 + 3cx$
    (iv) $12a^3b^3c^3 - 8a^2b^2c^2 + 4abc$

9. Factorise the following expressions:
    (i) $D^2 - d^2$
    (ii) $1 - a^2$
    (iii) $4x^2y^2 - 9z^2$
    (iv) $T_1{}^4 - T_2{}^4$

10. Factorise the following expressions:
    (i) $a^2 + 8a + 16$
    (ii) $d^2 - 10d + 25$
    (iii) $9v^2 + 12v + 4$
    (iv) $4x^2 - 12xy + 9y^2$

11. Simplify the following:
    (i) $\dfrac{x}{2} + \dfrac{x}{4} - \dfrac{2x}{3}$
    (ii) $\dfrac{2a - 1}{b} - \dfrac{2a + 3}{2b} - \dfrac{3a - 8}{3b}$
    (iii) $\dfrac{4}{x + 2} + \dfrac{18}{x^2 - 2x - 8} - \dfrac{3}{x - 4}$

12. Find the value of:

$$2x^3 - x^2y + xy^2 - 3y^3$$

when $x = 2$, and $y = -2$

13. Simplify the following and find the value if $x = -2$, and $y = -3$.

$$3[4x + 2\{x - 2y - (3x + y)\} - 3x]$$

14. Find the remainder when $2x^3 - 4x^2 + 5x - 6$ is divided by $(x - 3)$.

15. Find the value of b if, when $x^3 + 6x^2 + bx + 9$ is divided by $(x + 5)$ the remainder is 4.

16. Find the value of c if $(x + 4)$ is a factor of $x^3 + x^2 - 10x + c$.

17. Find the constants b and c in the expression $x^3 + 3x^2 - bx - c$ if, when it is divided by $(x + 1)$ there is no remainder, and when divided by $(x + 2)$ the remainder is 15.

18. By using the binomial theorem, find the cube root of 1·012 correct to 7 places of decimals.

CHAPTER 3

SIMPLE EQUATIONS

An equation is an expression consisting of two 'sides', one side being equal in value to the other. A simple equation contains one hidden number of the first order (e.g., x, and not x^2 or x^3, etc.) which is usually referred to as the *unknown* and to *solve* the equation means to find the value of the unknown.

Since one side of the equation is equal to the other side, it follows that if, in the process of solving, it is convenient to make some change to one side, exactly the same change must be made to the other side to ensure that the equation is still true. Hence, equality will be preserved if:

   (i) the same quantity is added to both sides;

  (ii) the same quantity is subtracted from both sides;

 (iii) every term on both sides is multiplied by the same quantity;

 (iv) every term on both sides is divided by the same quantity;

  (v) both sides are raised to the same power;

 (vi) the same root is taken of both sides;

and any one or more of the above steps may be necessary in solving an equation.

There can be any number of terms in an equation, some may be fractions, others may be bracketed quantities: the unknown quantity may be included in more than one term and perhaps on both sides of the equation. In such cases it will be necessary to simplify the equation, preferably one step at a time, following the usual rules of arithmetic and algebra thus:

   (i) eliminate fractions; this is done by multiplying every term on both sides by the L.C.M. of all the denominators;

  (ii) remove brackets; in doing so observe strictly the rules on removal of brackets explained in Chapter on Algebra;

 (iii) place all terms containing the unknown on one side, and pure numbers on the other side; terms taken over from one side to the other must have their signs changed;

 (iv) collect and summarise terms on each side;

  (v) find the value of the unknown; for the simplest of equations this is done by dividing both sides by the coefficient of the unknown, other equations may require further or different treatment such as taking the same root of both sides or raising both sides to the same power.

The above is a general purpose guide to the usual steps in solving simple equations. However, other processes can be introduced when most convenient, for instance, in some equations which include algebraic fractions, it may be possible to cancel common factors in the numerator and denominator of one or more of the fractions, if this is done in the initial stages labour will be saved later.

The following examples will help to clarify the above steps.

Example. $4x + 10 = 18$

Take 10 to the other side and change its sign, this is the same as subtracting 10 from each side,

$$4x = 18 - 10$$
$$4x = 8$$

Divide both sides by 4 (the coefficient of x)

$$x = 2 \quad \text{Ans.}$$

Example. $7(2x - 4) = 2(x + 4) - 5(3 - x)$

Remove brackets, multiplying the terms inside each bracket by the multiplier in front.

$$14x - 28 = 2x + 8 - 15 + 5x$$

Place all terms containing x on one side and pure members on the other, not forgetting to change signs when terms are taken over,

$$14x - 2x - 5x = 8 - 15 + 28$$

Summarise each side,

$$7x = 21$$

Divide both sides by 7,

$$x = 3 \quad \text{Ans.}$$

Example. $\dfrac{2x}{3} + 1 \cdot 5x = 16 - \dfrac{x}{2}$

L.C.M. of denominators is 6, multiply every term by 6,

$$\frac{6 \times 2x}{3} + 6 \times 1 \cdot 5x = 6 \times 16 - \frac{6 \times x}{2}$$

Cancel out denominators into the 6 on the top, and simplify each term,

$$4x + 9x = 96 - 3x$$
$$4x + 9x + 3x = 96$$
$$16x = 96$$
$$x = 6 \quad \text{Ans.}$$

Example.

$$\frac{3x + 2}{2} - \frac{5(x - 1)}{6} = \frac{5x}{4} - \frac{5 - x}{2}$$

L.C.M. of denominators is 12, multiplying each term by 12 and cancelling denominators in one step,

$$6(3x + 2) - 10(x - 1) = 15x - 6(5 - x)$$
$$18x + 12 - 10x + 10 = 15x - 30 + 6x$$
$$18x - 10x - 15x - 6x = -30 - 12 - 10$$
$$-13x = -52$$
$$x = 4 \quad \text{Ans.}$$

(Note that -52 divided by -13 is $+4$).

Example. $8 - \dfrac{9x}{2} - \dfrac{6}{x} = 2(4 - 3x)$

L.C.M. of denominators is $2x$, multiply every term by $2x$ and at the same time cancel out denominators,

$$16x - 9x^2 - 12 = 4x(4 - 3x)$$
$$16x - 9x^2 - 12 = 16x - 12x^2$$

Collect functions of x^2 and x on one side, numbers on the other side,

$$-9x^2 + 12x^2 + 16x - 16x = 12$$

Simplify, note that $+16x$ and $-16x$ cancel out,

$$3x^2 = 12$$

Divide both sides by 3,

$$x^2 = 4$$

Take square root of both sides,

$$x = \pm 2 \quad \text{Ans.}$$

Note. The square root of 4 can be $+2$ or -2, because -2 multiplied by -2 gives $+4$. Therefore when taking the square root of a number in the solution of equations write $\pm$, indicating 'plus or minus'. If either $+2$ or -2 be substituted for x in the original equation, it will be seen that either value of x satisfies the equation.

Example.

$$\frac{3x^2 + 10x + 3}{x + 3} = \frac{x^2 - 4x + 3}{x - 1}$$

On inspection of the numerators in this equation, it appears a possibility of their respective denominators dividing into them, this is always worth trying because it will greatly simplify the working. Instead of actual division try factorising the numerators, one of the factors being the same as the denominator. This example is such that it will factorise, cancel, and form an easy solution as shown below. If however this was not possible, the alternative procedure would be to multiply throughout by the L.C.M. of the denominators as previously explained.

$$\frac{3x^2 + 10x + 3}{x + 3} = \frac{x^2 - 4x + 3}{x - 1}$$

$$\frac{(x + 3)(3x + 1)}{x + 3} = \frac{(x - 1)(x - 3)}{x - 1}$$

$$3x + 1 = x - 3$$

$$3x - x = -3 - 1$$

$$2x = -4$$

$$x = -2 \quad \text{Ans.}$$

PROBLEMS INVOLVING SIMPLE EQUATIONS

From the facts given in the problem and what is required to be found, the first step is to make up a straightforward equation; this is the sorting-out part of the solution.

Make a sketch of the problem if it is at all possible and insert on this sketch all the given data and indicate the unknown quantity. If a sketch is not practicable it may help to write down the given quantities.

Give the unknown quantity a symbol, for example, 'let $r=$ internal radius in mm', or 'let $m=$ mass in kg', and so on.

Example. A port (left) tank and a starboard (right) tank, each of 200 t capacity, are each half full of oil. Find what mass of oil must be pumped out of the port tank and into the starboard tank so that there will be four times the mass of oil in one tank as in the other.

Fig. 2

Initial mass of oil in each tank $= 100$ t

Let $m=$ mass of oil pumped over, then,

final mass of oil in port tank $= (100 - m)$ t
final mass of oil in starboard tank $= (100 + m)$ t

Mass in the starboard tank is to be four times the mass in the port tank, therefore,

$$\text{Mass in starboard tank} = 4 \times \text{mass in port tank}$$
$$(100 + m) = 4 \times (100 - m)$$
$$100 + m = 400 - 4m$$
$$4m + m = 400 - 100$$
$$5m = 300$$
$$m = 60$$

∴ mass of oil to be transferred $= 60$ t   Ans.

(Then there will be 160 t of oil in the starboard tank and 40 t in the port tank.)

Example.   An electric train leaves station A bound for station B at the same instant that a diesel train leaves B for A on parallel lines along the same route. The speed of the electric train is 80 km/h, that of the diesel train 64 km/h, and the distance between stations is 72 km. Find the distance from A where the trains will pass each other.

Fig. 3

Let x = distance from A to passing point C

then $(72 - x)$ = distance from B to passing point C

As the trains leave at the same time and pass each other at the same instant, then the time taken from station to passing point is the same for each train. This gives the equation,

$$\left.\begin{matrix} \text{Time for electric train} \\ \text{to travel } x \text{ km} \end{matrix}\right\} = \left\{\begin{matrix} \text{Time for diesel train} \\ \text{to travel } (72 - x) \text{ km} \end{matrix}\right.$$

$$\text{Substituting, Time} = \frac{\text{distance}}{\text{speed}} \text{ for each train,}$$

$$\frac{\text{distance travelled by electric train}}{\text{speed of electric train}} = \frac{\text{distance travelled by diesel train}}{\text{speed of diesel train}}$$

$$\frac{x}{80} = \frac{72 - x}{64}$$

L.C.M. = 320, multiplying every term by 320,

$$4x = 5(72 - x)$$
$$4x = 360 - 5x$$
$$4x + 5x = 360$$
$$9x = 360$$
$$x = 40$$

∴ Trains pass each other at a point 40 km from A.   Ans.

Example. A ship travels up-river against the current for a distance of 25 naut. miles and then down-river with the current over the same distance, taking 3 h 30 min over the double journey. If the normal speed of the ship in still water is 15 knot, find the speed of the current.

An equation can be found from the total time being equal to the time for the ship to go up-river plus the time for it to return down-river, and time in hours can be expressed as distance (naut. miles) divided by speed (knot) to suit the quantities given in the problem.

Let x = speed of current (knot),

speed of ship against current = $(15 - x)$ knot,

then, speed of ship running with current = $(15 + x)$ knot.

Time to go up-river + Time to go down-river = Total time

$$\frac{\text{distance up-river}}{\text{speed up-river}} + \frac{\text{distance down-river}}{\text{speed down-river}} = 3\tfrac{1}{2} \text{ h}$$

$$\frac{25}{15 - x} + \frac{25}{15 + x} = 3.5$$

Multiply every term by $(15 - x)(15 + x)$, the L.C.M. of the denominators,

$$25(15 + x) + 25(15 - x) = 3.5(15 - x)(15 + x)$$
$$375 + 25x + 375 - 25x = 3.5(15^2 - x^2)$$
$$750 = 787.5 - 3.5x^2$$
$$3.5x^2 = 787.5 - 750$$
$$3.5x^2 = 37.5$$
$$x^2 = 10.71$$
$$x = \pm\sqrt{10.71}$$
$$x = \pm 3.273$$

$\therefore$ Speed of current = 3.273 knot   Ans.

TRANSPOSITION AND EVALUATION OF FORMULAE

A formula is a group of algebraic symbols which expresses a rule for determining the value of one of the symbols when values are substituted for the others. To transpose means to change the order of the symbols to produce a re-arranged equation giving the value of one of the other symbols in terms of the remainder. Being an equation, the procedure is the same as for equations in general.

Example.   Transpose the following formula to give p_2 in terms of the other quantities,

$$\frac{p_1 V_1}{T_1} = \frac{p_2 V_2}{T_2}$$

Note the usual practice of omitting multiplication signs between the quantities to be multiplied, for the first few examples the multiplication signs will be put in while working through the various steps.

$$\frac{p_1 \times V_1}{T_1} = \frac{p_2 \times V_2}{T_2}$$

Multiply both sides by the L.C.M. of the denominators which is $T_1 \times T_2$,

$$p_1 \times V_1 \times T_2 = p_2 \times V_2 \times T_1$$

Divide both sides by $V_2 \times T_1$, so that p_2 will be left on its own on one side,

$$\frac{p_1 \times V_1 \times T_2}{V_2 \times T_1} = p_2$$

It is usual to write expressions and formulae with the required unknown on the left side of the equation and to omit multiplication signs, thus,

$$p_2 = \frac{p_1 V_1 T_2}{V_2 T_1} \quad \text{Ans.}$$

Example.   Express S in terms of the other quantities in the following expression,

$$d = \sqrt[3]{\frac{S \times D}{C}}$$

Cube both sides,

$$d^3 = \frac{S \times D}{C}$$

Multiply both sides by C,

$$C \times d^3 = S \times D$$

Divide both sides by D,

$$\frac{C \times d^3}{D} = S$$

or,

$$S = \frac{Cd^3}{D} \quad \text{Ans.}$$

Example.   Transpose the following expression to give the value of r in terms of E and n. Find the value of r when $E = 60$, $n = 1 \cdot 4$.

$$E = 100\left[1 - \left\{\frac{1}{r}\right\}^{n-1}\right]$$

Note, $1^{n-1} = 1$

$$\therefore E = 100\left[1 - \frac{1}{r^{n-1}}\right]$$

Divide both sides by 100,

$$\frac{E}{100} = 1 - \frac{1}{r^{n-1}}$$

Take 1 to other side leaving unknown by itself,

$$\frac{E}{100} - 1 = -\frac{1}{r^{n-1}}$$

Multiply throughout by -1 to make unknown positive,

$$1 - \frac{E}{100} = \frac{1}{r^{n-1}}$$

Cross-multiply to bring unknown on top,

$$r^{n-1} = \frac{1}{1 - \dfrac{E}{100}}$$

Take $n - 1$ root of both sides,

$$r = \left\{\frac{1}{1 - \dfrac{E}{100}}\right\}^{\frac{1}{n-1}} \quad \text{Ans. (i)}$$

Insert numerical values,

$$r = \left\{ \cfrac{1}{1 - \cfrac{60}{100}} \right\}^{\frac{1}{1\cdot4-1}}$$

Simplify

$$\frac{1}{1\cdot4 - 1} = \frac{1}{0\cdot4} = 2\cdot5$$

$$1 - \frac{60}{100} = 1 - 0\cdot6 = 0\cdot4$$

$$\frac{1}{1 - \dfrac{60}{100}} = \frac{1}{0\cdot4} = 2\cdot5$$

Hence,

$$r = 2\cdot5^{2\cdot5}$$
$$= 9\cdot88 \quad \text{Ans. (ii)}$$

Example.   Transpose the following expression to give V_1 in terms of the other quantities,

$$p_1 \times V_1{}^n = p_2 \times V_2{}^n$$

and find the value of V_1 when $p_1 = 1\cdot035$, $p_2 = 4\cdot14$, $V_2 = 0\cdot5$ and $n = 1\cdot3$.

$$p_1 \times V_1{}^n = p_2 \times V_2{}^n$$

Divide both sides by p_1

$$V_1{}^n = \frac{p_2 \times V_2{}^n}{p_1}$$

Take n'th root of both sides,

$$V_1 = \sqrt[n]{\frac{p_2 \times V_2{}^n}{p_1}}$$

$$V_1 = V_2 \times \sqrt[n]{\frac{p_2}{p_1}}$$

$$\text{or,} \quad V_1 = V_2 \times \left(\frac{p_2}{p_1}\right)^{\frac{1}{n}} \quad \text{Ans. (i)}$$

Substituting for values,

$$V_1 = 0.5 \times {}^{1.3}\sqrt{\frac{4.14}{1.035}}$$

$$= 0.5 \times {}^{1.3}\sqrt{4}$$

$$= 1.453 \quad \text{Ans. (ii)}$$

LOGARITHMIC EQUATIONS

To illustrate the basic principles, two examples are now solved using logarithms (to base 10). Simultaneous logarithmic equations are covered in Chapter 4.

Example.   Given $ab^x = cd^x$, find x when: $a = 13.5$, $b = 1.8$, $c = 68$, $d = 0.55$.

$$a \times b^x = c \times d^x$$

$$13.5 \times 1.8^x = 68 \times 0.55^x$$

Bring all terms to the power of x to one side, and pure numbers to the other side,

$$\left(\frac{1.8}{0.55}\right)^x = \frac{68}{13.5}$$

$$3.273^x = 5.037$$

$$(\text{lg of } 3.273) \times x = \text{lg of } 5.037$$

$$0.5149 \times x = 0.7022$$

$$x = \frac{0.7022}{0.5149}$$

$$x = 1.363 \quad \text{Ans.}$$

Example.   Given $\dfrac{T_1}{T_2} = \left(\dfrac{p_1}{p_2}\right)^{\frac{n-1}{n}}$ find n when,

$$T_1 = 797, \quad T_2 = 301, \quad p_1 = 34\cdot4, \quad p_2 = 1\cdot05$$

$$\frac{797}{301} = \left(\frac{34\cdot4}{1\cdot05}\right)^{\frac{n-1}{n}}$$

$$2\cdot648 = (32\cdot76)^{\frac{n-1}{n}}$$

$$\lg \text{ of } 2\cdot648 = (\lg \text{ of } 32\cdot76) \times \frac{n-1}{n}$$

$$0\cdot4229 = (1\cdot5154) \times \frac{n-1}{n}$$

$$0\cdot4229n = 1\cdot5154n - 1\cdot5154$$

$$1\cdot5154 = 1\cdot5154n - 0\cdot4229n$$

$$n = \frac{1\cdot5154}{1\cdot0925}$$

$$n = 1\cdot387 \quad \text{Ans.}$$

Note. Logarithms to any base can be used to evaluate these types of example involving logarithmic (and exponential) equations and functions.

TEST EXAMPLES 3

1. Find the value of x which satisfies the following equation:

$$8 + 5x - 7 = 3x + 9$$

2. Find the value of a in the equation:

$$2(a + 3) + 3(2a - 4) = 4(11 - 3a)$$

3. Solve this equation:

$$3[3 - \{x + 2(1 - x)\} - 4x] = 2[x - 3(2 + x) - 4]$$

4. Find x from the following equation:

$$\frac{2x}{3} + \frac{x}{4} - \frac{5}{6} = \frac{4x}{5} + \frac{1}{3}$$

5. Find a in the following:

$$\frac{(1 - 2a^2)}{6a} - \frac{1}{4} + \frac{a}{3} = \frac{1}{6} - \frac{5}{2a}$$

6. If

$$\frac{2}{x - 3} + \frac{3}{x + 2} = \frac{4}{x^2 - x - 6} \quad \text{find } x.$$

7. A ship travelling at 17·5 knot leaves one port bound for another $4\frac{1}{2}$ h after another ship whose speed is 16 knot leaves the same port set on the same course. After how many hours and at what distance from port will the fast ship overtake the slower one?

8. A rectangular plate is to be cut so that the length is four times the breadth and having an area of 1 m². Find the length and breadth.

9. Transpose the following equation to give θ_2 in terms of the other quantities:

$$\frac{R_2}{R_1} = \frac{R_0(1 + \alpha\theta_2)}{R_0(1 + \alpha\theta_1)}$$

and find the value of θ_2 when:

$$R_1 = 200$$
$$R_2 = 240$$
$$\theta_1 = 15$$
$$\alpha = 0\cdot0042$$

10. The diameter in mm of coupling bolts should not be less than that given by the formula:

$$d = \sqrt{\frac{D^3}{3\cdot5 \times n \times R}}$$

where D = diameter of shafting in mm;
$\quad n$ = number of bolts per coupling;
$\quad R$ = pitch circle radius in mm.

Express R in terms of the other quantities and find the pitch circle radius when $d = 82\cdot5$ mm, $D = 381$ mm, and $n = 8$ bolts per coupling.

11. Given

$$\frac{T_1}{T_2} = \left\{\frac{p_1}{p_2}\right\}^{\frac{n-1}{n}}$$

find the value of n when $T_1 = 670$, $T_2 = 324$, $p_1 = 21$ and $p_2 = 1\cdot25$.

12. Find the values of x in each of the following equations:
    (a) $4^{0\cdot59x} = 56\cdot36$
    (b) $x^{1\cdot95} = 12\cdot4x^{0\cdot53}$
    (c) $\epsilon^{5x} = 46\cdot38^{2\cdot6}$
    (d) $^3\sqrt{x} = \epsilon^{2\cdot5}$

CHAPTER 4

SIMULTANEOUS LINEAR EQUATIONS

In the preceding chapter, equations containing only one unknown quantity were explained; now two (or more) unknown quantities are required to be found.

To find the values of two unknowns, two equations are required, each containing the same two unknown quantities, this pair of equations is called 'simultaneous'.

Various different methods may be used in the solution of these; three methods commonly employed will be explained here in the order, (i) by elimination, (ii) by substitution, (iii) by equating expressions of like unknowns. There is another method and that is by drawing a graph of each equation on a common base; the point of intersection of the graphs produces the solution of the unknowns; this method is included in Chapter 6.

Method (i). This process is to couple the two equations together in such a form that by either (*a*) adding them together, (*b*) subtracting one from the other, (*c*) multiplying them, or (*d*) dividing one by the other, one of the unknown quantities cancel out, leaving a single equation containing only one unknown which is then simply solved. When one of the quantities has thus been found its value is substituted into one of the original equations which will then become another single equation containing only the other one remaining unknown to be solved.

The following examples will serve to demonstrate some of the steps normally involved in this method of solution.

Example. When twice one number is added to five times another number, the result is 34, and when three times the latter number is subtracted from four times the former, the result is 16. Find the numbers.

$$\text{Let} \quad x = \text{one number,}$$

$$\text{and} \quad y = \text{other number,}$$

From the first statement, $2x + 5y = 34$ ... ... (i)

From the second statement, $4x - 3y = 16$ ... ... (ii)

Multiply equation (i) by 2 so that it will contain the same multiple
of x as in equation (ii), and set the pair down again,

$$4x + 10y = 68 \quad \ldots \quad \ldots \quad \ldots \quad \ldots \quad \text{(iii)}$$
$$4x - 3y = 16 \quad \ldots \quad \ldots \quad \ldots \quad \ldots \quad \text{(iv)}$$

By subtracting (iv) from (iii), $4x$ will cancel, leaving one equation
containing only y as the unknown. Remember that when subtracting a
minus quantity, change its sign and add, thus subtracting $-3y$ from
$+10y$ gives $+13y$.

$$4x + 10y = 68 \quad \ldots \quad \ldots \quad \ldots \quad \ldots \quad \text{(iii)}$$
$$\text{subtract} \quad 4x - 3y = 16 \quad \ldots \quad \ldots \quad \ldots \quad \ldots \quad \text{(iv)}$$
$$13y = 52$$
$$y = 4$$

Substitute the value of y, found to be 4, into any one of the original
equations which contain x and y; this will produce another equation
containing only x as the unknown.

Substituting $y = 4$ into equation (i)

$$2x + 5 \times 4 = 34$$
$$2x = 34 - 20$$
$$2x = 14$$
$$x = 7$$

Therefore the numbers are 7 and 4.   Ans.

Example.   Given $2p + 5q = 26\cdot5$
                  and $3p - 2q = 6\cdot5$

find the values of p and q.

$$2p + 5q = 26\cdot5 \quad \ldots \quad \ldots \quad \ldots \quad \ldots \quad \text{(i)}$$
$$3p - 2q = 6\cdot5 \quad \ldots \quad \ldots \quad \ldots \quad \ldots \quad \text{(ii)}$$

Multiply (i) by 3, and multiply (ii) by 2,

$$6p + 15q = 79\cdot5 \quad \ldots \quad \ldots \quad \ldots \quad \ldots \quad \text{(iii)}$$
$$6p - 4q = 13 \quad \ldots \quad \ldots \quad \ldots \quad \ldots \quad \text{(iv)}$$
Subtract (iv) from (iii) $19q = 66\cdot5$
$$q = 3\cdot5$$

Substitute $q = 3 \cdot 5$ into equation (ii)

$$3p - 2 \times 3 \cdot 5 = 6 \cdot 5$$
$$3p = 6 \cdot 5 + 7$$
$$3p = 13 \cdot 5$$
$$p = 4 \cdot 5$$

The values of p and q are 4·5 and 3·5 respectively.   Ans.

Example.   Find the values of x and y in the simultaneous equations,

$$\frac{x}{8} + \frac{y}{5} = \frac{7}{8}$$
$$\frac{2x}{3} - \frac{y}{2} = \frac{3}{4}$$

Simplify these equations by multiplying the first by the L.C.M. of its denominators which is 40, and the second by its L.C.M. which is 12,

$$5x + 8y = 35 \quad \ldots \quad \ldots \quad \ldots \quad \ldots \quad \text{(i)}$$
$$8x - 6y = 9 \quad \ldots \quad \ldots \quad \ldots \quad \ldots \quad \text{(ii)}$$

Multiply (i) by 3, and (ii) by 4,

$$15x + 24y = 105 \quad \ldots \quad \ldots \quad \ldots \quad \ldots \text{(iii)}$$
$$\underline{32x - 24y = 36} \quad \ldots \quad \ldots \quad \ldots \quad \ldots \text{(iv)}$$

Add (iii) and (iv) $47x = 141$

$$x = 3$$

Substitute $x = 3$ into equation (i),

$$5 \times 3 + 8y = 35$$
$$8y = 35 - 15$$
$$8y = 20$$
$$y = 2\tfrac{1}{2}$$

The values of x and y are 3 and $2\tfrac{1}{2}$ respectively.   Ans.

Example.   Given the simultaneous equations,

$$1 \cdot 5^x \times 2^y = 18$$
$$4^x \times 1 \cdot 5^y = 54$$

find the values of x and y.

Writing the two simultaneous equations in log form (base 10); see logarithmic equations (Chapter 3).

$$(\lg 1 \cdot 5) \times x + (\lg 2) \times y = \lg 18$$
$$(\lg 4) \times x + (\lg 1 \cdot 5) \times y = \lg 54$$

Inserting log values,

$$0 \cdot 1761x + 0 \cdot 301y = 1 \cdot 2553 \quad \dots \quad \dots \quad \dots \quad \dots \quad \text{(i)}$$
$$0 \cdot 6021x + 0 \cdot 1761y = 1 \cdot 7324 \quad \dots \quad \dots \quad \dots \quad \dots \quad \text{(ii)}$$

Dividing (i) by 0·1761, and dividing (ii) by 0·6021,

$$x + 1 \cdot 709y = 7 \cdot 127 \quad \dots \quad \dots \quad \dots \quad \dots \quad \text{(iii)}$$
$$x + 0 \cdot 2925y = 2 \cdot 877 \quad \dots \quad \dots \quad \dots \quad \dots \quad \text{(iv)}$$

Subtracting (iv) from (iii),

$$1 \cdot 4165y = 4 \cdot 25$$
$$y = 3$$

Substituting $y = 3$ into (iii),

$$x + 1 \cdot 709 \times 3 = 7 \cdot 127$$
$$x = 7 \cdot 127 - 5 \cdot 127$$
$$x = 2$$

The values of x and y are 2 and 3 respectively.   Ans.

Method (*ii*) of solving simultaneous equations is by transposing one of the equations to express one of the unknowns in terms of the other quantities, then substituting this expression for that unknown into the other equation, thus producing a single equation containing only the other unknown which can then be solved.

Repeating the first example to be solved by this method,

$$2x + 5y = 34$$
$$4x - 3y = 16$$

Transposing the first equation to express x in terms of the other quantities.

$$2x + 5y = 34$$
$$2x = 34 - 5y$$
$$x = 17 - 2 \cdot 5y$$

Substituting this value of x into the second equation, simplifying and solving.

$$4x - 3y = 16$$
$$4(17 - 2 \cdot 5y) - 3y = 16$$
$$68 - 10y - 3y = 16$$
$$-10y - 3y = 16 - 68$$
$$-13y = -52$$
$$y = 4$$

Substituting $y = 4$ into the first equation and solving,

$$2x + 5y = 34$$
$$2x + 20 = 34$$
$$2x = 34 - 20$$
$$2x = 14$$
$$x = 7$$

The values of x and y are 7 and 4 respectively.   Ans.

Method (iii) is to transpose both equations to express the same unknown in terms of the other quantities, the two expressions are then equated together, making one equation with one unknown.
Taking the same example again,

$$2x + 5y = 34 \quad \ldots \quad \ldots \quad \ldots \quad \ldots \quad \text{(i)}$$
$$4x - 3y = 16 \quad \ldots \quad \ldots \quad \ldots \quad \ldots \quad \text{(ii)}$$

Transposing both equations, in each case expressing x in terms of the other quantities,

From (i)
$$2x = 34 - 5y$$
$$x = 17 - 2\cdot5y \qquad \ldots \quad \ldots \quad \text{(iii)}$$

From (ii)
$$4x = 16 + 3y$$
$$x = 4 + 0\cdot75y \qquad \ldots \quad \ldots \quad \text{(iv)}$$

Since x in one equation has the same value as in the other, then, (iii) = (iv)

$$4 + 0\cdot75y = 17 - 2\cdot5y$$
$$2\cdot5y + 0\cdot75y = 17 - 4$$
$$3\cdot25y = 13$$
$$y = 4$$

Substituting $y = 4$ into equation (i)

$$2x + 20 = 34$$
$$2x = 14$$
$$x = 7$$

$x = 7$ and $y = 4$ as before.

The method to employ in solving a given simultaneous equation will be that which is easiest to apply depending upon the form in which the equation is given.

THREE UNKNOWNS

Just as two unknowns can be found from two equations, three unknowns can be solved if three equations be given.

Example. To find the values of x, y and z which satisfy the equations,

$$3x + 2y - z = 4 \quad \ldots \quad \ldots \quad \ldots \quad \ldots \quad \text{(i)}$$
$$2x + y + z = 7 \quad \ldots \quad \ldots \quad \ldots \quad \ldots \quad \text{(ii)}$$
$$x - y + z = 2 \quad \ldots \quad \ldots \quad \ldots \quad \ldots \quad \text{(iii)}$$

Eliminate one unknown at a time, take z first as it appears the easiest to get rid of.

Add equations (i) and (ii),

$$3x + 2y - z = 4$$
$$\underline{2x + y + z = 7}$$
$$5x + 3y \qquad = 11 \quad \ldots \quad \ldots \quad \ldots \quad \ldots \quad (iv)$$

Subtract (iii) from (ii),

$$2x + y + z = 7$$
$$\underline{x - y + z = 2}$$
$$x + 2y \qquad = 5 \quad \ldots \quad \ldots \quad \ldots \quad \ldots \quad (v)$$

Multiply (v) by 5 and subtract (iv) from the result,

$$5x + 10y = 25$$
$$\underline{5x + 3y = 11}$$
$$7y = 14$$
$$y = 2$$

Substitute $y = 2$ into (v),

$$x + 2 \times 2 = 5$$
$$x = 5 - 4$$
$$x = 1$$

Substitute $x = 1$ and $y = 2$ into (iii),

$$1 - 2 + z = 2$$
$$z = 2 + 2 - 1$$
$$z = 3$$

$\therefore x = 1$, $y = 2$ and $z = 3$.   Ans.

TEST EXAMPLES 4

1. When $2\frac{1}{2}$ times one number is added to $3\frac{1}{2}$ times another the result is 19; and when $3\frac{1}{2}$ times the first number is subtracted from $2\frac{1}{2}$ times the second, the result is 3. Find the numbers.

2. Find the values of x and y in the simultaneous equations:

$$\frac{2x}{3} - \frac{3y}{5} = \frac{3}{4} \quad \text{and} \quad \frac{x}{2} - \frac{y}{4} = \frac{13}{16}$$

3. Find the values of a and b which satisfy the equations:

$$a(1 + 2b) = 3 \quad \text{and} \quad a(1 - 3b) = 0 \cdot 5$$

4. A man and his wife are 72 and 68 years old respectively, and have one grandson and one grand-daughter. The man's age is equal to the sum of four times the grandson's age and three times the grand-daughter's. The woman's age is equal to the sum of three times the grandson's age and four times the grand-daughter's. Find the ages of the two grandchildren.

5. The difference between two numbers is 2 and the difference between their squares is 6. Find the numbers.

6. The linear law of a simple lifting machine is given by $F = a + bm$ where $m =$ mass lifted, $F =$ effort applied, a and b being constants. In a certain lifting machine it was found that when $m = 30$ kg, $F = 35$ N, and when $m = 70$ kg, $F = 55$ N. Find the constants a and b, express the law of this machine, and find the effort required to lift a mass of 60 kg.

7. Two ships, A and B, leave one port bound for another on the same course. B leaves 1 h later than A and overtakes in 8 h. If the speeds of each ship had been 4 knot slower, B would have overtaken A 2 h earlier. Find the original speeds of the ships.

8. Given the simultaneous equations,

$$\frac{x}{2-y} + \frac{6}{x} = 4 \quad \text{and} \quad \frac{2x}{2-y} - \frac{9}{x} = 1$$

find the values of

$$\frac{x}{2-y}, \frac{1}{x}, x \quad \text{and} \quad y.$$

9. Find the values of x and y in the simultaneous equations,

$$2^x = 4^y \quad \text{and} \quad 4^{x-1} = 2^{y+1}$$

10. Find the values of x and y in the simultaneous equations,

$$1 \cdot 259^{x+1} \times 1 \cdot 175^{y-1} = 2 \cdot 323$$
$$3 \cdot 162^x \times 1 \cdot 778^y = 25 \cdot 12$$

11. Given the following relationship,

$$\frac{d^2}{x^2} = \frac{x^2}{y^2} = \frac{y^2}{D^2}$$

express x in terms of d and D, and find the values of x and y when $D = 75$ and $d = 25$.

12. Find the values of a, b and c in the simultaneous equations,

$$3a + 6b - 2c = 7 \cdot 25$$
$$2a + 3b + 4c = 26$$
$$4a - 2b + c = 10 \cdot 25$$

CHAPTER 5

QUADRATIC AND CUBIC EQUATIONS

A **quadratic** equation is one which contains the square of the unknown quantity, thus, $x^2 = 36$ is a quadratic equation in its very elementary form and solved simply by taking the square root of both sides, $x = \pm 6$.

The form usually associated with the title quadratic equation contains the first power of the unknown as well as its square, the general form being,

$$ax^2 + bx + c = 0$$

where a (the coefficient of x^2), b (which is the coefficient of x), and c are given quantities, and x is the unknown. These may be solved by various methods, those which will be explained here are (i) by factorisation, (ii) by completing the square, (iii) by formula. Another method is by graphical means and this is explained in Chapter 6.

Method (i) by factorisation. This method is applied only when the expression can be readily factorised.

Example.

$$x^2 - 5x + 6 = 0 \quad \ldots \quad \ldots \quad \ldots \quad \ldots \quad \text{(i)}$$

Factorise, as explained in Chapter 2,

$$(x - 2)(x - 3) = 0 \quad \ldots \quad \ldots \quad \ldots \quad \ldots \quad \text{(ii)}$$

From previous, when any quantity is multiplied by zero, the result is zero. It therefore follows that if the result of the product of two quantities is zero, one of those quantities must be zero. In equation (ii) the product of $(x - 2)$ and $(x - 3)$ is zero, hence either $(x - 2)$ or $(x - 3)$ must be a zero quantity.

$$\text{If} \qquad x - 2 = 0$$
$$\text{then} \qquad x = 2$$
$$\text{or, if} \qquad x - 3 = 0$$
$$\text{then} \qquad x = 3$$

The value of x in the equation can therefore be 2 or 3. By trying each of these values in the original equation (i) it will be seen that either will satisfy the equation.

$$\therefore x = 2 \quad \text{or} \quad 3 \quad \text{Ans.}$$

Example. $2x^2 - 5x - 12 = 0$

Factorise: $(2x + 3)(x - 4) = 0$

either $2x + 3 = 0$ or $x - 4 = 0$

then $2x = -3$ then $x = 4$

$$x = -1\tfrac{1}{2}$$

Therefore, $x = 4$ or $-1\tfrac{1}{2}$ Ans.

Method (ii) by completing the square.   Any quadratic expression, whether it can be factorised or not, can be solved by this method. It is based upon the process of changing the expression into one which is a 'perfect square', that is, one whose square root can be readily obtained, then, by taking the square root, the expression so found contains only the first power of the unknown, thus producing a simple equation which can be easily solved.

Example. $4x^2 + 12x - 7 = 0$

Divide throughout by 4 to reduce coefficient of x^2 to unity,

$$x^2 + 3x - \frac{7}{4} = 0$$

The square root of this expression cannot be taken therefore move $-\tfrac{7}{4}$ over to the other side,

$$x^2 + 3x = \frac{7}{4}$$

and add such a quantity that will make the left hand side into a perfect square, not forgetting that whatever is added to one side the same quantity must also be added to the other side to preserve equality. In Chapter 2, section on factorisation, paragraph (iii), it was pointed out that an expression is a perfect square when the third term is equal to the square of half the coefficient of x. The coefficient of x here is 3, half of 3 is $\frac{3}{2}$, and this squared is $(\frac{3}{2})^2$. Therefore add $(\frac{3}{2})^2$ to both sides,

$$x^2 + 3x + \left(\frac{3}{2}\right)^2 = \frac{7}{4} + \left(\frac{3}{2}\right)^2$$

Now take the square root of both sides, and solve

$$x + \frac{3}{2} = \pm\sqrt{\frac{7}{4} + \frac{9}{4}}$$

$$x + \frac{3}{2} = \pm\sqrt{\frac{16}{4}}$$

$$x + \tfrac{3}{2} = \pm 2$$

$$x = \pm 2 - 1\tfrac{1}{2}$$

$$x = \tfrac{1}{2} \quad \text{or} \quad -3\tfrac{1}{2} \quad \text{Ans.}$$

Note the $\pm$ sign. As previously seen, the square root of a number can be plus or minus, and both values must be taken into account. The root of a minus quantity is inadmissible.

Example. $12x^2 + x - \tfrac{1}{2} = 0$

Dividing throughout by 12,

$$x^2 + \frac{x}{12} - \frac{1}{24} = 0$$

Shifting third term to other side and completing the square,

$$x^2 + \frac{x}{12} + \left(\frac{1}{24}\right)^2 = \frac{1}{24} + \left(\frac{1}{24}\right)^2$$

Taking square root of both sides and simplifying,

$$x + \frac{1}{24} = \pm\sqrt{\frac{1}{24} + \frac{1}{24^2}}$$

$$x + \frac{1}{24} = \pm\sqrt{\frac{24 + 1}{24^2}}$$

$$x + \frac{1}{24} = \pm\sqrt{\frac{25}{24^2}}$$

$$x + \frac{1}{24} = \pm\frac{5}{24}$$

$$x = \pm\frac{5}{24} - \frac{1}{24}$$

$$x = \frac{4}{24} \quad \text{or} \quad -\frac{6}{24}$$

$$x = \frac{1}{6} \quad \text{or} \quad -\frac{1}{4} \quad \text{Ans.}$$

Method (*iii*) *by formula.* Let 'a' be the coefficient of x^2, 'b' the coefficient of x, and 'c' the third term, gives the general form of a quadratic equation:

$$ax^2 + bx + c = 0$$

and solving for x by the method of completing the square, a ready-made formula is produced for solving any quadratic equation.

$$ax^2 + bx + c = 0$$

Dividing throughout by a,

$$x^2 + \frac{bx}{a} + \frac{c}{a} = 0$$

Taking the third term to the other side and adding to both sides the square of half the coefficient of x, to complete the square,

$$x^2 + \frac{bx}{a} + \left(\frac{b}{2a}\right)^2 = \left(\frac{b}{2a}\right)^2 - \frac{c}{a}$$

Taking square root of both sides and simplifying,

$$x + \frac{b}{2a} = \pm\sqrt{\frac{b^2}{4a^2} - \frac{c}{a}}$$

$$x + \frac{b}{2a} = \pm\sqrt{\frac{b^2 - 4ac}{4a^2}}$$

$$x + \frac{b}{2a} = \frac{\pm\sqrt{b^2 - 4ac}}{2a}$$

$$x = -\frac{b}{2a} \pm \frac{\sqrt{b^2 - 4ac}}{2a}$$

$$x = \frac{-b \pm \sqrt{b^2 - 4ac}}{2a}$$

This is a very useful formula which provides a straightforward solution to any quadratic equation and should be committed to memory.

Example. $1 \cdot 5x^2 + 2x - 10 = 0$

Applying the formula,

$$x = \frac{-b \pm \sqrt{b^2 - 4ac}}{2a}$$

Substituting,

$$a = 1 \cdot 5, b = 2, c = -10,$$

$$x = \frac{-2 \pm \sqrt{2^2 - 4 \times 1 \cdot 5 \times (-10)}}{2 \times 1 \cdot 5}$$

$$x = \frac{-2 \pm \sqrt{4 + 60}}{3}$$

$$x = \frac{-2 \pm \sqrt{64}}{3}$$

$$x = \frac{-2 \pm 8}{3}$$

$$x = \frac{6}{3} \quad \text{or} \quad \frac{-10}{3}$$

$$x = 2 \quad \text{or} \quad -3\tfrac{1}{3} \quad \text{Ans.}$$

Great care must be taken with the signs. Note that the value of c in the above examples is -10, and the term $-4ac$ becomes $(-4) \times 1.5 \times (-10)$ which is $+60$.

Another point to note is when the value of b is a minus quantity, in the next example the value of b is -9, the term $-b$ in the formula then becomes $-(-9)$ which is $+9$.

Example. $2x^2 - 9x - 35 = 0$

$$x = \frac{-b \pm \sqrt{b^2 - 4ac}}{2a}$$

where $a = 2$, $b = -9$, $c = -35$

$$x = \frac{+9 \pm \sqrt{9^2 - 4 \times 2 \times (-35)}}{2 \times 2}$$
$$x = \frac{9 \pm \sqrt{81 + 280}}{4}$$
$$x = \frac{9 \pm \sqrt{361}}{4}$$
$$x = \frac{9 \pm 19}{4}$$
$$x = \frac{28}{4} \quad \text{or} \quad \frac{-10}{4}$$
$$x = 7 \quad \text{or} \quad -2\tfrac{1}{2} \quad \text{Ans.}$$

EQUATIONS REDUCIBLE TO QUADRATICS

Equations of the form,

$$ax^{2n} + bx^n + c = 0$$

where n is a power of x, and $2n$ is twice that power, can be solved as a normal quadratic by substituting another symbol of the first order for x^n such as y, consequently x^{2n} would then be represented by y^2, thus,

$$ay^2 + by + c = 0$$

y is solved by one of the usual methods of solving quadratic equations then the value of x is obtained from the substitution $y = x^n$.

Example. $x^4 - 8\tfrac{1}{2}x^2 + 14\tfrac{1}{16} = 0$

Let y represent x^2, then $y^2 = x^4$,

$$y^2 - 8\tfrac{1}{2}y + 14\tfrac{1}{16} = 0$$

Solving by formula,

$$y = \frac{-b \pm \sqrt{b^2 - 4ac}}{2a}$$

where $a = 1$, $b = -8\tfrac{1}{2}$, $c = 14\tfrac{1}{16}$

$$y = \frac{8 \cdot 5 \pm \sqrt{72 \cdot 25 - 56 \cdot 25}}{2}$$

$$y = \frac{8 \cdot 5 \pm \sqrt{16}}{2}$$

$$y = \frac{8 \cdot 5 \pm 4}{2}$$

$$y = \frac{12 \cdot 5}{2} \quad \text{or} \quad \frac{4 \cdot 5}{2}$$

$$y = 6 \cdot 25 \quad \text{or} \quad 2 \cdot 25$$

$$y = x^2 \quad \therefore \quad x = \sqrt{y}$$

$$x = \pm\sqrt{6 \cdot 25} \quad \text{or} \quad \pm\sqrt{2 \cdot 25}$$

$$x = \pm 2 \cdot 5 \quad \text{or} \quad \pm 1 \cdot 5 \quad \text{Ans.}$$

Example. $0 \cdot 3 V^{2 \cdot 8} - 1 \cdot 56 V^{1 \cdot 4} + 1 \cdot 98 = 0$

Note first that every term is divisible by 3, therefore take advantage of this by dividing every term by $0 \cdot 3$ to produce an equation with a simpler set of figures,

$$V^{2 \cdot 8} - 5 \cdot 2 V^{1 \cdot 4} + 6 \cdot 6 = 0$$

Let $x = V^{1 \cdot 4}$ then $x^2 = V^{2 \cdot 8}$

$$x^2 - 5 \cdot 2x + 6 \cdot 6 = 0$$

By formula, $\qquad x = \dfrac{-b \pm \sqrt{b^2 - 4ac}}{2a}$

where $a = 1$, $b = -5 \cdot 2$, $c = 6 \cdot 6$

$$x = \frac{5 \cdot 2 \pm \sqrt{27 \cdot 04 - 26 \cdot 4}}{2}$$

$$x = \frac{5 \cdot 2 \pm \sqrt{0 \cdot 64}}{2}$$

$$x = \frac{5 \cdot 2 \pm 0 \cdot 8}{2}$$

$$x = \frac{6}{2} \quad \text{or} \quad \frac{4 \cdot 4}{2}$$

$$x = 3 \quad \text{or} \quad 2 \cdot 2$$

$$x = V^{1 \cdot 4} \quad \therefore \quad V = {}^{1 \cdot 4}\sqrt{x}$$

$$V = {}^{1 \cdot 4}\sqrt{3} \quad \text{or} \quad {}^{1 \cdot 4}\sqrt{2 \cdot 2}$$

$$= 2 \cdot 192 \quad \text{or} \quad 1 \cdot 756 \quad \text{Ans.}$$

SIMULTANEOUS QUADRATIC EQUATIONS

In the previous chapter methods of solving simultaneous linear equations were explained, but the examples were such that only simple equations (linear) were involved. Further examples can now be dealt with where quadratic equations are either given in the first place or are produced in the process of solving.

Example.   Find the values of x and y which satisfy the equations,

$$2x^2 - 3y = 3$$
$$x + 5y = 4$$

Multiplying the first equation by 5 and the second equation by 3, then adding the results together to eliminate y,

$$10x^2 - 15y = 15$$
$$\underline{3x + 15y = 12}$$
$$10x^2 + 3x = 27$$

Re-arranging,

$$10x^2 + 3x - 27 = 0$$

Solving this quadratic by formula,

$$x = \frac{-b \pm \sqrt{b^2 - 4ac}}{2a}$$

where $a = 10$, $b = 3$, $c = -27$

$$x = \frac{-3 \pm \sqrt{9 + 1080}}{20}$$

$$x = \frac{-3 \pm \sqrt{1089}}{20}$$

$$x = \frac{-3 \pm 33}{20}$$

$$x = \frac{30}{20} \quad \text{or} \quad \frac{-36}{20}$$

$$x = 1 \cdot 5 \quad \text{or} \quad -1 \cdot 8$$

Substituting $x = 1 \cdot 5$ into the second equation,

$$1 \cdot 5 + 5y = 4$$
$$5y = 2 \cdot 5$$
$$y = 0 \cdot 5$$

Substituting $x = -1 \cdot 8$ into the second equation,

$$-1 \cdot 8 + 5y = 4$$
$$5y = 5 \cdot 8$$
$$y = 1 \cdot 16$$

$$\left. \begin{array}{l} x = 1 \cdot 5 \quad \text{and} \quad y = 0 \cdot 5 \\ \text{or} \quad x = -1 \cdot 8 \quad \text{and} \quad y = 1 \cdot 16 \end{array} \right\} \quad \text{Ans.}$$

An alternative method to the above is to find the value of one unknown in terms of the other from the simplest equation, and substitute this into the other equation. Thus, in the previous example,

$$2x^2 - 3y = 3 \quad \dots \quad \dots \quad \dots \quad \dots \quad \text{(i)}$$
$$x + 5y = 4 \quad \dots \quad \dots \quad \dots \quad \dots \quad \text{(ii)}$$

From (ii)

$$y = \tfrac{1}{5}(4 - x)$$

Substitute this value of y into equation (i) and simplify,

$$2x^2 - 3 \times \tfrac{1}{5}(4 - x) = 3$$

Multiply throughout by 5,

$$10x^2 - 12 + 3x = 15$$
$$10x^2 + 3x - 27 = 0$$

the same quadratic to be solved as before.

   Example.   Find the values of x and y which satisfy the simultaneous equations:

$$2x^2 + xy - y^2 = 8 \quad \ldots \quad \ldots \quad \ldots \quad \ldots \qquad \text{(i)}$$
$$3x + 2y = 5 \quad \ldots \quad \ldots \quad \ldots \quad \ldots \qquad \text{(ii)}$$

Find the value of y in terms of x from (ii),

$$3x + 2y = 5$$
$$y = 2 \cdot 5 - 1 \cdot 5x \quad \ldots \quad \ldots \qquad \text{(iii)}$$

Substitute for y into equation (i) and simplify,

$$2x^2 + xy - y^2 = 8$$
$$2x^2 + x(2 \cdot 5 - 1 \cdot 5x) - (2 \cdot 5 - 1 \cdot 5x)^2 = 8$$
$$2x^2 + 2 \cdot 5x - 1 \cdot 5x^2 - (6 \cdot 25 - 7 \cdot 5x + 2 \cdot 25x^2) = 8$$
$$2x^2 + 2 \cdot 5x - 1 \cdot 5x^2 - 6 \cdot 25 + 7 \cdot 5x - 2 \cdot 25x^2 = 8$$
$$2x^2 - 1 \cdot 5x^2 - 2 \cdot 25x^2 + 2 \cdot 5x + 7 \cdot 5x - 6 \cdot 25 - 8 = 0$$
$$-1 \cdot 75x^2 + 10x - 14 \cdot 25 = 0$$
$$1 \cdot 75x^2 - 10x + 14 \cdot 25 = 0$$

Solving by quadratic formula,

$$x = \frac{-b \pm \sqrt{b^2 - 4ac}}{2a}$$

$$= \frac{10 \pm \sqrt{10^2 - 4 \times 1 \cdot 75 \times 14 \cdot 25}}{2 \times 1 \cdot 75}$$

$$= \frac{10 \pm \sqrt{100 - 99 \cdot 75}}{3 \cdot 5} = \frac{10 \pm 0 \cdot 5}{3 \cdot 5}$$

$$= 3 \quad \text{or} \quad 2 \cdot 714$$

From (iii) $\qquad\qquad y = 2 \cdot 5 - 1 \cdot 5x$

If $x = 3$, $\qquad\qquad y = 2 \cdot 5 - 1 \cdot 5 \times 3$
$$= -2$$

If $x = 2 \cdot 714$, $\qquad\qquad y = 2 \cdot 5 - 1 \cdot 5 \times 2 \cdot 714$
$$= -1 \cdot 571$$

Hence, values of x and y are, respectively,

$$\left. \begin{array}{rcr} 3 & \text{and} & -2 \\ \text{or,} \quad 2 \cdot 714 & \text{and} & -1 \cdot 571 \end{array} \right\} \text{ Ans.}$$

PROBLEMS INVOLVING QUADRATIC EQUATIONS

As explained in Chapter 3 on the solution of problems, the first procedure is to look for and compose an equation from the facts given in the problem, letting some symbol such as x representing the required unknown, the equation is then simplified and worked out. If there are two unknowns express one in terms of the other at the first opportunity.

When simplifying equations which contain terms of the unknown to other powers than unity, it is usual to arrange all terms on the left hand side in order of descending powers of the unknown, leaving zero on the other side. If this produces a quadratic equation it is solved by the most convenient of the methods just explained. If a more complicated equation is produced, other means can be employed such as solving by a graph which will be explained later.

Example. Two ships sail from one port to another, a distance of 825 naut. miles, on the same course, the speed of one ship being 4 knot faster than the other. The fast ship leaves port 2 h after the slow ship and arrives at their destination 14 h sooner. Find the speeds of the two ships.

Let x knot = speed of slow ship

then $(x + 4)$ knot = speed of fast ship

Difference in times for the two ships to cover the journey,

$$= 2 + 14 = 16 \text{ h}$$

An equation can be formed from the times taken on the journey:
Time taken by slow ship − Time taken by fast ship = 16 h

$$\text{time} = \frac{\text{distance}}{\text{speed}}, \quad \text{therefore,}$$

$$\frac{\text{distance travelled by slow ship}}{\text{speed of slow ship}} - \frac{\text{distance by fast ship}}{\text{speed of fast ship}} = 16$$

$$\frac{825}{x} - \frac{825}{(x+4)} = 16$$

Multiplying every term by $x(x + 4)$ and simplifying,

$$825(x + 4) - 825x = 16x(x + 4)$$
$$825x + 3300 - 825x = 16x^2 + 64x$$
$$3300 = 16x^2 + 64x$$
$$16x^2 + 64x - 3300 = 0$$

Dividing throughout by 16,

$$x^2 + 4x - 206\tfrac{1}{4} = 0$$

Solving this quadratic by method of completing the square,

$$x^2 + 4x = 206\tfrac{1}{4}$$

$$x^2 + 4x + (2)^2 = 206\tfrac{1}{4} + (2)^2$$

$$x + 2 = \pm\sqrt{206\tfrac{1}{4} + 4}$$

$$x + 2 = \pm\sqrt{210\tfrac{1}{4}}$$

$$x + 2 = \pm 14\tfrac{1}{2}$$

$$x = \pm 14\tfrac{1}{2} - 2$$

$$x = 12\tfrac{1}{2} \quad \text{or} \quad -16\tfrac{1}{2}$$

The minus quantity is inadmissable, the practical value of x is therefore $12\tfrac{1}{2}$.

$$\left.\begin{array}{l} \text{Speed of slow ship} = 12\tfrac{1}{2} \text{ knot} \\ \text{Speed of fast ship} = 12\tfrac{1}{2} + 4 = 16\tfrac{1}{2} \text{ knot} \end{array}\right\} \text{Ans.}$$

CUBIC EQUATIONS

A **cubic** equation is one which contains the cube of the unknown, thus, $x^3 = 8$ is a cubic equation of the most elementary form and solved simply by taking the cube root of both sides, $x = \sqrt[3]{8} = 2$.

However, the form usually associated with the title cubic equation contains either or both of the first and second powers of the unknown as well as its cube, such as $x^3 + 2x^2 - x = 2$.

One method of solution is to bring all terms of the equation to the left hand side and leaving zero on the other side, resolve the expression into its three factors, each of these factors are then, in turn, equated to zero which produces a value of the unknown that will satisfy the given equation.

Example. $x^3 + 2x^2 - x - 2 = 0$

The three factors of this expression are,

$$(x - 1)(x + 1)(x + 2)$$

By equating each factor to zero, the three roots are obtained.

$$x - 1 = 0 \quad \therefore x = 1$$
$$x + 1 = 0 \quad \therefore x = -1$$
$$x + 2 = 0 \quad \therefore x = -2$$

The roots of this equation are $+1$, -1, and -2, and any one of these values of x will satisfy the given equation.

If the equation is not a very easy one like the above, the factors will not be readily seen. In such cases, attempt to get one root by trial, from this get the first factor. Dividing the cubic equation by this factor will produce a quadratic equation which can be solved by factors or by quadratic formula. The following examples show how this is done.

Example.   Find the roots of the equation,

$$x^3 - x^2 = 5{\cdot}75x - 7{\cdot}5$$

Re-arrange with all terms on the left hand side, in descending powers of x,

$$x^3 - x^2 - 5{\cdot}75x + 7{\cdot}5 = 0$$

Find the first root by trial, try $x = 1$,

$$1^3 - 1^2 - 5{\cdot}75 \times 1 + 7{\cdot}5$$
$$= 1 - 1 - 5{\cdot}75 + 7{\cdot}5$$
$$= 1{\cdot}75$$

Try $x = 2$,

$$2^3 - 2^2 - 5{\cdot}75 \times 2 + 7{\cdot}5$$
$$= 8 - 4 - 11{\cdot}5 + 7{\cdot}5$$
$$= 0 \quad \text{this is it.}$$

$x = 2$ satisfies the equation, therefore this is a root, and $x - 2$ must be a factor. Divide this factor into the cubic expression, this will produce a quadratic whose roots can be found.

$$x - 2)x^3 - x^2 - 5{\cdot}75x + 7{\cdot}5(x^2 + x - 3{\cdot}75$$
$$\underline{x^3 - 2x^2}$$
$$x^2 - 5{\cdot}75x + 7{\cdot}5$$
$$\underline{x^2 - 2x}$$
$$- 3{\cdot}75x + 7{\cdot}5$$
$$\underline{- 3{\cdot}75x + 7{\cdot}5}$$

Equate the resulting quadratic to zero and, if the factors cannot be seen, solve by formula,

$$x^2 + x - 3{\cdot}75 = 0$$

$$x = \frac{-b \pm \sqrt{b^2 - 4ac}}{2a}$$

$$= \frac{-1 \pm \sqrt{1^2 - 4 \times 1 \times (-3{\cdot}75)}}{2 \times 1}$$

$$= \frac{-1 \pm \sqrt{16}}{2} = \frac{-1 \pm 4}{2}$$

$$= 1{\cdot}5 \quad \text{or} \quad -2{\cdot}5$$

The roots of the given equation are,

$$2, \quad 1{\cdot}5, \quad \text{and} \quad -2{\cdot}5 \quad \text{Ans.}$$

The result could be checked by substituting for x, in the given cubic equation, each of these roots.

Example. Solve the following equation,

$$2x^2 = 17 + \frac{3}{x}$$

Multiply throughout by the least common denominator, which is x, to eliminate the fraction,

$$2x^3 = 17x + 3$$

Arrange all terms on left hand side and equate to zero,

$$2x^3 - 17x - 3 = 0$$

Find the first root by trial, try $x = 1$,

$$2 \times 1^3 - 17 \times 1 - 3$$
$$= 2 - 17 - 3$$
$$= -18$$

Try $x = 2$,
$$2 \times 2^3 - 17 \times 2 - 3$$
$$= 16 - 34 - 3$$
$$= -21$$

Try $x = 3$,
$$2 \times 3^3 - 17 \times 3 - 3$$
$$= 54 - 51 - 3$$
$$= 0$$

Hence $x = 3$ is a root and $x - 3$ must be a factor. Divide the cubic equation by this factor to obtain a quadratic which can be solved,

$$
\begin{array}{r}
x - 3 \overline{)2x^3 - 17x - 3} \, (2x^2 + 6x + 1 \\
\underline{2x^3 - 6x^2} \\
6x^2 - 17x - 3 \\
\underline{6x^2 - 18x} \\
x - 3 \\
\underline{x - 3}
\end{array}
$$

Equate the resulting quadratic to zero and solve by formula,

$$2x^2 + 6x + 1 = 0$$

$$x = \frac{-b \pm \sqrt{b^2 - 4ac}}{2a}$$

$$= \frac{-6 \pm \sqrt{6^2 - 4 \times 2 \times 1}}{2 \times 2}$$

$$= \frac{-6 \pm \sqrt{28}}{4} = \frac{-6 \pm 5 \cdot 292}{4}$$

$$= -0 \cdot 177 \quad \text{or} \quad -2 \cdot 823$$

The roots of the given cubic equation are,

$$3, \quad -0 \cdot 177 \quad \text{and} \quad -2 \cdot 823 \quad \text{Ans.}$$

Note the last two examples. In the former the last term of the cubic equation is 7·5 and easy factors of this number which come readily to mind are 1, 7·5; 2, 3·75; 3, 2·5; 5, 1·5, all plus or minus, and the first root of the equation, by trial, was one of these. In the latter example, the last term of the cubic equation is 3 and its ready factors are 1, 3; 2, 1·5, all plus or minus, and the first root of this equation, by trial, was one of these. Trial figures for the first root should therefore be chosen with this in mind.

If the first root is not a number which can readily be found by trial as in the foregoing examples, the above process could be quite laborious   and the equation would probably be more easily solved by a graphical solution.

TEST EXAMPLES 5

1. Find the value of x in each of the following equations,
    (i) $(2x + 8)(3x - 5) = 0$
    (ii) $(0 \cdot 5x - 10)(0 \cdot 25x + 5) = 0$
    (iii) $(5x + 0 \cdot 5)(4x + 0 \cdot 8) = 0$

2. Solve the following equations by the method of factorising,
    (i) $3x^2 + 2x - 33 = 0$
    (ii) $4x^2 - 17x + 4 = 0$
    (iii) $12x^2 + 10x - 12 = 0$

3. Solve the following equations by the method of completing the square,
    (i) $x^2 - x - 3\frac{3}{4} = 0$
    (ii) $3x^2 + 2x - 1 = 0$
    (iii) $4x^2 - 9x + 2 = 0$

4. Solve the following equations by the quadratic formula,
    (i) $3x^2 - 2x + 0 \cdot 25 = 0$
    (ii) $5x^2 + 4x - 5 \cdot 52 = 0$
    (iii) $10x^2 - x - 0 \cdot 2 = 0$

5. Find the value of x when:

$$\log 0{\cdot}5x = 2 \times \log(x - 6)$$

6. Find the value of b in the equation,

$$6b^4 - 2{\cdot}46b^2 + 0{\cdot}24 = 0$$

7. Find the value of V in the equation,

$$V^{2{\cdot}8} - 5{\cdot}1V^{1{\cdot}4} + 5{\cdot}6 = 0$$

8. Find the values of x and y in the following simultaneous equations,

$$x^2 - xy + 2y^2 = 16$$
$$x + 2y = 8$$

9. In 5 h less time than it takes a certain ship to travel 330 naut. miles, another ship which is $3\frac{1}{2}$ knot faster can travel 4 naut. miles further. What are the speeds of the two ships?

10. The area of a rectangle is 76 cm^2 and the perimeter is 350 mm. Find the length and breadth.

11. Find the roots of the following cubic equation,

$$2x^3 + 3x^2 - 17x = 30$$

12. Find the values of x to satisfy the following equation,

$$2x - \frac{16}{x}\left\{2 - \frac{3}{x}\right\} = 3$$

CHAPTER 6

GRAPHS

A graph is a diagram which shows the relation between two quantities. Graphs are usually plotted on squared paper (metric). Taking the related quantities to be x and y, Fig. 4 shows the elements of plotting graphs.

Both quantities vary in value throughout the graph and the value of one depends upon the value of the other. In practice there are often cases where the values of one of the quantities is entirely dependent upon how the other is varied. Take for example the stretching of a spring, if a load is hung on the spring hook a certain amount of stretch takes place, if a heavier load is hung a greater stretch occurs, thus the amount of stretch depends on the magnitude of the load. In this example the load would be referred to as the *independent variable* and the stretch as the *dependent variable*. In the drawing of a graph of a function of x such as $x^2 - 2x + 5$, let the value of this be denoted by y and write $y = x^2 - 2x + 5$, then for a series of chosen values of x the values of y are calculated to obtain a number of plotting points to enable the graph to be drawn. Choose the values of x and the values of y depend upon these, hence x is the independent variable and y the dependent variable.

The larger the scale to which the graph is drawn the more accurate the results obtained when reading points from the graph, therefore the scale chosen should be as large as possible depending upon the highest and lowest values to be represented.

The various values of x and y (or other similar pairs of variable quantities) are plotted thus, referring to Fig. 4:

The point of intersection of the horizontal and vertical base lines, marked 0, is the common zero point for both quantities and therefore represents zero value for both x and y. Positive values of x are measured horizontally to the right from 0 and negative values are measured horizontally to the left. The horizontal base line is referred to as the xx axis. Horizontal measurements are termed abscissae (singular: abscissa). Positive values of y are measured vertically above 0 and negative values are measured vertically downwards from 0. The vertical base line is the yy axis. Vertical measurements are termed ordinates.

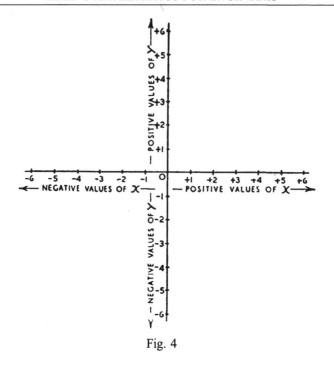

Fig. 4

PLOTTING OF STRAIGHT-LINE GRAPHS

Consider an equation of the form $y = a + bx$ where a and b are any constant quantities and may be positive or negative and as an example take such an equation where the value of the constant a is 2 and that of b is 1·5, thus

$$y = 2 + 1·5x$$

Working out the values of y for various values of x between the extreme limits of, say, $x = -2$ and $x = +4$,

When	$x = -2$,	$y = 2 - 3$	$= -1$
When	$x = -1$,	$y = 2 - 1·5$	$= +0·5$
When	$x = 0$,	$y = 2 + 0$	$= +2$
When	$x = +1$,	$y = 2 + 1·5$	$= +3·5$
When	$x = +2$,	$y = 2 + 3$	$= +5$
When	$x = +3$,	$y = 2 + 4·5$	$= +6·5$
When	$x = +4$,	$y = 2 + 6$	$= +8$

Plotting these points and drawing a graph through the plotted points as in Fig. 5:

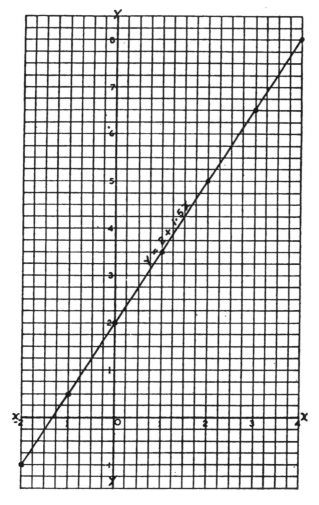

Fig. 5

Note. (i) that the graph is a *straight line*, and with this knowledge the graph of any equation of the form $y = a + bx$ may be plotted with two pairs of values only to give two points through which to draw the straight line.

(ii) From left to right the graph *slopes upwards* and the value of b determines the gradient of the slope. In this case, for every unit increase of x the increase of y is 1·5; if b had been greater than 1·5 the slope would have been greater and vice- versa. The graph slopes upwards because b is *positive*, if b had been negative the graph would have sloped downwards.

(iii) The value of y when x is zero is 2, and this is the value of a. It is the intercept on the y axis.

Now consider the equations,

$$y = 4 + x$$
$$y = 3 + 0\cdot5x$$
$$y = 2 - 0\cdot25x$$
$$y = -0\cdot5x$$
$$y = -2 - 0\cdot5x$$

All of these are of the general form $y = a + bx$. Graphs of these equations are plotted in Fig. 6 between the limits $x = 0$ and $x = 12$. Examine these graphs carefully.

Note.   It is also useful to reduce the equation of a curve, by substitution, to a linear graph to evaluate the constants, for example:

$$y = a + bx^2 \qquad \text{let} \quad z = x^2$$
$$y = a + bz \qquad \text{i.e.} \quad \text{linear}$$

similarly $y = a + b\sqrt{x} \qquad \text{let} \quad z = \sqrt{x}$

and $y = a + \dfrac{b}{x^2} \qquad \text{let} \quad z = \dfrac{1}{x^2}, \quad \text{etc.}$

DETERMINING THE EQUATION TO A STRAIGHT LINE GRAPH

Instead of drawing a graph to a given equation proceed to find the equation to a given straight line graph.

Example.   Find the equation to a straight line graph which passes through the points (2, 4), (10, 7).

Plot the two points, $x = 2$, $y = 4$, and $x = 10$, $y = 7$, and draw the straight line through them, extending the line to cut the axis oy as shown in Fig. 7. The equation is of the form $y = a + bx$. The value of y when $x = 0$ is the constant a, from the graph we read $a = 3\cdot25$. The increase of

Fig. 6

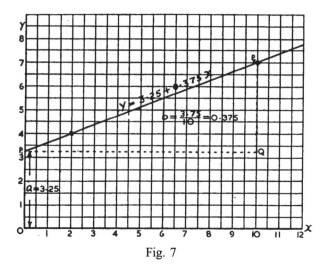

Fig. 7

y per unit increase of x is the value b, to obtain an accurate value take two points on the graph as far apart as convenient, say at the points indicated by P_1 and P_2. From Q to P_2 is the increase of y when the increase of x is P_1 to Q. Thus y increases by 3·75 when x is increased by 10, dividing 3·75 by 10 gives 0·375, hence y will increase by 0·375 when x is increased by 1 and therefore the value of b is 0·375. See Fig. 7.

The equation to the graph is $y = 3·25 + 0·375x$.   Ans.

There are many practical applications of determining the equation to a given graph such as when performing a series of experiments on a machine, an engine, or a piece of material under a strength test, to ascertain how one quantity varies with another. For instance, various loads can be hung from the lifting hook of a lifting machine and the effort required to lift each load found experimentally and tabulated, a graph is then drawn showing how the effort varies with the load, the equation to the graph is determined and this is the law of that particular machine.

Example. In an experiment on a certain lifting machine the following data were observed,

Load	20	40	60	80	100	120
Effort	4·5	6·1	7·8	8·9	10·4	12·1

If the law of this machine expressing the relationship between effort applied (F) and load lifted (m) be expressed by the linear equation $F = a + bm$, plot a graph representing the above experimental values on a base of load and from it determine the linear law of this machine.

After plotting the experimental values a straight line is drawn as near as possible through these points as shown in Fig. 8. Those points not exactly on this line are probably due to irregularities of the machine or errors of observation during the experiment.

The value of a reads 3.

The value of b is the increase of effort per unit increase of load.

Choosing two points on the line, P_1 and P_2, Q to P_2 measures 7·5, P_1 to Q measures 100, therefore $b = 7·5 \div 100 = 0·075$.

Hence the linear law of this machine is

$$F = 3 + 0·075m \quad \text{Ans.}$$

Fig. 8

GRAPHICAL SOLUTION OF SIMULTANEOUS LINEAR EQUATIONS

The method of solving simultaneous equations by graphical means can best be demonstrated by an example:

To find the values of x and y which satisfy the equations,

$$2x + 5y = 34$$
$$\text{and} \quad 4x - 3y = 16$$

Find the value of y in the first equation,

$$2x + 5y = 34$$
$$5y = 34 - 2x$$
$$y = 6 \cdot 8 - 0 \cdot 4x \quad \ldots \quad \ldots \quad \ldots \quad \text{(i)}$$

Find the value of y in the second equation,

$$4x - 3y = 16$$
$$-3y = 16 - 4x$$
$$3y = 4x - 16$$
$$y = 1\tfrac{1}{3}x - 5\tfrac{1}{3} \quad \ldots \quad \ldots \quad \ldots \quad \text{(ii)}$$

Finding two plotting points for each equation,

$$y = 6 \cdot 8 - 0 \cdot 4x$$

when $x = \;\;0,$ $y = 6 \cdot 8 - 0 = 6 \cdot 8$
when $x = 10,$ $y = 6 \cdot 8 - 4 = 2 \cdot 8$

$$y = 1\tfrac{1}{3}x - 5\tfrac{1}{3}$$

when $x = \;\;0,$ $y = 0 - 5\tfrac{1}{3} = -5\tfrac{1}{3}$
when $x = \;\;9,$ $y = 12 - 5\tfrac{1}{3} = 6\tfrac{2}{3}$

The points $x = 0$ and $x = 10$ for the first equation, and $x = 0$ and $x = 9$ for the second equation were chosen simply because they appeared to be easy figures for substituting and to produce reasonably sized graphs. $x = 0$ is obviously the first choice for a plotting point of any graph, the other point could be any value of x but it should be chosen with a view to produce simple figures.

The graphs are now plotted as shown in Fig. 9. At the point of intersection of the graphs read the values $x = 7$ and $y = 4$ and these are the only values which are true for both equations.

Hence, $x = 7$ and $y = 4$.   Ans.

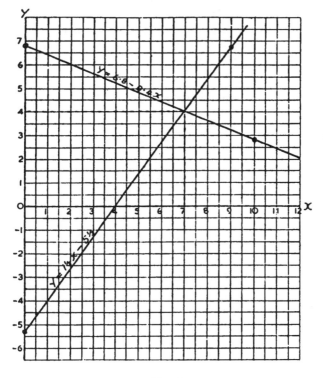

Fig. 9

GRAPHICAL SOLUTION OF QUADRATIC EQUATIONS

Graphs of equations containing x to the first power are all straight lines. Graphs of equations containing x to other powers, such as x^2 (quadratic equations) and x^3 (cubic equations) are curves and obviously more than two plotting points are necessary as a guide to the drawing of a curve; the more plotting points the more accurate can the curve be drawn.

As in previous cases the equation to be solved is first simplified, all terms are brought to one side in order of descending powers of the unknown, say x, leaving zero on the other side. Replace the nought by y, that is, let $y =$ the given expression and plot a graph for a series of values of x. Where this graph reads $y = 0$ gives the value of x which will satisfy the equation. The values of x when $y = 0$ are those points where the graph cuts the x axis, the values of y in proximity to these points therefore change from positive to negative or from negative to positive, the trial values of x for calculating the plotting points for the curve should therefore be chosen with this in mind. The following worked examples will clarify this explanation.

Example. Find, graphically, the values of x in the equation,

$$x^2 + 2x = 5 \cdot 5x - 1 \cdot 96$$

Simplify and bring all terms to one side,

$$x^2 - 3 \cdot 5x + 1 \cdot 96 = 0$$
$$\text{Let } y = x^2 - 3 \cdot 5x + 1 \cdot 96$$

Calculate values of y for selected values of x,

$$\begin{aligned}
\text{when} \quad x &= 0 & y &= 0 - 0 + 1 \cdot 96 & &= +1 \cdot 96 \\
\text{when} \quad x &= 1 & y &= 1 - 3 \cdot 5 + 1 \cdot 96 & &= -0 \cdot 54 \\
\text{when} \quad x &= 2 & y &= 4 - 7 + 1 \cdot 96 & &= -1 \cdot 04 \\
\text{when} \quad x &= 3 & y &= 9 - 10 \cdot 5 + 1 \cdot 96 & &= +0 \cdot 46 \\
\text{when} \quad x &= 4 & y &= 16 - 14 + 1 \cdot 96 & &= +3 \cdot 96
\end{aligned}$$

Note that the value of y changes sign between $x = 0$ and $x = 1$, and again between $x = 2$ and $x = 3$, therefore the two values of x will be obtained from the graph at these two intersections of the x axis and hence there is no need to plot the graph beyond the limits of $x = 0$ and $x = +3$. The larger the scale of the graph the more accurate will be the reading of the values of x therefore the graph should be plotted to the largest scale possible on the paper.

Results of greater accuracy could be obtained by calculating values of y for a few points between $x = 0$ and $x = +1$, and also between $x = +2$ and $x = +3$ and drawing to a larger scale only those two parts of the curve which cross the x axis.

By drawing the graph as shown in Fig. 10, when $y = 0$, $x = 0 \cdot 7$ and $2 \cdot 8$. The graph is concave upwards (i.e. $+x^2$).

Therefore, $x = 0 \cdot 7$ or $2 \cdot 8$.   Ans.

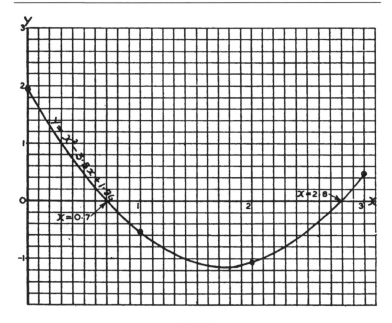

Fig. 10

Example.   Solve, $x^2 - 0.8x - 3.84 = 0$
Let $y = x^2 - 0.8x - 3.84$

when $x = 0$, $y = 0 - 0 - 3.84 \quad = -3.84$
when $x = 1$, $y = 1 - 0.8 - 3.84 = -3.64$
when $x = 2$, $y = 4 - 1.6 - 3.84 = -1.44$
when $x = 3$, $y = 9 - 2.4 - 3.84 = +2.76$

Note that the value of y changes sign from negative to positive between $x = 2$ and $x = 3$, therefore there is no need to proceed further in this direction. The other value where change of sign takes place, i.e. from positive to negative, must be when x is a negative quantity. Proceeding then in this direction,

when $x = -1$, $y = 1 + 0.8 - 3.84 = -2.04$
when $x = -2$, $y = 4 + 1.6 - 3.84 = +1.76$

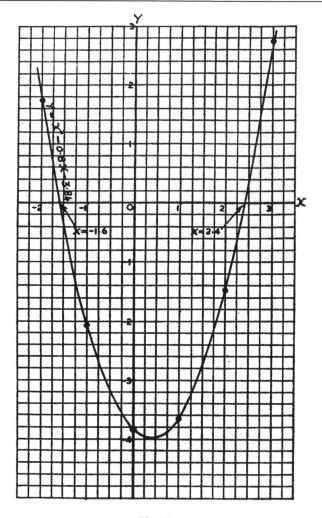

Fig.11

Knowing that $y=0$ between $x=-1$ and -2, there is sufficient data to plot the graph. It may be of assistance to clear up the above by tabulating these results before attempting to plot them, thus,

x	-2	-1	0	$+1$	$+2$	$+3$
y	$+1\cdot76$	$-2\cdot04$	$-3\cdot84$	$-3\cdot64$	$-1\cdot44$	$+2\cdot76$

Plotting the graph as in Fig. 11 and reading the values of x when $y=0$,

$$x = 2\cdot4 \quad \text{or} \quad -1\cdot6 \quad \text{Ans.}$$

Another method of solving quadratic equations, and one which can often be applied to solve cubic and more complicated equations is demonstrated by the following example.

To solve $$x^2 - 4x + 1\tfrac{3}{4} = 0$$

This can be written

$$x^2 - (4x - 1\tfrac{3}{4}) = 0$$

Let y_1 represent x^2
and y_2 represent $(4x - 1\tfrac{3}{4})$
then, $$x^2 - (4x - 1\tfrac{3}{4}) = 0$$
is represented by, $$y_1 - y_2 = 0$$

Graph plotting points are found for each part:

$$y_1 = x^2 \quad \dots \quad \dots \quad \dots \quad \dots \quad (i)$$

when $x = 0,$ $y_1 = 0$
when $x = 1,$ $y_1 = 1$
when $x = 2,$ $y_1 = 4$
when $x = 3,$ $y_1 = 9$
when $x = 4,$ $y_1 = 16$

$$y_2 = 4x - 1\tfrac{3}{4} \quad \dots \quad \dots \quad \dots \quad (ii)$$

This is a straight line equation and two plotting points only are required.

when $x = 0,$ $y_2 = 0 - 1\tfrac{3}{4}$ $= -1\tfrac{3}{4}$
when $x = 4,$ $y_2 = 16 - 1\tfrac{3}{4}$ $= 14\tfrac{1}{4}$

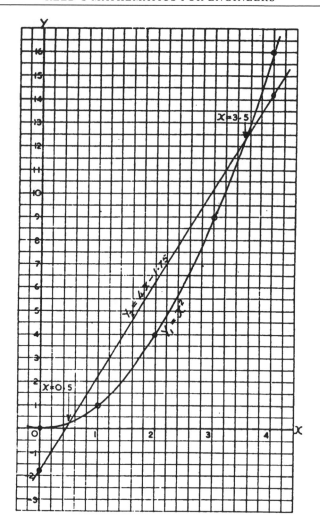

Fig. 12

The curve of $y_1 = x^2$ and the straight line representing $y_2 = 4x - 1\frac{3}{4}$ are now plotted as shown in Fig. 12.

From the graph it is seen that the difference between the values of y_1 and y_2 is zero (i.e., $y_1 - y_2 = 0$) where the straight line intersects the curve.

$y_1 - y_2 = 0$ which means $x^2 - 4x + 1\frac{3}{4} = 0$ when $x = \frac{1}{2}$ and $x = 3\frac{1}{2}$,

therefore $x = \frac{1}{2}$ or $3\frac{1}{2}$.   Ans.

Always check results by substituting them into the original equation to see if they are correct.

GRAPHICAL SOLUTION OF SIMULTANEOUS QUADRATICS

These are dealt with in a similar manner as previously explained with regard to simultaneous linear equations. Two quadratic equations could be involved, or one quadratic and one linear equation.

Example.   Find the values of x and y which satisfy the equations,

$$y = 12 + 3x - 0 \cdot 5x^2$$
$$\text{and} \quad y = 14 - 1 \cdot 25x$$

The extreme values of x to be taken for calculating the plotting points are chosen by making mental estimates with a view to the two graphs crossing.

Taking the linear equation first, being a straight line graph only two points are needed,

$$y = 14 - 1 \cdot 25x$$

when	$x = 0$,	$y = 14 - 0$	$= 14$
when	$x = 10$,	$y = 14 - 12 \cdot 5$	$= 1 \cdot 5$

Taking the quadratic,

$$y = 12 + 3x - 0 \cdot 5x^2$$

when	$x = 0$,	$y = 12 + 0 - 0$	$= 12$
when	$x = 1$,	$y = 12 + 3 - 0 \cdot 5$	$= 14 \cdot 5$
when	$x = 2$,	$y = 12 + 6 - 2$	$= 16$
when	$x = 3$,	$y = 12 + 9 - 4 \cdot 5$	$= 16 \cdot 5$
when	$x = 4$,	$y = 12 + 12 - 8$	$= 16$
when	$x = 5$,	$y = 12 + 15 - 12 \cdot 5$	$= 14 \cdot 5$
when	$x = 6$,	$y = 12 + 18 - 18$	$= 12$
when	$x = 7$,	$y = 12 + 21 - 24 \cdot 5$	$= 8 \cdot 5$
when	$x = 8$,	$y = 12 + 24 - 32$	$= 4$
when	$x = 9$,	$y = 12 + 27 - 40 \cdot 5$	$= -1 \cdot 5$

This appears to be sufficient. Graph is convex upwards (i.e. $-0 \cdot 5x^2$).

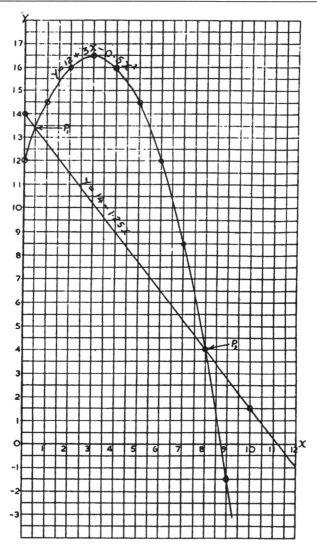

Fig.13

Drawing the graphs as in Fig. 13 the points of intersection P_1 and P_2 produce the values of x and y, thus,

$$\left.\begin{array}{lll} x = 0 \cdot 5 & \text{and} & y = 13 \cdot 375 \\ \text{or} \quad x = 8 & \text{and} & y = 4 \end{array}\right\} \quad \text{Ans.}$$

DETERMINATION OF LAWS

One case has already been shown, that of determining the law connecting effort and load in a lifting machine, this relation was expressed by a straight line equation and the law found quite simply. However, in engineering many cases arise where the variation of one quantity with another are more complicated, most of them are represented by curves, but some of these may be reduced to a straight line from which the law can be found.

One typical example is that of a mass of a gas being expanded or compressed in a cylinder, the law connecting the variation of pressure as the volume of the gas is increased or decreased by the movement of the piston is:

$$pV^n = \text{a constant}$$

Writing this equation in log form (see logarithmic equations, Chapter 3):

$$\log p + n \log V = \log C$$

and transposing to express $\log p$ in terms of the other quantities:

$$\log p = \log C - n \log V$$

It is now reduced to a straight-line equation similar to $y = a + bx$

the variable $\log p$ taking the place of the variable y

the variable $\log V$ taking the place of the variable x

the constant $\log C$ taking the place of the constant a

the constant n taking the place of the constant b

A graph of $\log p$ on a base of $\log V$ is now plotted and the value of n is determined in the same manner as the value of b would be found in the equation $y = a + bx$.

Example. The following ordinates and abscissae were measured from part of the expansion curve of an indicator diagram off an I.C. engine, where p is the pressure and V the volume of the gases in the cylinder. If the law of expansion can be expressed by $pV^n = C$, estimate the value of n.

p	28	24	16.6	13	9·7	6·8	4·7
V	0·6	0·7	0·9	1·1	1·4	1·8	2·4

Tabulating the values of p and V with their respective logarithms:

p	$\lg p$	V	$\lg V$	
28	1·4472	0·6	$\bar{1}$·7782	$= -0·2218$
24	1·3802	0·7	$\bar{1}$·8451	$= -0·1549$
16·6	1·2201	0·9	$\bar{1}$·9542	$= -0·0458$
13	1·1139	1·1	0·0414	
9·7	0·9868	1·4	0·1461	
6·8	0·8325	1·8	0·2553	
4·7	0·6721	2·4	0·3802	

When the values of V are less than unity, their logarithms have negative characteristics, to plot these they are expressed as all-negative values. Base 10 logarithms have been used here.

The graph is now plotted as shown in Fig. 14. Note that the lowest value of $\lg p$ is 0·6721, the graph can be drawn to a larger scale by starting with a value of $\lg p$ just a little lower than this, say 0·6, instead of commencing with zero origin.

Choosing two points on the graph,

$$n = \frac{\text{decrease of } \lg p}{\text{increase of } \lg V} = \frac{0·65}{0·5} = 1·3$$

Therefore, $n = 1·3$ Ans.

Thus, $\lg p = \lg C - 1·3 \lg V$

Written in nominal form this is,

$$p = C \times V^{-1·3}$$

or, as in the original setting,

$$pV^{1·3} = C$$

CURVE SKETCHING

It is often informative to sketch the graph by inspection of the algebraic equation. For example, from previous, general form $y = a + bx$: this is a straight line graph, $+b$ slopes upwards, $-b$ slopes downwards, the greater the b value the steeper the slope (gradient), $+$ or $-a$ is the intercept on the y axis (when $x = 0$).

For the quadratic equation, general form $y = cx^2 + bx + a$: this is a parabolic graph, $+c$ concave upwards, $-c$ convex upwards, the greater the c value the steeper the slope (gradient), $+$ or $-a$ as above, $+b$ gives vertical axis of symmetry to the left of the y axis and $-b$ to the right, roots evaluation gives points on the x axis where $y = 0$.

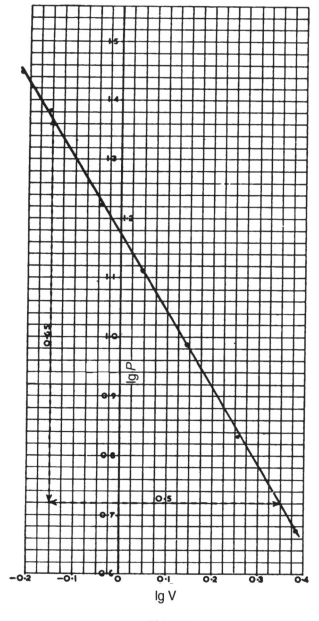

Fig. 14

TEST EXAMPLES 6

1. On a common base, plot graphs representing the equations,

(i)	$y = 2 + x$
(ii)	$y = 12 - 1 \cdot 5x$
(iii)	$y = -1 - 0 \cdot 5x$
(iv)	$y = -4 + 1 \cdot 25x$

all between the limits of $x = 0$ and $x = 12$.

2. Draw a straight line through the two pairs of points $(-2, 14 \cdot 5)$, $(8, -3)$ and from it derive the equation to the graph.

3. Plot a graph using the following values and find the law of the graph.

x	-2	-1	0	1	2	3
y	10	7	4	1	-2	-5

4. The following data were taken during an experiment on a small turbine where P represents the power developed and m the rate of consumption of steam. Assuming that the relationship between P and m can be represented by the straight line equation $m = a + bP$, draw a straight line as near as possible through the plotted points of the experimental results, estimate the values of a and b and hence the law connecting P and m.

P	20	25	30	35	40	45	50
m	220	265	315	365	410	455	505

5. Find, graphically, the values of x and y which satisfy the simultaneous equations,

$$3x + 5y = 23$$
$$\text{and} \quad 5x - 2y = 12 \cdot 5$$

6. Find, graphically, the values of p and q in the simultaneous equations,

$$5p - 2q = 5 \cdot 6$$
$$\text{and} \quad 2p - 3q = -4 \cdot 8$$

7. Find, graphically, the value of x in the equation,

$$x^2 - 5x + 5\tfrac{1}{4} = 0$$

8. Draw the graph of $y = 0 \cdot 5x^2 - 2x - 6$ between the values of $x = -4$ and $x = +8$.

   From the graph read the values of x in the following equations:

   (i) $0 \cdot 5x^2 - 2x - 6 = 0$

   (ii) $0 \cdot 5x^2 - 2x - 4 = 0$

   (iii) $0 \cdot 5x^2 - 2x - 1 = 0$

   (iv) $0 \cdot 5x^2 - 2x = 0$

   (v) $0 \cdot 5x^2 - 2x + 1 = 0$

9. On a common base draw graphs of $y_1 = x^2$, and $y_2 = 3 \cdot 5 + 2 \cdot 5x$, between the values of $x = -2$ and $x = +4$; find the values of x in the equation $x^2 - 2 \cdot 5x - 3 \cdot 5 = 0$.

10. Find, by graphical means, the values of x and y which satisfy the simultaneous equations,

$$y = 0 \cdot 4x^2 - 3x + 2$$
$$y = 1 \cdot 4x - 2$$

11. Using graphical means only and taking values of x between 0 and $+6$, solve for x and y in the following pair of simultaneous equations:

$$y^2 = 16x$$
$$y = 5 + 8x - 2x^2$$

   Note. $y^2 = 16x$ can be expressed as $y = \pm 4\sqrt{x}$.

               suggested scales: x axis 2 cm = 1

                                     y axis 2 cm = 4

12. By drawing a graph of $y = e^{-x}$ and $y = x^2$ solve the equation:

$$x^2 e^x = 1$$

   Note: plot values between $x = 0$ and $x = 1$.

TRIGONOMETRY AND GEOMETRY

An *angle* is the corner of two joining lines and the magnitude of an angle is measured in either degrees or radians.

MEASUREMENT OF ANGLES

A degree is one three-hundred-and-sixtieth part of a circle, hence there are 360° in a circle.

Figure 15 shows a quarter of a circle which is 90° and is termed a *right-angle*, an angle which is less than 90° (Fig. 16) is called an *acute* angle, greater than 90° but less than 180° (Fig. 17) is an *obtuse* angle, and greater than 180° (Fig. 18) is a *reflex* angle.

| Fig. 15 | Fig. 16 | Fig. 17 | Fig. 18 |

One sixtieth part of a degree is termed one *minute* and the sixtieth part of a minute is one *second*, thus,

$$60 \text{ s} = 1 \text{ min}$$
$$60 \text{ min} = 1°$$
$$360° = 1 \text{ circle.}$$

Symbols are used to represent degrees, minutes and seconds. An angle of 35 degrees 23 minutes and 15 seconds is written 35°23'15''. In this work, accuracy to the nearest minute is all that is required.

A *radian* is the angle subtended by a circular arc of length equal to the radius.

In Fig. 19, the length of the arc A to B is equal to the radius OB and OA, and the enclosed angle AOB is 1 rad.

The length of an arc to subtend 2 rad is 2 × radius, in symbols:

If θ = number of radians

and r = radius

then,   arc length = $\theta \times r$

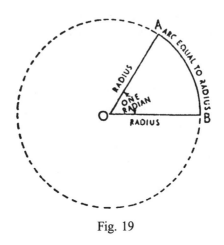

Fig. 19

Similarly, if a wheel of 0·3 m radius turns through 4 rad in 1 s, then a point on the rim moves a linear distance of 4 × 0·3 = 1·2 m/s. In symbols:

If ω = angular velocity

v = linear velocity,

r = radius

then, $v = \omega r$

Circumference of a circle = $\pi \times$ diameter

= $2\pi \times$ radius

Therefore one circle contains 2π rad

$$2\pi \text{ rad} = 360°$$
$$1 \text{ rad} = \frac{360°}{2\pi}$$
$$= 57·3°$$

The angular velocity of a rotating part of a mechanism is often more conveniently expressed in rad/s instead of in the practical units of rev/min; to convert from one to the other:

$$\text{If} \quad N = \text{rev/min}$$
$$\text{and} \quad \omega = \text{rad/s}$$
$$\text{angular velocity} = N \text{ rev/min}$$
$$= 2\pi N \text{ rad/min}$$
$$= \frac{2\pi N}{60} \text{ rad/s}$$
$$\therefore \omega = \frac{2\pi N}{60}$$

Example.   Express in (a) rad, (b) deg, the angles subtended at the centre of a circle of 50 mm radius, by arc lengths of 50, and 140 mm respectively.

(i) Arc length of 50 mm:

$$\theta = \frac{\text{arc length}}{\text{radius}} = \frac{50}{50} = 1 \text{ rad.} \quad \text{Ans. (a)(i)}$$
$$= 57 \cdot 3° \quad \text{Ans. (b)(i)}$$

(ii) Arc length of 140 mm:

$$\theta = \frac{140}{50} = 2 \cdot 8 \text{ rad.} \quad \text{Ans. (a)(ii)}$$
$$2 \cdot 8 \times 57 \cdot 3 = 160 \cdot 44°. \quad \text{Ans. (b)(ii)}$$

Example.   A flywheel of 1 m diameter is rotating at 120 rev/min.
(i) express this in rad/s.
(ii) find the linear velocity, in m/s, of a point on the rim.

$$\omega = \frac{120 \times 2\pi}{60}$$
$$= 12 \cdot 568 \text{ rad/s} \quad \text{Ans. (i)}$$
$$v = \omega r$$
$$= 12 \cdot 568 \times 0 \cdot 5$$
$$= 6 \cdot 284 \text{ m/s} \quad \text{Ans. (ii)}$$

TRIGONOMETRIC RATIOS

A right angled triangle is one which contains an angle of 90°, the longest side (opposite the right angle) is termed the *hypotenuse*, the other two sides are termed the *opposite* and *adjacent* depending upon which of the other two angles are under consideration.

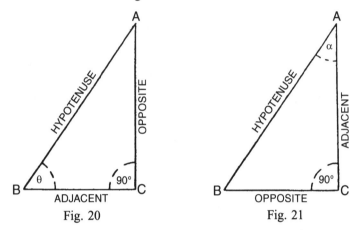

Fig. 20   Fig. 21

Considering angle θ (Fig. 20), side AC is opposite the angle and therefore referred to as such, the other side BC is the adjacent.

If angle α is being considered (Fig. 21), BC is the opposite and AC is the adjacent.

The ratios of the lengths of the sides of a right angled triangle are expressed by *sine* (abbreviated to sin), *cosine* (abbreviated cos) and *tangent* (abbreviated tan), as follows:

$$\text{sine of angle} = \frac{\text{opposite}}{\text{hypotenuse}}$$

$$\text{cosine of angle} = \frac{\text{adjacent}}{\text{hypotenuse}}$$

$$\text{tangent of angle} = \frac{\text{opposite}}{\text{adjacent}}$$

Referring to Fig. 20,

$$\sin \theta = \frac{AC}{AB}$$

$$\cos \theta = \frac{BC}{AB}$$

$$\tan \theta = \frac{AC}{BC}$$

These ratios are the most often used.

The reciprocals of the above ratios are:

$$\text{cosecant } \theta, \text{ abbreviated cosec } \theta = \frac{1}{\sin \theta} = \frac{AB}{AC}$$

$$\text{secant } \theta, \text{ abbreviated sec } \theta = \frac{1}{\cos \theta} = \frac{AB}{BC}$$

$$\text{cotangent } \theta, \text{ abbreviated cot } \theta = \frac{1}{\tan \theta} = \frac{BC}{AC}$$

Every angle has its own value of sine, cosine and tangent.

The sum of the angles in any triangle is 180°, therefore if one angle of a right angled triangle is 30° the other must be 60° and if one angle is 45° the other must be 45°.

Referring to Fig. 22,

$$\sin 30° = \frac{100}{200} = 0\cdot 5$$

$$\cos 30° = \frac{173\cdot 2}{200} = 0\cdot 866$$

$$\tan 30° = \frac{100}{173\cdot 2} = 0\cdot 5773$$

Note that the sides are in the ratio, $1 : 2 : \sqrt{3}$

Fig. 22

$$\sin 60° = \frac{173\cdot 2}{200} = 0\cdot 866$$

$$\cos 60° = \frac{100}{200} = 0\cdot 5$$

$$\tan 60° = \frac{173\cdot 2}{100} = 1\cdot 732$$

Fig. 23

Referring to Fig. 23,

$$\sin 45° = \frac{100}{141 \cdot 1} = 0 \cdot 7071$$

$$\cos 45° = \frac{100}{141 \cdot 1} = 0 \cdot 7071$$

$$\tan 45° = \frac{100}{100} = 1 \cdot 000$$

COMPLEMENTARY ANGLES

If the sum of any two angles is 90° they are said to be *complementary angles*. 60° is the complementary angle to 30°, 50° is complementary to 40°, 70° is complementary to 20°, and so on. In all such cases *the sine of an angle is equal to the cosine of its complement*. The notes referring to Fig. 22 show that the sine of 30° is the same as the cosine of 60°, and cos 30° is the same as sin 60°.

In general, referring to Fig. 24,

$$\sin \theta = \cos \alpha = \cos (90 - \theta)$$

$$\cos \theta = \sin \alpha = \sin (90 - \theta)$$

$$\tan \theta = \cot \alpha = \cot (90 - \theta)$$

Fig. 24

SUPPLEMENTARY ANGLES

If the sum of two angles is 180° they are said to be *supplementary* to each other. Thus 80° is the supplementary angle of 100°, 53° is the supplementary angle of 127°, and so on.

THEOREM OF PYTHAGORAS

In a right angled triangle, *the square of the hypotenuse is equal to the sum of the squares of the other two sides.*

This may be shown by a small square of side c contained in a larger square of side $(a + b)$ arranged as in Fig. 25.

The area of a right angled triangle is $\dfrac{\text{base} \times \text{perpendicular height}}{2}$

In the triangles of sides a, b and c,

$$\text{area of one triangle} = \tfrac{1}{2}ab$$
$$\text{area of four triangles} = 4 \times \tfrac{1}{2}ab = 2ab$$
$$\text{area of large square} = (a + b)^2 = a^2 + 2ab + b^2$$
$$\text{area of small square} = c^2$$

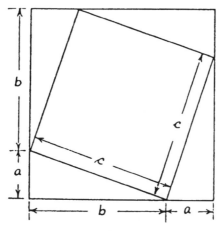

Fig. 25

Area of small square = area of large square − area of 4 triangles

$$c^2 = a^2 + 2ab + b^2 - 2ab$$
$$c^2 = a^2 + b^2$$

The simplest example is that of a right angled triangle with a height of 3 and base 4,

$$(\text{hypotenuse})^2 = (\text{height})^2 + (\text{base})^2$$
$$\therefore \text{hypotenuse} = \sqrt{3^2 + 4^2}$$
$$= \sqrt{25} = 5$$

This is illustrated in Fig. 26.

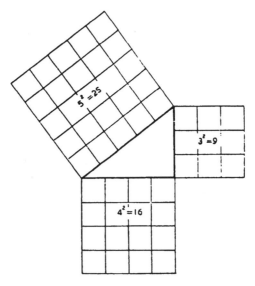

Fig. 26

RELATIONSHIPS BETWEEN SINE, COSINE AND TANGENT OF ANGLES

Referring to Fig. 20,

$$\sin\theta = \frac{AC}{AB} \quad \text{and} \quad \cos\theta = \frac{BC}{AB}$$

$$\sin\theta \div \cos\theta = \frac{AC}{AB} \div \frac{BC}{AB} = \frac{AC}{AB} \times \frac{AB}{BC} = \frac{AC}{BC}$$

and $\dfrac{AC}{BC}$ is $\tan\theta$

$$\therefore \ \tan\theta = \frac{\sin\theta}{\cos\theta} \qquad \dots \quad \dots \quad \dots \quad \text{(i)}$$

$$(\text{hypotenuse})^2 = (\text{opposite})^2 + (\text{adjacent})^2$$

$$(AB)^2 = (AC)^2 + (BC)^2$$

Dividing every term by $(AB)^2$,

$$1 = \left(\frac{AC}{AB}\right)^2 + \left(\frac{BC}{AB}\right)^2$$

$$1 = \sin^2\theta + \cos^2\theta$$

usually written, $\sin^2\theta + \cos^2\theta = 1$ $\qquad \dots \quad \dots \quad \dots \quad \text{(ii)}$

The ratios of the reciprocals are also useful,

$$(AB)^2 = (AC)^2 + (BC)^2$$

Dividing every term by $(AC)^2$

$$\left(\frac{AB}{AC}\right)^2 = \left(\frac{AC}{AC}\right)^2 + \left(\frac{BC}{AC}\right)^2$$

$$\operatorname{cosec}^2\theta = 1 + \cot^2\theta \qquad \dots \quad \dots \quad \text{(iii)}$$

$$(AB)^2 = (AC)^2 + (BC)^2$$

Dividing every term by $(BC)^2$

$$\left(\frac{AB}{BC}\right)^2 = \left(\frac{AC}{BC}\right)^2 + \left(\frac{BC}{BC}\right)^2$$

$$\sec^2\theta = \tan^2\theta + 1 \qquad \dots \quad \dots \quad \text{(iv)}$$

Example.   Without using calculator or tables, find the cosine and tangent of an angle whose sine is 0·8.

$$\sin^2 \theta + \cos^2 \theta = 1$$
$$\cos^2 \theta = 1 - \sin^2 \theta$$
$$\cos \theta = \sqrt{1 - \sin^2 \theta} = \sqrt{1 - 0·8^2}$$
$$= \sqrt{1 - 0·64} = \sqrt{0·36}$$
$$= 0·6 \text{ Ans. (i)}$$
$$\tan \theta = \frac{\sin \theta}{\cos \theta} = \frac{0·8}{0·6}$$
$$= 1·333 \text{ Ans. (ii)}$$

Take care, $\sin \theta \times \sin \theta$ is written $\sin^2 \theta$ and not $\sin \theta^2$,
$\quad\quad\quad\quad \cos \theta \times \cos \theta$ is written $\cos^2 \theta$ and not $\cos \theta^2$,
$\quad\quad\quad\quad$ and so on,
thus it is the *sine* or *cosine which is squared, and not the angle.*

IDENTITIES

An *identity* is an equation that is true for all values of the quantities involved in the equation, thus:

$$x^2 - y^2 = (x + y)(x - y)$$
$$(x + y)^2 = x^2 + 2xy + y^2$$

are examples of identities because they are true for any values of x and y.

A *trigonometric identity* is an equation that is true for any angle, thus the four expressions derived in the previous paragraph:

$$\sin \theta / \cos \theta = \tan \theta$$
$$\sin^2 \theta + \cos^2 \theta = 1$$
$$\operatorname{cosec}^2 \theta = 1 + \cot^2 \theta$$
$$\sec^2 \theta = 1 + \tan^2 \theta$$

are all trigonometric identities because they are true for any value of angle θ, and many more can be proved from the knowledge of these fundamental identities and the trigonometric ratios. A few simple examples are shown below.

(i) Prove that

$$\operatorname{cosec} \theta + \cot \theta = \frac{1 + \cos \theta}{\sin \theta}$$

Simplifying left hand side of the equation:

$$\operatorname{cosec} \theta + \cot \theta = \frac{1}{\sin \theta} + \frac{\cos \theta}{\sin \theta}$$

$$= \frac{1 + \cos \theta}{\sin \theta}$$

$$= \text{right hand side of equation.} \quad \text{Ans. (i)}$$

(ii) Prove that

$$\frac{\sec A - \cos A}{\sin A} = \tan A$$

Simplifying left hand side of equation:

$$\frac{\sec A - \cos A}{\sin A} = \frac{\dfrac{1}{\cos A} - \cos A}{\sin A}$$

$$= \frac{\dfrac{1 - \cos^2 A}{\cos A}}{\sin A} = \frac{1 - \cos^2 A}{\cos A . \sin A}$$

$$= \frac{\sin^2 A}{\cos A . \sin A} = \frac{\sin A}{\cos A}$$

$$= \tan A$$

$$= \text{right hand side of equation.} \quad \text{Ans. (ii)}$$

(iii) Prove that

$$\sin \theta = \frac{\tan \theta}{\sqrt{1 + \tan^2 \theta}}$$

Simplifying right hand side of equation:

$$\frac{\tan \theta}{\sqrt{1 + \tan^2 \theta}} = \frac{\tan \theta}{\sqrt{\sec^2 \theta}} = \frac{\tan \theta}{\sec \theta}$$

$$= \frac{\sin \theta}{\cos \theta} \times \frac{\cos \theta}{1} = \sin \theta$$

$$= \text{left hand side of equation.} \quad \text{Ans. (iii)}$$

Note. See also Compound and Double Angles in Chapter 8.

READING TRIGONOMETRIC RATIOS

The values of the sine, cosine and tangent for angles 0° to 90° are included in Tables (which often contain logarithms). They can also be obtained directly from a suitable calculator.

SINE VALUES. Note that as the angle increases from 0° to 90°, the sine increases from 0 to 1. All values of sines are therefore decimal fractions except for 90° where the sine is of maximum value, i.e., unity.

COSINE VALUES. Note that as the angle increases, the value of the cosine gets smaller. The maximum value of the cosine is unity for an angle of 0°, decreasing to zero for an angle of 90°.

TANGENT VALUES. Note that the value of the tangent increases from zero for 0° to infinity for 90°, below 45° the tangents are decimal fractions, the tangent of 45° is unity.

ANGLES GREATER THAN 90°

Figures 27b, 27c and 27d show circles of 360° with a radius arm swept around through given angles, in all cases the angle between the arm and the horizontal diameter has the same numerical values of sine, cosine and tangent as the given angle. For angles between 0° and 90° all the ratios have positive values; for angles between 90° and 180° only the sine is positive, the cosine and tangent are negative for angles between 270° and 360° only the cosine is positive, the sine and tangent are negative. As an aid to remember whether the ratios are positive or negative, divide a circle into its four quadrants and memorise the positive values only, thus, All, Sin, Tan, Cos, respectively, as illustrated in Fig. 27a, the remainder being negative values.

ANGLES BETWEEN 90° AND 180°. Subtract the angle from 180° and read the values of the resultant angle, these are numerically the same as for the given angle but, although the sine of the given angle is positive, its cosine and tangent have negative values. See Figs. 27a and 27b.

Fig. 27a

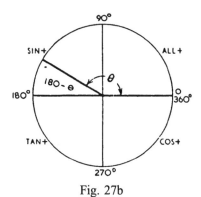

Fig. 27b

Example.

$$\sin 124°23' = \sin(180° - 124°23')$$
$$= \sin 55°37'$$
$$= 0.8253$$
$$\cos 124°23' = -\cos(180° - 124°23')$$
$$= -\cos 55°37'$$
$$= -0.5648$$
$$\tan 124°23' = -\tan(180° - 124°23')$$
$$= -\tan 55°37'$$
$$= -1.4614$$

Fig. 27c

ANGLES BETWEEN 180° AND 270°. Subtract 180° from the angle and read the values of the resultant angle. In this case only the tangent of the given angle is positive, the sine and cosine are negative. See Figs. 27a and 27c.

Example.
$$\sin 203°14' = -\sin(203°14' - 180°)$$
$$= -\sin 23°14'$$
$$= -0.3944$$
$$\cos 203°14' = -\cos(203°14' - 180°)$$
$$= -\cos 23°14'$$
$$= -0.9189$$
$$\tan 203°14' = \tan(203°14' - 180°)$$
$$= \tan 23°14'$$
$$= 0.4293$$

Fig. 27d

ANGLES BETWEEN 270° AND 360°. Subtract the angle from 360° and read the values of the resultant angle. The cosine is now the only positive value, the sine and tangent are negative. See Figs. 27a and 27d.

Example.
$$\sin 304°44' = -\sin(360° - 304°44')$$
$$= -\sin 55°16'$$
$$= -0\cdot8218$$
$$\cos 304°44' = \cos(360° - 304°44')$$
$$= \cos 55°16'$$
$$= 0\cdot5697$$
$$\tan 304°44' = -\tan(360° - 304°44')$$
$$= -\tan 55°16'$$
$$= -1\cdot4424$$

From the foregoing there is more than one possible solution for a given sine, cosine or tangent value.

Example (i), given that the sine of an angle is 0·3636, to find the angle.

The sine being of positive value for all angles from 0° to 180°, the angle can lie in the first or second quadrant. Read 0·3636 as the sine of 21°19', but it is also the sine of (180° − 21°19') which is 158°41'. Angle is 21°19' or 158°41'.   Ans. (i)

Example (ii), given that the cosine of an angle is −0·3352, to find the angle.

The cosine is negative for all angles from 90° to 270° therefore the angle can be in the second or third quadrants. Read 0·3352 as the cosine of 70°25', therefore,

$$-0\cdot3352 \text{ is the cosine of } (180° - 70°25')$$
$$= 109°35' \quad \text{Ans. (ii)}$$
$$\text{or } 180° + 70°25'$$
$$= 250°25' \quad \text{Ans. (ii)}$$

Example (iii), given that the tangent of an angle is 2·4876, to find the angle.

The tangent is positive for angles between 0° and 90°, and also between 180° and 270°, therefore the angle can be in the first or third quadrants. Read 2·4876 as the tangent of 68°6′, therefore,

2·4876 is the tangent of 68°6′   Ans. (iii)

or (180° + 68°6′)

= 248°6′   Ans. (iii)

From the above the values of the sine and cosine are between zero and ± 1, never numerically greater than unity. The tangent varies from zero to ± infinity.

It is sometimes useful to express some angles in radians instead of degrees.

$$360° = 2\pi \text{ rad}$$
$$180° = \pi \text{ rad}$$
$$90° = \pi/2 \text{ rad etc.}$$

GRAPHICAL REPRESENTATION

A little more study of the previous circle diagrams, and also Fig. 28, will show that if the radius arm of the circle is unity, then the vertical

Fig. 28

Fig. 29

height above the horizontal axis represents the value of sine θ when θ is the angle between the arm and the horizontal. Since the cosine of an angle is equal to the sine of its complement, the vertical height above the horizontal will represent the value of cosine θ if θ is taken as the angle between the arm and the *vertical axis*. Thus, although graphs of sine and cosine can be plotted by taking values from the calculator or tables, a quicker and more convenient method is to project their values from a circle diagram as shown in Fig. 29.

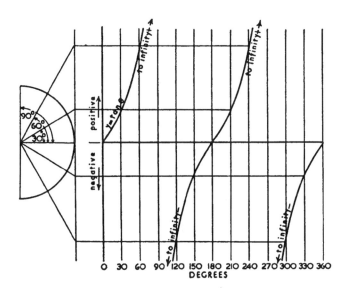

Fig. 30

It will be seen that, with a proper understanding of the positive and negative values, a half-circle only is required from which to project all points from 0° to 360°.

Further, the tangent of an angle being opposite ÷ adjacent, then the vertical height (opposite) = adjacent × tan θ. Hence if the base line Ox is made constant at unity, the vertical height of the radius-arm projected as shown in Fig. 28 will represent tan θ. The graph of $y = \tan \theta$ is shown in Fig. 30.

LATITUDE AND LONGITUDE

The shape of the earth is approximately spherical, a straight line joining the North and South Poles and passing through the centre of the earth is called the Polar Axis. The earth rotates about its polar axis in the direction from West to East, that is, anticlockwise looking down on to the North Pole, and makes one complete revolution once in (approximately) every 24 h.

Parallels of Latitude are circles around the earth, perpendicular to the polar axis. The parallel of latitude midway between the two poles is the Equator and this is the standard from which other parallels of latitude are measured, North and South of it, from 0° to 90° either way.

Fig. 31a

Meridians of Longitude are circles around the earth passing through the two poles and cutting the equator at right angles. The Greenwich Meridian is the meridian of longitude which passes through Greenwich and this is taken as the standard from which other meridians of longitude are measured, East and West of it, from 0° to 180°.

Thus any position on the earth's surface can be defined by its latitude and its longitude. Referring to Fig. 31b, let NGLS be the Greenwich Meridian. Angle QOP is the degrees latitude of point P, North of the equator. Angle LOQ (which is the same as GMP) is the degrees longitude of P, East of Greenwich.

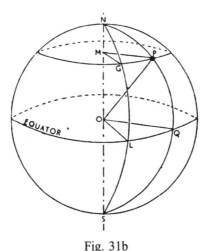

Fig. 31b

Since the earth rotates in the direction West to East and the sun being a fixed body, any point on the earth's surface East of another will pass a direct line of the sun first. Hence at places East of Greenwich the time is ahead of the time at Greenwich, and at places West of Greenwich the time is behind.

Taking the earth to rotate once in 24 h:

$$360° = 24 \text{ h}$$
$$15° = 1 \text{ h}$$
$$1° = \tfrac{1}{15} \text{ h} = 4 \text{ min}$$

As an example, the longitude of Karachi is 67° East, therefore the difference in time between Greenwich and Karachi is 67 × 4 min = 4 h 28 min, and if the clocks were set by the sun, it would be 4·28 p.m. in Karachi when it is 12 noon at Greenwich.

It is obvious that different parts of one country should not have different times by the clock to other parts of the same country, modifications are therefore made. The time by the sun at Greenwich is referred to as Greenwich Mean Time (G.M.T.), all clocks in Britain are set to G.M.T. in the winter, and put forward one hour in the summer.

THE NAUTICAL MILE. This is the length of an arc on the earth's surface subtending an angle of 1 min $(\frac{1}{60}^°)$ at the centre of the earth.

Taking the circumference of the earth as 40 000 km

$$360° \text{ around surface} = 40\ 000 \text{ km}$$
$$1 \text{ min around surface} = \frac{40\ 000}{360 \times 60}$$
$$= 1{\cdot}852 \text{km}$$

This is the international nautical mile which is the nautical unit of distance.

Aircraft and ship speeds are expressed in naut. miles/h, which are termed *knots*, one international knot being equal to 1·852 km/h.

COMPASS BEARINGS

A direction expressed with regard to the points of the compass is termed a *bearing* and it is usual to give a bearing in one of the two following methods.

  (i) Stating the angle in degrees less than 90° from either North or South (whichever of the two is the nearer direction), the angle thus lies within one of the four quadrants and is therefore called a *quadrant bearing*.

 (ii) Stating the angle in degrees measured clockwise from North and expressing this in three figures, using noughts for hundred, tens or units when there are none. This is called a *three-figure bearing*.

To illustrate these terms, Fig. 32 shows the direction of movement in relation to the four cardinal points of the compass.

Figure 32a is the quadrant bearing and may be stated as 83° East of South, or South 83° East which is abbreviated to S 83° E.

Fig. 32a   Fig. 32b

Figure 32b shows the same direction expressed as a three-figure bearing, 097°.

GEOMETRICAL CONSTRUCTION OF TRIANGLES

Example.   To construct a triangle of sides 64 and 48 mm and an angle of 42° opposite the 48 mm side, and to measure the remaining side and angles.

Referring to Fig. 33, draw the base Ox, measure 42° and draw Oy. Mark A at 64 mm from O. With centre A and compasses set to a radius of 48 mm, describe an arc to cut Oy, here the arc will cut Oy at two points B and C. Join AB and there is one triangle OAB which satisfies the description. Join AC and now there is another triangle OAC

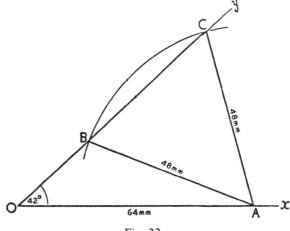

Fig. 33

which also satisfies the description. Hence there are two possible solutions to this example.

Measuring the remaining side and angles:

For one triangle,

Remaining side, OB = 26 mm

Remaining angles, OAB = 21° and OBA = 117°

For the other triangle,

Remaining side, OC = 69 mm

Remaining angles, OAC = 75° and OCA = 63°

SOME IMPORTANT GEOMETRICAL FACTS

The opposite angles of the intersection of two straight lines are equal. See Fig. 34 and note also that $\alpha = 180° - \theta$.

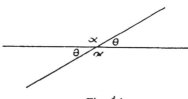

Fig. 34

The alternate angles produced by a straight line cut of a pair of parallel lines are equal to each other. See Fig. 35.

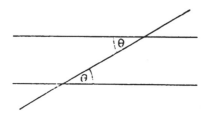

Fig. 35

The exterior angle formed by extending one side of a triangle is equal to the sum of the two opposite internal angles. Figure 36 illustrates this.

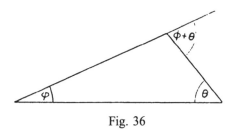

Fig. 36

If an angle between two sides of a triangle is bisected and the bisecting line produced to meet the opposite side, the opposite side is divided into two parts having lengths of the same ratio as the two sides which form the bisected angle. Thus, referring to Fig. 37, angle B is bisected and side b is divided into two parts x and y, and the ratio x to y is equal to the ratio a to c.

Fig. 37

CROSSED CHORDS

Referring to Fig. 38, the triangles CAB and CDB have the common base CB which is a chord of the circle, therefore the angles at the apices of these triangles where they touch the circumference of the circle are equal (see Fig. 42). Angle CAB = Angle CDB. Also, at the intersection of the two straight lines AB and CD, angle COA = angle BOD (see Fig. 34). Now considering triangles COA and BOD, since two angles of each of these are equal, the remaining angle of each must be equal, therefore angle ACO = angle DBO.

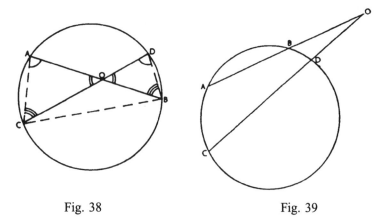

Fig. 38   Fig. 39

In such similar triangles, the sides opposite the corresponding angles must be in the same ratio, hence for two non-parallel chords of a circle:

$$\frac{AO}{CO} = \frac{DO}{BO}$$

$$\therefore AO \times BO = CO \times DO$$

where A and B are the points where the two ends of the chord AB touch the circle, C and D the points where the two ends of another chord CD touch the circle, and O is the point of intersection of these two chords.

This rule of crossed chords is also true when the intersection of the chords occurs outside the circle as illustrated in Fig. 39.

A useful application of the case where the chords intersect inside the circle is the estimation of the diameter of a circular vessel when a rule of sufficient length is not available. Thus, one chord is made the diameter itself and this cuts another chord perpendicular to it as in Fig. 40. As an example, let AB be the diameter of a vessel, a 1 m straight-edge is laid horizontally across to form the chord CD, the vertical distance between bottom of vessel and straight-edge is measured to be 100 mm, this is BO, then:

$$AO \times BO = CO \times DO$$

$$AO \times 100 = 500 \times 500$$

$$AO = 2500 \text{ mm}$$

$$\text{Diameter of vessel} = AB = AO + BO$$

$$= 2500 + 100$$

$$= 2600 \text{ mm or } 2 \cdot 6 \text{ m}$$

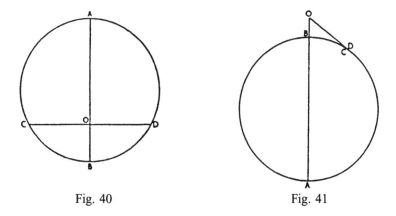

Fig. 40   Fig. 41

An interesting example of the case where the chords meet outside the circle is to estimate the distance of observation from a given point above the earth's surface to the horizon. Figure 41 shows a circle representing the earth, AB is one chord which is the diameter, say 12 750 km, this is extended to the observation point O, let this be 24 m above the earth's surface. The other chord is imagined to be so small that it becomes tangential to the circle, i.e., the length of CD is nil and points C and D are at one. The extension of this chord meets the other at O. CO (or DO) is the distance from the point of observation to the horizon.

$$24 \text{ m} = 0 \cdot 024 \text{ km}$$
$$\text{AO} \times \text{BO} = \text{CO} \times \text{DO}$$
$$(12\,750 \cdot 024) \times (0 \cdot 024) = \text{CO} \times \text{DO}$$

Adding 0·024 to 12 750 makes no difference in four-figure accuracy, i.e., 12 750·024 can be taken as 12 750.

$$\text{CO} \times \text{DO} = (\text{CO})^2 \text{ because CO is equal to DO}$$
$$\therefore \ 12\,750 \times 0 \cdot 024 = (\text{CO})^2$$
$$\text{CO} = \sqrt{12\,750 \times 0 \cdot 024}$$
$$= 17 \cdot 49 \text{ km}$$

CYCLIC TRIANGLES AND QUADRILATERALS

The apex angles of all triangles at the circumference within the same segment of a circle and having the same chord as a base, are equal. Stated briefly: Angles in the same segment of a circle are equal. See Fig. 42.

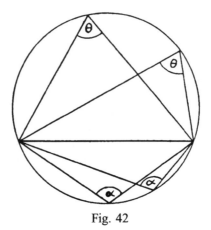

Fig. 42

If the base of the triangle is the diameter of the circle, then the apex angle at the circumference is 90°. Stated briefly: The angle in a semi-circle is a right angle. See Fig. 43.

If two triangles be drawn within the same segment of a circle and having one chord as their common base, the apex of one being at the

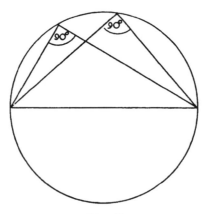

Fig. 43

centre of the circle and the apex of the other touching the circumference, the angle at the centre is twice the angle at the circumference. Briefly: The angle at the centre of a circle is double the angle at the circumference for triangles in the same segment standing on the same chord. See Fig. 44.

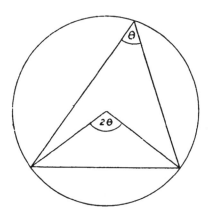

Fig. 44

The sum of either pair of opposite angles in a quadrilateral (i.e., a four-sided figure) inscribed in a circle is equal to 180°. This is illustrated in Fig. 45 with measured angles. Briefly: The opposite angles of a cyclic quadrilateral are supplementary. It can also be seen that any exterior angle produced by extending one side, is equal to the opposite interior angle.

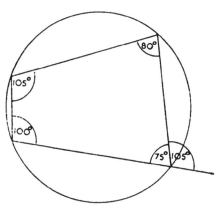

Fig. 45

As an exercise on the last few cases, measure the angles from Fig. 46.

$$\text{ADB} = \text{AEB}, \quad \text{ACB} = 2 \times \text{ADB}, \quad \text{AFB} = \text{AGB}.$$

There are a number of cyclic quadrilaterals here, ADBF, ADBG, AEBF and AEBG.

Measure any remaining angles in these quadrilaterals and check that all opposite angles are supplementary.

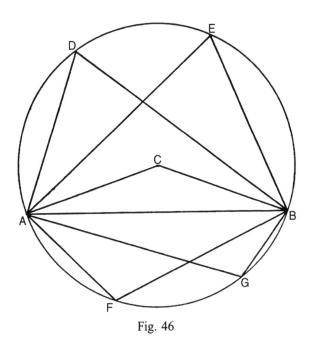

Fig. 46

CIRCUMSCRIBED CIRCLE

If a triangle is drawn inside a circle with its three corners touching the circumference, the perpendicular bisectors of the three sides meet at the centre of the circle. See Fig. 47.

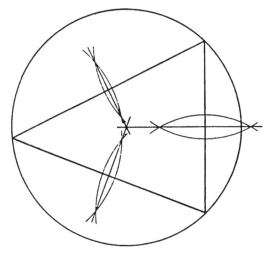

Fig. 47

INSCRIBED CIRCLE

If a triangle is drawn around a circle such that the three sides of the triangle just touch the circumference of the circle, the bisectors of the three angles meet at the centre of the circle. See Fig. 48.

SIMILAR TRIANGLES

Triangles are *similar* when they are equiangular (i.e., contain the same angles). It follows that their corresponding sides are in the same proportion and the shape of the triangles are the same.

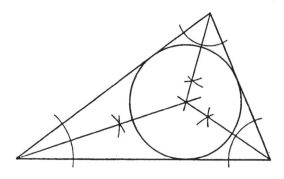

Fig. 48

To ascertain whether two triangles are similar, apply any of the following tests to see if:

   (i) they are equiangular,

  (ii) their corresponding sides are in proportion,

 (iii) one angle in each triangle are equal and the sides containing these angles are in proportion.

Figure 49 shows some pairs of similar triangles, in each pair triangle ABC is similar to triangle XYZ.

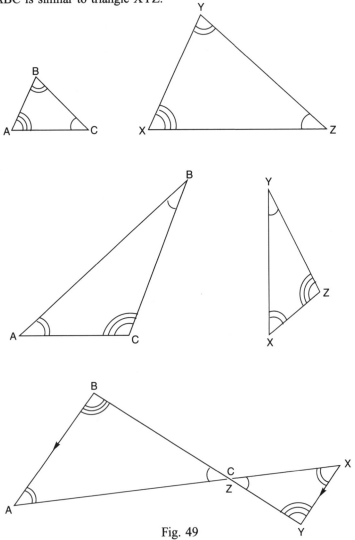

Fig. 49

A given triangle can be divided into two or more similar triangles by drawing one or more lines parallel to one of the sides. When lines are drawn parallel to one side, they divide the other two sides into parts of the same ratio. This is illustrated in Fig. 50, the usual method of indicating parallel lines by arrows is used.

ABC, XYZ and PQR are similar triangles and their sides are in the same ratio.

Fig. 50

Congruent triangles have the same shape and *size*, and thus contain the same area. Figure 51 illustrates some congruent triangles.

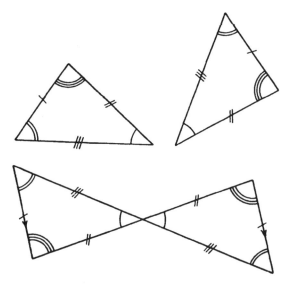

Fig. 51

TEST EXAMPLES 7

1. (i) Express the following angles in rad,

   $$114°36', \qquad 286°30'.$$

   (ii) Express in (a) rad, (b) deg, the angles subtended by arc lengths of 10, and 30·4 m respectively, on a circle of 10 m diameter.

2. A disc flywheel is rotating at a speed of 10·52 rad/s. Calculate the linear velocity, in m/s, of points on the wheel at radii of 100 and 500 mm respectively. Find the linear velocity in m/s of the rim at 2 m diameter when rotating at 125 rev/min.

3. In a right angled triangle ABC, length AC is 36 mm, length BC is 27 mm, and the angle at C is 90°. Calculate the length of the hypotenuse AB and the sine, cosine and tangent of the angle at B.

4. Find, without the use of calculator or tables, the sine and tangent of an angle whose cosine is 0·4924.

5. Write down the sine, cosine and tangent of the following angles,

   $$10°33' \qquad 46°55' \qquad 150°47' \qquad 201°21' \qquad 287°14'$$

   Sketch sine and cosine curves for angles between 0° and 360°.

6. The following refer to angles between 0° and 360°,
   (a) find the angles whose sines are:

   $$0·3783, \qquad -0·7005,$$

   (b) find the angles whose cosines are:

   $$0·9687, \qquad -0·8769,$$

   (c) find the angles whose tangents are:

   $$0·2010, \qquad -3·2006,$$

7. If $\theta = 80°$, find the values of:

   $$\sin \theta, \qquad \cos \theta, \qquad \sin 2\theta, \qquad \cos 2\theta, \qquad \sin^2 \theta, \qquad \cos^2 \theta$$

8. Find the values of θ between $0°$ and $360°$ which satisfy the equation,

$$\cos\theta - \sin^2\theta = 0$$

9. If $a = 2\sin\theta$, and $b = 5\cos\theta$, find the values of θ for angles between $0°$ and $180°$ when:

$$\frac{a^2}{2} = \frac{2b^2}{5} - 4$$

10. Prove that $\operatorname{cosec}^2 A + \sec^2 A = \operatorname{cosec}^2 A \sec^2 A$

11. Prove that

$$\frac{1 - \sin A}{1 + \sin A} = (\sec A - \tan A)^2$$

12. Prove that:

$$(\sec A - \cos A)(\operatorname{cosec} A - \sin A) = \frac{1}{\tan A + \cot A}$$

13. The velocity of the piston in a reciprocating engine is given by:

$$v = \omega r\left(\sin\theta + \frac{\sin 2\theta}{2n}\right) \text{ m/s}$$

and the acceleration is given by:

$$a = \omega^2 r\left(\cos\theta + \frac{\cos 2\theta}{n}\right) \text{ m/s}^2$$

where ω = angular velocity of crank in rad/s,
r = throw of crank ($\frac{1}{2}$ stroke) in m,
θ = angle of crank past top centre, in deg,
n = ratio of connecting rod length to crank length.
Calculate (i) the velocity, (ii) the acceleration, of the piston of an engine of 1 m stroke, connecting rod length 2 m, at the instant the crank is $80°$ past top centre and running at 150 rev/min.

14. Construct a triangle, ABC, such that AB = 48 mm, BC = 39 mm and the angle at A = $50°$, measure the remaining side and angles. A geometrically similar triangle has AB = 60 mm. What does BC equal?

15. A trammel gauge supplied by the makers of an engine as a measurement of the diameter of a cylinder when new, was exactly 750 mm. The cylinder is now gauged and, with one end of the trammel held against the cylinder wall, there is 78 mm chord travel at the other end. Find the wear (increase in diameter).

16. Find the distance from an observation point 30 m above sea level, to the horizon, assuming the earth is 12 750 km diameter.

17. Construct a triangle of sides 56, 48 and 40 mm long respectively, bisect each side to find the centre of a circle which will pass through the three points of the triangle, draw the circle and state its radius.

18. Construct a triangle of sides 68, 58 and 42 mm long respectively, bisect the angles to find the centre of a circle which will touch the three sides of the triangle, draw the circle and state its radius.

CHAPTER 8

SOLUTION OF TRIANGLES

To solve a triangle means to find the other sides and angles of the triangle remaining from the data given. Of the three sides and three angles of any triangle, at least one side must be given with two other quantities; the two other quantities may be the other two sides, or one other side and one angle, or two of the angles.

A sketch of the triangle is advisable to understand the problem clearly and a scale drawing, especially in the early stages of learning, gives a check on calculations.

RATIOS FOR RIGHT ANGLED TRIANGLES

Figure 52 is a right angled triangle because one of its angles is 90° and one of the angles (other than the right angle) is given, therefore the side opposite this angle is referred to as the opposite and the other side is the adjacent.

The ratio of the sides are (see Chapter 7):

$$\text{Sine} = \frac{\text{opposite}}{\text{hypotenuse}}$$

$$\text{Cosine} = \frac{\text{adjacent}}{\text{hypotenuse}}$$

$$\text{Tangent} = \frac{\text{opposite}}{\text{adjacent}}$$

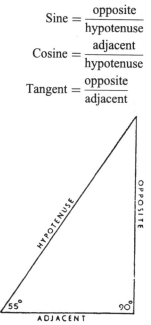

Fig. 52

Example.   One of the angles in a right angled triangle is 59°42′ and the hypotenuse is 55 mm. Find the remaining angle and sides.

Fig. 53

Referring to Fig. 53

$$\frac{\text{opposite}}{\text{hypotenuse}} = \sin 59°42′$$

$$\text{opposite} = \text{hypotenuse} \times \sin 59°42′$$

$$= 55 \times 0·8634$$

$$= 47·49 \text{ mm   Ans.}$$

The remaining side can now be found by the Theorem of Pythagoras:

$$(\text{hypotenuse})^2 = (\text{opposite})^2 + (\text{adjacent})^2$$

$$\therefore \text{ adjacent} = \sqrt{55^2 - 47·49^2}$$

$$= 27·74 \text{ mm   Ans.}$$

or by using the cosine ratio:

$$\frac{\text{adjacent}}{\text{hypotenuse}} = \cos 59°42′$$

$$\text{adjacent} = 55 \times \cos 59°42′$$

$$= 27·75 \text{ mm   Ans.}$$

Since the three angles of any triangle add up to 180°, the third angle is found by subtracting the sum of the other two from 180°.

$$\text{Third angle} = 180° - (90° + 59°42')$$
$$= 90° - 59°42'$$
$$= 30°18' \quad \text{Ans.}$$

Example.   A light on a cliff is viewed from a position at sea, the angle of elevation being 32°15'. At a point 100 m further away from the cliff and in direct line with the first observation point, the light is viewed again and the angle of elevation is now 20°44'. Find (*a*) the height of the light above sea level, and (*b*) the horizontal distance from the second observation point to the light.

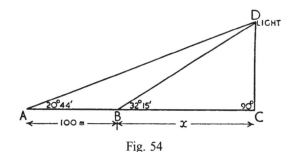

Fig. 54

Referring to Fig. 54,

$$\frac{CD}{x} = \tan 32°15'$$
$$\therefore CD = x \times 0\cdot6309 \qquad \ldots \quad \ldots \quad \text{(i)}$$
$$\frac{CD}{100 + x} = \tan 20°44'$$
$$\therefore CD = (100 + x) \times 0\cdot3786$$
$$CD = 37\cdot86 + 0\cdot3786x \qquad \ldots \quad \text{(ii)}$$

From (i) and (ii),

$$0\cdot6309x = 37\cdot86 + 0\cdot3786x$$
$$0\cdot2523x = 37\cdot86$$
$$x = 150\cdot1 \text{ m}$$
$$AC = 100 + 150\cdot1$$
$$\text{Horizontal distance} = 250\cdot1 \text{ m} \quad \text{Ans. } (b)$$

From (i),

$$CD = x \times 0\cdot6309$$
$$= 150\cdot1 \times 0\cdot6309$$
$$\text{Height} = 94\cdot69 \text{ m} \quad \text{Ans.} \quad (a)$$

TRIANGLES OTHER THAN RIGHT ANGLED

If the triangle does not contain one angle of 90°, the sine, cosine and tangent ratios of the sides cannot be applied as in the above right angled triangles. Other rules are employed which will now be explained.

The commonest method of notation of triangles is to let capital letters represent the angles and their corresponding small letters represent the sides opposite to these triangles. Thus in Fig. 55 the three corners are lettered A, B and C, this means that the three angles at these corners are represented by these letters. The side opposite angle A is represented by its lower case a, the side opposite angle B is represented by b, and the side opposite C is represented by c. A perpendicular erected from the base of the triangle to its apex is usually denoted by h, this perpendicular divides the triangle into two right angled triangles which can often provide a solution by the knowledge of right angled triangles only.

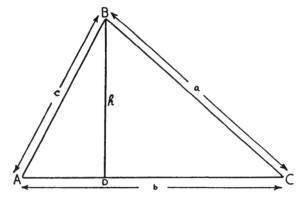

Fig. 55

SINE RULE

Referring to Fig. 55, and considering the right angled triangular part BCD,

$$\frac{h}{a} = \sin C \quad \therefore h = a \sin C$$

Considering the right angled triangular part ABD,

$$\frac{h}{c} = \sin A \quad \therefore h = c \sin A$$

hence,

$$a \sin C = c \sin A$$

or,

$$\frac{a}{\sin A} = \frac{c}{\sin C} \qquad \cdots \quad \cdots \quad (i)$$

Figure 56 represents the same triangle as Fig. 55, but with a perpendicular h_2 from side c to angle C.

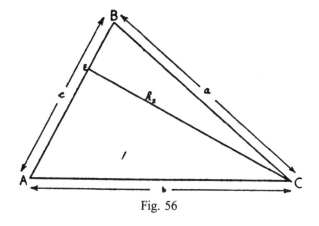

Fig. 56

Considering the right angled triangular part BCE,

$$\frac{h_2}{a} = \sin B \quad \therefore h_2 = a \sin B$$

Considering the right angled triangular part ACE,

$$\frac{h_2}{b} = \sin A \quad \therefore \ h_2 = b \sin A$$

hence,

$$a \sin B = b \sin A$$

or,

$$\frac{a}{\sin A} = \frac{b}{\sin B} \qquad \ldots \quad \ldots \quad \ldots \quad \text{(ii)}$$

From (i) and (ii): $\dfrac{a}{\sin A} = \dfrac{b}{\sin B} = \dfrac{c}{\sin C}$

This is the SINE RULE which is very important and most useful in trigonometrical calculations. Note that the length of any side is proportional to the sine of the angle opposite that side, the longest side is opposite the largest angle, and the shortest side is opposite the smallest angle.

Example. The vertical post of a jib crane is 10 m long. The angle between jib and post is 40°, and between jib and tie the angle is 45°. Find the length of the tie and the length of the jib.

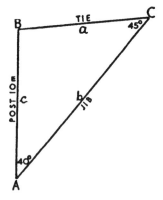

Fig. 57

Referring to Fig. 57,

$$\frac{a}{\sin A} = \frac{c}{\sin C}$$

$$a = \frac{c \sin A}{\sin C}$$

$$= \frac{10 \times 0.6428}{0.7071} = 9.088 \text{ m}$$

$$B = 180° - (40° + 45°) = 95°$$

$$\frac{b}{\sin B} = \frac{c}{\sin C}$$

$$b = \frac{c \sin B}{\sin C}$$

$$= \frac{10 \times 0.9962}{0.7071} = 14.09 \text{ m}$$

Length of tie = 9.088 m
Length of jib = 14.09 m   } Ans.

Example. Two ships leave the same port at the same time on courses which diverge at 29°. When one ship had travelled 40 naut. miles the two ships were then 21 naut. miles apart, find how far the other ship had travelled from port.

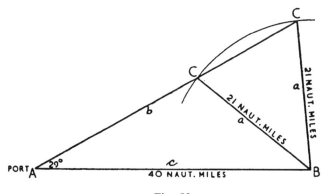

Fig. 58

Referring to Fig. 58,

$$\frac{a}{\sin A} = \frac{c}{\sin C}$$

$$\sin C = \frac{c \sin A}{a}$$

$$= \frac{40 \times 0.4848}{21} = 0.9234$$

0·9234 is the sine of 67°26′ but is also the sine of
180° − 67°26′ = 112°34′.

Therefore there are two possible answers to this problem, as
illustrated in Fig. 58.

If $C = 67°26′$:

$B = 180° − (29° + 67°26′) = 83°34′$

$$\frac{a}{\sin A} = \frac{b}{\sin B}$$

$$b = \frac{a \sin B}{\sin A}$$

$$= \frac{21 \times 0.9937}{0.4848} = 43.04 \qquad \text{(i)}$$

If $C = 112°34′$

$B = 180° − (29° + 112°34′) = 38°26′$

$$b = \frac{a \sin B}{\sin A}$$

$$= \frac{21 \times 0.6216}{0.4848} = 26.93 \qquad \text{(ii)}$$

For the two ships to be 21 naut. miles apart and one having travelled
40 naut. miles, the other ship has travelled:

either   43·04   or   26·93 naut. miles.   Ans.

COSINE RULE

Inspection of the Sine Rule will show that it would not solve a
triangle when two sides and the included angle between these sides
were the only given quantities, nor if the given quantities were the
three sides without any angles. Such cases can be solved by the
Cosine Rule which will now be explained.

Referring to Fig. 55 and considering the right angled triangular part ABD, let AD be represented by x, then by the Theorem of Pythagoras,

$$h^2 = c^2 - x^2 \quad \dots \quad \dots \quad \dots \quad \dots \quad \text{(i)}$$

Now considering the right angled triangular part BCD,

$$\begin{aligned} \text{DC} &= b - x \\ h^2 &= a^2 - (b - x)^2 \\ &= a^2 - (b^2 - 2bx + x^2) \\ &= a^2 - b^2 + 2bx - x^2 \quad \dots \quad \dots \quad \text{(ii)} \end{aligned}$$

From (i) and (ii)

$$a^2 - b^2 + 2bx - x^2 = c^2 - x^2$$
$$a^2 = b^2 + c^2 - 2bx$$

but $x = c \times \cos A$, therefore,

$$a^2 = b^2 + c^2 - 2bc \cos A$$

This is the COSINE RULE and equally important as the sine rule for solving triangles. It will be obvious that this can be written in either of the three forms:

$$a^2 = b^2 + c^2 - 2bc \cos A$$
$$b^2 = a^2 + c^2 - 2ac \cos B$$
$$c^2 = a^2 + b^2 - 2ab \cos C$$

Note that the last term is a negative value, if the angle involved is between 90° and 180°, its cosine is negative, and $-2bc$ multiplied by a minus quantity will produce a positive term.

Transposing the cosine rule to find one angle given the three sides:

$$a^2 = b^2 + c^2 - 2bc \cos A$$
$$2bc \cos A = b^2 + c^2 - a^2$$
$$\cos A = \frac{b^2 + c^2 - a^2}{2bc}$$

this can also be written:

$$\cos B = \frac{a^2 + c^2 - b^2}{2ac}$$

$$\text{or,} \quad \cos C = \frac{a^2 + b^2 - c^2}{2ab}$$

Example.   A ship going due North at 16 knot runs into a 5 knot current moving North-East. Find the resultant speed and direction of the ship.

Reference Fig. 59,

$$\text{Angle } A = 90° + 45° = 135°$$

$$a^2 = b^2 + c^2 - 2bc \cos A$$

$$= 16^2 + 5^2 - 2 \times 16 \times 5 \times \cos 135°$$

$$= 256 + 25 - 160 \times (-0.7071)$$

$$= 256 + 25 + 113.1$$

$$a = \sqrt{394.1}$$

$$= 19.85 \text{ knot}$$

$$\frac{a}{\sin A} = \frac{c}{\sin C}$$

$$\sin C = \frac{c \times \sin A}{a}$$

$$= \frac{5 \times 0.7071}{19.85} = 0.1781$$

$$C = 10°15'$$

$$\left.\begin{array}{l} \text{Resultant speed} = 19.85 \text{ knot} \\ \text{Resultant direction} = 10°15' \text{ East of North} \end{array}\right\} \quad \text{Ans.}$$

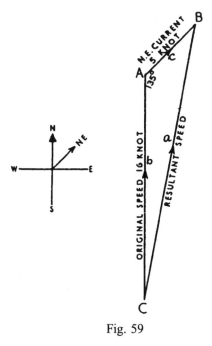

Fig. 59

Example.   The three sides of a triangle measure 8, 6 and 4 cm respectively. Find the angles.

$$\cos A = \frac{b^2 + c^2 - a^2}{2bc}$$

$$= \frac{4^2 + 8^2 - 6^2}{2 \times 4 \times 8} = 0 \cdot 6875$$

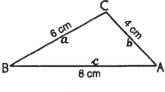

Fig. 60

Angle $A = 46°34'$

$$\frac{a}{\sin A} = \frac{b}{\sin B}$$

$$\sin B = \frac{b \sin A}{a}$$

$$= \frac{4 \times 0.7262}{6} = 0.4841$$

Angle $B = 28°57'$

Angle $C = 180° - (46°34' + 28°57')$

$$= 180° - 75°31'$$

$$= 104°29'$$

The three angles are:

$46°34'$, $28°57'$ and $104°29'$ Ans.

Summarising the formulae given so far for solving triangles, the sine, cosine and tangent ratios of sides are used for right angled triangles, and either the sine rule or cosine rule for other triangles. The sine rule is easier to calculate than the cosine rule and is therefore used wherever possible, the two cases where the sine rule cannot be applied and the cosine rule becomes necessary are when the only data available is:

(i) two sides and the angle between these sides,
(ii) the three sides.

AREAS OF TRIANGLES

It can be seen from any of the previous illustrations of triangles, or from Figs. 61 and 62 that the area of a triangle is half of the area of its circumscribing rectangle, therefore,

Area of triangle $= \frac{1}{2}$(base $\times$ perpendicular height)

Fig. 61

Fig. 62

Referring to Fig. 62,

$$\text{Perpendicular height} = a \times \sin C$$

$$\text{Area} = \tfrac{1}{2}(b \times a \sin C)$$

$$\therefore \text{Area} = \frac{ab \sin C}{2}$$

Note this formula, in words it is 'half the product of two sides and the sine of the angle between these sides'. An easy formula to apply and a very useful one.

Another important formula for finding the area of a triangle is one which calculates the area directly from the three sides of the triangle:

$$\text{Area} = \sqrt{s(s-a)(s-b)(s-c)}$$

where a, b and c = the three lengths of the sides respectively,

and s = semi-sum of sides,

$$= \tfrac{1}{2}(a+b+c)$$

Example. The three sides of a triangle measure 8, 10 and 14 cm respectively, find the area enclosed.

$$s = \tfrac{1}{2}(a+b+c)$$

$$= \tfrac{1}{2}(8+10+14)$$

$$= 16$$

$$s - a = 16 - 8 = 8$$

$$s - b = 16 - 10 = 6$$

$$s - c = 16 - 14 = 2$$

$$\text{Area} = \sqrt{s(s-a)(s-b)(s-c)}$$

$$= \sqrt{16 \times 8 \times 6 \times 2} = \sqrt{1536}$$

$$= 39 \cdot 2 \text{ cm}^2 \quad \text{Ans.}$$

EQUILATERAL TRIANGLE

An equilateral triangle is one which has three equal sides and three equal angles. Each angle is therefore 60° (Fig. 63).

$$\text{Perpendicular height} = \text{side} \times \sin 60°$$
$$= \text{side} \times 0.866$$
$$\text{Area} = \tfrac{1}{2}(\text{base} \times \text{perp. ht.})$$
$$= \tfrac{1}{2}(\text{side} \times \text{side} \times 0.866)$$
$$= 0.433 \text{ side}^2$$

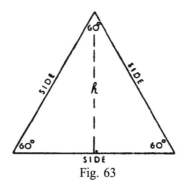

Fig. 63

ISOSCELES TRIANGLE

An isosceles triangle is one which has two equal sides and two equal angles.

In Fig. 64 angles A and C are equal, therefore the lengths of the sides a and c are equal.

$$A = C = \tfrac{1}{2}(180 - B)$$

It is thus an easy matter to calculate the perpendicular height or other data required to find the area by any of the general formulae.

CIRCUMSCRIBED CIRCLE

To find the radius of a circle whose circumference will pass through the three angular points of a triangle. This construction was shown in Chapter 7 (Fig. 47). Let the given triangle be ABC as shown in Fig. 65.

Fig. 64

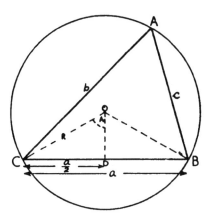

Fig. 65

Since the angle at the centre is twice the angle at the apex, that is, angle $COB = 2A$, then angle $COD = A$.

$$\frac{a}{2} \div R = \sin A$$

$$\frac{a}{2R} = \sin A$$

$$\therefore 2R = \frac{a}{\sin A}$$

Therefore, by sine rule,

$$2R = \frac{a}{\sin A} = \frac{b}{\sin B} = \frac{c}{\sin C} \quad \cdots \quad \cdots \quad (i)$$

Also, area of triangle $= \frac{1}{2} ab \sin C$

Substituting the value of $\sin C = \dfrac{c}{2R}$

Area of triangle $= \frac{1}{2} \times a \times b \times \dfrac{c}{2R}$

$$\therefore R = \frac{abc}{4 \times \text{area of triangle}} \quad \cdots \quad (ii)$$

INSCRIBED CIRCLE

To find the radius of a circle inscribed within a triangle, this construction was shown in Chapter 7 (Fig. 48).

Let R = radius of the circle

Let a, b and c = lengths of the sides of the triangle.

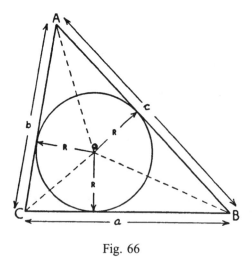

Fig. 66

Dividing the triangle ABC into three small triangles BOC, COA and AOB as shown in Fig. 66, the radius of the circle R is the perpendicular height in each of these.

Finding the area of each triangle by the rule,

area $= \frac{1}{2}$(base $\times$ perp. height) and then adding together,

$$\text{Area of BOC} = \tfrac{1}{2} \times a \times R$$
$$\text{Area of COA} = \tfrac{1}{2} \times b \times R$$
$$\text{Area of AOB} = \tfrac{1}{2} \times c \times R$$
$$\text{Area of whole triangle ABC} = \tfrac{1}{2}R(a+b+c)$$
$$\therefore R = \frac{2 \times \text{area of triangle}}{a+b+c}$$

or, $\quad R = \dfrac{2 \times \text{area of triangle}}{\text{perimeter of triangle}}$

COMPOUND ANGLES

In some problems it is often convenient to express the relationship between the trigonometrical ratios of a compound angle and those of the two single component angles.

Referring to Fig. 67,

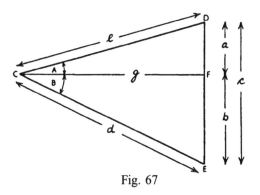

Fig. 67

$$\text{Area of CED} = \text{area of CFD} + \text{area of CFE}$$
$$\tfrac{1}{2}[ed \sin(A+B)] = \tfrac{1}{2}(ge \sin A) + \tfrac{1}{2}(gd \sin B)$$

Dividing throughout by $\frac{1}{2}ed$,

$$\sin(A+B) = \frac{g}{d}\sin A + \frac{g}{e}\sin B$$
$$= \cos B \sin A + \cos A \sin B$$

Usually written,

$$\sin(A + B) = \sin A \cos B + \cos A \sin B \quad \dots \quad \dots \quad (i)$$

By a similar process it can be shown that,

$$\sin(A - B) = \sin A \cos B - \cos A \sin B \quad \dots \quad \dots \quad (ii)$$

Again referring to Fig. 67 and applying the cosine rule,

$$\cos C = \frac{e^2 + d^2 - c^2}{2ed}$$

$$\cos(A + B) = \frac{e^2 + d^2 - (a + b)^2}{2ed}$$

$$= \frac{e^2 + d^2 - a^2 - 2ab - b^2}{2ed}$$

but, by Pythagoras, $e^2 - a^2 = g^2$

and $d^2 - b^2 = g^2$

$$\therefore \cos(A + B) = \frac{2g^2 - 2ab}{2ed}$$

$$= \frac{g^2}{ed} - \frac{ab}{ed}$$

$$= \frac{g}{e} \times \frac{g}{d} - \frac{a}{e} \times \frac{b}{d}$$

$$= \cos A \times \cos B - \sin A \times \sin B$$

Usually written,

$$\cos(A + B) = \cos A \cos B - \sin A \sin B \quad \dots \quad \dots \quad (iii)$$

By a similar kind of process it can also be shown that,

$$\cos(A - B) = \cos A \cos B + \sin A \sin B \quad \dots \quad \dots \quad (iv)$$

The tangent of an angle being the sine divided by its cosine, the relationship for the tangent of a compound angle can be obtained by dividing $\sin(A + B)$ by $\cos(A + B)$,

$$\tan(A + B) = \frac{\sin(A + B)}{\cos(A + B)}$$

$$= \frac{\sin A \cos B + \cos A \sin B}{\cos A \cos B - \sin A \sin B}$$

Dividing all terms, top and bottom, by $\cos A \cos B$,

$$= \dfrac{\dfrac{\sin A \cos B}{\cos A \cos B} + \dfrac{\cos A \sin B}{\cos A \cos B}}{\dfrac{\cos A \cos B}{\cos A \cos B} - \dfrac{\sin A \sin B}{\cos A \cos B}}$$

$$= \frac{\tan A + \tan B}{1 - \tan A \tan B} \qquad \dots \quad \dots \quad \dots \quad \text{(v)}$$

and by a similar process,

$$\tan(A - B) = \frac{\tan A - \tan B}{1 + \tan A \tan B} \qquad \text{(vi)}$$

Collecting the above formulae:

$$\sin(A \pm B) = \sin A \cos B \pm \cos A \sin B$$
$$\cos(A \pm B) = \cos A \cos B \mp \sin A \sin B$$
$$\tan(A \pm B) = \frac{\tan A \pm \tan B}{1 \mp \tan A \tan B}$$

DOUBLE ANGLES

Formulae expressing the relationship between the ratios of angles and double the angles are useful and can be obtained from those above by letting $A = B$, thus,

$$\sin(A + B) = \sin A \cos B + \cos A \sin B$$

$B = A$, therefore,

$$\sin 2A = \sin A \cos A + \cos A \sin A$$
$$\sin 2A = 2 \sin A \cos A \qquad \dots \quad \dots \quad \dots \quad \text{(i)}$$
$$\cos(A + B) = \cos A \cos B - \sin A \sin B$$

$B = A$, therefore,

$$\cos 2A = \cos A \cos A - \sin A \sin A$$
$$\cos 2A = \cos^2 A - \sin^2 A \qquad \dots \quad \dots \quad \dots \quad \text{(iia)}$$

Also, since

$$\sin^2 A + \cos^2 A = 1 \quad \text{(see Chapter 7)}$$
$$\text{then,} \quad \cos^2 A = 1 - \sin^2 A$$
$$\text{and,} \quad \sin^2 A = 1 - \cos^2 A$$

Substituting for $\cos^2 A$ and $\sin^2 A$ in turn into (iia):

$$\cos 2A = \cos^2 A - \sin^2 A$$
$$= (1 - \sin^2 A) - \sin^2 A$$
$$\cos 2A = 1 - 2\sin^2 A \qquad \dots \quad \dots \quad \dots \quad \text{(iib)}$$

and,

$$\cos 2A = \cos^2 A - \sin^2 A$$
$$= \cos^2 A - (1 - \cos^2 A)$$
$$= \cos^2 A - 1 + \cos^2 A$$
$$\cos 2A = 2\cos^2 A - 1 \qquad \dots \quad \dots \quad \dots \quad \text{(iic)}$$

$$\tan(A + B) = \frac{\tan A + \tan B}{1 - \tan A \tan B}$$

$B = A$, therefore,

$$\tan 2A = \frac{\tan A + \tan A}{1 - \tan A \tan A}$$
$$\tan 2A = \frac{2\tan A}{1 - \tan^2 A} \qquad \dots \quad \dots \quad \dots \quad \text{(iii)}$$

Note.   Also see Identities in Chapter 7.

TEST EXAMPLES 8

1. The top of a vertical mast is viewed from a position at 15 m from its base on a level ground and the angle of elevation measured to be 45°34′. Find the height of the mast.

2. A boat is sighted from a point on a cliff 95 m above the sea, the angle of depression of the line of view being 14°25′. Find (i) the horizontal distance from cliff to boat, and (ii) the distance from observation point to boat.

3. A right angled triangular plate has one angle of 28°37′ and the length of the hypotenuse is 120 mm. Find the lengths of the other two sides and the area of the triangle.

4. The top of a flagstaff is viewed from a point on a level ground at some distance from the foot of the staff, and the angle of elevation is 48°30′. At another point 10 m further away from the foot, the staff top is viewed again and this time the angle of elevation is 37°38′.

Find the distance from the foot of staff to the first observation point and also the height of the flagstaff.

5. The length of the sides of a cube is 60 mm. Find the length of the diagonal across the face and the length of the cross diagonal from one corner to the opposite corner passing through the centre of the cube.

6. The length of the vertical post of a jib crane is 15 m. The angle between jib and post is 35°30′ and between tie and post the angle is 105°30′. Calculate the lengths of the jib and tie.

7. In a reciprocating engine of 800 mm stroke, the connecting rod is 1600 mm long. Find how far the crosshead has moved from the top of its stroke when the crank is 35° past its top dead centre.

8. The fuel valve of a diesel engine closes when the piston has moved one-tenth of its stroke from the top. If the length of the connecting rod is twice the length of the stroke, find the angular position of the crank from top dead centre when the valve closes.

9. A ship going due South at 17 knot runs into a 4 knot current running 50° East of North. Find the resultant speed and direction of the ship.

10. Two ships approach a port, their courses converging at an angle of 23°. At a certain time one ship is twice as far from port as the other and their distance apart is 32 naut. miles; find how far each ship is from port.

11. Two ships are 50 naut. miles apart and going towards the same port at the same speed of 18 knot, on courses which converge at 73°39′. If one ship will arrive in port half-an-hour before the other, find their distances from port.

12. Three sides of a triangle measure 16·4, 10·2 and 9·8 m respectively. Find the angles.

13. Two sides of a triangle measure 6·5 and 7·5 m respectively and the angle included between these two sides is 46°51′. Find the area of the triangle.

14. Find the area in cm^2 of a triangular plate of sides 71, 42 and 53 mm long respectively.

15. The area of an equilateral triangle is 57·27 cm^2. Find the length of its sides.

16. From,

$$\sin^2 \theta + \cos^2 \theta = 1$$

and, $\cos 2\theta = \cos^2 \theta - \sin^2 \theta$

Prove that (i) $\cos 2\theta = 1 - 2 \sin^2 \theta$

(ii) $\cos 2\theta = 2 \cos^2 \theta - 1$

and,   (iii)   find the value of $(1 + \cot^2 \theta)(1 - \cos 2\theta)$

17. Given that,

$$\sin 2\theta = 2 \sin \theta \cos \theta$$

and, $\cos 2\theta = \cos^2 \theta - \sin^2 \theta$

prove: (i) $\sin 2\theta = \dfrac{2 \tan \theta}{1 + \tan^2 \theta}$

(ii) $\cos 2\theta = \dfrac{1 - \tan^2 \theta}{1 + \tan^2 \theta}$

and,   (iii)   find the value of θ between $0°$ and $90°$
which satisfies the equation:

$\sin 2\theta + 2 \cos 2\theta = 1$

18. Prove,

$$\sin 3\theta = 3 \sin \theta - 4 \sin^3 \theta$$

MENSURATION OF AREAS

Cm^2 is a very practical size, between m^2 and mm^2, and is often used. Note the scale of areas:

$$1 \text{ cm} = 10 \text{ mm} \quad \therefore 1 \text{ cm}^2 = 10^2 \text{ mm}^2$$
$$1 \text{ m} = 10^2 \text{ cm} \quad \therefore 1 \text{ m}^2 = 10^4 \text{ cm}^2$$
$$1 \text{ m} = 10^3 \text{ mm} \quad \therefore 1 \text{ m}^2 = 10^6 \text{ mm}^2$$

Note also

$$1 \text{ cm}^2 = 10^{-4} \text{ m}^2$$
$$1 \text{ mm}^2 = 10^{-6} \text{ m}^2 = 10^{-2} \text{ cm}^2$$

A PARALLELOGRAM is a four-sided figure whose opposite sides are parallel and equal in length to each other. It therefore follows that opposite angles are equal, one pair of opposite angles being obtuse, and the other pair acute and supplementary to the obtuse angles. It may be considered as a rectangular framework leaning over to one side as in Fig. 68 wherein it can be seen that the outer triangular area (shown dotted) at one end is equal to the inner triangular area at the other end. Hence the area of the parallelogram is equal to that of a rectangle of the same base and same perpendicular height. Also, if a diagonal is drawn from one corner to the opposite corner, it will bisect the parallelogram into two equal triangles, the area of each being half that of the parallelogram.

Area of Parallelogram = base × perp. height

Fig. 68

A RHOMBUS is a special kind of parallelogram. It is a diamond-shaped four-sided figure with all sides of equal length and opposite sides parallel to each other. See Fig. 69. The diagonals of a rhombus are perpendicular to each other and their intersection form right angles; the diagonals bisect each other and each bisects its corner angles. The area of a rhombus is half of the product of its diagonals.

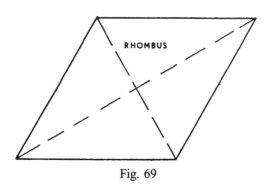

Fig. 69

A TRAPEZIUM is a four-sided figure, two sides only of which are parallel. Referring to Fig. 70, if a and b are the respective lengths of the two parallel sides and h is the perpendicular height, then,

$$\text{Area of Trapezium} = \text{average length} \times \text{perp. height}$$
$$= \tfrac{1}{2}(a + b) \times h$$

The equivalent rectangle of the trapezium is shown in dotted lines.

The area of any four-sided figure, such as shown in Fig. 71, wherein all sides are different length and all angles different, can be found by

Fig. 70

dividing the figure into two triangles by a diagonal, calculating the
area of each triangle and adding them together.

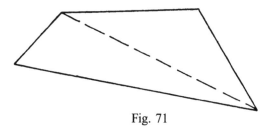

Fig. 71

TRIANGLES

A diagonal drawn joining two opposite corners of a parallelogram
(Fig. 72) divides the figure into two *equal* triangles, therefore the area of
a triangle is half that of a parallelogram of the same base and
perpendicular height. This and other rules for the areas of triangles were
given in the previous chapter, thus,

$$\text{Area of triangle} = \tfrac{1}{2}(\text{base} \times \text{perp. height})$$
$$= \tfrac{1}{2}(ab \sin C)$$
$$= \sqrt{s(s - a)(s - b)(s - c)}$$

where a, b and c are the lengths of the three sides and s is their semi-
sum.

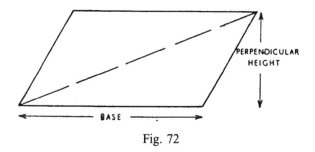

Fig. 72

POLYGONS

A Polygon is a figure bounded by more than four straight sides. A
regular polygon has all its sides equal in length and all its angles equal,

any regular polygon is therefore made up of as many equal triangles as there are sides and the method of finding the area of a polygon is to first find the area of one triangle and then multiply by the number of triangles which constitute the polygon.

Special names are given to some regular polygons as follows,

A Five-sided figure is called a   Pentagon

A Six-sided figure is called a   Hexagon

A Seven-sided figure is called a   Heptagon

An Eight-sided figure is called an   Octagon

A Nine-sided figure is called a   Nonagon

A Ten-sided figure is called a   Decagon

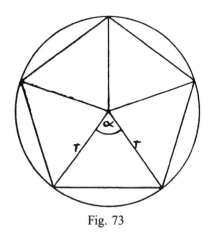

Fig. 73

For any polygon, if n = number of sides, then,

$$\text{number of triangles} = n$$

$$\text{Apex angle of each triangle} = \alpha = \frac{360°}{n}$$

If r = radius of the circumscribing circle, then r is also the slant height of each triangle. Note that all the triangles are isosceles, see Figs. 73 to 75.

$$\text{Area of each triangle} = \tfrac{1}{2}(ab \sin C)$$
$$= \tfrac{1}{2}r^2 \sin \alpha$$
$$\therefore \text{Area of polygon} = \tfrac{1}{2}nr^2 \sin \alpha$$

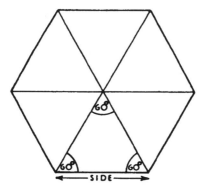

Fig. 74

It is, however, also convenient to express the area of the more common polygons in terms of the length of the 'sides' or 'flats'.

As there are six sides to the hexagon, it is composed of six triangles, the apex of each triangle is $360° \div 6 = 60°$.

The base angles are each $\frac{1}{2}(180° - 60°) = 60°$.

Therefore the triangles must be equilateral (see Fig. 74).

The area of an equilateral triangle $= 0.433$ side^2 (previously shown)

$$\therefore \text{Area of Hexagon} = 6 \times 0.433 \text{ side}^2$$
$$= 2.598 \text{ side}^2$$

The OCTAGON being composed of eight isosceles triangles, the apex angle of each is $360° \div 8 = 45°$ (see Fig. 75).

The base angles are each $\frac{1}{2}(180° - 45°) = 67\frac{1}{2}°$

$$\text{Perp. height of triangle} = \frac{1}{2} \text{ side} \times \tan 67\frac{1}{2}°$$
$$\text{Area of triangle} = \frac{1}{2} (\text{base} \times \text{perp. height})$$
$$= \frac{1}{2} \times \text{base} \times \frac{1}{2} \times \text{side} \times \tan 67\frac{1}{2}°$$
$$= \frac{1}{2} \times \text{side} \times \frac{1}{2} \times \text{side} \times \tan 67\frac{1}{2}°$$
$$= 0.60355 \text{ side}^2$$
$$\text{Area of Octagon} = 8 \times 0.60355 \text{ side}^2$$
$$= 4.8284 \text{ side}^2$$

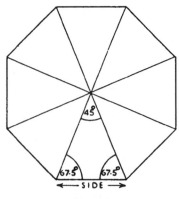

Fig. 75

THE CIRCLE

The Circumference is the outer rim of the circle, an Arc is part of the Circumference, other common terms are illustrated in Fig. 76.

$$Circumference = \pi \times diameter = \pi d$$
$$= 2\pi \times radius = 2\pi r$$
$$where \quad \pi = 3 \cdot 142 \text{ to nearest four figures.}$$

In many cases π may be conveniently taken as the vulgar fraction, which is $3\frac{1}{7}$ or $\frac{22}{7}$.

Fig. 76

The Area of a circle can be considered as being made up of a great number of small triangles, like a polygon of an infinite number of sides,

$$r = \text{height of each triangle}$$

$$\text{Area of each triangle} = \frac{r \times \text{base}}{2}$$

$$\text{Area of circle} = \text{sum of areas of all triangles}$$

$$= \text{sum of} \left\{ \frac{r \times \text{base}}{2} \right\}$$

$\dfrac{r}{2}$ is a common multiplier,

$$\therefore \text{Area of circle} = \frac{r}{2} \times \text{sum of bases}$$

but the sum of the bases constitute the whole circumference $= 2\pi r$

$$\therefore \text{Area of circle} = \frac{r}{2} \times 2\pi r = \pi r^2$$

$$\text{Also, since } r = \frac{d}{2}$$

$$\text{Area of circle} = \frac{\pi}{4} d^2 = 0.7854 d^2$$

ANNULUS OR CIRCULAR RING

Area of Annulus = area of outer circle − area of inner circle

$$= \pi R^2 - \pi r^2 \quad (\text{See Fig. 77})$$
$$= \pi (R^2 - r^2)$$

$$\text{or} \quad \frac{\pi}{4}(D^2 - d^2)$$
$$\text{or} \quad 0.7854(D^2 - d^2)$$

Note that the factors of $R^2 - r^2$ are $(R + r)(R - r)$
and that the factors of $D^2 - d^2$ are $(D + d)(D - d)$

Use of the factors make calculations of annular areas much quicker.

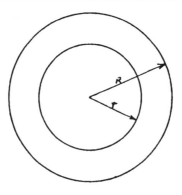

Fig. 77

Example.   Find the effective under-face area of a reciprocating pump piston 41·5 mm diameter if the piston rod diameter is 8·5 mm.

$$\text{Area of Annulus} = 0{\cdot}7854(D^2 - d^2)$$
$$= 0{\cdot}7854(D + d)(D - d)$$
$$= 0{\cdot}7854(41{\cdot}5 + 8{\cdot}5)(41{\cdot}5 - 8{\cdot}5)$$
$$= 0{\cdot}7854 \times 50 \times 33$$
$$= 1296 \text{ mm}^2 \quad \text{Ans.}$$

SECTOR OF A CIRCLE

A Sector of a circle is shown in Fig. 78. As in the case of the whole circle we can consider the sector as being made up of a number of small triangles:

$$\text{Area of Sector} = \frac{r}{2} \times \text{sum of bases}$$
$$= \frac{r}{2} \times \text{length of arc}$$

alternatively, if θ is the angle at the centre, in *degrees*,

$$\text{area of circle of } 360° = \pi r^2$$
$$\text{area of sector of } 1° = \frac{\pi r^2}{360}$$
$$\text{area of sector of } \theta° = \frac{\theta}{360} \times \pi r^2$$

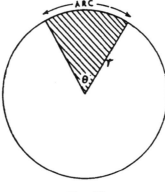

Fig. 78

Further, if the angle θ at the centre be measured in *radians*,

$$\text{area of circle } (= 2\pi \text{ rad}) = \pi r^2$$

$$\text{area of sector of 1 rad} = \frac{\pi r^2}{2\pi} = \frac{r^2}{2}$$

$$\text{area of sector of } \theta \text{ rad} = \frac{\theta r^2}{2}$$

SEGMENT OF A CIRCLE

Referring to Fig. 79,

Area of Segment = area of sector − area of triangle

$$\text{area of sector (shown above)} = \frac{\theta r^2}{2}$$

where θ is the centre angle in rad.

$$\text{Area of triangle} = \frac{ab \sin C}{2} \text{ in this case, } a = r,$$

$b = r$, and C is the centre angle θ in deg.

$$\therefore \text{ Area of triangle} = \frac{r^2 \sin \theta}{2}$$

Area of segment = area of sector − area of triangle

$$= \frac{\theta r^2}{2} - \frac{r^2 \sin \theta}{2}$$

$$= \frac{r^2}{2}[\theta - \sin \theta]$$

Note carefully that in this apparently simple formula, the first θ in the brackets is the angle expressed in *radians*, whereas the second θ is in *degrees*.

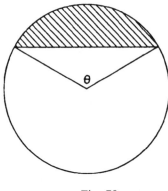

Fig. 79

Example.   Calculate the area of a segment which subtends an angle of 150° at the centre of a circle 150 mm diameter.

$$\theta = \frac{150}{57 \cdot 3} \quad \text{or} \quad \frac{150 \times 2\pi}{360}$$
$$= 2 \cdot 618 \text{ rad}$$

$$\sin 150° = \sin(180° - 150°) = \sin 30° = 0 \cdot 5$$

$$\text{Area of Segment} = \frac{r^2}{2}[\theta - \sin\theta]$$
$$= \frac{75^2}{2}[2 \cdot 618 - 0 \cdot 5]$$
$$= \frac{75^2 \times 2 \cdot 118}{2}$$
$$= 5957 \text{ mm}^2 \quad \text{Ans.}$$

ELLIPSE

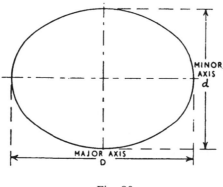

Fig. 80

If D = major axis, and d = minor axis of an ellipse (as in Fig. 80),

Circumference = $\pi \times$ average diameter (approx.)

$$= \pi\left(\frac{D+d}{2}\right)$$

$$\text{Area} = \frac{\pi}{4} \times D \times d$$

SURFACE OF CYLINDER

Imagine the shell of a cylinder being un-rolled as in Fig. 81 it can be seen that,

Curved surface area of a cylinder = $\pi d \times h$

Fig. 81

SURFACE OF SPHERE

The curved surface area of a sphere is equal to the curved surface area of its circumscribing cylinder, that is, a cylinder of equal diameter and height.

The curved surface area of a segment of the sphere or any such sliced portion, is equal to the curved surface area of the corresponding slice off the circumscribing cylinder.

In all cases, referring to Fig. 82,

$$\text{Curved Surface Area} = \pi d \times h$$

$$\text{For the whole sphere, } h = d,$$

$$\text{Curved Surface Area of Sphere} = \pi d^2$$

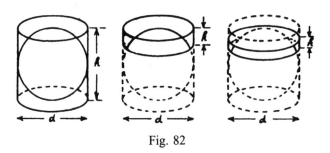

Fig. 82

THEOREM OF PAPPUS OR GULDINUS

This theorem is one of the most useful to employ in finding areas and volumes of objects of circular shapes, or if the area or volume is known it can be used to determine the position of the centroid, or centre

Fig. 83

of gravity (mass), of many sections. With regard to areas the theorem is stated thus:

If a line, lying wholly on one side of a fixed axis, be rotated about that axis in its own plane, it will sweep out a surface area equal to the length of the line multiplied by the distance its centre of gravity moves.

Consider a 'line' such as a straight piece of wire of length l (Fig. 83), positioned at r from an axis parallel to the wire, if the wire is moved around through a complete circle about the axis $o\ o$ as centre, a surface area like a thin cylinder will be swept out. The centre of gravity of the piece of wire is at its mid-length, the distance moved by the centre of gravity in one revolution is the circumference $= 2\pi r$, therefore:

$$\text{Area swept out} = \text{length of line} \times \text{distance c.g. moves}$$
$$= l \times 2\pi r$$
$$= 2\pi r l$$

SURFACE OF CONE

Now let the line be inclined with one end touching the fixed axis, as in Fig. 84. If this line is rotated through one complete revolution the area swept out is that of the curved surface area of a cone. The centre of gravity of the line is at its mid-length, let this be x from $o\ o$.

$$\text{Area swept out} = \text{length of line} \times \text{distance c.g. moves}$$
$$= l \times 2\pi x$$

Fig. 84

If the radius of the base of the swept out cone be represented by r, it can be seen that x is half of r, therefore:

$$\text{Curved surface area of cone} = l \times 2\pi \times \frac{r}{2}$$

$$= \pi r l$$

l being the slant height of the cone.

Fig. 85

As an alternative to the above, referring to Fig. 85, imagine a paper cone being unrolled, the curved surface area develops into a flat sector of a circle. The slant height of the cone, l, forms the radius of this sector, and the circumference of the base of the cone (which is $2\pi r$) forms the arc of the sector.

The area of a sector of a circle is $r/2 \times$ length of arc, therefore if this is now expressed in terms of the dimensions of the corresponding cone:

$$\text{Curved surface area of cone} = \text{area of sector}$$

$$= \frac{l}{2} \times 2\pi r$$

$$= \pi r l \text{ (as before)}.$$

SURFACE OF FRUSTUM OF CONE

Fig. 86

A Frustum of a cone is the part left after a portion of the top of the cone has been sliced off. Referring to Fig. 86, the line to be rotated is equivalent to the slant height of the frustum, $= l$. If the radii of the frustum at bottom and top be represented by R and r respectively, these are the distances of the bottom and top ends of the line, respectively, from the axis. The centre of gravity of the line is at its mid-length, the position of this point from the axis is the mean of R and r which is $\frac{1}{2}(R + r)$, hence,

Area swept out = length of line × distance c.g. moves

Curved surface area of frustum $= l \times 2\pi \times \frac{1}{2}(R + r)$

$$= \pi l(R + r)$$

SURFACE OF A CIRCULAR RING OF CIRCULAR SECTION

Now consider a line as a piece of wire bent around into a circle of radius r, the centre of this circle being at R from the axis (Fig. 87), when this circle is swept through a complete revolution about the axis $o\ o$, the area swept out is the curved surface area of a ring. A practical example of this is the surface area of a ring i.e. that area exposed to the air.

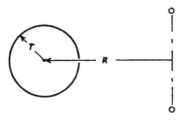

Fig. 87

Area swept out = length of line × distance c.g. moves

Curved surface area of ring $= 2\pi r \times 2\pi R$

$$= 4\pi^2 Rr$$

SURFACE OF A CIRCULAR RING OF ELLIPTICAL SECTION

If the line is an ellipse of major axis D and minor axis d, the centre being at R from the axis, the area swept out in one revolution is the curved surface area similar to that of a circular lifebuoy of elliptical section (see Fig. 88).

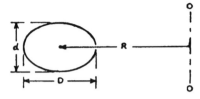

Fig. 88

Area swept out = length of line × distance c.g. moves

$$\text{Curved surface of lifebuoy} = \pi\left(\frac{D+d}{2}\right) \times 2\pi R$$

$$= \pi^2 R(D+d)$$

From the foregoing examples the importance of this Theorem will be appreciated. Not only can curved surface areas be easily calculated, but if the area is known in the first place, the centre of gravity of the line could be determined, this is demonstrated in the example:

To find the centre of gravity of a piece of wire bent into the shape of a semi-circle of diameter d.

If this semi-circular piece of wire is swept through one revolution about a fixed axis on its own diameter (Fig. 89) the area swept out will be the surface area of a sphere, this has already been shown to be πd^2.

Let the centre of gravity be at x from the axis, that is, the position of a knife-edge for the wire to rest upon and be balanced.

Fig. 89

Area swept out = length of line × distance c.g. moves

$$\pi d^2 = \tfrac{1}{2} \times \pi d \times 2\pi x$$

$$x = \frac{\pi \times d^2 \times 2}{\pi \times d \times 2 \times \pi} = \frac{d}{\pi}$$

Hence the centre of gravity of this piece of wire lies on a line parallel to the diameter, at d/π from the diameter.

SIMILAR FIGURES

Areas of similar figures vary as the square of their corresponding linear dimensions.

Similar figures mean that they are of the same shape and proportions, although their sizes are different.

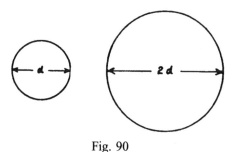

Fig. 90

Consider two circles, one of diameter d, the other twice as big in diameter $= 2d$, as in Fig. 90.

$$\text{Area of small circle} = 0{\cdot}7854 d^2$$

$$\text{Area of large circle} = 0{\cdot}7854 \times (2d)^2$$

Therefore the ratio of their areas is,

$$d^2 : (2d)^2$$
$$= d^2 : 2^2 \times d^2$$
$$= 1 : 2^2$$

Thus, if the diameter of the larger circle is twice the diameter of the smaller circle, all linear dimensions (i.e., radius, circumference) will be twice as much, but the area is 2^2 which is *four* times the area of the small circle.

If the diameter of one circle is three times that of another, the radius and circumference of the larger is three times the radius and circumference of the smaller, but the area is $3^2 = nine$ times as much.

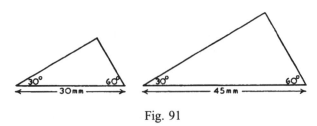

Fig. 91

Figure 91 shows two similar triangles, the ratio of the base dimensions is $30 : 45$ which is $1 : 1\cdot5$, hence the base of the larger triangle is $1\frac{1}{2}$ times greater than the base of the smaller.

Therefore all linear dimensions of the larger triangle are $1\frac{1}{2}$ times greater than the corresponding linear dimension of the smaller. The ratio of their areas is proportional to the square of their corresponding dimensions thus:

$$\text{Ratio of dimensions} = 1 : 1\cdot5$$
$$\therefore \text{Ratio of areas} = 1^2 : 1\cdot5^2$$
$$= 1 : 2\cdot25$$

Hence the area of the larger triangle is $2\frac{1}{4}$ times the area of the smaller.

Example. A hexagonal plate is cut out of a sheet. Due to an error in marking off, the sides were all made 10% longer than intended, find the percentage of error in area.

$$\text{Ratio correct dimensions to wrong} = 100 : 110$$
$$= 1 : 1\cdot1$$
$$\text{Ratio correct area to wrong} = 1^2 : 1\cdot1^2$$
$$= 1 : 1\cdot21$$
$$= 100 : 121$$

$\therefore$ Area is 21% too large.   Ans.

IRREGULAR FIGURES

SIMPSON'S FIRST RULE. This is a method of finding the area of an irregular figure. Briefly it is stated:

'To the sum of the first and last ordinates, add four times the even ordinates and twice the odd ordinates, multiply this sum by one-third the common interval and the result is the area of the figure.'

An odd number of ordinates, equally spaced, must be used for this rule. Step by step, the procedure is as follows, referring to Fig. 92,

1. Divide this given figure into an even number of equally spaced parts, this gives an odd number of ordinates.
2. Measure the ordinates and the common distance between them.
3. Add together: the first ordinate, the last ordinate, four times the even ordinates and twice the odd ordinates.
4. Multiply the above sum by one-third of the common distance between the ordinates.

Fig. 92

Example.   A flat plate is shaped as shown in Fig. 92, the dimensions being in mm, find its area (cm^2) by Simpson's rule.

Working in cm and setting out in tabulated form:

Ordinates	Simpson's Multipliers	Products
0	1	0
3·54	4	14·16
6·32	2	12·64
8·34	4	33·36
9·6	2	19·20
10·2	4	40·80
9·96	2	19·92
8·68	4	34·72
5·8	1	5·80
		Sum = 180·60

$$\text{Common interval} = \text{length} \div \text{number of spaces}$$
$$= 320 \div 8$$
$$= 40 \text{ mm} = 4 \text{ cm}$$
$$\text{Area} = \frac{180\cdot6 \times 4}{3}$$
$$= 240\cdot8 \text{ cm}^2 \quad \text{Ans.}$$

From the explanation of Simpson's Rule, the multipliers of the ordinates are:

For 3 ordinates	1, 4, 1
For 5 ordinates	1, 4, 2, 4, 1
For 7 ordinates	1, 4, 2, 4, 2, 4, 1
For 9 ordinates	1, 4, 2, 4, 2, 4, 2, 4, 1 and so on

This rule is often expressed in formula fashion thus:

$$\text{Area} = \frac{h}{3}(a + 4b + 2c + 4d + e)$$

h being the common interval,
a, b, c, etc., being the ordinates.

The mean (average) height of an irregular figure can be obtained by dividing the area by its length, or can be found direct by Simpson's rule by dividing the sum of the products of the ordinates and their mutipliers, by the total of multipliers.

In the foregoing example the two methods of obtaining the mean height would be:

(i)

$$\text{Area} = 240\cdot8 \text{ cm}^2$$
$$\text{Length} = 32 \text{ cm}$$
$$\text{Mean height} = 240\cdot8 \div 32 = 7\cdot525 \text{ cm}$$

(ii)

$$\text{Sum of products} = 180\cdot6$$
$$\text{Sum of multipliers} = 1 + 4 + 2 + 4 + 2 + 4 + 2 + 4 + 1$$
$$= 24$$
$$\text{Mean height} = 180\cdot6 \div 24 = 7\cdot525 \text{ cm}$$

Example.   The ordinates measured athwartships across a ship at
the load water line are: 0·2, 9, 15·5, 20, 21·5, 20·5, 18·5, 12·5 and 1·3 m
respectively, and the length is 180 m. Find the water plane area.

Ordinates	Simpson's Multipliers	Products
0·2	1	0·2
9	4	36
15·5	2	31
20	4	80
21·5	2	43
20·5	4	82
18·5	2	37
12·5	4	50
1·3	1	1·3
		Sum = 360·5

$$\text{Number of ordinates} = 9$$

$$\therefore \quad \text{Number of spaces} = 8$$

$$\text{Common interval} = \text{length} \div \text{no. of spaces}$$
$$= 180 \div 8$$
$$= 22 \cdot 5 \text{ m}$$
$$\text{Water plane area} = \frac{360 \cdot 5 \times 22 \cdot 5}{3}$$
$$= 2704 \text{ m}^2 \quad \text{Ans.}$$

For shapes such as the water plane area of a ship which are
symmetrical about the longitudinal centre-line, measurements from the
centre-line to the hull may be taken and referred to as 'half-ordinates'.
These half-ordinates are put through Simpson's rule, the half-area
calculated, then multiplied by two to obtain the full area.

MID-ORDINATE RULE

Another method of finding the area or the mean height of an irregular
figure is by the mid-ordinate rule.

The method is to divide the figure into any number of equally spaced
parts, erecting lines midway between these ordinates, these being the

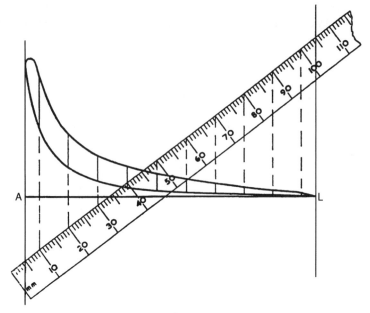

Fig. 93

mid-ordinates; the mid-ordinates are measured, added together and the sum is divided by the number of mid-ordinates to get their average height.

If the area is required, this can be obtained by multiplying the mean height by the length.

The simplest method of dividing the diagram into ten parts and employing the mid-ordinate rule to determine the mean height is explained in the following example.

Referring to Fig. 93 which is a copy of an indicator diagram from the cylinder of an internal combustion engine:

1. Erect a line at each of the two extreme ends of the diagram, perpendicular to the atmospheric line (that is the straight horizontal base line marked AL).

2. Place a rule so that it measures 100 mm between these perpendiculars, if the length of the diagram was exactly 100 mm, the rule would lie parallel with the atmospheric line, but almost all diagrams are less than this therefore the rule must be inclined until it registers 100 mm between the lines.

3. Instead of marking the ten spaces and then the middle of these
   spaces to indicate the mid-ordinates, it is quicker to slide the
   rule until it registers 5 mm at the first perpendicular and 105 mm
   at the other, then mark off every 10 mm point, this gives the
   position of the mid-ordinates direct.
4. Erect perpendicular lines through these marks across the diagram,
   these are the mid-ordinates.
5. Measure the mid-ordinates, in this case they are 13·5, 9, 7, 6,
   4·5, 3·5, 2·5, 2, 1 and 0·5 mm. Add these measurements together,
   this gives 49·5 mm. Divide by the number of mid-ordinates,
   in this case 10, to obtain the mean height of the diagram, thus,
   $49·5 \div 10 = 4·95$ mm.

To obtain the mean effective pressure in the engine cylinder from
which this diagram was taken, the mean height is multiplied by the
pressure scale of the spring used in the indicator. In this diagram,
the spring stiffness was such that one mm of height represents a
pressure of 180 kN/m^2. Hence, the mean effective pressure is
$4·95 \times 180 = 891$ kN/m^2.

TEST EXAMPLES 9

1. In a parallelogram ABCD, the opposite parallel sides AD and BC
   are each 100 mm long, the other sides are each 60 mm long, and
   the diagonal AC is 140 mm. Calculate the angles, the short
   diagonal, the perpendicular height, and the area.

2. The sides of a rhombus are each 32 mm long and the length of the
   long diagonal is 48 mm. Calculate the angles, the length of the
   short diagonal, and the area.

3. In a trapezium ABCD, the two parallel sides are AB and CD, and
   their lengths are 100 and 60 mm respectively. Side BC is
   perpendicular to the parallel sides and its length is 50 mm.
   (i) Find the area of the trapezium (cm^2).
   (ii) Find the position of a dividing line EF parallel to AB to divide
        the trapezium into two equal half areas.

4. The lengths of the sides of a four-sided figure ABCD, are, in m,
   $AB = 1$, $BC = 2$, $CD = 1·5$, $DA = 3·5$, and the angle BCD is
   117° 17′. Find the area of the figure.

5. The length of the sides of a regular hexagonal plate is 80 mm. The plate is cut parallel to one of its sides and this reduces the area by 10%, calculate the thickness of the piece cut off.

6. An octagonal plate, the sides of which are each 30 mm long, has a circular hole 50 mm diameter cut out of it. Find the net area of the plate in mm^2.

7. Find the length of the sides and the area of the largest equilateral triangular plate that can be cut out of a circular plate 120 mm diameter.

8. The outer and inner diameters of the collar of a single-collar thrust shaft are 755 and 415 mm respectively, and the effective area of contact with the thrust pads is 0·7 of the face of the collar. Calculate (i) the effective area of contact, in m^2, and (ii) the total force on the collar, in kN, when the thrust pressure is 2000 kN/m^2.

9. Find the area, in cm^2, of the smaller segment of a circle of 200 mm diameter if the length of chord is 180 mm.

10. Find the diameter of a solid hemisphere whose total surface area (including the flat circular base) is 58·9 cm^2.

11. The ball of a Brinell hardness testing machine is 10 mm diameter. Calculate the depth and curved surface area of an indentation in a material under test when the surface diameter of the indentation is 5 mm.

12. It is required to make a hollow cone out of thin flat sheet steel, the base diameter of the cone to be 150 mm and the perpendicular height 125 mm. Find the dimensions of the sector to be cut out of the sheet to make this cone and sketch the pattern.

13. A lampshade has the form of a frustum of a cone, the diameters at the base and top are 320 and 180 mm respectively and the perpendicular height is 170 mm. Calculate the curved surface area.

14. A circular ring made of round bar is 640 mm outside diameter and 440 mm inside diameter. Calculate the surface area to be painted.

15. An equilateral triangular plate has sides 125 mm long, and another similarly shaped plate has sides 175 mm long. By what percentage is the larger plate greater in area than the smaller plate?

16. Regularly spaced semi-ordinates measured transversely across a ship at the load-water-line are as follows: 0·1, 3, 5·85, 7·2, 8·1, 8·4, 8·4, 8·25, 8·1, 7·5, 6·3, 3·75 and 0·5 m respectively, and the length is 150 m. Find the area of the water-plane by Simpson's rule.

17. (a) Plot the two curves $y = x^2 + 3x + 6$ and $y = 2x^2 - x + 1$ on common axes between the limits $x = 0$ and $x = 4$.

   (b) By Simpson's rule find the area enclosed between the two curves.

18. An internal combustion engine indicator diagram is divided into ten mid-ordinates and their measurements are: 26, 15, 9·5, 8, 7, 5·5, 4·5, 4, 3 and 0 mm respectively. Find (i) the mean height in mm by the mid-ordinate rule, (ii) the mean effective pressure if 1 mm represents a pressure of 160 kN/m².

CHAPTER 10

MENSURATION OF VOLUMES AND MASSES

VOLUME (V) is the result of the product of three dimensions measured in similar units. Units m^3, mm^3 and, often, cm^3.

$$1 \text{ cm}^3 = 1 \text{ ml} = 10^3 \text{ mm}^3$$
$$1 \text{ l} = 10^3 \text{ cm}^3 = 10^6 \text{ mm}^3$$
$$1 \text{ m}^3 = 10^3 \text{ l} = 10^6 \text{ cm}^3$$

MASS (m) is the quantity of matter possessed by a body and is proportional to the volume and the density of the body. It is a constant quantity, that is, the mass can only be changed by adding more matter or taking matter away. Units g, kg, Mg. The latter is 1 tonne (t).

DENSITY (ρ) is a measure of the mass per unit volume. The unit of density is kg/m^3. Other units are, g/cm^3 for solid materials, g/ml for liquids, g/l for gases. In some cases t/m^3 and kg/l may be used.

$$m = V\rho$$

The density of pure water may be taken as 1000 kg/m^3 which is equal to 1 t/m^3, 1 kg/l, and 1 g/ml.

The total mass of a body is therefore the product of the volume and the density. Units must be consistent throughout, such as,

$$\text{mass [kg]} = \text{volume [m}^3\text{]} \times \text{density [kg/m}^3\text{]}$$

or

$$\text{mass [g]} = \text{volume [cm}^3\text{]} \times \text{density [g/cm}^3\text{]}$$

The cm, between mm (small) and m (large), is often used.

RELATIVE DENSITY or SPECIFIC GRAVITY of a substance is the ratio of the mass of a volume of the substance to the mass of an equal volume of pure water. In other words, it is the ratio of the density of the substance to the density of pure water.

PRISMS

A regular prism is a bar of regular cross-section, some examples are given in Fig. 94.

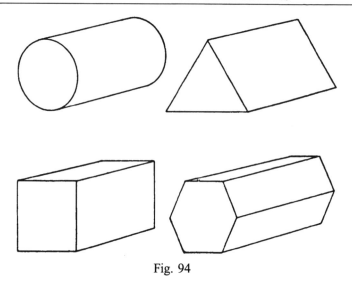

Fig. 94

In all these cases,

Volume = area of cross-section × length

Hence, to find the volume of a prism, calculate the area of the end and multiply this by length (or height) of the prism.

Example.   A brass bar 250 mm long has a constant hexagonal cross-section measuring 90 mm across the face from one corner to the

Fig. 95

opposite corner. Find (i) the volume of the bar, (ii) the mass in kg
if the density of brass is 8·4 g/cm³.

Side of each equilateral triangle = 45 mm   (See Fig. 95)

$$\text{Perpendicular height} = 45 \times \sin 60°$$

$$\text{Area of each equilateral triangle} = \tfrac{1}{2}(\text{base} \times \text{perp. ht.})$$

$$= \tfrac{1}{2} \times 45 \times 45 \times \sin 60°$$

$$= 0.433 \times 45^2$$

$$\text{Area of hexagon} = 6 \times 0.433 \times 45^2$$

$$\text{Volume of prism} = \text{area} \times \text{length}$$

$$= 6 \times 0.433 \times 45^2 \times 250$$

$$= 1.315 \times 10^6 \text{ mm}^3$$

$$\text{or} \quad 1315 \text{ cm}^3 \quad \text{Ans.} \qquad \dots \quad \text{(i)}$$

$$\text{Mass (m)} = \text{Volume (V)} \times \text{Density } (\rho)$$

$$= 1315 \times 8.4 \text{ g}$$

$$\text{Mass} = 1315 \times 8.4 \times 10^{-3} \text{ kg}$$

$$= 11.05 \text{ kg} \quad \text{Ans.} \qquad \dots \quad \dots \quad \text{(ii)}$$

PYRAMIDS

A pyramid is a body standing on a triangular, square or polygonal
base, its sides tapering to a point at the apex, some examples are
illustrated in Fig. 96. The cone may be considered as a pyramid with a
circular base.

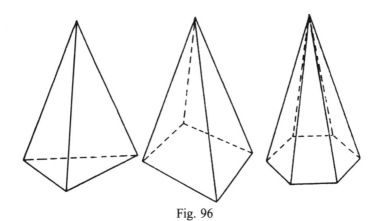

Fig. 96

The volume of a pyramid is one-third of the volume of its circumscribing prism. Thus, the volume of a cone is one-third of the volume of a solid cylinder of the same section as the base of the cone and having the same height; the volume of a square pyramid is one-third the volume of a bar of square section equal to the base of the pyramid and of the same height (or length). In all cases:

Volume of pyramid $= \frac{1}{3}$ (area of base × perpendicular height)

OBLIQUE PRISMS AND PYRAMIDS

If the prism or pyramid be imagined as being made up of a number of discs or laminations and pushed over to one side, it can be seen by reference to Fig. 97 that the same rule for finding the volumes of regular prisms or regular pyramids can be applied provided the *perpendicular* height is used.

Fig. 97

FRUSTUMS

A frustum of a pyramid or cone is the bottom piece left, after a portion has been sliced off the top (Fig. 98).

The volume can be found by subtracting the volume of the sliced-off top part from the volume of the complete pyramid.

Example.   A frustum of a square pyramid has a height of 4 m and the lengths of the sides of the square base and top are 5 and 2 m respectively. Find the volume of the frustum.

Fig. 98

By similar triangles, from Fig. 99:

$$\frac{h}{2} = \frac{h+4}{5}$$
$$5h = 2h + 8$$
$$h = 2\tfrac{2}{3} \text{ m}$$
$$H = 2\tfrac{2}{3} + 4 = 6\tfrac{2}{3} \text{ m}$$

Volume of whole pyramid $= \tfrac{1}{3} \times 5^2 \times 6\tfrac{2}{3}$ m^3

Volume of top cut off $= \tfrac{1}{3} \times 2^2 \times 2\tfrac{2}{3}$ m^3

$\therefore$ Volume of frustum $= \tfrac{1}{3}(5^2 \times 6\tfrac{2}{3} - 2^2 \times 2\tfrac{2}{3})$

$$= 52 \text{ m}^3 \quad \text{Ans.}$$

Fig. 99

SPHERE

The sphere may be considered as being made up of a great number of very small pyramids whose bases lie on the surface of the sphere and their apexes all meeting at the centre of the sphere.

Volume of each pyramid

$$= \tfrac{1}{3}(\text{area of base} \times \text{perpendicular height})$$

Volume of sphere

$= $ sum of volume of all pyramids

$= \tfrac{1}{3} \times$ perpendicular height $\times$ sum of areas of bases

$= \tfrac{1}{3} \times$ radius of sphere $\times$ curved surface area of sphere

$$= \frac{1}{3} \times \frac{d}{2} \times \pi d^2$$

$$= \frac{\pi}{6}d^3 \quad \text{or} \quad \frac{4}{3}\pi r^3$$

Volume of hollow sphere

$= $ vol. of outer sphere $-$ vol. of inner spherical space

$$= \frac{\pi}{6}D^3 - \frac{\pi}{6}d^3$$

$$= \frac{\pi}{6}(D^3 - d^3)$$

Example.   A solid lead cone, 40 mm diameter at the base and 120 mm perpendicular height is to be melted down and cast into a hollow sphere of 10 mm uniform thickness. Find the inside and outside diameters of the sphere.

Working in cm:

Let $d = $ inside diameter,

then $(d + 2)$ cm $= $ outside diameter.

Volume of hollow sphere $= \dfrac{\pi}{6}(D^3 - d^3)$

$$= \dfrac{\pi}{6}[(d+2)^3 - d^3]$$

$$= \dfrac{\pi}{6}[d^3 + 6d^2 + 12d + 8 - d^3]$$

$$= \dfrac{\pi}{6}(6d^2 + 12d + 8)$$

Volume of material from cone $= \dfrac{1}{3} \times \dfrac{\pi}{4} \times 4^2 \times 12 = \pi \times 16 \text{ cm}^3$

$$\dfrac{\pi}{6}(6d^2 + 12d + 8) = \pi \times 16$$

$$6d^2 + 12d + 8 = 96$$

$$3d^2 + 6d - 44 = 0$$

Solving this quadratic:

$$\left. \begin{array}{l} d = 2 \!\cdot\! 958 \text{ cm} \quad \text{or} \quad 29 \!\cdot\! 58 \text{ mm} \\ D = 4 \!\cdot\! 958 \text{ cm} \quad \text{or} \quad 49 \!\cdot\! 58 \text{ mm} \end{array} \right\} \text{ Ans.}$$

SPHERICAL SEGMENT

A segment of a sphere is shown by ABCDA in Fig. 100. Let its radius $DC = r$, thickness $BD = h$, and diameter of sphere $= d$. The volume of

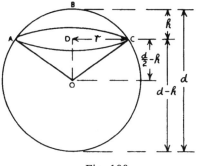

Fig. 100

the spherical segment can be obtained by subtracting the volume of the cone OADCO from the volume of the spherical sector OABCO.

Volume of the sector of sphere. Consider this as being made up of a great number of very small pyramids whose bases lie on the spherical surface of the sector and their apexes all meeting at the centre of the sphere.

Volume of pyramid $= \frac{1}{3}$ area of base $\times$ perp. height

Volume of sector $= \frac{1}{3} \times$ perp. height $\times$ sum of areas of bases.

The sum of the areas of the bases is the curved surface area of the slice of the sphere and this has been shown (Chapter 9) to be equal to the curved surface area of the corresponding slice of the circumscribing cylinder, which is πdh.

$$\text{Volume of sector} = \frac{1}{3} \times \frac{1}{2}d \times \pi dh$$

$$= \frac{\pi}{6}d^2 h$$

It will be seen that the volume of the spherical sector and the volume of the whole sphere are in the ratio of their spherical surface areas, thus,

$$\frac{\text{Volume of sector}}{\text{Volume of sphere}} = \frac{\text{Surface area of sector}}{\text{Surface area of sphere}}$$

$$\text{Volume of sector} = \frac{\pi}{6}d^3 \times \frac{\pi dh}{\pi d^2}$$

$$= \frac{\pi}{6}d^2 h \quad \text{as above}$$

$$\text{Volume of cone} = \frac{1}{3} \text{area of base} \times \text{perp. height}$$

$$= \frac{1}{3}\pi r^2 \left(\frac{d}{2} - h\right)$$

$$= \frac{\pi}{6}r^2(d - 2h)$$

Substituting r^2 in terms of d and h, by crossed chords,

$$r^2 = h(d - h)$$

$$\text{Volume of cone} = \frac{\pi}{6} h(d - h)(d - 2h)$$

$$= \frac{\pi}{6} h(d^2 - 3dh + 2h^2)$$

$$\text{Volume of segment} = \text{Vol. of sector} - \text{Vol. of cone}$$

$$= \frac{\pi}{6} d^2 h - \frac{\pi}{6} h(d^2 - 3dh + 2h^2)$$

$$= \frac{\pi}{6} h(d^2 - d^2 + 3dh - 2h^2)$$

$$= \frac{\pi}{6} h^2(3d - 2h)$$

Example. A segment 2 cm thick is cut off a sphere 10 cm diameter. Find the volumes of the segment cut off, the remaining segment, and the whole sphere.

$$\text{Volume of segment cut off} = \frac{\pi}{6} h^2(3d - 2h)$$

$$= \frac{\pi}{6} \times 2^2(3 \times 10 - 2 \times 2)$$

$$= \frac{\pi}{6} \times 4 \times 26 = 54 \cdot 46 \text{ cm}^3 \quad \text{Ans. (i)}$$

$$\text{Thickness of remaining segment} = 10 - 2 = 8 \text{ cm}$$

$$\text{Volume} = \frac{\pi}{6} h^2(3d - 2h)$$

$$= \frac{\pi}{6} \times 8^2(3 \times 10 - 2 \times 8)$$

$$= \frac{\pi}{6} \times 64 \times 14 = 469 \cdot 2 \text{ cm}^3 \quad \text{Ans. (ii)}$$

$$\text{Volume of sphere} = \text{sum of vols. of the two segments}$$

$$= 54 \cdot 46 + 469 \cdot 2$$

$$= 523 \cdot 66 \text{ cm}^3 \quad \text{Ans. (iii)}$$

As a check:

$$\text{Volume of sphere} = \frac{\pi}{6} d^3 = \frac{\pi}{6} \times 10^3$$

$$= 523 \cdot 66 \text{ cm}^3 \quad \text{as above}$$

Example.   A sphere is sliced into three pieces by two parallel cuts. The top segment is 8 cm thick and 24 cm diameter at its base, the bottom segment is 5 cm thick. Calculate the volume of the zone of sphere between the segments.

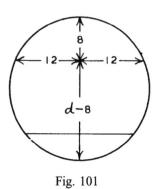

Fig. 101

Let d = diameter of sphere, by crossed chords (Fig. 101):

$$8 \times (d - 8) = 12 \times 12$$
$$8d - 64 = 144$$
$$d = 26 \text{ cm}$$
$$\text{Volume of sphere} = \frac{\pi}{6}d^3$$
$$= \frac{\pi}{6} \times 26^3 = 9204 \text{ cm}^3$$
$$\text{Volume of spherical segment} = \frac{\pi}{6}h^2(3d - 2h)$$
$$\text{Volume of top segment} = \frac{\pi}{6} \times 8^2(3 \times 26 - 2 \times 8)$$
$$= \frac{\pi}{6} \times 64 \times 62 = 2078 \text{ cm}^3$$
$$\text{Volume of bottom segment} = \frac{\pi}{6} \times 5^2(3 \times 26 - 2 \times 5)$$
$$= \frac{\pi}{6} \times 25 \times 68 = 890 \text{ cm}^3$$
$$\text{Volume of zone} = \text{volume of sphere} - \text{top and bottom}$$
$$\text{segments}$$
$$= 9204 - 2078 - 890$$
$$= 6236 \text{ cm}^3 \quad \text{Ans.}$$

THEOREM OF PAPPUS OR GULDINUS APPLIED
TO VOLUMES

If an *area*, situated wholly on one side of a fixed axis, be rotated in its own plane about this axis, it will sweep out a *volume* equal to the product of the area and the distance its centroid moves.

In the majority of cases areas are being swept around one complete revolution and the resultant volumes are referred to as 'solids of revolution'.

For example, consider a flat circular disc of radius r, its centre being at R from the axis o o as in Fig. 102, if this area is swept around the axis through one complete revolution, it will sweep out a solid ring of circular section, the mean radius of the ring being R, and the radius of the cross-section of the material being r.

Fig. 102

A practical example of this is the volume of a ring, thus:

Volume swept out = area × distance its centroid moves

$$\text{Volume of ring} = \pi r^2 \times 2\pi R$$
$$= 2\pi^2 R r^2$$

Now consider an elliptical area of major diameter D, minor diameter d, swept around through one revolution, R being the radius from the axis o o to the centre of the ellipse (Fig. 103).

Fig. 103

The volume swept out is the shape of a circular lifebuoy of elliptical cross-section.

Volume swept out = area × distance its centroid moves

$$\text{Volume of lifebuoy} = \frac{\pi}{4} Dd \times 2\pi R$$

$$= \frac{\pi^2}{2} DdR$$

It is best to work from first principles making use of this theorem rather than applying formulae.

Example. The inside diameter of a solid circular cork lifebuoy is 500 mm and the section is elliptical 160 mm major diameter by 120 mm minor diameter. Find (i) its volume in m^3, (ii) its mass if the density of cork is 240 kg/m^3.

Referring to Fig. 103, working in m:

$$D = 160 \text{ mm} = 0.16 \text{ m}$$

$$d = 120 \text{ mm} = 0.12 \text{ m}$$

$$R = 250 + 80 = 330 \text{ mm} = 0.33 \text{ m}$$

Volume swept out = area × distance its centroid moves

$$= 0.7854 \times D \times d \times 2\pi R$$

$$= 0.7854 \times 0.16 \times 0.12 \times 2\pi \times 0.33$$

$$= 0.03127 \text{ m}^3 \quad \text{Ans. (i)}$$

$$\text{Mass (m)} = \text{volume (V)} \times \text{density } (\rho)$$

$$= 0.03127 \times 240$$

$$= 7.504 \text{ kg} \quad \text{Ans. (ii)}$$

FORCE, WEIGHT AND CENTRE OF GRAVITY

FORCE is that which produces or tends to produce motion in a body. The unit of force is the *newton* (N) and may be defined as the force required to give unit acceleration (a gain of velocity of 1 m/s every second the force is applied) to unit mass (one kg).

The WEIGHT (W) of a body is the gravitational force on the mass of that body, that is, the force of attraction exerted on the body by the earth.

If a body is allowed to fall freely, it will fall with an acceleration of 9.81 m/s^2, this is termed *gravitational acceleration* and is represented by g. Since 1 N of force will give 1 kg of mass an acceleration of

1 m/s^2, then the force (N) to give m kg of mass an acceleration of 9.81 m/s^2 is $m \times 9 \cdot 81$. Hence, at the earth's surface, the gravitational force on a mass of m kg is mg newtons, therefore:

$$\text{Weight [N]} = \text{mass [kg]} \times g \ [\text{m/s}^2]$$
$$W = mg$$

The CENTRE OF GRAVITY of a body is that point through which the whole weight of the mass can be considered as acting (Centre of Mass). For instance, imagine a body to be compressed in volume into one tiny particle without losing mass, the position of this small heavy particle would be at the centre of gravity of the body to have the same effect. If the body was suspended from this point, or supported on it, it would balance perfectly without tilting.

When dealing with an *area* instead of a solid, an area theoretically has no mass, therefore it is not *strictly* correct to use the term centre of gravity, in such cases the term *centroid* can be used.

PARALLELOGRAM

A parallelogram would balance if laid on a knife edge along either one of its two diagonals, therefore its centre of gravity (for a plate) or centroid (for a plane area) is at the intersection of its diagonals as shown in Fig. 104.

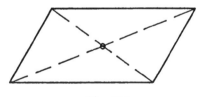

Fig. 104

TRAPEZIUM

The centroid of a trapezium is at the intersection of EF and HG as shown in Fig. 105, found graphically as follows:

Join EF (the mid points)

Produce AD to G, length DG being equal to BC

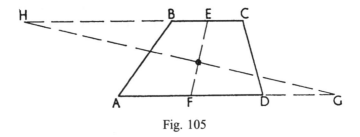

Fig. 105

Produce BC to H, length BH being equal to AD

Join HG

The intersection of EF and HG is the centroid.

TRIANGLE

The centroid of a triangle lies on a line joining a corner of the triangle with the mid-point of its opposite side, at a point at one-third of the height from that side. See Fig. 106.

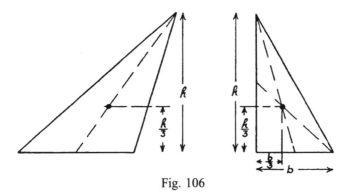

Fig. 106

PYRAMID

The centre of gravity of a pyramid or cone is at one-quarter of the height above the base. See Fig. 107.

Fig. 107

SEMI-CIRCULAR AREA

The centroid of a semi-circular area is at $0.424r$ from its diameter, as shown in Fig. 108. This can easily be shown by the Theorem of Pappus:

If the semi-circular area is swept around through one revolution about an axis on its own diameter, the volume swept out will be that of a sphere. Referring to Fig. 108, let the centroid be at x from the diameter.

Fig. 108

Volume swept out = area × distance its centroid moves

$$\tfrac{4}{3}\pi r^3 = \tfrac{1}{2}\pi r^2 \times 2\pi y$$

$$y = \frac{4 \times \pi \times r^3 \times 2}{3 \times \pi \times r^2 \times 2\pi}$$

$$= \frac{4r}{3\pi}$$

$$= 0.424r$$

HEMISPHERE

The centre of gravity of a hemisphere is at three-eighths of the radius above the diameter. See Fig. 109.

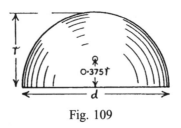

Fig. 109

VOLUME OF CONE

Now that the position of the centroid of a triangle is known, it can be shown that the volume of a cone can be determined by the Theorem of Pappus.

If a triangular area is swept about an axis *o o* which coincides with its side as shown in Fig. 110, it will, in one revolution, sweep out the

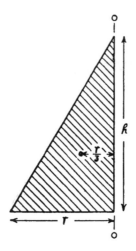

Fig. 110

volume of a cone. If the radius of the base of the cone is r, the centroid of the triangle is at $\frac{1}{3}r$ from o o.

Volume swept out = area of triangle × distance its centroid moves

Volume of cone $= \frac{1}{2}$(base × perp. ht.) × $(2\pi \times \frac{1}{3}r)$

$$= \frac{r \times h \times 2\pi \times r}{2 \times 3}$$

$$= \frac{1}{3}\pi r^2 h \quad \text{(as shown previously)}$$

VOLUME OF FRUSTUM OF A CONE

To derive a formula for the volume of a frustum of a cone, let $r =$ radius at top, $R =$ radius at bottom, and $h =$ perpendicular height.

Consider a trapezium made up of a rectangle and a triangle as shown in Fig. 111. If this area is rotated one revolution about the axis o o, a frustum of a cone will be swept out.

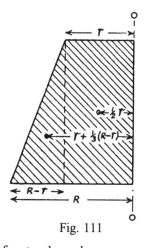

Fig. 111

Area of rectangle $= rh$

Centroid from o o $= \frac{1}{2}r$

Area of triangle $= \frac{1}{2}$(base × perp. height)

$$= \frac{1}{2}(R - r)h$$

Centroid from o o $= r + \frac{1}{3}(R - r)$

$$= r + \frac{1}{3}R - \frac{1}{3}r$$

$$= \frac{1}{3}R + \frac{2}{3}r$$

Volume swept out by rectangle $= rh \times 2\pi \times \frac{1}{2}r$

$$= \pi r^2 h \qquad \ldots \quad \ldots \quad \ldots \quad \text{(i)}$$

$$\text{Volume swept out by triangle} = \tfrac{1}{2}(R - r)h \times 2\pi(\tfrac{1}{3}R + \tfrac{2}{3}r)$$
$$= \pi h(R - r)(\tfrac{1}{3}R + \tfrac{2}{3}r)$$
$$= \pi h(\tfrac{1}{3}R^2 + \tfrac{1}{3}Rr - \tfrac{2}{3}r^2) \qquad \ldots \quad \text{(ii)}$$
$$\text{Total volume} = \pi r^2 h + \pi h(\tfrac{1}{3}R^2 + \tfrac{1}{3}Rr - \tfrac{2}{3}r^2)$$
$$= \pi h(r^2 + \tfrac{1}{3}R^2 + \tfrac{1}{3}Rr - \tfrac{2}{3}r^2)$$
$$= \pi h(\tfrac{1}{3}R^2 + \tfrac{1}{3}Rr + \tfrac{1}{3}r^2)$$
$$= \tfrac{1}{3}\pi h(R^2 + Rr + r^2)$$

or, since $R = \tfrac{1}{2}D$, and $r = \tfrac{1}{2}d$,

$$\text{Volume} = \tfrac{1}{12}\pi h(D^2 + Dd + d^2)$$

SIMILAR SOLIDS

Volumes of similar objects vary as the cube of their corresponding linear dimensions.

Similar objects mean that they are of the same shape and proportions, but of different size.

Consider two solid spheres, one of diameter d, the other having a diameter of $2d$, as in Fig. 112,

$$\text{Volume of small sphere} = \frac{\pi}{6}d^3$$
$$\text{Volume of large sphere} = \frac{\pi}{6} \times (2d)^3$$

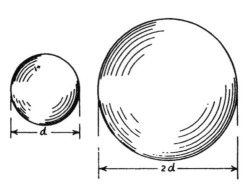

Fig. 112

Thus, the ratio of their volumes is:

$$d^3 : (2d)^3$$
$$= d^3 : 2^3 \times d^3$$
$$= 1 : 2^3$$

Hence, the diameter of the larger sphere being twice the diameter of the smaller, all linear dimensions such as the radius and circumference are twice as much, all areas such as the sectional area and curved surface area are $2^2 = 4$ times as much (as explained in last chapter), the volume is $2^3 = 8$ times the volume of the smaller, and consequently, the mass of the larger is 8 times the mass of the smaller if they are made of the same kind of material.

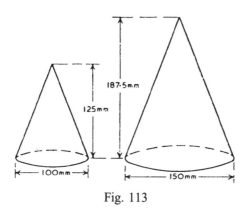

Fig. 113

Figure 113 shows two similar cones, they are similar because they have the same proportions, for instance, in each case the perpendicular height is 1·25 times the diameter of the base. The dimensions of the larger cone is 1·5 times the corresponding dimensions of the smaller, thus:

$$\text{Ratio of corresponding dimensions} = 1 : 1{\cdot}5$$
$$\text{Ratio of corresponding areas} = 1^2 : 1{\cdot}5^2$$
$$= 1 : 2{\cdot}25$$
$$\text{Ratio of corresponding volumes} = 1^3 : 1{\cdot}5^3$$
$$= 1 : 3{\cdot}375$$

Hence, all linear dimensions (such as diameter of base, circumference of base, perpendicular height, slant height) of the larger cone are 1·5 times those of the smaller cone; all areas (such as area of base, curved surface area, sectional area) of the larger cone are $1·5^2 = 2·25$ times the corresponding areas of the smaller; and the volume of the larger cone is $1·5^3 = 3·375$ times the volume of the smaller.

SIMPSON'S RULE APPLIED TO VOLUMES

The procedure of finding the volume of an irregular object by Simpson's rule is the same as for the area of an irregular figure, it is merely a matter of substituting cross-sectional areas for ordinates. Thus:

To the first and last cross-sectional areas, add four times the even cross-sectional areas and twice the odd; multiply this sum by one-third the common interval and the result is the volume of the object.

Example.   A casting of light alloy, 750 mm long, has a variable cross-sectional area throughout its length. At regular distances of 125 mm apart, starting from one end, the sectional areas are, 12·2, 17·5, 23·2, 27·9, 21·0, 11·2 and 0 cm^2 respectively. Find the volume and its mass if the density of the material is 3·2 g/cm^3.

Sectional Areas (cm^2)	Simpson's Multipliers	Products
12·2	1	12·2
17·5	4	70·0
23·2	2	46·4
27·9	4	111·6
21·0	2	42·0
11·2	4	44·8
0	1	0
		Sum = 327·0

Common interval = 12·5 cm

$$\text{Volume} = \text{sum of products} \times \tfrac{1}{3} \text{ common interval}$$
$$= 327 \times \tfrac{1}{3} \times 12·5$$
$$= 1362·5 \text{ cm}^3 \quad \text{Ans. (i)}$$

$$\text{Mass (m)} = \text{volume (V)} \times \text{density } (\rho)$$
$$= 1362·5 \times 3·2$$
$$= 4360 \text{ g} = 4·36 \text{ kg} \quad \text{Ans. (ii)}$$

Example.   A barrel is 960 mm long; the diameter at each end is 600 mm, at quarter and three-quarter lengths the diameter is 720 mm, and at mid-length the diameter is 800 mm. Find the capacity of the barrel in m^3 and also in l.

Working in m (see Fig. 114):

Sectional Areas	Multipliers	Products
$0{\cdot}7854 \times 0{\cdot}6^2$	1	$0{\cdot}7854 \times 0{\cdot}36$
$0{\cdot}7854 \times 0{\cdot}72^2$	4	$0{\cdot}7854 \times 2{\cdot}0736$
$0{\cdot}7854 \times 0{\cdot}8^2$	2	$0{\cdot}7854 \times 1{\cdot}28$
$0{\cdot}7854 \times 0{\cdot}72^2$	4	$0{\cdot}7854 \times 2{\cdot}0736$
$0{\cdot}7854 \times 0{\cdot}6^2$	1	$0{\cdot}7854 \times 0{\cdot}36$

$$\text{Sum} = 0{\cdot}7854 \times 6{\cdot}1472$$

$$\text{Common interval} = 0{\cdot}96 \div 4 = 0{\cdot}24 \text{ m}$$

$$\text{Volume} = 0{\cdot}7854 \times 6{\cdot}1472 \times \tfrac{1}{3} \times 0{\cdot}24$$

$$= 0{\cdot}3863 \text{ m}^3 \quad \text{Ans. (i)}$$

$$= 386{\cdot}3 \text{ l} \quad \text{Ans. (ii)}$$

Note that the common multiplier of $0{\cdot}7854$ is carried through to the final sum of the products.

This could be expressed in formula fashion thus:

$$\text{Volume} = \frac{h}{3} \times 0{\cdot}7854(d_1^2 + 4d_2^2 + 2d_3^2 + \text{etc.})$$

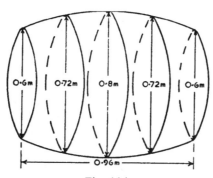

Fig. 114

where d_1, d_2, d_3, etc., are the diameters, and h is the common interval between measurements, or

$$\text{Volume} = \frac{h}{3} \times \pi(r_1^2 + 4r_2^2 + 2r_3^2 + \text{etc.})$$

where r_1, r_2, r_3, etc., are the radii.

Example.   Plot the graph $xy = 6$ between the limits $x = 2$ and $x = 6$. If the area under this graph is rotated about its x-axis through one complete revolution, calculate, by Simpson's rule, the volume swept out.

$$xy = 6 \qquad \therefore y = \frac{6}{x}$$

Plotting points for values of x between the limits $x = 2$ and $x = 6$,

$x =$	2	3	4	5	6
$y = \dfrac{6}{x}$	3	2	1·5	1·2	1

Fig. 115a

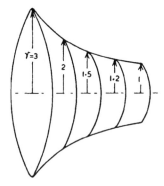

Fig. 115b

The graph is shown in Fig. 115a. When the area under this graph is rotated about its x-axis through one revolution, the volume swept out appears as shown in Fig. 115b. The y-ordinates of the graph become the radii of the solid at regular intervals along its length. Putting the cross-sectional areas at these regular intervals through Simpson's rule as in the previous example:

Radii r	Cross-sectional Areas $= \pi r^2$	Simpson's Multipliers	Products
3	$\pi \times 9$	1	$\pi \times \ \ 9$
2	$\pi \times 4$	4	$\pi \times 16$
1·5	$\pi \times 2·25$	2	$\pi \times \ \ 4·5$
1·2	$\pi \times 1·44$	4	$\pi \times \ \ 5·76$
1	$\pi \times 1$	1	$\pi \times \ \ 1$

$$\text{Sum} = \pi \times 36·26$$

Common interval between ordinates $= 1$

$$\text{Volume} = \pi \times 36·26 \times \tfrac{1}{3} \times 1$$
$$= 37·98 \ \text{units}^3 \quad \text{Ans.}$$

FLOW OF LIQUID THROUGH PIPES, ETC.

VOLUME FLOW ($\dot{V}$) is the volume of a fluid flowing past a given point in unit time (m^3/s).

The velocity or speed of flow is the 'length' of liquid which passes in a given time. For instance, if the velocity of the liquid is 2 m/s it means that a column of the liquid 2 m long passes every s, hence, volume flow is the product of the cross-sectional area of the flowing liquid and its velocity. In basic units:

$$\text{Volume flow } [m^3/s] = \text{cross-sect. area } [m^2] \times \text{velocity } [m/s]$$
$$\dot{V} = A \ v$$

MASS FLOW ($\dot{m}$) is the mass of fluid flowing past a given point in unit time.

Since density is the mass per unit volume, then the mass flow is the product of the volume flow and the density.

$$\text{Mass flow } [kg/s] = \text{volume flow } [m^3/s] \times \text{density } [kg/m^3]$$
$$\dot{m} = \dot{V}\rho$$

Example.   Oil of density 0·85 g/ml flows full bore through a pipe 50 mm diameter at a velocity of 1·5 m/s. Find the quantity flowing,

(i) in m³/h, (ii) kg/h, (iii) t/h.

$$\text{Velocity} = 1{\cdot}5 \text{ m/s} = 1{\cdot}5 \times 3600 \text{ m/h}$$

$$\text{Volume flow } [\text{m}^3/\text{h}] = \text{area } [\text{m}^2] \times \text{velocity } [\text{m/h}]$$

$$\dot{V} = 0{\cdot}7854 \times 0{\cdot}05^2 \times 1{\cdot}5 \times 3600$$

$$= 10{\cdot}6 \text{ m}^3/\text{h} \quad \text{Ans. (i)}$$

$$\text{Density} = 0{\cdot}85 \text{ g/ml} = 0{\cdot}85 \times 10^3 \text{ kg/m}^3$$

$$\text{Mass flow } [\text{kg/h}] = \text{volume flow } [\text{m}^3/\text{h}] \times \text{density } [\text{kg/m}^3]$$

$$\dot{m} = 10{\cdot}6 \times 0{\cdot}85 \times 10^3$$

$$= 9012 \text{ kg/h} \quad \text{Ans. (ii)}$$

$$= 9{\cdot}012 \text{ t/h} \quad \text{Ans. (iii)}$$

FLOW THROUGH VALVES. When a liquid flows out of the open end of a pipe, the maximum quantity of liquid escaping depends upon the area of the bore of the pipe end. The flow can be restricted by a cover over the pipe end so that the area of escape is less than the area of the pipe bore.

Referring to Fig. 116, the area of escape is the circumferential opening, circumference × lift. The maximum effective lift will be when this circumferential area of escape is equal to the area of the bore, thus,

$$\text{circumference} \times \text{lift} = \text{area of bore}$$

$$\pi \times d \times \text{lift} = \frac{\pi}{4} \times d^2$$

$$\text{lift} = \frac{d}{4}$$

Fig. 116

A practical example is a valve over a valve seat, neglecting the area taken up by the wings of the valve, the maximum effective lift is one-quarter of the valve diameter. If the lift is more than this, no more liquid can flow through than that which is allowed by the area of the bore of the seat, but if the lift is less than one-quarter of the diameter, the circumferential area of escape is less than the area of the seat bore, and the quantity of liquid flowing through depends upon the area, circumference × lift.

Example.   Calculate the quantity of water flowing, in l/min, through a valve 100 mm diameter when the lift is 15 mm and the velocity of the water is 3 m/s, assuming that the wings of the valve take up one-sixth of the circumference.

One sixth of the area is obstructed by the wings, this leaves five-sixths of the area for the water to flow through. Working in m:

Circumferential area of escape between valve and seat

$$= \frac{5}{6} \times \pi \times 0 \cdot 1 \times 0 \cdot 015 \text{ m}^2$$

$$\dot{V} = \frac{5}{6} \times \pi \times 0 \cdot 1 \times 0 \cdot 015 \times 3 \text{ m}^3/\text{s}$$

$\text{lm}^3 = 10^3 \text{ l hence}$

$$\dot{V} = \frac{5}{6} \times \pi \times 0 \cdot 1 \times 0 \cdot 015 \times 3 \times 10^3 \times 60 \text{ l/min}$$

$$= 706 \cdot 9 \text{ l/min}   \text{Ans.}$$

CENTRES OF GRAVITY BY FIRST MOMENTS

The moment of a force about a given point is the product of the force and the perpendicular distance of its line of action from that point.

Fig. 117

Figure 117 illustrates a force of 300 N acting on the end of a lever, at a perpendicular distance of 2 m from o, its moment therefore is $300 \times 2 = 600$ Nm. This is the effect of the force which tends to turn

Fig. 118

the lever in a clockwise direction around the axis O. A force of
400 N acting at 1·5 m, or 600 N at 1 m leverage, would have the
same turning effect.

Consider a piece of plate cut to shape shown in Fig. 118. Imagine
this plate supported horizontally on one single support, call this
support the fulcrum. The fulcrum (F) must be positioned exactly at the
centre of gravity of the plate if the plate is to be perfectly balanced
because 'the centre of gravity is that position through which the whole
weight can be considered as acting'.

Now take moments about the end o o, this means to imagine the plate
to be temporarily hinged at this end, for perfect equilibrium the moments
of all the forces tending to turn the plate clockwise around the hinge
must be equal to the moments of the forces tending to turn the plate
anticlockwise about the hinge.

Let W_1, W_2 and W_3 represent the weights of the top, centre and
bottom parts.

Let x_1, x_2 and x_3 represent the distances of the centres of gravity of
these parts from oo.

Let $\bar{x}$ represent the position of the fulcrum (F) from o o, and as
previously stated this is the centre of gravity of the whole plate.

Moments about o o:

Clockwise moments = Anticlockwise moments

$$W_1 \times x_1 + W_2 \times x_2 + W_3 \times x_3 = F \times \bar{x}$$

Since the total upward force F must be equal to the total downward force, then $F = W_1 + W_2 + W_3$

$$\therefore\ W_1 \times x_1 + W_2 \times x_2 + W_3 \times x_3 = (W_1 + W_2 + W_3) \times \bar{x}$$

$$\bar{x} = \frac{W_1 x_1 + W_2 x_2 + W_3 x_3}{W_1 + W_2 + W_3}$$

In words this is:

$$\bar{x} = \frac{\text{Summation of all moments of weights}}{\text{Summation of all weights}}$$

$$\bar{x} = \frac{\Sigma \text{ moments of weight}}{\Sigma \text{ weights}} \qquad \dots \quad \dots \quad \dots \quad \text{(i)}$$

As previously explained, weight is equal to mass $\times$ g, and since g is constant, then weight can be represented by mass:

$$\bar{x} = \frac{\Sigma \text{ moments of masses}}{\Sigma \text{ masses}} \qquad \dots \quad \dots \quad \dots \quad \text{(ii)}$$

Mass is obtained from, volume $\times$ density, so that if the material is the same kind throughout, the same value for the density of the material will be in every term of the above expression and will cancel out, hence:

$$\bar{x} = \frac{\Sigma \text{ moments of volumes}}{\Sigma \text{ volumes}} \qquad \dots \quad \dots \quad \dots \quad \text{(iii)}$$

Further, volume = area $\times$ thickness, therefore if the thickness of the material is uniform throughout as well as its density, then the thickness will also cancel from every term,

$$\bar{x} = \frac{\Sigma \text{ moments of areas}}{\Sigma \text{ areas}} \qquad \dots \quad \dots \quad \dots \quad \text{(iv)}$$

Hence, for convenience take moments of masses, moments of volumes and moments of areas. The above expressions provide methods of finding the position of the centre of gravity of objects and figures made up from regular shapes.

Moments as used above are usually referred to as 'first moments' to distinguish them from 'second moments' which are used in applied mechanics.

Fig. 119

Example.   To find the position of the centre of gravity of the plate illustrated in Fig. 119 which is of uniform thickness throughout, the dimensions shown being all in mm.

Working in cm:

$$\text{Area of top flange} = 11 \times 2 = 22 \text{ cm}^2$$

$$\text{Area of centre web} = 10 \times 1\cdot5 = 15 \text{ cm}^2$$

$$\text{Area of bottom flange} = 16 \times 3 = 48 \text{ cm}^2$$

$$\text{Distance of c.g. of top flange from base} = 14 \text{ cm}$$

$$\text{Distance of c.g. of centre web from base} = 8 \text{ cm}$$

$$\text{Distance of c.g. of bottom flange from base} = 1\cdot5 \text{ cm}$$

Taking moments about base,

$$\bar{y} = \frac{\Sigma \text{ moments of areas}}{\Sigma \text{ areas}}$$

$$= \frac{22 \times 14 + 15 \times 8 + 48 \times 1\cdot5}{22 + 15 + 48} = \frac{500}{85}$$

$$= 5\cdot88 \text{ cm or } 58\cdot8 \text{ mm above the base.}\quad \text{Ans.}$$

Example.   A hole 30 mm diameter is bored through a solid disc 90 mm diameter, the centre of the hole being 25 mm from the centre of the disc. (Fig. 120) Find the position of the centre of gravity of the disc after the hole has been cut out.

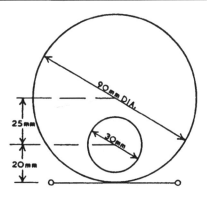

Fig. 120

Moments about base o o, working in cm:

$$\bar{y} = \frac{\Sigma \text{ moments of areas}}{\Sigma \text{ areas}}$$

$$\bar{y} = \frac{0 \cdot 7854 \times 9^2 \times 4 \cdot 5 - 0 \cdot 7854 \times 3^2 \times 2}{0 \cdot 7854 \times 9^2 - 0 \cdot 7854 \times 3^2}$$

$$\bar{y} = \frac{3^2 \times 4 \cdot 5 - 2}{3^2 - 1} = \frac{38 \cdot 5}{8}$$

$$= 4 \cdot 8125 \text{ cm from bottom, } = 48 \cdot 125 \text{ mm}$$

or, $48 \cdot 125 - 45$

$$= 3 \cdot 125 \text{ mm from disc centre. \quad Ans.}$$

(Alternatively, moments can be taken about centre of disc.)

Note, in this example area is lost by boring the hole, therefore the summation of areas is the net area obtained by subtracting the area of the hole from the area of the disc; also, the summation of moments of areas is the difference between the moments of areas of the disc and hole.

In each of the above two cases, it is obvious that the centre of gravity lies on the vertical centre line because the figures are symmetrical, therefore it is sufficient to calculate the position of the centre of gravity in one direction only. For figures that are not symmetrical, it is necessary to express the position of the centre of gravity in two directions at right angles to each other, say from the base and from one side, this is done by taking moments about these two datum lines separately.

IRREGULAR FIGURES. Simpson's rule can be employed to find the moment of an irregular area in a similar manner to which it is applied in finding the area.

To express the moment about a given point, the perpendicular distance of each ordinate is measured from that point, then:

Add together, the moment of the first ordinate, the moment of the last ordinate, four times the moments of the even ordinates, and twice the moments of the odd ordinates; multiply this sum by one-third of the common interval.

The centroid can then be found by dividing the moment of the area by the area.

As an example, take a right angled triangle of 80 mm base and 48 mm height as illustrated in Fig. 121, to find the area and position of centroid, from base o o by Simpson's rule. By taking a regular shape such as this it enables us to compare the results so obtained with those calculated from formulae.

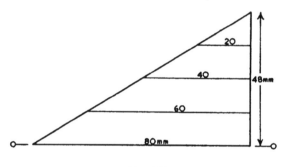

Fig. 121

Measurements from base, in cm.

i	ii	iii	iv	v
Ordinates	Simpson's multipliers	Products of i and ii	Distances of ordinates from base	Products of iii and iv
8	1	8	0	0
6	4	24	1·2	28·8
4	2	8	2·4	19·2
2	4	8	3·6	28·8
0	1	0	4·8	0
		Sum = 48		Sum = 76·8

$$\text{Common interval} = 4\cdot8 \div 4 = 1\cdot2 \text{ cm}$$
$$\text{Area} = 48 \times \tfrac{1}{3} \times 1\cdot2 = 19\cdot2 \text{ cm}^2 \quad \dots \quad \text{(i)}$$
$$\text{Moment of area about base} = 76\cdot8 \times \tfrac{1}{3} \times 1\cdot2 = 30\cdot72 \text{ cm}^3$$
$$\text{Centroid from base} = \frac{\text{moment of area}}{\text{area}}$$
$$= \frac{30\cdot72}{19\cdot2} = 1\cdot6 \text{ cm or 16 mm} \quad \text{(ii)}$$

It will be seen that the position of the centroid can be obtained by dividing the sum of column v by the sum of column iii thus,

$$\frac{76\cdot8}{48} = 1\cdot6 \text{ cm}$$

Further, if this triangle is swept through one complete revolution about its base o o it will sweep out the volume of a cone of dimensions 48 mm radius of base and 80 mm perpendicular height.

By Theorem of Pappus:

$$\text{Volume swept out} = \text{area} \times \text{distance its centroid moves}$$
$$= 19\cdot2 \times 2\pi \times 1\cdot6$$
$$= 193\cdot1 \text{ cm}^3 \quad \dots \quad \dots \quad \dots \quad \text{(iii)}$$

The above agrees with results by formulae:

$$\text{Area} = \tfrac{1}{2}(\text{base} \times \text{perpendicular height})$$
$$= \tfrac{1}{2} \times 8 \times 4\cdot8 = 19\cdot2 \text{ cm}^2$$
$$\text{Centroid} = \tfrac{1}{3} \text{ of perpendicular height}$$
$$= \tfrac{1}{3} \times 4\cdot8 = 1\cdot6 \text{ cm}$$
$$\text{Volume of cone} = \tfrac{1}{3} \times \text{area of base} \times \text{perpendicular height}$$
$$= \tfrac{1}{3} \times \pi \times 4\cdot8^2 \times 8 = 193\cdot1 \text{ cm}^3$$

SHIFT OF CENTRE OF GRAVITY DUE TO SHIFT OF LOADS

Consider a system composed of loads which weigh w_1, w_2 and w_3 as shown in Fig. 122, the centre of gravity of each being h_1, h_2 and h_3

respectively from the base $o\ o$. Let $\bar{y}_1$ be the distance of the centre of gravity of the whole system from the base, then:

$$\bar{y}_1 = \frac{\Sigma \text{ moments of weights}}{\Sigma \text{ weights}}$$
$$= \frac{w_1h_1 + w_2h_2 + w_3h_3}{w_1 + w_2 + w_3}$$

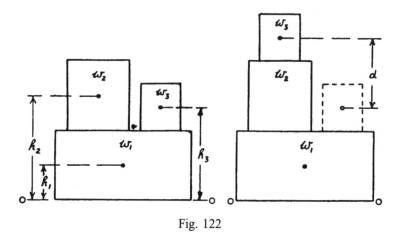

Fig. 122

If w_3 be lifted into the position shown, through a height of d the new centre of gravity of the whole system from the base, represented by $\bar{y}_2$ is:

$$\bar{y}_2 = \frac{w_1h_1 + w_2h_2 + w_3(h_3 + d)}{w_1 + w_2 + w_3}$$
$$= \frac{w_1h_1 + w_2h_2 + w_3h_3 + w_3d}{w_1 + w_2 + w_3}$$

The shift of the centre of gravity of the whole system in the direction measured from the base is $\bar{y}_2 - \bar{y}_1$ which is:

$$\bar{y}_2 - \bar{y}_1 = \frac{w_3d}{w_1 + w_2 + w_3}$$

In words this is:

$$\text{Shift of c.g.} = \frac{\text{weight shifted} \times \text{distance it is moved}}{\textit{total} \text{ weight}}$$

As shown previously, weight can be represented by mass, therefore write:

$$\text{Shift of c.g.} = \frac{\text{mass shifted} \times \text{distance it is moved}}{total \text{ mass}}$$

TEST EXAMPLES 10

1. An I-section steel girder of 150 mm overall depth has unequal flanges, the top flange is 100 mm wide by 12 mm thick and the bottom flange is 140 mm wide by 14 mm thick. The centre web is 10 mm thick. Considering the flanges as rectangular in section by neglecting radii and fillets, calculate the mass in kg/m run if the density of the material is 7·86 g/cm^3.

2. A hollow steel shaft, 400 mm outside diameter and 200 mm inside diameter, has a coupling 75 mm thick and 760 mm diameter at each end, and the overall length is 6 m. Neglecting fillets and coupling bolt holes, find the mass of the shaft in t taking the density of steel as 7·86 × 10^3 kg/m^3.

3. A cylinder and sphere and base of a cone are all the same diameter, and the heights of the cylinder and cone are each equal to the diameter of the sphere. Find the ratio of the volumes of the cylinder and sphere relative to the volume of the cone.

4. A piece of flat steel plate, having a mass of 6·5 kg/m^2, is cut to the shape of a sector of a circle of radius 180 mm and subtended angle at the centre 240°, and the sector is rolled into a cone. Find (i) the mass of material used, (ii) the diameter of the base of the cone, (iii) the perpendicular height of the cone, (iv) the capacity of the cone in l.

5. An object is constructed by brazing the base of a solid cone to the flat surface of a solid hemisphere, the diameter of the base of the cone and the diameter of the hemisphere both being 60 mm, and the perpendicular height of the cone 50 mm. Find the mass of the object if the density of the materials is 8·4 g/cm^3.

6. A hollow lead sphere has a uniform thickness of 10 mm and its mass is 3 kg. Taking the specific gravity of lead as 11·4, find its outside diameter.

7. A hole 24 mm diameter is bored centrally through a sphere 51 mm diameter. Calculate the volume of the drilled sphere in cm^3 and its mass if the density of the material is $7·86 \times 10^3$ kg/m^3.

8. A tapered hole is bored through a right circular cone, concentric with the axis of the cone. The base diameter of the cone is 64 mm and the perpendicular height is 60 mm. The diameter of the hole at the base of the cone is 28 mm and the diameter where it breaks through the surface of the cone is 16 mm. Calculate the volume and mass of the remaining hollow frustum, taking the density of the material as $8·4$ g/cm^3.

9. The lengths of the sides of the base of a regular hexagonal pyramid is 25 mm and the perpendicular height is 60 mm. Find the volume in cm^3. If this pyramid is cut through a plane parallel to its base at half the height, find the volume of the remaining frustum.

10. A vessel in the form of a hollow cone with vertex downwards, is partially filled with water. The volume of the water is 200 cm^3 and the depth of the water is 50 mm. Find the volume of water which must be added to increase the depth to 70 mm.

11. The diameter of the base of a hollow cone is 300 mm and its perpendicular height is 500 mm. It is partly filled with water so that when resting on its base the depth of the water is 250 mm. If the cone is inverted and balanced on its apex, what will then be the depth of the water?

12. The surface area of a solid sphere is $1\frac{1}{2}$ times the surface area of a smaller sphere, and the difference in their volumes is 10 cm^3. Find the volume and diameter of the smaller sphere.

13. The diameters of a barrel are 395 mm at each end, 477 mm at quarter and three-quarter lengths, and 500 mm at mid-length, and the total length is 581 mm. Using Simpson's rule calculate the capacity of the barrel in l.

14. Plot the graph $y = 5 + 4x - x^2$ between the limits $x = -1$ and
    $x = +5$. If the area under this curve is rotated about its x-axis, find
    the volume swept out.

15. A water-trough has a regular isosceles triangular section, the
    angle at the bottom being 80°. Calculate the volume flow of water
    along the trough, in m³/h, when the depth of the water in the
    trough is 180 mm and it is flowing at a velocity of 0·5 m/s.

16. Find the height of the centre of gravity of a frustum of a cone which
    is 80 mm diameter at the base, 60 mm diameter at the top, and
    40 mm perpendicular height.

17. Find the position of the centre of gravity of the beam knee plate
    illustrated in Fig. 123 giving the distances from the 375 and
    300 mm straight sides as represented by $\bar{x}$ and $\bar{y}$ respectively.

Fig. 123

18. A bolt has a round head and plain round shank, the head is 60 mm
    diameter and 40 mm deep, the shank is 40 mm diameter and the
    overall length of the bolt is 270 mm. A ring of the same material as
    the bolt, and of the same dimensions as the bolt head, is made to
    slide on the shank to a position of 131 mm from the shank end to
    the mid-point of the ring. Find the position of the centre of gravity
    of the whole from end of shank.

DIFFERENTIAL CALCULUS

The development and application of the differential calculus may be explained by the relation between equations and their graphs.

The meaning of the *gradient* at any point on such a graph is of particular importance in this context and it is therefore dealt with first.

GRADIENT OF A LINE

It will be recalled, from previous work on graphs, that the *gradient* (or *slope*) of a line is the $\dfrac{change\ in\ y}{change\ in\ x}$ between any two points on the line.

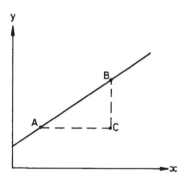

Fig. 124

For the line shown in Fig. 124,

$$\text{gradient} = \frac{\text{change in } y}{\text{change in } x} \quad \text{between points } A \text{ and } B$$

$$= \frac{BC}{AC}$$

The following examples are given by way of revision, to show how the gradient of a line is calculated:

Example.   Plot the graph of the equation $y = 3x$ between the limits $x = 0$ and $x = 4$ and find the gradient of the graph.

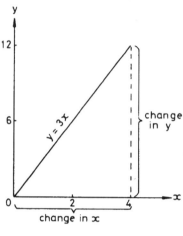

Fig. 125

Referring to Fig. 125:

$$\text{Gradient} = \frac{\text{change in } y}{\text{change in } x}$$
$$= \frac{12}{4}$$
$$= \frac{3}{1}$$
$$= 3 \quad \text{Ans.}$$

Note: The change in y is three times the change in x.

Thus the *gradient* indicates the *rate of change* of one quantity, *with respect to* another, related, quantity.

Example.   Plot the graph of the equation $y = 2 - 0.25x$ between the limits $x = 0$ and $x = 8$. Find the gradient of this graph. The graph is shown in, Fig. 126

$$\text{Gradient} = \frac{\text{change in } y}{\text{change in } x}$$

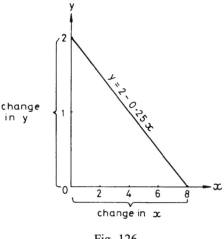

Fig. 126

(Note that the value of y changes from 2 to zero, i.e. the change in y is -2.)

$$\therefore \text{Gradient} = \frac{-2}{8}$$
$$= -\frac{0 \cdot 25}{1}$$
$$= -0 \cdot 25 \quad \text{Ans.}$$

Two important points are noted from the previous examples:

Fig. 127

Fig. 128

(i) If y *increases* as x increases (Fig. 127), the gradient is *positive*.
(ii) If y *decreases* as x increases (Fig. 128), the gradient is *negative*.

ZERO GRADIENT

The gradient of a horizontal straight line is zero, since the change in y is zero for any given change in the value of x (Fig. 129).

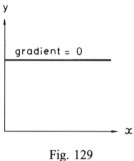

Fig. 129

GRADIENT OF A CURVE

The gradient of a curve is not constant, but is changing from point to point along the length of the curve.

The gradient of a curve at any given point is the gradient of the *tangent* to the curve at that point.

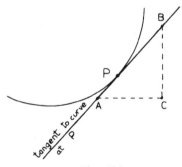

Fig. 130

Referring to Fig. 130:

Gradient of the *curve* at P = gradient of the *tangent* at P

The gradient of a curve may be obtained by drawing the tangent and measuring the gradient, or mathematically, by the *differential calculus*.

DIFFERENTIATION FROM FIRST PRINCIPLES

From Fig. 130 it was seen that the gradient of the tangent at P was required, in order to determine the gradient of the curve at P.
Chord PA is now constructed, as shown (Fig. 131).

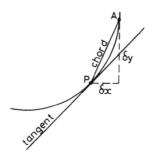

Fig. 131

δ is used, for convenience, to express mathematically the change in the value of y and x between points P and A.

Thus, δx, pronounced 'delta ex', means a small change in the value of x. It does *not* mean $\delta \times x$.

Similarly, δy means the corresponding change in the value of y. From Fig. 131,

$$\text{gradient of chord } PA = \frac{\delta y}{\delta x}$$

The gradient of this chord is obviously quite different to the gradient of the tangent to the curve.

However, if point A is now allowed to move along the curve towards point P, it is seen (Figs. 132a and 132b), that the slope of the *chord* more and more resembles the slope of the *tangent* as A gets closer to P.

In fact, when point A gets very close to point P, the slope of the chord and the tangent are virtually the same.

As A gets very close to P, so length δx is becoming very small, until it finally approaches zero value.

i.e. δx approaches zero value (denoted by $\delta x \to 0$).

From the above reasoning, it follows that, when δx has become infinitely small, the ratio $\delta y / \delta x$ has reached a special value, or *limit*, where it represents the gradient of the curve at point P.

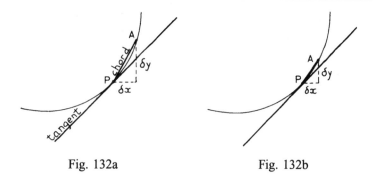

Fig. 132a   Fig. 132b

In order to indicate that this is a special value of $\delta y/\delta x$, it is identified by changing the notation from $\delta y/\delta x$ to dy/dx. This relationship is expressed mathematically as:

$$\underset{\delta x \to 0}{\text{limit}} \; \frac{\delta y}{\delta x} = \frac{dy}{dx}$$

The term dy/dx is called the *differential coefficient* of y with respect to x and the process of finding dy/dx is called *differentiation*.

Example.   From first principles, derive an expression for the gradient of the curve $y = x^2$ at any point on the curve.

The sketch of the graph of $y = x^2$ is shown in Fig. 133. Point P represents any point on the curve.

Chord PA is drawn as shown.

1. The co-ordinates for point P are (x, y).
2. Hence, the co-ordinates for point A are $(x + \delta x)$, $(y + \delta y)$.
3. Now, the equation of this curve is $y = x^2$

$$\therefore \text{At point}, P, y = x^2 \quad \ldots \quad \ldots \quad \ldots \quad \ldots \quad \text{(i)}$$

and, at point A, $(y + \delta y) = (x + \delta x)^2$

$$\therefore y + \delta y = x^2 + 2x \, \delta x + (\delta x)^2 \quad \ldots \quad \text{(ii)}$$

Subtract equation (i) from equation (ii),

$$y + \delta y = x^2 + 2x\delta x + (\delta x)^2$$
$$\underline{y \qquad = x^2}$$
$$\delta y = \qquad 2x\delta x + (\delta x)^2 \qquad \ldots \quad \text{(iii)}$$

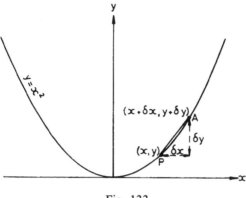

Fig. 133

Divide equation (iii) by δx, thus obtaining *gradient*,

$$\frac{\delta y}{\delta x} = \frac{2x\,\delta x}{\delta x} + \frac{(\delta x)^2}{\delta x}$$

$$\therefore \frac{\delta y}{\delta x} = 2x + \delta x \qquad \ldots \qquad \ldots \qquad \ldots \qquad (iv)$$

If point A now moves very close to point P, so length δx will approach zero value.

$$\text{i.e.} \quad \underset{\delta x \to 0}{\text{limit}} \frac{\delta y}{\delta x} = 2x$$

$$\therefore \frac{dy}{dx} = 2x$$

Hence, at any point on the curve $y = x^2$

the gradient of the curve $= 2x$ Ans.

Note: Since δx becomes very close to zero value, it can be omitted from the right-hand side of equation (iv) as being negligible compared to the term $2x$. This does not happen on the left side of equation (iv), because, as δx becomes very small, so too does δy, hence the ratio $\delta y / \delta x$ remains a significant quantity.

Example.   Calculate the gradient of the curve $y = x^2$ at the points $x = -3$ and $x = +2$.

From the previous example,

$$\text{gradient at any point on the curve} = \frac{dy}{dx} = 2x.$$

$$\therefore \text{ At the point } x = -3$$
$$\text{gradient} = 2 \times (-3)$$
$$= -6 \quad \text{Ans. (i)}$$
$$\text{At the point } x = 2,$$
$$\text{gradient} = 2 \times (2)$$
$$= 4 \quad \text{Ans. (ii)}$$

These results can be confirmed by drawing tangents to the curve $y = x^2$ at $x = -3$ and $x = 2$.

The gradient of each of these tangents, when measured, should be reasonably close to the calculated values. (The tangents can be drawn on Fig. 134.)

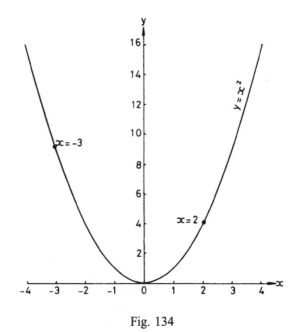

Fig. 134

Example.   From first principles, find the differential coefficient of y, with respect to x, for the equation $y = 3x^3$.

(The differential coefficient or gradient may be calculated without actually drawing a graph, although a sketch of the graph is often useful when solving problems.)

$$y = 3x^3 \quad \ldots \qquad \ldots \qquad \ldots \tag{i}$$

$$\therefore (y + \delta y) = 3(x + \delta x)^3$$

$$= 3\{x^3 + 3x^2\,\delta x + 3x(\delta x)^2 + (\delta x)^3\}$$

$$= 3x^3 + 9x^2\,\delta x + 9x(\delta x)^2 + 3(\delta x)^3 \quad \ldots \tag{ii}$$

Subtract equation (i) from equation (ii),

$$y + \delta y = 3x^3 + 9x^2\,\delta x + 9x(\delta x)^2 + 3(\delta x)^3$$
$$\underline{\quad y = 3x^3 \qquad\qquad\qquad\qquad\qquad\qquad}$$
$$\delta y = \qquad 9x^2\,\delta x + 9x(\delta x)^2 + 3(\delta x)^3$$

Divide by δx,

$$\frac{\delta y}{\delta x} = 9x^2 + 9x\,\delta x + 3(\delta x)^2$$

$$\lim_{\delta x \to 0} \frac{\delta y}{\delta x} = 9x^2$$

$$\text{i.e.} \quad \frac{dy}{dx} = 9x^2$$

$\therefore$ For the equation $y = 3x^3$,

differential coefficient $= 9x^2$ Ans.

GENERAL RULE FOR DIFFERENTIATION

From the previous section, the following results were obtained:

$$\text{when } y = x^2 \qquad \frac{dy}{dx} = 2x$$

$$\text{and, when } y = 3x^3, \qquad \frac{dy}{dx} = 9x^2$$

From the form of these results (which is confirmed by solving further examples), the following general rule is noted:

$$\text{when} \quad y = ax^n$$

$$\frac{dy}{dx} = nax^{n-1}$$

$$\text{e.g. when} \quad y = 9x^4 \ \dots \ (\text{i.e. } a = 9, n = 4)$$

$$\frac{dy}{dx} = (4 \times 9)x^{(4-1)}$$

$$\therefore \frac{dy}{dx} = 36x^3 \quad \text{Ans.}$$

Example.   Differentiate the following equations with respect to x:

(a) $y = x^8$ (b) $y = 2x^{-3}$ (c) $y = -7x^{-4}$

(d) $y = x$ (e) $y = \dfrac{1}{x}$ (f) $y = \dfrac{x^3}{12}$

(a) $$y = x^8$$

$$\therefore \frac{dy}{dx} = 8x^7 \quad \text{Ans.} \quad (a)$$

(b) $$y = 2x^{-3}$$

$$\therefore \frac{dy}{dx} = -6x^{-4}$$

$$= -\frac{6}{x^4} \quad \text{Ans.} \quad (b)$$

(c) $$y = -7x^{-4}$$

$$\therefore \frac{dy}{dx} = 28x^{-5}$$

$$= \frac{28}{x^5} \quad \text{Ans.} \quad (c)$$

(d) $$y = x$$

$$(\text{i.e.} \quad y = x^1)$$

$$\therefore \frac{dy}{dx} = x^0$$

$$= 1 \quad \text{Ans.} \quad (d)$$

(e)
$$y = \frac{1}{x}$$

$$(\text{i.e.} \quad y = x^{-1})$$

$$\therefore \frac{dy}{dx} = -x^{-2}$$

$$= -\frac{1}{x^2} \quad \text{Ans.} \quad (e)$$

(f)
$$y = \frac{x^3}{12}$$

$$\therefore \frac{dy}{dx} = \frac{3 \times x^2}{12}$$

$$= \frac{x^2}{4} \quad \text{Ans.} \quad (f)$$

DIFFERENTIAL COEFFICIENT OF A CONSTANT

As shown previously, when y is a constant, the resulting graph has zero gradient (see Fig. 129).

i.e. if $y = a$ (where a is any constant)

$$\frac{dy}{dx} = 0$$

e.g. if $y = 7$

$$\frac{dy}{dx} = 0$$

DIFFERENTIAL COEFFICIENT OF A SUM OF TERMS

The differential coefficient of a sum of terms is obtained by differentiating each term separately.

e.g. if $y = x^3 - 2x^2 + 4x - 9$

$$\frac{dy}{dx} = 3x^2 - 4x + 4$$

Example. Differentiate the equation

$$y = \frac{x^3}{3} - \frac{3}{x^2} + 3x$$

with respect to x.

Rearranging the equation,

$$y = \frac{x^3}{3} - 3x^{-2} + 3x$$

$$\frac{dy}{dx} = x^2 + 6x^{-3} + 3$$

$$= x^2 + \frac{6}{x^3} + 3 \quad \text{Ans.}$$

Example.   Differentiate the equation $s = 3t^2 - 20t + 40$ with respect to t. (Note: Symbols s and t represent two related quantities, as do x and y.)

$$s = 3t^2 - 20t + 40$$

$$\frac{ds}{dt} = 6t - 20 \quad \text{Ans.}$$

SECOND DIFFERENTIAL COEFFICIENT

In some cases, having differentiated an expression once, it is necessary to differentiate a second time.

The notation d^2y/dx^2 is used to denote the second differentiation of an expression.

e.g.   Consider the equation $y = x^4$

differentiating once, $\dfrac{dy}{dx} = 4x^3$

differentiating twice, $\dfrac{d^2y}{dx^2} = 12x^2$

Example.   Determine the second differential coefficient of the following equation:

$$y = x^3 - 4x^2 + 3x - 7$$

$$\frac{dy}{dx} = 3x^2 - 8x + 3$$

$$\frac{d^2y}{dx^2} = 6x - 8 \quad \text{Ans.}$$

DISTANCE, VELOCITY AND ACCELERATION

For a moving body,

$$\text{average velocity} = \frac{\text{distance travelled}}{\text{time taken}}$$

Using symbol v for velocity, s for distance and t for time, this equation may be expressed in calculus notation:

$$\text{average velocity} = \frac{\delta s}{\delta t}$$

If the velocity at a given instant (the *instantaneous* velocity) is required, the time interval δt must be very small, i.e. δt must approach zero value (Fig. 135).

Fig. 135

Thus,

$$\underset{\delta t \to 0}{\text{limit}} \frac{\delta s}{\delta t} = \frac{ds}{dt}$$

Hence, at any given time t, the *instantaneous velocity* of a moving body may be expressed as:

$$v = \frac{ds}{dt}$$

Similarly,

$$\text{average acceleration} = \frac{\text{change of velocity}}{\text{time to change}}$$

By the same reasoning as that above, the *instantaneous acceleration a* is given by the expression:

$$a = \frac{dv}{dt}$$

Example.   The distance s moved by a body in time t is given by the formula $s = t^3 - 3t^2$. Find expressions for the velocity and acceleration of the body at any instant.

$$s = t^3 - 3t^2$$

$$\left.\begin{array}{l} \text{velocity, } v = \dfrac{ds}{dt} = 3t^2 - 6t \\[2mm] \text{acceleration } a = \dfrac{dv}{dt} = 6t \end{array}\right\} \text{ Ans.}$$

Note: The expression for the acceleration of the body is seen to be the second differential equation of the original equation relating distance s to time t.

$$\text{i.e.} \quad s = t^3 - 3t^2$$

$$\frac{ds}{dt} = 3t^2 - 6t$$

$$\frac{d^2s}{dt^2} = 6t$$

Example.   A body moves s metres in t seconds according to the relationship $s = t^3 - 7t^2 + 3$.
   (a) Derive expressions for the velocity and acceleration of the body at any instant.
   (b) Use these expressions to find the velocity and acceleration of the body after 5 s.

(a) $$s = t^3 - 7t^2 + 3$$

$$v = \frac{ds}{dt} = 3t^2 - 14t$$

$$a = \frac{dv}{dt} = 6t - 14$$

   $\therefore$ At any instant

$$\left.\begin{array}{l}\text{velocity} = 3t^2 - 14t \ \text{m/s} \\ \text{acceleration} = 6t - 14 \ \text{m/s}^2 \end{array}\right\} \quad \text{Ans. (a)}$$

(b) When

$$t = 5,$$

$$v = 3 \times (5)^2 - 14 \times (5)$$

$$= 5 \ \text{m/s} \quad \text{Ans. (b)}$$

$$a = 6 \times (5) - 14$$

$$= 16 \ \text{m/s}^2 \quad \text{Ans. (b)}$$

Example.   The distance (displacement) s moved by a body in time t is given by the expression

$$s = 40t - 5t^2$$

Calculate (a) the velocity after 2 s; (b) the time taken for the body to come to rest.

(a)
$$s = 40t - 5t^2$$
$$v = \frac{ds}{dt} = 40 - 10t$$
when $t = 2$
$$v = 40 - 20$$
$$= 20 \text{ m/s.}\quad \text{Ans. (a)}$$

(b)   When the body comes to rest, $v = 0$
$$\therefore 40 - 10t = 0$$
$$\therefore t = \frac{40}{10}$$
$$= 4 \text{ s}\quad \text{Ans. (b)}$$

MAXIMA AND MINIMA

An important application of differential calculus involves functions which have maximum or minimum values.

The graph shown below (Fig. 136) represents a function which has a local *maximum* value of y at point A and a local *minimum* value of y at B.

Such points are called *turning points* and have zero gradient.

i.e. at a turning point, $\dfrac{dy}{dx} = 0.$

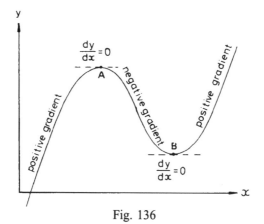

Fig. 136

Example.   The curve $y = 3x - x^2 + 1$ has a turning point.
(a) Find the value of x at which this occurs.
(b) Determine whether the turning point is a maximum or minimum value.
(c) Find the value of y at the turning point.

(a)
$$y = 3x - x^2 + 1$$
$$\frac{dy}{dx} = 3 - 2x$$

for turning points,
$$3 - 2x = 0$$
$$2x = 3$$
$$\therefore x = 1 \cdot 5 \quad \text{Ans. (a)}$$

(b) The nature of the turning point can be determined by sketching the curve:
From the sketch (Fig. 137), at $x = 1 \cdot 5$, a *maximum* value occurs.   Ans. (b).

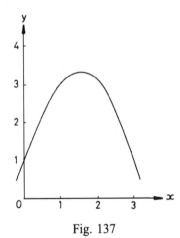

Fig. 137

(c) To find the maximum value of y, substitute $x = 1 \cdot 5$ in the original equation:

i.e. $y = (3 \times 1 \cdot 5) - (1 \cdot 5)^2 + 1$

$\therefore$ Maximum value of $y = 3 \cdot 25$.   Ans. (c)

Inspection of Fig. 136 shows that the gradient changes sign when passing through a turning point.

This presents an alternative test for maximum or minimum values:

(i) At a *maximum* value, the gradient dy/dx is *positive* before the turning point and *negative* after it.

Hence, dy/dx is *decreasing* in value, as x increases, i.e. the *rate of change* of dy/dx is negative.

$$\therefore \quad \frac{d^2y}{dx^2} \text{ is negative.}$$

(Note: since dy/dx is a gradient, the rate of change of the gradient is d^2y/dx^2).

(ii) At a *minimum* value, the gradient is *negative* before the turning point and *positive* after it.

Hence, dy/dx is *increasing* in value and the rate of change of dy/dx is positive.

$$\therefore \quad \frac{d^2y}{dx^2} \text{ is positive.}$$

Note: If a curve has a *point of inflexion* the gradient does not change sign when passing through this point, i.e. it is *stationary*, then both dy/dx and d^2y/dx^2 equal zero.

Summing up:

At a maximum value,

$$\frac{dy}{dx} = 0, \qquad \frac{d^2y}{dx^2} \text{ is negative.}$$

At a minimum value,

$$\frac{dy}{dx} = 0, \qquad \frac{d^2y}{dx^2} \text{ is positive.}$$

Example.

(a) Determine the values of x which give maximum or minimum values of y in the equation

$$y = x^3 - 6x^2 + 9x$$

(b) Calculate these maximum or minimum values of y.

(a)
$$\frac{dy}{dx} = 3x^2 - 12x + 9$$
$$\frac{d^2y}{dx^2} = 6x - 12.$$

For maximum or minimum values,

$$\frac{dy}{dx} = 0$$

i.e. $3x^2 - 12x + 9 = 0$

$x^2 - 4x + 3 = 0$

$\therefore (x - 1)(x - 3) = 0$

i.e. $(x - 1) = 0$ or $(x - 3) = 0$

$\therefore x = 1$ or $x = 3$

$\therefore$ Maximum or minimum values of y occur when $x = 1$ or $x = 3$.   Ans. (a).

(b) When $x = 1$,

$$\frac{d^2y}{dx^2} = 6 - 12 \quad \text{(i.e. negative)}$$

When $x = 3$,

$$\frac{d^2y}{dx^2} = 18 - 12 \quad \text{(positive)}$$

$\therefore$ When $x = 1$,

$$y = (1)^3 - 6(1)^2 + 9(1)$$

$\therefore$ Maximum value of $y = 4$ Ans. (b)

When $x = 3$

$$y = (3)^3 - 6(3)^2 + 9(3)$$

$\therefore$ Minimum value of $y = 0$ Ans. (b)

Note: These results are confirmed by the sketch of the graph shown in Fig. 138.

Example.   A rectangular sheet of steel is 60 cm wide and 28 cm long. Four square portions are to be removed at the corners and the sides turned up to form an open rectangular box.

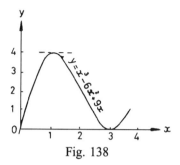

Fig. 138

Prove that, for this box to have maximum volume, its depth should be 6 cm.

Fig. 139a   Fig. 139b

Referring to Fig. 139a

let x = side of square removed

With the corner portions removed, the box is formed, with the dimensions shown (Fig. 139b)

let V = volume of box

then, $V = x(28 - 2x)(60 - 2x)$

$$V = 4x^3 - 176x^2 + 1680x$$

$$\therefore \frac{dV}{dx} = 12x^2 - 352x + 1680$$

for maximum (or minimum) value of V,

$$12x^2 - 352x + 1680 = 0$$

solve for x : $3x^2 - 88x + 420 = 0$

$$\therefore (3x - 70)(x - 6) = 0$$

hence, $3x - 70 = 0$ or, $x - 6 = 0$

$x = 23 \cdot 33$ or, $x = 6$

$\therefore x = 6$ cm   (rejecting the inadmissable solution)

Note: in a problem of this type, it is evident that $x = 6$ cm must give a *maximum* volume, and not a *minimum*.

The result can of course, be confirmed by differentiating again:

$$\frac{d^2y}{dx^2} = 24x - 352$$

When $x = 6$

$$\frac{d^2y}{dx^2} = 144 - 352$$
$$= -208 \quad \text{(negative)}$$

$\therefore$ Maximum volume is obtained when depth is 6 cm.   Ans.

DIFFERENTIATION OF SIN x, COS x

For any angle x,

$$\text{If} \quad y = \sin x, \qquad \frac{dy}{dx} = \cos x$$
$$\text{If} \quad y = \cos x, \qquad \frac{dy}{dx} = -\sin x$$

These differential coefficients can be demonstrated by reference to the sketch graphs of $\sin x$ and $\cos x$ (Fig. 140).

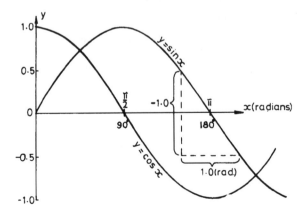

Fig. 140

For example, when $x = 180°$ (i.e. π rad):

$$\text{from the } \sin x \text{ curve, gradient} = \frac{-1}{1}$$

$$\text{i.e.} \quad \frac{dy}{dx} = -1$$

and, from the $\cos x$ curve, $\cos x = -1$

i.e. differential coefficient of $\sin x = \cos x$

Similarly, the gradient at any point on the $\cos x$ curve is numerically equal to the corresponding value of $\sin x$. In this case, however, the sign must be reversed, because the $\cos x$ curve has a *negative* gradient where $\sin x$ has *positive* values.

Example.   Differentiate the following expressions with respect to x:

(a) $y = -\sin x$

(b) $y = 2 \sin x$

(c) $y = 4 \sin x - 3 \cos x$

(a) $y = -\sin x$

$$\frac{dy}{dx} = -\cos x \quad \text{Ans. (a)}$$

(b) $y = 2 \sin x$

$$\frac{dy}{dx} = 2 \times \cos x$$

$$= 2 \cos x \quad \text{Ans. (b)}$$

(c) $y = 4 \sin x - 3 \cos x$

$$\frac{dy}{dx} = 4 \cos x + 3 \sin x \quad \text{Ans. (c)}$$

The *second differential coefficients* of $\sin x$ and $\cos x$ can be determined quite easily by repeated differentiation:

$$y = \sin x$$

$$\frac{dy}{dx} = \cos x$$

$$\frac{d^2y}{dx^2} = -\sin x$$

Similarly,
$$y = \cos x$$
$$\frac{dy}{dx} = -\sin x$$
$$\frac{d^2y}{dx^2} = -\cos x$$

Example.   Obtain the second differential coefficients of (a) $4\cos x$, (b) $\cos x - 2\sin x$.

(a) $y = 4\cos x$

$$\frac{dy}{dx} = -4\sin x$$

$$\frac{d^2y}{dx^2} = -4\cos x \quad \text{Ans. (a)}$$

(b) $y = \cos x - 2\sin x$

$$\frac{dy}{dx} = -\sin x - 2\cos x$$

$$\frac{d^2y}{dx^2} = -\cos x + 2\sin x \quad \text{Ans. (b)}$$

Note: It is seen that, for sines and cosines, the second differential coefficient is equal to the original function, but of the opposite sign.

DIFFERENTIAL COEFFICIENT OF $\ln x$ AND e^x

Naperian logarithms (ln) have special applications, for example, when finding the work done by an expanding gas.

When $y = \ln x$

$$\frac{dy}{dx} = \frac{1}{x}$$

When $y = e^x$

$$\frac{dy}{dx} = e^x$$

The proof of those relationships are beyond the scope of this work.

Example.   Obtain the second differential coefficient of the equations $y = \ln x$ and $y = e^x$.

$$y = \ln x$$

$$\frac{dy}{dx} = \frac{1}{x}$$

$$= x^{-1}$$

$$\frac{d^2y}{dx^2} = -x^{-2}$$

$$= -\frac{1}{x^2} \quad \text{Ans.}$$

$$y = e^x$$

$$\frac{dy}{dx} = e^x$$

$$\frac{d^2y}{dx^2} = e^x \quad \text{Ans.}$$

FUNCTIONAL NOTATION

In an equation such as $y = 2x$ or $y = 5x^3 + 3x$, the value of y obviously depends upon the value chosen for x. Hence, y is said to be a *function* of x and the general expression for such a relationship is:

$$y = f(x)$$

Functional notation may also be used to indicate the differentiation process, using the symbols shown below:

$$y = f(x)$$

$$\frac{dy}{dx} = f'(x)$$

$$\frac{d^2y}{dx^2} = f''(x)$$

For example if $\qquad\qquad y = 5x^3 + 2x$

then $\qquad\qquad\qquad f(x) = 5x^3 + 2x$

$$f'(x) = 15x^2 + 2$$

$$f''(x) = 30x.$$

TEST EXAMPLES 11

1. Differentiate the following equations with respect to x:
   (a) $y = x^3 + 3x^2 - 9x + 4$
   (b) $y = \dfrac{2x^3}{3} - \dfrac{7}{x^2} + x$
   (c) $y = \sqrt[5]{x^3} + 1$
   (d) $y = 5\cos x - 7\cos x + 2\sin x$

2. Calculate the gradient of the curve $x^2 + 3x - 7$ at the points where $x = 3$ and $x = -2$.

3. The displacement s metres of a body from a fixed point is given by the equation $s = 20t - 5t^2 + 4$ where t is the time in seconds. Find:
   (a) The velocity after 2 s
   (b) The displacement when the velocity is zero
   (c) The acceleration.

4. Determine the gradient of a tangent to any point in the curve
$$y = 4x + \frac{1}{x}$$
   Show that there are two points where the gradient is zero.

5. Find the co-ordinates of the point on the graph of $y = 3x^2 - x + 2$ at which the gradient is equal to -7.

6. The angle θ rad through which a shaft has turned after time t seconds is given by the equation
$$\theta = 2 + 16t - \frac{t^2}{2}.$$
   Find the angular velocity after 2 s and the time for the shaft to come to rest. (Note: angular velocity $\omega = d\theta/dt$).

7. (a) Determine the second differential coefficient of the expression $y = x^3 + 3_x + \ln x$ with respect to x.
   (b) Determine the second differential coefficient of the expression $y = 3\cos\theta - 7\cos\theta + \theta$ with respect to θ.

8. Determine the maximum value of y in the equation
$y = 12x + 3x^2 - 2x^3$.

9. For a beam of length l, the bending moment M at any distance x from one end is given by the equation

$$M = \frac{wlx}{2} - \frac{wx^2}{2}$$

where w is the uniform load per unit length. Show that bending moment is a maximum at the centre of the beam.

10. Differentiate the following equations:

(a) $t = 2 \cdot 1 \sqrt[3]{\frac{1}{\theta^2}} - \frac{4}{5\sqrt{\theta}}$ (b) $z = \frac{au^n - 1}{c}$

(c) $y = 3x(x^2 - 4)$ (d) $y = 2 \cos \theta + 5$

11. Determine the minimum value of $f(x)$ for the equation

$$f(x) = \frac{x^3}{3} - 2x^2 + 3x + 1$$

12. Power (P) and Voltage (V) of a lamp are related by $P = aV^b$, where a and b are constants. Find an expression for (a) the rate of change of power with voltage and (b) power per volt at 100 volts, when $a = 0 \cdot 5 \times 10^{-10}$ and $b = 6$.

13. A line of length l is to be cut up into four parts and put together as a rectangle. Show that the area of the rectangle will be a maximum if each of its sides is equal to one quarter of l (i.e. a square).

14. Determine the second differential coefficient of:
(a) $f(\theta) = \cos \theta - \ln \theta$
(b) $f(t) = at^2 + 2 \ln t$
(c) $f(x) = 5e^x$

15. A body moves so that its displacement (distance) x metres, which it travels from a certain point 0, is given by: $x = 0 \cdot 2t^2 + 10 \cdot 4$ where t is the time in seconds. Find the velocity and acceleration (a) 5 s

after the body begins to move and (b) when the displacement is 100 m.

16. Angular displacement (θ rad) from rest of a revolving wheel is given by: $\theta = 2{\cdot}1 - 3{\cdot}2t + 4{\cdot}8t^2$ where t is the time in seconds. Find the angular velocity and angular acceleration after 1·5 s.

17. Verify that the equation $f(x) = x^5 - 5x$ has a maximum and a minimum value and determine the value of x and $f(x)$ at these points.

18. The gradient function of $y = ax^2 + bx + c$ is $4x + 2$. The function has a minimum value of 1. Find the values of a, b and c.

CHAPTER 12

INTEGRAL CALCULUS

Integration may be considered as *reversing* the process of differentiation.

That is, given the differential coefficient of a function, we are required to find the original function.

The symbol $\int$ is used to denote the integration process. This is the old-fashioned letter 'S' and the reason for its use becomes evident when integration is used to find the 'sum' of a number of quantities.

CONSTANT OF INTEGRATION

Consider the three equations below:

$$y = x^2, \qquad y = x^2 + 3, \qquad y = x^2 + 7$$

For each of these equations,

$$\frac{dy}{dx} = 2x$$

Obviously, when reversing the differentiation process (i.e. *integrating*), provision must be made for the *possibility* of a *constant* in the original equation.

This is achieved by adding a constant, C, called the *constant of integration*.

$$\text{i.e.} \quad \int 2x \, dx = x^2 + C,$$

which may be interpreted as:
(the integral of) $2x$ (with respect to x) $= x^2 + C$.

GENERAL RULE FOR INTEGRATION

Consider the following differential equations:

$$\text{if} \quad y = \frac{x^2}{2}, \qquad \frac{dy}{dx} = x$$

$$\text{if} \quad y = \frac{x^3}{3}, \qquad \frac{dy}{dx} = x^2$$

$$\text{if} \quad y = \frac{x^4}{4}, \qquad \frac{dy}{dx} = x^3$$

From these equations, the following integrals are obtained:

$$\int x \, dx = \frac{x^2}{2} + C$$

$$\int x^2 \, dx = \frac{x^3}{3} + C$$

$$\int x^3 \, dx = \frac{x^4}{4} + C$$

It is seen that in each case, the procedure is to raise the power of x by 1 and divide by this raised power.

Expressing this mathematically, a general rule for integration is obtained, which includes a constant of integration:

$$\int x^n \, dx = \frac{x^{n+1}}{n+1} + C$$

Note: there is an important exception to this rule, the integral of x^{-1} or $1/x$, which is dealt with later.

Example.   Evaluate the following integrals:

(a) $\int x^7 dx$ (b) $\int 3x^5 dx$ (c) $\int \frac{x^{-4}}{3} dx$ (d) $\int 8dx$

(a)
$$\int x^7 dx = \frac{x^8}{8} + C \quad \text{Ans. (a)}$$

(b)
$$\int 3x^5 dx = 3 \times \frac{x^6}{6} + C$$
$$= \frac{x^6}{2} + C \quad \text{Ans. (b)}$$

(c)
$$\int \frac{x^{-4}}{3} dx = -\frac{x^{-3}}{9} + C$$
$$= -\frac{1}{9x^3} + C \quad \text{Ans. (c)}$$

(d)
$$\int 8 \, dx = 8x + C \quad \text{Ans. (d)}$$

This last result may be confirmed by differentiating the answer, or by applying the general rule, as shown:

$$\int 8 \, dx \quad \text{may be written as} \quad \int (8 \times x^0) \, dx, \quad \text{since } x^0 = 1.$$

Applying the general rule,

$$\int (8 \times x^0) \, dx = 8 \times \frac{x^1}{1} + C$$
$$= 8x + C$$

INTEGRATION OF A SUM OF TERMS

The integral of a sum of terms is equal to the sum of their separate integrals.

e.g.
$$\int (3x^2 + 7x - 10) \, dx = \int 3x^2 \, dx + \int 7x \, dx - \int 10 \, dx$$
$$= x^3 + \frac{7x^2}{2} - 10x + C$$

Note: the constants which should be added to each separate term are combined as a single constant.

Example.   Evaluate the integral

$$\int (x^2 - 3x^3 + 2) \, dx$$

$$\int (x^2 - 3x^3 + 2) \, dx = \frac{x^3}{3} - \frac{3x^4}{4} + 2x + C \quad \text{Ans.}$$

Example.   Integrate the expression $3t^2 + t + 1$ with respect to t.

$$\int (3t^2 + t + 1) \, dt = t^3 + \frac{t^2}{2} + t + C \quad \text{Ans.}$$

Example.   Integrate the expression $3x^2 - 6x + \frac{1}{2}$ with respect to x.

$$\int \left(3x^2 - 6x + \frac{1}{2}\right) dx = x^3 - 3x^2 + \frac{x}{2} + C \quad \text{Ans.}$$

EVALUATING THE CONSTANT OF INTEGRATION

The value of the constant of integration, for a given function, can be calculated, provided a corresponding pair of values of x and y are known.

Example.   The gradient of a curve is $4x + 5$. If the curve passes through the point $(x = 0, y = -4)$, find the equation of the curve.

$$\text{Gradient of curve} = \frac{dy}{dx} = 4x + 5$$

$$\therefore y = \int \left(\frac{dy}{dx}\right) dx$$

$$y = \int (4x + 5) \, dx$$

$$\therefore y = 2x^2 + 5x + C \qquad \text{(i)}$$

To find the constant of integration C, substitute $x = 0$, $y = -4$, in equation (i):

$$-4 = 2 \times (0)^2 + 5 \times (0) + C$$
$$\therefore C = -4$$

The equation of the curve is $y = 2x^2 + 5x - 4$.   Ans.

Example.   The curve of a graph has a gradient of $10x - x^2$. If the curve passes through the point (3, 52), find the equation of the graph.

$$\frac{dy}{dx} = 10x - x^2$$

$$y = \int (10x - x^2)\, dx$$

$$\therefore y = 5x^2 - \frac{x^3}{3} + C$$

Substituting $x = 3$, $y = 52$,

$$52 = 5(3)^2 - \frac{(3)^3}{3} + C$$

$$52 = 45 - 9 + C$$

$$\therefore C = 16$$

The equation is $y = 5x^2 - \dfrac{x^3}{3} + 16$ Ans.

INTEGRATION OF SIN x, COS x, $1/x$, e^x

The following differential coefficients are known:

$$y = \sin x, \qquad \frac{dy}{dx} = \cos x$$

$$y = \cos x, \qquad \frac{dy}{dx} = -\sin x$$

$$y = \ln x, \qquad \frac{dy}{dx} = \frac{1}{x}$$

$$y = e^x \qquad \frac{dy}{dx} = e^x$$

Reversing the process, the following integrals are obtained:

$$\int \cos x\, dx = \sin x + C$$

$$\int \sin x\, dx = -\cos x + C$$

$$\int \frac{1}{x}\, dx = \ln x + C$$

$$\int e^x\, dx = e^x + C$$

Example.   Evaluate the integral $\int (2\cos x - \sin x)dx$

$$\int (2\cos x - \sin x)\,dx = 2\sin x - (-\cos x) + C$$
$$= 2\sin x + \cos x + C \quad \text{Ans.}$$

Example.   Evaluate the integral $\int (\cos\theta + 5\sin\theta)$ with respect to θ.

$$\int (\cos\theta + 5\sin\theta)\,d\theta = \sin\theta - 5\cos\theta + C \quad \text{Ans.}$$

Example.   Evaluate the integral $\int (5/x)\,dx$.

$$\int \left(\frac{5}{x}\right) dx = \int \left(5 \times \frac{1}{x}\right) dx$$
$$= 5\ln x + C \quad \text{Ans.}$$

AREA BY INTEGRATION, DEFINITE INTEGRAL

In Fig. 141, the curve ac represents the sketch of a function of x. The area abc may be divided into a large number of strips, or *elements*, one of which is shown.

$$\text{Let } A = \text{area } abc$$
$$\delta A = \text{area of one strip}$$

If δx is made very small, the effect of the curve at the top of the strip becomes negligible. The strip may then be considered as a rectangle of height y and width δx.

$$\text{i.e.} \quad \delta A = y\,dx$$
$$\therefore \frac{\delta A}{\delta x} = y$$
$$\frac{dA}{dx} = \underset{\delta x \to 0}{\text{limit}} \frac{\delta A}{\delta x} = y$$

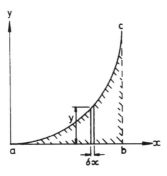

Fig. 141

Integrating both sides of this expression with respect to x,

$$\int \left(\frac{dA}{dx}\right) dx = \int (y) \, dx$$

$$\therefore A = \int y \, dx, \quad \text{between the limits}$$

$$x = a \quad \text{and} \quad x = b$$

This general rule is expressed mathematically as:

$$\text{Area} = \int_a^b y \, dx$$

Example.   Find the area between the curve $y = x^2$, the x axis and the ordinates $x = 2$ and $x = 4$ (Fig. 142).

$$\text{Area} = \int_a^b y \, dx$$

$$= \int_2^4 x^2 \, dx$$

$$= \frac{x^3}{3} + C \quad \text{between } x = 4 \text{ and } x = 2.$$

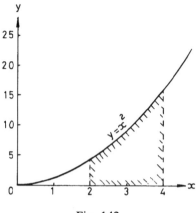

Fig. 142

when $x = 4$, $\dfrac{x^3}{3} + C = 21\frac{1}{3} + C$

when $x = 2$, $\dfrac{x^3}{3} + C = 2\frac{2}{3} + C$

Subtract:

$$\begin{aligned}
\text{Area} &= [21\tfrac{1}{3} + C] - [2\tfrac{2}{3} + C] \\
&= 21\tfrac{1}{3} + C - 2\tfrac{2}{3} - C \\
&= 18\tfrac{2}{3} \quad \text{units}^2. \quad \text{Ans.}
\end{aligned}$$

Note: The constant of integration C *always* disappears when integrating between limits.

Because of this, when an integral has limits, it is called a *definite integral*.

Example.   Find the area enclosed by the curve $y = x^2 + 2x + 1$, the x-axis, and the ordinates $x = 5$, $x = 2$.

The sketch graph of the equation is shown (Fig. 143).

$$\begin{aligned}
\text{Area} &= \int_a^b y\,dx \\
&= \int_2^5 (x^2 + 2x + 1)\,dx
\end{aligned}$$

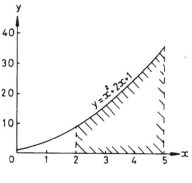

Fig. 143

Integrate: $\text{Area} = \left[\dfrac{x^3}{3} + x^2 + x\right]_2^3$

(The integral is inserted in square brackets, with upper and lower limits of x placed as shown above.)

Solve: $\text{Area} = \left[\dfrac{(5)^3}{3} + (5)^2 + 5\right] - \left[\dfrac{(2)^3}{3} + (2)^2 + 2\right]$

$= [41\tfrac{2}{3} + 25 + 5] - [2\tfrac{2}{3} + 4 + 2]$

$= 71\tfrac{2}{3} - 8\tfrac{2}{3}$

$= 63 \text{ units}^2. \quad \text{Ans.}$

Note: When an *area* is to be calculated, a sketch of the graph should always be made.

Other problems involving definite integrals may not require a sketch. In either case, the use of upper and lower limits eliminates the constant of integration.

Example.   Evaluate the definite integral $\int_{-1}^{1} (x^4 - 2x^2 + 1)\, dx$

$$\int_{-1}^{1} (x^4 - 2x^2 + 1)\, dx = \left[\frac{x^5}{5} - \frac{2x^3}{3} + x \right]_{-1}^{1}$$

$$= \left[\frac{(1)^5}{5} - \frac{2(1)^3}{3} + 1 \right]$$

$$- \left[\frac{(-1)^5}{5} - \frac{2(-1)^3}{3} + (-1) \right]$$

$$= \left[\frac{1}{5} - \frac{2}{3} + 1 \right] - \left[-\frac{1}{5} + \frac{2}{3} - 1 \right]$$

$$= \left[\frac{8}{15} \right] - \left[-\frac{8}{15} \right]$$

$$= \frac{16}{15}   \text{Ans.}$$

The arrangement of these solutions should be carefully noted.

The *lower* value of x must be placed at the *bottom* of the integral sign and the bracket.

The *upper* value of x must be at the *top* of the integral sign and bracket.

Example.   Evaluate the definite integral $\int_{0}^{\pi} (\sin x)\, dx$

Note: For this integral, upper limit $= \pi$ rad (i.e. 180°),
lower limit $= 0$ rad (i.e. 0°).

$$\int_{0}^{\pi} (\sin x)\, dx = [- \cos x]_{0}^{\pi}$$

$$= [- \cos \pi] - [- \cos 0]$$

$$= [-(-1)] - [-1]$$

$$= 1 + 1$$

$$= 2   \text{Ans.}$$

INTEGRATION AS A SUMMATION

In the previous section, it was shown that the area under a curve could be determined by dividing the area into very narrow strips.

Fig. 144

One such strip is shown in Fig. 144. The width of the strip may be represented by symbol dx if its width approaches zero value.

$$\text{Area of one strip} = y \times dx$$

The total area *abcd* could be obtained by adding together all these small areas, such as the one shown.

i.e.   Area *abcd* = the summation of all the areas such as ydx
between the limits $x = a$ and $x = b$

$$\therefore \text{Area} = \int_a^b y \, dx$$

Thus, the symbol $\int$ may be interpreted as meaning the summation of the quantities to which it is applied.

VOLUME OF A SOLID OF REVOLUTION

If a curve is rotated about the *x*-axis as shown, (Figs. 145a and 145b), the shape generated is called a *solid of revolution*.

The area under the curve is divided into a large number of elemental strips, such as the one shown (Fig. 145a).

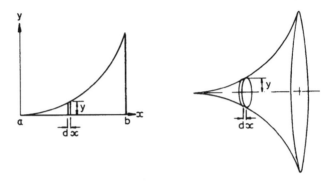

Fig. 145a   Fig. 145b

By rotating this element about the x-axis, a solid disc is generated (Fig. 145b).

Volume of one disc = cross-section area × thickness

$$= \pi y^2 \, dx$$

Total volume = the summation of the volumes of all such discs, between $x = a$ and $x = b$.

i.e.   Volume $= \displaystyle\int_a^b \pi y^2 \, dx$

Since the constant factor π is not affected by the integration process, the equation may be written:

$$\text{Volume of a solid of revolution} = \pi \int_a^b y^2 \, dx$$

Example.   Calculate the volume generated by rotating the curve $y = x^3$ about the x-axis between $x = 0$ and $x = 2$.

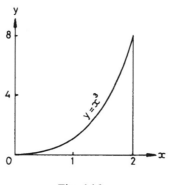

Fig. 146

Referring to Fig. 146:

$$V = \pi \int_a^b y^2 \, dx$$

where $y = x^3$, $a = 0$, $b = 2$.

$$\therefore V = \pi \int_0^2 (x^3)^2 \, dx$$

$$= \pi \int_0^2 x^6 \, dx$$

$$= \pi \left[\frac{x^7}{7} \right]_0^2$$

$$= \pi \left[\frac{2^7}{7} \right] - \pi[0]$$

$$= \pi[18 \cdot 28]$$

$$\therefore \text{Volume} = 57 \cdot 45 \text{ units}^3. \quad \text{Ans.}$$

Example. Use integral calculus to prove that the volume of a sphere is $\frac{4}{3}\pi r^3$ where r is the radius of the sphere.

Note: For convenience, the volume of a *hemisphere* is initially calculated.

From Figs 147a and 147b:

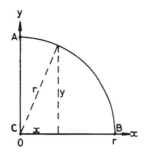

Fig. 147a   Fig. 147b

If the quadrant ABC is rotated about the x-axis, a hemisphere is generated. (Lower and upper limits of curve AB are $x = 0$, $x = r$.)

For any point on the curve AB:

by Pythagoras theorem: $y^2 = r^2 - x^2$

$$\therefore \text{ Volume of hemisphere} = \pi \int_a^b y^2 \, dx$$

$$= \pi \int_0^r (r^2 - x^2) \, dx$$

$$= \pi \left[r^2 x - \frac{x^3}{3} \right]_0^r$$

$$= \pi \left[r^3 - \frac{r^3}{3} \right] - 0$$

$$= \frac{2}{3} \pi r^3$$

$$\therefore \text{ Volume of sphere} = 2 \times \frac{2}{3} \pi r^3$$

$$= \frac{4}{3} \pi r^3 \quad \text{Ans.}$$

DISTANCE AND VELOCITY BY INTEGRATION

In the previous chapter, it was shown that the relation between distance s, time t and velocity v could be expressed as:

$$\frac{ds}{dt} = v$$

Integrating both sides of this equation with respect to t, the following equation is obtained:

$$s = \int v\, dt \qquad \ldots \quad \ldots \quad \ldots \quad \text{(i)}$$

Likewise, the relation between acceleration a, velocity and time was defined as:

$$\frac{dv}{dt} = a$$

Integrating both sides of this equation gives the following expression:

$$v = \int a\, dt \qquad \ldots \quad \ldots \quad \ldots \quad \text{(ii)}$$

Example. The velocity v of a body after time t is given by the expression $v = 10 - 2t$. If displacement (distance) $s = 24$ when $t = 2$, obtain an expression for distance s in terms of t.

$$s = \int v\, dt$$

$$= \int (10 - 2t)dt$$

$$\therefore s = 10t - t^2 + C \qquad \ldots \quad \ldots \quad \ldots \quad \text{(i)}$$

Substituting $s = 24$, $t = 2$, in equation (i),

$$24 = 20 - 4 + C$$

$$\therefore C = 8 \qquad \ldots \quad \ldots \quad \ldots \quad \ldots \quad \text{(ii)}$$

From equations (i) and (ii),

$$s = 10t - t^2 + 8 \quad \text{Ans.}$$

Example. The velocity v m/s after t seconds for a body is given by $v = 4 + 7t$. Find the distance travelled by the body in the interval from $t = 0$ to $t = 5$ s.

$$s = \int_0^5 v \, dt \quad \text{(note: definite integral)}$$

$$\therefore s = \int_0^5 (4 + 7t) \, dt$$

$$= \left[4t + \frac{7t^2}{2} \right]_0^5$$

$$= [107 \cdot 5] - [0]$$

$$\therefore \text{Distance} = 107 \cdot 5 \text{ m.} \quad \text{Ans.}$$

Example. A body moves such that its acceleration a m/s^2 after time t seconds is given by $a = 18 - 2t$.

(a) Derive an expression for the velocity v m/s of the body, given that $v = 20$ m/s when $t = 0$.

(b) Use the expression to find the velocity of the body after 3 s.

(a)
$$v = \int a \, dt$$

$$v = \int (18 - 2t) \, dt$$

$$\therefore v = 18t - t^2 + C \qquad \ldots \quad \ldots \quad \ldots \quad \text{(i)}$$

Substitute $v = 20$, $t = 0$ in equation (i),

$$20 = 0 - 0 + C$$

$$\therefore C = 20 \qquad \ldots \quad \ldots \quad \ldots \quad \ldots \quad \text{(ii)}$$

From equations (i) and (ii),

$$v = 18t - t^2 + 20 \quad \text{Ans. (a)}$$

(b) When
$$t = 3$$
$$v = 54 - 9 + 20$$
$$\therefore \text{Velocity} = 65 \text{ m/s.} \quad \text{Ans. (b)}$$

TEST EXAMPLES 12

1. Evaluate the following integrals:

    (a) $\int (x^4 + x^2 - 8x + 5)\, dx$

    (b) $\int \left(\dfrac{4}{x^2} + \dfrac{1}{x} \right) dx$

    (c) $\int_1^3 (2x - 3x^2 - 1)\, dx$

2. A curve has a gradient of $x^2 + x - 2$. If the curve passes through the point $x = 2$, $y = 5$, find its equation.

3. Evaluate the integrals:

    (a) $\int (3\cos x - 2\sin x + 4)\, dx$

    (b $\int (4\cos x - \cos x + x)\, dx$

    (c) $\int_0^{\pi/2} \cos x\, dx$

4. Find the area between the curve $y = x^3 - 4x^2 + 3x$ and the x-axis between the limits $x = 1$ and $x = 3$.

5. The curve shown overleaf (Fig. 148) was plotted during the isothermal expansion of a gas, following the law $pV = C$, between volume V_1 and V_2. Show that the area under the graph $= pV \ln V_2/V_1$.

6. The acceleration a m/s^2 of a body is given by the equation $a = 6t$.
    (a) Use calculus to obtain an expression for velocity v after t seconds given that $v = 0$ when $t = 0$.
    (b) Calculate the *average* velocity during the period $t = 2$ to $t = 3$.
    (c) Calculate the *instantaneous* velocity at $t = 2 \cdot 5$.

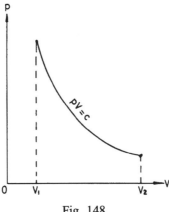

Fig. 148

7. The velocity v m/s of a body after time t seconds is given by the equation $v = 3t^2 + 8t + 12$. Find the displacement of s metres for the body after 10 s, given that $s = 10$ when $t = 0$.

8. A cone is generated by rotating the line $y = x/2$ about the x-axis from $x = 0$ to $x = 6$. Calculate the volume of the cone.

9. Find the volume generated by rotating about the x-axis that part of the curve $y = x^2 - x$ which lies between its intersections with the x-axis.

10. Evaluate the following integrals:

(a) $\int (x+1)(x+2)\,dx$ (b) $\int \left(\frac{1}{x} - \frac{1}{x^2}\right)dx$

(c) $\int_1^2 (a+2b)(x+1)\,dx$ (d) $\int 3e^x\,dx$

11. Evaluate the area enclosed by the curve $f(x) = 0.06x^2 + 10$, the x axis and the ordinates $x = 6$ and $x = 8$.

12. A gas is compressed from a volume of V_1 to a volume of V_2 according to the law $pV^n = C$, where p is the pressure and C is a constant. Show that the area under the compression curve on a

pressure-volume diagram, between the stated volume limits, is given by:

$$\text{Area} = \frac{-C}{n-1}\left(\frac{1}{V_2^{n-1}} - \frac{1}{V_1^{n-1}}\right)$$

13. Evaluate the following integrals:

(a) $\int\left(\sin\theta - \frac{1}{2}\right)\frac{d\theta}{3}$

(b) $\int_0^\pi \sin x \, dx$

(c) $\int_0^{\pi/2} (5\cos x + 3\sin x - x)\, dx$

14. Find the volume of the ellipsoid formed by rotating the ellipse $x^2/a^2 + y^2/b^2 = 1$, of major axis 2a and minor axis 2b, about the major axis.

15. A particle is projected with a horizontal velocity (u) and moves into a resisting medium so that at time (t) its acceleration (dv/dt) equals a constant (k) multiplied by its velocity (v). Show that:

$$\ln\frac{v}{u} = -kt$$

16. Sketch the curve and find an expression for the area between the limits $x=0$ and $x=1$, the curve $y = b/x + a$ and the x axis. Evaluate this area when $a=1$ and $b=2$.

17. Evaluate the following integrals:

(a) $\int \frac{3}{x}dx$ (b) $\int \frac{1}{a}x^3 dx$

(c) $\int (4z^3 + 3z^2 + 2z + 1)dz$ (d) $\int (2\cos\theta - 5\sin\theta)d\theta$

18. A particle P starts from rest at 0 with a velocity of 5 m/s and moves along a straight line OX with an acceleration of $-2t^2$ at time t seconds after leaving 0. Describe the motion after 3 s.

SELECTION OF RULES AND FORMULAE

FROM THE CHAPTERS OF THIS BOOK

LAWS OF INDICES

$$x^m \times x^n = x^{m+n}$$

$$x^m \div x^n = x^{m-n}$$

$$(x^m)^n = x^{m \times n} \text{ written } x^{mn}$$

$$x^{-n} = \frac{1}{x^n}$$

$$x^{1/n} = \sqrt[n]{x}$$

$$x^{m/n} = \sqrt[n]{x^m}$$

$$1^m = 1 \text{ for all values of } m$$

$$x^1 = x$$

$$x^0 = 1 \text{ for all values of } x \text{ except when } x = 0$$

LOGARITHMS

$$\log_x N = n \text{ means } x^n = N$$

$$\log(x \times y) = \log x + \log y$$

$$\log(x \div y) = \log x - \log y$$

$$\log(x^m) = (\log x) \times m$$

$$\log \sqrt[m]{x} = (\log x) \div m$$

$$\log_b N = \frac{\log_a N}{\log_a b}$$

$$\ln N = 2{\cdot}3026 \times \lg N$$

ALGEBRA

$$x^2 - y^2 = (x + y)(x - y)$$
$$x^4 - y^4 = (x^2 + y^2)(x^2 - y^2)$$
$$x^3 + y^3 = (x + y)(x^2 - xy + y^2)$$
$$x^3 - y^3 = (x - y)(x^2 + xy + y^2)$$
$$(x + y)^2 = x^2 + 2xy + y^2$$
$$(x - y)^2 = x^2 - 2xy + y^2$$
$$(x + y)^3 = x^3 + 3x^2y + 3xy^2 + y^3$$
$$(x - y)^3 = x^3 - 3x^2y + 3xy^2 - y^3$$

Linear equation: $y = a + bx$

Quadratic equation: $y = ax^2 + bx + c$

Roots of quadratic equation of the form:

$$ax^2 + bx + c = 0$$

are:

$$x = \frac{-b \pm \sqrt{b^2 - 4ac}}{2a}$$

TRIGONOMETRY AND GEOMETRY

$$\sin\theta = \frac{\text{opposite}}{\text{hypotenuse}}$$

$$\cos\theta = \frac{\text{adjacent}}{\text{hypotenuse}}$$

$$\tan\theta = \frac{\text{opposite}}{\text{adjacent}}$$

$$\operatorname{cosec}\theta = \frac{1}{\sin\theta} = \frac{\text{hypotenuse}}{\text{opposite}}$$

$$\sec\theta = \frac{1}{\cos\theta} = \frac{\text{hypotenuse}}{\text{adjacent}}$$

$$\cot\theta = \frac{1}{\tan\theta} = \frac{\text{adjacent}}{\text{opposite}}$$

$$\text{Hypotenuse}^2 = \text{opposite}^2 + \text{adjacent}^2$$

$$\tan \theta = \frac{\sin \theta}{\cos \theta}$$

$$\sin^2 \theta + \cos^2 \theta = 1$$

$$\operatorname{cosec}^2 \theta - \cot^2 \theta = 1$$

$$\sec^2 \theta - \tan^2 \theta = 1$$

$$\sin (A + B) = \sin A \cos B + \cos A \sin B$$

$$\sin (A - B) = \sin A \cos B - \cos A \sin B$$

$$\cos (A + B) = \cos A \cos B - \sin A \sin B$$

$$\cos (A - B) = \cos A \cos B + \sin A \sin B$$

$$\tan (A + B) = \frac{\tan A + \tan B}{1 - \tan A \tan B}$$

$$\tan (A - B) = \frac{\tan A - \tan B}{1 + \tan A \tan B}$$

$$\sin 2A = 2 \sin A \cos A$$

$$\cos 2A = \cos^2 A - \sin^2 A$$

$$\cos 2A = 1 - 2 \sin^2 A$$

$$\cos 2A = 2 \cos^2 A - 1$$

$$\tan 2A = \frac{2 \tan A}{1 - \tan^2 A}$$

SINE RULE:
$$\frac{a}{\sin A} = \frac{b}{\sin B} = \frac{c}{\sin C}$$

COSINE RULE:
$$a^2 = b^2 + c^2 - 2bc \cos A$$

$$\cos A = \frac{b^2 + c^2 - a^2}{2bc}$$

CROSSED CHORDS:
$$ao \times bo = co \times do$$

CYCLIC TRIANGLES:

Angles in the same segment of a circle are equal.

The angle in a semi-circle is a right angle.

The angle at the centre of a circle is double the angle at the circumference for triangles in the same segment and on the same chord.

CIRCULAR MEASURE:

$$\pi = 3 \cdot 142 = \tfrac{22}{7}$$

$$\frac{\pi}{4} = 0 \cdot 7854 = \tfrac{11}{14}$$

Circumference of circle $= \pi d = 2\pi r$

Circumference of ellipse $= \pi \left\{ \dfrac{D + d}{2} \right\}$ approx:

One circle $= 360° = 2\pi$ rad.

One rad $= 57 \cdot 3°$

Length of arc $= \theta r$

Linear velocity $= \omega r$

PLANE AREAS

$$\text{Area of circle} = \pi r^2 = \frac{\pi}{4} d^2$$

$$\text{Area of annulus} = \pi (R^2 - r^2) = \frac{\pi}{4} (D^2 - d^2)$$

$$\text{Area of ellipse} = \pi R r = \frac{\pi}{4} D d$$

Area of parallelogram $=$ base $\times$ perp. height

Area of rhombus $= \tfrac{1}{2}$ product of diagonals

Area of trapezium $= \tfrac{1}{2}$ sum of parallel sides
$\times$ perp. distance between

$$\text{Area of sector} = \frac{\theta°}{360} \times \pi r^2$$

Area of segment $= \tfrac{1}{2} r^2 (\theta - \sin \theta)$

Area of triangle $= \tfrac{1}{2} ($base $\times$ perp. height$)$

$$= \tfrac{1}{2} (ab \sin C)$$

$$= \sqrt{s(s - a)(s - b)(s - c)}$$

Area of equilateral triangle $= 0 \cdot 433$ side^2

Area of hexagon $=$ six equilateral triangles

Area of irregular figure by Simpson's rule: To the first and last ordinates add four times the even ordinates and twice the odd, multiply this sum by one-third the common interval between ordinates. In symbols:

$$= \frac{h}{3}(a + 4b + 2c + 4d + e)$$

SURFACE AREAS

$$\text{Curved surface of cylinder} = \pi dh$$
$$\text{Curved surface of sphere} = \pi d^2$$
$$\text{Curved surface of cone} = \pi rl$$
$$\text{Curved surface of frustum} = \pi l(R + r)$$

VOLUMES

$$\text{Volume of prism} = \text{area of end} \times \text{length.}$$
$$\text{Volume of cone and pyramid} = \tfrac{1}{3}(\text{area of base} \times \text{perp. height})$$
$$\text{Volume of sphere} = \frac{\pi}{6}d^3 = \frac{4}{3}\pi r^3$$
$$\text{Volume of spherical segment} = \frac{\pi}{6}h^2(3d - 2h)$$
$$\text{Volume of frustum of cone} = \tfrac{1}{12}\pi h(D^2 + Dd + d^2)$$
$$= \tfrac{1}{3}\pi h(R^2 + Rr + r^2)$$

CENTROIDS AND CENTRES OF GRAVITY

$$\text{Triangle} = \tfrac{1}{3} \text{ height from base}$$
$$\text{Pyramid} = \tfrac{1}{4} \text{ height from base}$$
$$\text{Semi-circular area} = 0 \cdot 424 \, r \text{ from diameter}$$
$$\text{Hemisphere} = 0 \cdot 375 \, r \text{ from diameter}$$

CALCULUS

$\dfrac{dy}{dx}$	y	$\displaystyle\int y\,dx$
1	x	$\dfrac{x^2}{2} + C$
0	a	$ax + C$
1	$x + a$	$\dfrac{x^2}{2} + ax + C$
a	ax	$\dfrac{ax^2}{2} + C$
nx^{n-1}	x^n	$\dfrac{x^{n+1}}{n+1} + C$
$\cos x$	$\sin x$	$-\cos x + C$
$-\sin x$	$\cos x$	$\sin x + C$
$-x^{-2}$	$\dfrac{1}{x}$ (i.e. x^{-1})	$\ln x + C$
e^x	e^x	$e^x + C$

$$\text{Maximum} \quad \frac{dy}{dx} = 0 \quad \frac{d^2y}{dx^2} \text{ is negative}$$

$$\text{Minimum} \quad \frac{dy}{dx} = 0 \quad \frac{d^2y}{dx^2} \text{ is positive}$$

$$\text{Area} = \int_a^b y\,dx$$

$$\text{Volume} = \pi \int_a^b y^2\,dx$$

$$\frac{ds}{dt} = v \quad \text{and} \quad s = \int v\,dt$$

$$\frac{dv}{dt} = a \quad \text{and} \quad v = \int a\,dt$$

SOLUTIONS TO TEST EXAMPLES 1

1.
$$\frac{10^{\frac{3}{2}} \times 10^4 \times 10^{\frac{3}{4}}}{10^3 \times 10^{\frac{1}{4}} \times 10^2}$$

$$= \frac{10^{6\frac{1}{4}}}{10^{5\frac{1}{4}}} = 10^1 = 10 \quad Ans.$$

2.
$$\frac{4^2 \times 4^{\frac{2}{3}} \times 4^{-2}}{4^{\frac{1}{2}} \times 4^{\frac{1}{6}}}$$

$$= \frac{4^{\frac{2}{3}}}{4^{\frac{2}{3}}} = 4^\circ = 1 \quad Ans.$$

3.
$$\frac{8^{-2}}{8^{-5}}$$

(Note result of subtracting -5 from -2 is $+3$)

$$= 8^3 = 512 \quad Ans.$$

4.
$$\frac{(3^{\frac{2}{5}})^{\frac{5}{3}} \times \sqrt{3} \times 3}{3^{-\frac{4}{3}} \times 3^3}$$

$$= \frac{3^{\frac{2}{3}} \times 3^{\frac{1}{2}} \times 3}{3^{-\frac{4}{3}} \times 3^3}$$

$$= \frac{3^{\frac{13}{6}}}{3^{\frac{5}{3}}} = 3^{\frac{1}{2}} = \sqrt{3} = 1 \cdot 732 \quad Ans.$$

5.
$$(1\tfrac{2}{3})^2 + \sqrt{\tfrac{4}{81}} + \sqrt{200}$$

$$= \left(\frac{5}{3}\right)^2 + \frac{\sqrt{4}}{\sqrt{81}} + \sqrt{2} \times \sqrt{100}$$

$$= \frac{25}{9} + \frac{2}{9} + 1 \cdot 414 \times 10$$

$$= \frac{27}{9} + 14 \cdot 14 = 3 + 14 \cdot 14$$

$$= 17 \cdot 14 \quad Ans.$$

6.
$$\frac{(2^2)^3 \times \sqrt{3} \times 27^{\frac{2}{3}} \times \sqrt{12}}{\sqrt[4]{81} \times 4^{\frac{3}{2}}}$$

$$= \frac{2^6 \times \sqrt{3} \times 3^2 \times \sqrt{3} \times \sqrt{4}}{3 \times 2^3}$$

$$= \frac{2^6 \times 3 \times 3^2 \times 2}{3 \times 2^3}$$

$$= 2^4 \times 3^2 = 16 \times 9 = 144 \quad \text{Ans.}$$

7. Let x represent volume of second sphere

1st vol. : 2nd vol. : : 1st dia.^{3} : 2nd dia.^{3}

$$24 \cdot 25 \quad : \quad x \quad : : \quad 1^3 \quad : 2^3$$

$$24 \cdot 25 \quad : \quad x \quad : : \quad 1 \quad : 8$$

$$x \times 1 \ = 24 \cdot 25 \times 8$$

$$x = 194 \text{ cm}^3 \quad \text{Ans.}$$

8.   Quantity pumped by 1st pump in 1 h $= \frac{1}{12}$ of tank

Quantity pumped by 2nd pump in 1 h $= \frac{1}{4}$ of tank

Quantity pumped by 3rd pump in 1 h $= \frac{1}{9}$ of tank

When all three pumps are working together,

$$\text{Quantity pumped per hour} = \frac{1}{12} + \frac{1}{4} + \frac{1}{9}$$

$$= \frac{3+9+4}{36} = \frac{16}{36}$$

$$= \frac{4}{9} \text{ of tank}$$

$\therefore$ Time to empty whole tank $= \frac{9}{4}$ h $= 2\frac{1}{4}$ h.   Ans.

9. $$\text{Strength} \propto \text{breadth} \times \text{depth}^2 \times \frac{1}{\text{length}}$$

$$\therefore \quad \frac{\text{Strength} \times \text{length}}{\text{breadth} \times \text{depth}^2} = \text{constant}$$

$$\frac{S_1 \times l_1}{b_1 \times d_1{}^2} = \frac{S_2 \times l_2}{b_2 \times d_2{}^2} \quad S_1 = S_2 \text{ and cancels}$$

$$\frac{5}{40 \times 100^2} = \frac{3}{b_2 \times 80^2}$$

$$b_2 = \frac{40 \times 10\ 000 \times 3}{5 \times 6400}$$

$$= 37 \cdot 5 \text{ mm} \quad \text{Ans.}$$

10. $$\text{Elongation} = 62 \cdot 5 - 50$$

$$= 12 \cdot 5 \text{ mm}$$

$$\% \text{ elongation} = \frac{\text{elongation}}{\text{original length}} \times 100$$

$$= \frac{12 \cdot 5}{50} \times 100 = 25 \quad \text{Ans. (i)}$$

$$\text{Reduction in area} = 80 - 48$$

$$= 32 \text{ mm}^2$$

$$\% \text{ reduction in area} = \frac{\text{reduction}}{\text{original area}} \times 100$$

$$= \frac{32}{80} \times 100 = 40 \quad \text{Ans. (ii)}$$

11. Ratio of powers,

	No. 1	No. 2	No. 3
$=$	115	: 95	: 100
$=$	1·15	: 0·95	: 1

$$1 \cdot 15 + 0 \cdot 95 + 1 = 3 \cdot 1$$

% of total power developed in No. 1 cylinder

$$= \frac{1 \cdot 15}{3 \cdot 1} \times 100 = 37 \cdot 1 \quad \text{Ans. (i)}$$

% of total power developed in No. 2 cylinder

$$= \frac{0 \cdot 95}{3 \cdot 1} \times 100 = 30 \cdot 6 \quad \text{Ans. (ii)}$$

% of total power developed in No. 3 cylinder

$$= \frac{1}{3 \cdot 1} \times 100 = 32 \cdot 3 \quad \text{Ans. (iii)}$$

12.   % zinc content $= 100 - (71 + 1 + 3)$

$$= 100 - 75 = 25$$

Total mass of alloy $= 500$ kg

$$\text{Mass of copper} = \frac{71}{100} \times 500 = 355 \text{ kg}$$

$$\text{Mass of tin} = \frac{1}{100} \times 500 = 5 \text{ kg}$$

$$\text{Mass of lead} = \frac{3}{100} \times 500 = 15 \text{ kg} \quad \Bigg\} \quad \text{Ans.}$$

$$\text{Mass of zinc} = \frac{25}{100} \times 500 = 125 \text{ kg}$$

$$\text{Total} = 500 \text{ kg}$$

13. Sum of measurements

$$= 27 + 39 + 47 + 51 + 48 + 32 + 20 + 11 + 8 + 5$$

$$= 288 \text{ mm}$$

Total number of readings $= 10$

$$\text{Mean height} = \frac{\text{total of measurements}}{\text{total number of readings}}$$

$$= \frac{288}{10}$$

$$= 28 \cdot 8 \text{ mm} \quad \text{Ans.}$$

14.   Cost of 200 t @ £60/t $= £12\ 000$

Cost of 600 t @ £70/t $= £42\ 000$

$$\text{Total cost} = £54\ 000$$

Total number of tonnes $= 200 + 600 = 800$

$$\text{Average cost} = \frac{\text{total cost}}{\text{total number of tonnes}}$$

$$= \frac{54\ 000}{800}$$

$$= £67 \cdot 50/t \quad \text{Ans.}$$

As explained in the text it is essential to divide one *total* quantity by another *total* quantity to obtain an average. Note that the average cost is *not*

$$\frac{£60 + £70}{2} = £65$$

15.
$$\ln\frac{850}{492} + \frac{840}{850} + 0 \cdot 6\ln\frac{1160}{850}$$
$$= \ln 1 \cdot 728 + 0 \cdot 9883 + 0 \cdot 6\ln 1 \cdot 365$$
$$= 0 \cdot 5469 + 0 \cdot 9883 + 0 \cdot 1867$$
$$= 1 \cdot 7219 \quad \text{Ans.}$$

16.
$$\log_b N = \frac{\log_a N}{\log_a b}$$
$$\log_2 N = \frac{\lg N}{\lg 2}$$
$$= \frac{\lg N}{0 \cdot 3010} = \lg N \times \frac{1}{0 \cdot 3010}$$
$$= \lg N \times 3 \cdot 322$$

$\therefore$ Converting multiplier is $3 \cdot 322$ Ans.

17. By common logs:

$$\lg 0 \cdot 06326^{-0 \cdot 25} = \bar{2} \cdot 8011 \times (-0 \cdot 25)$$
$$= -1 \cdot 1989 \times (-0 \cdot 25)$$
$$= 0 \cdot 2997$$
$$\text{Antilog} = 1 \cdot 994 \quad \text{Ans. } (a)$$

By natural logs:

$$\ln 0 \cdot 06326^{-0 \cdot 25} = (\ln 6 \cdot 326 + \ln 10^{-2}) \times (-0 \cdot 25)$$
$$= (1 \cdot 8446 + \bar{5} \cdot 3948) \times (-0 \cdot 25)$$
$$= \bar{3} \cdot 2394 \times (-0 \cdot 25)$$
$$= -2 \cdot 7606 \times (-0 \cdot 25)$$
$$= 0 \cdot 6901$$
$$\text{Antilog} = 1 \cdot 994 \quad \text{Ans. } (b)$$

Note. In Example 17 (and 18) tables have been used. A calculator simplifies the work as the minus number can be entered directly and the use of bar quantities is avoided.

18. Finding the logs:

$$\ln 2 \cdot 55 = 0 \cdot 9361$$

$$\ln 0 \cdot 08234 = \ln 8 \cdot 234 + \ln 10^{-2}$$

$$= 2 \cdot 1083 + \bar{5} \cdot 3948$$

$$= \bar{3} \cdot 5031 \quad \text{(i.e. } -2 \cdot 4969)$$

$$\ln 0 \cdot 36 = \ln 3 \cdot 6 + \ln 10^{-1}$$

$$= 1 \cdot 2809 + \bar{3} \cdot 6974$$

$$= \bar{2} \cdot 9783 \quad \text{(i.e. } -1 \cdot 0217)$$

$$\ln 10 \cdot 2 = \ln 1 \cdot 02 + \ln 10$$

$$= 0 \cdot 0198 + 2 \cdot 3026$$

$$k = 2 \cdot 55 \times \sqrt{\frac{0 \cdot 08234}{0 \cdot 36 \times 10 \cdot 2}}$$

$$\ln k = 0 \cdot 9361 + \{\bar{3} \cdot 5031 - (\bar{2} \cdot 9783 + 2 \cdot 3224)\} \div 2$$

$$= 0 \cdot 9361 + \{\bar{3} \cdot 5031 - 1 \cdot 3007\} \div 2$$

$$= 0 \cdot 9361 + \bar{4} \cdot 2024 \div 2$$

$$= 0 \cdot 9361 + \bar{2} \cdot 1012$$

$$= \bar{1} \cdot 0373 \quad \text{(i.e. } -0 \cdot 9627)$$

To find antilog:

subtract $\ln 10^{-1}$ i.e. $\bar{3} \cdot 6974$ (i.e. $-2 \cdot 3026$)

$$\bar{1} \cdot 0373 - \bar{3} \cdot 6974 = 1 \cdot 3399$$

$$\text{Antilog of } 1 \cdot 3399 = 3 \cdot 819$$

$$\text{Antilog of } \bar{1} \cdot 0373 = 3 \cdot 819 \times 10^{-1}$$

$$k = 0 \cdot 3819 \quad \text{Ans.}$$

SOLUTIONS TO TEST EXAMPLES 2

1. (i)

$$3x + 4y - 5z$$
$$\text{add} \quad -2x - 5y + 4z$$
$$\overline{\quad x - \ y - \ z} \quad \text{Ans.}$$

(ii)

$$2a^2b - ab + 3ab^2$$
$$\text{add} \quad -a^2b + ab + 5ab^2$$
$$\overline{\quad a^2b + \qquad 8ab^2} \quad \text{Ans.}$$

(iii)

$$\text{From} \quad 5x + 3y - 4z$$
$$\text{subtract} \quad 2x + 5y - 3z$$
$$\overline{\quad 3x - 2y - \ z} \quad \text{Ans.}$$

(iv)

$$\text{From} \quad 3a - 2b + \ 6c$$
$$\text{subtract} \quad -a - 5b - \ 4c$$
$$\overline{\quad 4a + 3b + 10c} \quad \text{Ans.}$$

2. (i)

$$5x - 3z - 4x - 2y + 4y + 2z - y$$
$$= 5x - 4x - 2y + 4y - y - 3z + 2z$$
$$= x + y - z \quad \text{Ans.}$$

(ii)

$$2{\cdot}5a + c - 1{\cdot}2a + 2{\cdot}5b - 3c + b + 1{\cdot}7a$$
$$= 2{\cdot}5a - 1{\cdot}2a + 1{\cdot}7a + 2{\cdot}5b + b + c - 3c$$
$$= 3a + 3{\cdot}5b - 2c \quad \text{Ans.}$$

(iii)

$$b^2 - 3ab^2 + 2a^2b - 4a^2 - 2b^2 + 5a^2 - 2ab^2$$
$$= -4a^2 + 5a^2 + 2a^2b - 3ab^2 - 2ab^2 + b^2 - 2b^2$$
$$= a^2 + 2a^2b - 5ab^2 - b^2 \quad \text{Ans.}$$

3. (i)
$$\frac{x \times x^3 \times x^5}{x^2 \times x^4}$$
$$= x^{1+3+5-2-4}$$
$$= x^3 \quad \text{Ans. (i)}$$

(ii)
$$x^5 \times x^{-3} \times x^{-2}$$
$$= x^{5-3-2} = x^0$$
$$= 1 \quad \text{Ans. (ii)}$$

(iii)
$$\sqrt{x} \times x^{\frac{1}{2}} \times x^{-\frac{1}{3}}$$
$$= x^{\frac{1}{2}+\frac{1}{2}-\frac{1}{3}} = x^{\frac{2}{3}}$$
$$\text{or } \sqrt[3]{x^2} \quad \text{Ans. (iii)}$$

(iv)
$$\sqrt[2]{(x^4 y^2)}$$
$$= x^2 y \quad \text{Ans. (iv)}$$

(v)
$$\frac{x^3}{x^3 - 0 \cdot 5x^3} = \frac{x^3}{0 \cdot 5x^3}$$
$$= \frac{1}{0 \cdot 5} = 2 \quad \text{Ans. (v)}$$

4. (i) $(x + 2y)(2x + y) = 2x^2 + 5xy + 2y^2$ Ans. (i)
    (ii) $(2x + y)(3x - 2y) = 6x^2 - xy - 2y^2$ Ans. (ii)
    (iii) $(3x - 4y)(2x - 3y) = 6x^2 - 17xy + 12y^2$ Ans. (iii)

5. (i) $(a + b)^2 = (a + b)(a + b) = a^2 + 2ab + b^2$ Ans. (i)
    (ii) $(a - b)^2 = (a - b)(a - b) = a^2 - 2ab + b^2$ Ans. (ii)
    (iii) $(a + b)^3 = (a + b)^2 \times (a + b) = (a^2 + 2ab + b^2) \times (a + b)$

$$
\begin{array}{l}
a^2 + 2ab + b^2 \\
\underline{ a \; + \; b} \\
a^3 + 2a^2b + ab^2 \\
\underline{ a^2b + 2ab^2 + b^3} \\
a^3 + 3a^2b + 3ab^2 + b^3 \quad \text{Ans. (iii)}
\end{array}
$$

(iv) $(a-b)^3 = (a-b)^2 \times (a-b) = (a^2 - 2ab + b^2) \times (a-b)$

$$a^2 - 2ab + b^2$$
$$a \quad - \quad b$$
$$\overline{a^3 - 2a^2b + ab^2}$$
$$- \quad a^2b + 2ab^2 - b^3$$
$$\overline{a^3 - 3a^2b + 3ab^2 - b^3} \quad \text{Ans. (iv)}$$

6. (i) $2a - 3b)8a^2 - 8ab - 6b^2(4a + 2b$ Ans. (i)

$$\overline{8a^2 - 12ab}$$
$$4ab - 6b^2$$
$$\overline{4ab - 6b^2}$$

(ii) $3x - 4y)9x^3 - 9x^2y - 10xy^2 + 8y^3(3x^2 + xy - 2y^2$ Ans. (ii)

$$\overline{9x^3 - 12x^2y}$$
$$3x^2y - 10xy^2$$
$$\overline{3x^2y - 4xy^2}$$
$$- \quad 6xy^2 + 8y^3$$
$$\overline{- \quad 6xy^2 + 8y^3}$$

(iii) $x - y)x^3 - y^3(x^2 + xy + y^2)$ Ans. (iii)

$$\overline{x^3 - x^2y}$$
$$+ \quad x^2y - y^3$$
$$\overline{x^2y - xy^2}$$
$$+ \quad xy^2 - y^3$$
$$\overline{xy^2 - y^3}$$

7. (i) $(a+b) + (c-d) - (a-b) - (c+d) + (a-b)$
$$= a+b+c-d-a+b-c-d+a-b$$
$$= a-a+a+b+b-b+c-c-d-d$$
$$= a+b-2d \quad \text{Ans. (i)}$$

(ii)

$$2\{a - 3(a + 2) + 4(2a - 1) + 5\}$$
$$= 2\{a - 3a - 6 + 8a - 4 + 5\}$$
$$= 2a - 6a - 12 + 16a - 8 + 10$$
$$= 12a - 10 \quad \text{Ans. (ii)}$$

(iii)

$$2x - [2x - \{2x - (2x - 2) - 2\} - 2] - 2$$
$$= 2x - [2x - \{2x - 2x + 2 - 2\} - 2] - 2$$
$$= 2x - [2x - 2x + 2x - 2 + 2 - 2] - 2$$
$$= 2x - 2x + 2x - 2x + 2 - 2 + 2 - 2$$
$$= 0 \quad \text{Ans. (iii)}$$

8. (i)

$$3b^2 - 6b + 9$$
$$= 3(b^2 - 2b + 3) \quad \text{Ans. (i)}$$

(ii)

$$pv + pvx$$
$$= pv(1 + x) \quad \text{Ans. (ii)}$$

(iii)

$$ax^3 - 2bx^2 + 3cx$$
$$= x(ax^2 - 2bx + 3c) \quad \text{Ans. (iii)}$$

(iv)

$$12a^3b^3c^3 - 8a^2b^2c^2 + 4abc$$
$$= 4abc(3a^2b^2c^2 - 2abc + 1) \quad \text{Ans. (iv)}$$

9. (i) $D^2 - d^2 = (D + d)(D - d) \quad \text{Ans. (i)}$
    (ii) $1 - a^2 = (1 + a)(1 - a) \quad \text{Ans. (ii)}$
    (iii) $4x^2y^2 - 9z^2 = (2xy + 3z)(2xy - 3z) \quad \text{Ans. (iii)}$
    (iv) $T_1^4 - T_2^4 = (T_1^2 + T_2^2)(T_1^2 - T_2^2)$
            or $(T_1^2 + T_2^2)(T_1 + T_2)(T_1 - T_2) \quad \text{Ans. (iv)}$

10. (i) $a^2 + 8a + 16 = (a + 4)(a + 4)$
             or $(a + 4)^2 \quad \text{Ans. (i)}$

(ii) $d^2 - 10d + 25 = (d - 5)(d - 5)$
         or $(d - 5)^2 \quad \text{Ans. (ii)}$

(iii)
$$9v^2 + 12v + 4 = (3v + 2)(3v + 2)$$
$$\text{or } (3v + 2)^2 \quad \text{Ans. (iii)}$$

(iv)
$$4x^2 - 12xy + 9y^2 = (2x - 3y)(2x - 3y)$$
$$\text{or } (2x - 3y)^2 \quad \text{Ans. (iv)}$$

11. (i)
$$\frac{x}{2} + \frac{x}{4} - \frac{2x}{3}$$
$$= \frac{6x + 3x - 8x}{12}$$
$$= \frac{x}{12} \quad \text{Ans. (i)}$$

(ii)
$$\frac{2a - 1}{b} - \frac{2a + 3}{2b} - \frac{3a - 8}{3b}$$
$$= \frac{6(2a - 1) - 3(2a + 3) - 2(3a - 8)}{6b}$$
$$= \frac{12a - 6 - 6a - 9 - 6a + 16}{6b}$$
$$= \frac{1}{6b} \quad \text{Ans. (ii)}$$

(iii)
$$\frac{4}{x + 2} + \frac{18}{x^2 - 2x - 8} - \frac{3}{x - 4}$$
$$= \frac{4(x - 4) + 18 - 3(x + 2)}{(x + 2)(x - 4)}$$
$$= \frac{4x - 16 + 18 - 3x - 6}{(x + 2)(x - 4)}$$
$$= \frac{x - 4}{(x + 2)(x - 4)}$$
$$= \frac{1}{x + 2} \quad \text{Ans. (iii)}$$

12. $2x^3 - x^2y + xy^2 - 3y^3 \quad x = 2, y = -2$
    $= 2(2)^3 - (2)^2(-2) + (2)(-2)^2 - 3(-2)^3$
    $= 2(8) - (4)(-2) + (2)(4) - 3(-8)$
    $= 16 - (-8) + 8 + 24$
    $= 16 + 8 + 8 + 24$
    $= 56$ Ans.

13. $3[4x + 2\{x - 2y - (3x + y)\} - 3x]$
    $= 3[4x + 2\{x - 2y - 3x - y\} - 3x]$
    $= 3[4x + 2x - 4y - 6x - 2y - 3x]$
    $= 12x + 6x - 12y - 18x - 6y - 9x$
    $= -9x - 18y$

substituting $x = -2, y = -3$
    $-9(-2) - 18(-3)$
    $= +18 + 54$
    $= 72$ Ans.

14. Remainder theorem:

$R = f(a)$ when $f(x)$ is divided by $(x - a)$

Let $x - a = x - 3$
then $a = +3$
$f(x) = 2x^3 - 4x^2 + 5x - 6$
$R = f(a) = 2(3)^3 - 4(3)^2 + 5(3) - 6$
    $= 54 - 36 + 15 - 6$
    $= 27$ Ans.

15.   Let $x - a = x + 5$
then $a = -5$
$f(x) = x^3 + 6x^2 + bx + 9$
$R = f(a) = (-5)^3 + 6(-5)^2 + b(-5) + 9$
    $4 = -125 + 150 - 5b + 9$
    $5b = 150 + 9 - 125 - 4 = 30$
    $b = 6$ Ans.

16. Factor theorem: If $(x - a)$ is a factor of $f(x)$, the remainder is zero, and $f(a) = 0$

$$\text{Let} \quad x - a = x + 4$$
$$\text{then} \quad a = -4$$

$x + 4$ is a factor, $\therefore f(-4) = 0$

$$f(x) = x^3 + x^2 - 10x + c$$
$$f(-4) = (-4)^3 + (-4)^2 - 10(-4) + c$$
$$0 = -64 + 16 + 40 + c$$
$$c = 64 - 16 - 40$$
$$= 8 \quad \text{Ans.}$$

17. Factor theorem:

$$\text{Let} \quad x - a = x + 1$$
$$\text{then} \quad a = -1$$

$x + 1$ is a factor, $\therefore f(-1) = 0$

$$f(x) = x^3 + 3x^2 - bx - c$$
$$f(-1) = (-1)^3 + 3(-1)^2 - b(-1) - c$$
$$0 = -1 + 3 + b - c$$
$$c = b + 2 \quad \dots \quad \dots \quad \dots \quad \dots \quad \dots \quad \text{(i)}$$

Remainder theorem:

$$\text{Let} \quad x - a = x + 2$$
$$\text{then} \quad a = -2$$
$$f(x) = x^3 + 3x^2 - bx - c$$
$$f(-2) = (-2)^3 + 3(-2)^2 - b(-2) - c$$
$$15 = -8 + 12 + 2b - c$$
$$c = 2b - 11 \quad \dots \quad \dots \quad \dots \quad \dots \quad \dots \quad \text{(ii)}$$

From (i) and (ii),

$$2b - 11 = b + 2$$
$$b = 13$$

Substituting for b into (i)

$$c = 13 + 2 = 15$$

Constants are 13 and 15.   Ans.

18. $$(1+x)^{\frac{1}{3}} = 1 + \frac{x}{3} + \frac{\frac{1}{3}(\frac{1}{3}-1)x^2}{2 \times 1} + \frac{\frac{1}{3}(\frac{1}{3}-1)(\frac{1}{3}-2)x^3}{3 \times 2 \times 1} + \cdots$$

$$= 1 + \frac{x}{3} - \frac{x^2}{9} + \frac{5x^3}{81} - \cdots$$

$$(1+0\cdot012)^{\frac{1}{3}} = 1 + \frac{0\cdot012}{3} - \frac{(0\cdot012)^2}{9} + \frac{5(0\cdot012)^3}{81} - \cdots$$

$$= 1 + 0\cdot004 - 0\cdot000016 + 0\cdot0000001$$

$$= 1\cdot0039841 \quad \text{Ans.}$$

SOLUTIONS TO TEST EXAMPLES 3

1.
$$8 + 5x - 7 = 3x + 9$$
$$5x - 3x = 9 + 7 - 8$$
$$2x = 8$$
$$x = 4 \quad \text{Ans.}$$

2.
$$2(a + 3) + 3(2a - 4) = 4(11 - 3a)$$
$$2a + 6 + 6a - 12 = 44 - 12a$$
$$2a + 6a + 12a = 44 + 12 - 6$$
$$20a = 50$$
$$a = 2\tfrac{1}{2} \quad \text{Ans.}$$

3.
$$3[3 - \{x + 2(1 - x)\} - 4x] = 2[x - 3(2 + x) - 4]$$
$$3[3 - \{x + 2 - 2x\} - 4x] = 2[x - 6 - 3x - 4]$$
$$3[3 - x - 2 + 2x - 4x] = 2[x - 6 - 3x - 4]$$
$$9 - 3x - 6 + 6x - 12x = 2x - 12 - 6x - 8$$
$$-3x + 6x - 12x - 2x + 6x = -12 - 8 - 9 + 6$$
$$-5x = -23$$
$$x = 4 \cdot 6 \quad \text{Ans.}$$

4.
$$\frac{2x}{3} + \frac{x}{4} - \frac{5}{6} = \frac{4x}{5} + \frac{1}{3}$$

multiplying throughout by 60,

$$40x + 15x - 50 = 48x + 20$$
$$40x + 15x - 48x = 20 + 50$$
$$7x = 70$$
$$x = 10 \quad \text{Ans.}$$

5.
$$\frac{(1 - 2a^2)}{6a} - \frac{1}{4} + \frac{a}{3} = \frac{1}{6} - \frac{5}{2a}$$

multiplying throughout by 12a,

$$2(1 - 2a^2) - 3a + 4a^2 = 2a - 30$$
$$2 - 4a^2 - 3a + 4a^2 = 2a - 30$$

$-4a^2$ and $+4a^2$ cancels,

$$-3a - 2a = -30 - 2$$
$$-5a = -32$$
$$a = 6\cdot4   \text{Ans.}$$

6.
$$\frac{2}{x-3} + \frac{3}{x+2} = \frac{4}{x^2 - x - 6}$$

Note that $(x - 3)(x + 2)$ are the factors of $x^2 - x - 6$, therefore the L.C.M. of the denominators is $x^2 - x - 6$, or more conveniently $(x - 3)(x + 2)$ for the purposes of multiplying throughout this equation.

Multiplying by $(x - 3)(x + 2)$,

$$2(x + 2) + 3(x - 3) = 4$$
$$2x + 4 + 3x - 9 = 4$$
$$2x + 3x = 4 + 9 - 4$$
$$5x = 9$$
$$x = 1\cdot8   \text{Ans.}$$

7. The equality of the ships is that the *distance* from port to meeting place is the same, therefore the equation is: Distance travelled by fast ship = Distance travelled by slow ship, and for distance write speed × time.

Let x = time taken by fast ship (h)
then $x + 4\frac{1}{2}$ = time taken by slow ship (h)

speed × time (of fast ship) = speed × time (of slow ship)

$$17 \cdot 5 \times x = 16 \times (x + 4\tfrac{1}{2})$$
$$17 \cdot 5x = 16x + 72$$
$$17 \cdot 5x - 16x = 72$$
$$1 \cdot 5x = 72$$
$$x = 48$$

∴ time for fast ship to overtake = 48 h   Ans. (i)

$$\text{distance} = \text{speed} \times \text{time}$$
$$= 17 \cdot 5 \times 48$$
$$= 840 \text{ naut. miles}$$

∴ Distance from port = 840 naut. miles   Ans. (ii)

8.   Let b = breadth of plate, in m, then
$4b$ = length of plate, in m,

$$\text{length} \times \text{breadth} = \text{area}$$
$$4b \times b = 1$$
$$4b^2 = 1$$
$$b^2 = 0 \cdot 25$$
$$b = \sqrt{0 \cdot 25} = 0 \cdot 5$$

∴ breadth is = 0·5 m
length = 4 × 0·5 = 2 m $\Big\}$ Ans.

9. Note that R_0 cancels,

$$\frac{R_2}{R_1} = \frac{1 + \alpha\theta_2}{1 + \alpha\theta_1}$$
$$R_1(1 + \alpha\theta_2) = R_2(1 + \alpha\theta_1)$$
$$1 + \alpha\theta_2 = \frac{R_2}{R_1}(1 + \alpha\theta_1)$$
$$\alpha\theta_2 = \frac{R_2}{R_1}(1 + \alpha\theta_1) - 1$$
$$\theta_2 = \frac{1}{\alpha}\left[\frac{R_2}{R_1}(1 + \alpha\theta_1) - 1\right] \quad \text{Ans. (i)}$$

Inserting values,

$$\theta_2 = \frac{1}{0.0042}\left[\frac{240}{200}(1 + 0.0042 \times 15) - 1\right]$$

$$= \frac{1}{0.0042}[1.2 \times 1.063 - 1]$$

$$= \frac{1}{0.0042} \times 0.2756$$

$$= 65.6 \quad \text{Ans. (ii)}$$

10.

$$d = \sqrt{\frac{D^3}{3.5 \times n \times R}}$$

Square both sides,

$$d^2 = \frac{D^3}{3.5 \times n \times R}$$

Multiply both sides by R and divide by d^2,

$$R = \frac{D^3}{3.5\, nd^2} \quad \text{Ans. (i)}$$

Substituting values,

$$R = \frac{381^3}{3.5 \times 8 \times 82.5^2}$$

$$= 290 \text{ mm} \quad \text{Ans. (ii)}$$

11.

$$\frac{T_1}{T_2} = \left\{\frac{p_1}{p_2}\right\}^{\frac{n-1}{n}}$$

$$\frac{670}{324} = \left\{\frac{21}{1.25}\right\}^{\frac{n-1}{n}}$$

$$2.068 = 16.8^{\frac{n-1}{n}}$$

$$\lg \text{ of } 2.068 = \lg \text{ of } 16.8 \times \left(\frac{n-1}{n}\right)$$

$$0.3156 = 1.2253 \times \left(\frac{n-1}{n}\right)$$

$$0.3156n = 1.2253(n - 1)$$

$$0.3156n = 1.2253n - 1.2253$$

$$1.2253 = 1.2253n - 0.3156n$$

$$1.2253 = 0.9097n$$

$$n = \frac{1.2253}{0.9097} = 1.347 \quad \text{Ans.}$$

12.

$$4^{0.59x} = 56 \cdot 36$$

$$\lg 4 \times 0.59x = \lg 56 \cdot 36$$

$$0 \cdot 6021 \times 0 \cdot 59x = 1 \cdot 751$$

$$x = \frac{1 \cdot 751}{0 \cdot 6021 \times 0 \cdot 59}$$

$$= 4 \cdot 929 \quad \text{Ans. (a)}$$

$$x^{1 \cdot 95} = 12 \cdot 4x^{0 \cdot 53}$$

$$1 \cdot 95 \lg x - 0 \cdot 53 \lg x = \lg 12 \cdot 4$$

$$1 \cdot 42 \lg x = 1 \cdot 0934$$

$$\lg x = \frac{1 \cdot 0934}{1 \cdot 42}$$

$$\lg x = 0 \cdot 7700$$

$$x = 5 \cdot 888 \quad \text{Ans. (b)}$$

$$\epsilon^{5x} = 46 \cdot 38^{2 \cdot 6}$$

$$2 \cdot 718^{5x} = 46 \cdot 38^{2 \cdot 6}$$

$$\lg 2 \cdot 718 \times 5x = \lg 46 \cdot 38 \times 2 \cdot 6$$

$$0 \cdot 4343 \times 5x = 1 \cdot 6663 \times 2 \cdot 6$$

$$x = \frac{1 \cdot 6663 \times 2 \cdot 6}{0 \cdot 4343 \times 5}$$

$$= 1 \cdot 995 \quad \text{Ans. (c)}$$

$$\sqrt[3]{x} = \epsilon^{2 \cdot 5}$$

$$\sqrt[3]{x} = 2 \cdot 718^{2 \cdot 5}$$

$$\lg x \div 3 = \lg 2 \cdot 718 \times 2 \cdot 5$$

$$\lg x = 0 \cdot 4343 \times 2 \cdot 5 \times 3$$

$$\lg x = 3 \cdot 2573$$

$$x = 1808 \quad \text{Ans. (d)}$$

Note. Logarithms to any base can be used to solve Examples 11 and 12.

SOLUTIONS TO TEST EXAMPLES 4

1. Let x = first number, and y = second number.

   From the first statement,

   $$2\tfrac{1}{2}x + 3\tfrac{1}{2}y = 19 \quad \ldots \quad \ldots \quad \ldots \quad \ldots \quad \text{(i)}$$

   From the second statement,

   $$2\tfrac{1}{2}y - 3\tfrac{1}{2}x = 3 \quad \ldots \quad \ldots \quad \ldots \quad \ldots \quad \text{(ii)}$$

   Re-arranging terms in (i) in the same order as (ii),

   $$3\tfrac{1}{2}y + 2\tfrac{1}{2}x = 19 \quad \ldots \quad \ldots \quad \ldots \quad \ldots \quad \text{(iii)}$$
   $$2\tfrac{1}{2}y - 3\tfrac{1}{2}x = 3 \quad \ldots \quad \ldots \quad \ldots \quad \ldots \quad \text{(iv)}$$

   Multiplying (iii) by 5 and multiplying (iv) by 7,

   $$17\tfrac{1}{2}y + 12\tfrac{1}{2}x = 95 \quad \ldots \quad \ldots \quad \ldots \quad \ldots \quad \text{(v)}$$
   $$17\tfrac{1}{2}y - 24\tfrac{1}{2}x = 21 \quad \ldots \quad \ldots \quad \ldots \quad \ldots \quad \text{(vi)}$$

   Subtracting (vi) from (v)

   $$37x = 74$$
   $$x = 2$$

   Substituting $x = 2$ into (i)

   $$2\tfrac{1}{2} \times 2 + 3\tfrac{1}{2}y = 19$$
   $$3\tfrac{1}{2}y = 19 - 5$$
   $$3\tfrac{1}{2}y = 14$$
   $$y = 4$$

   The numbers are 2 and 4.   Ans.

2.
   $$\frac{2x}{3} - \frac{3y}{5} = \frac{3}{4} \quad \ldots \quad \ldots \quad \ldots \quad \ldots \quad \text{(i)}$$
   $$\frac{x}{2} - \frac{y}{4} = \frac{13}{16} \quad \ldots \quad \ldots \quad \ldots \quad \ldots \quad \text{(ii)}$$

Multiplying (i) by 60, and multiplying (ii) by 16,

$$40x - 36y = 45 \quad \ldots \quad \ldots \quad \ldots \quad \ldots \quad \text{(iii)}$$
$$8x - 4y = 13 \quad \ldots \quad \ldots \quad \ldots \quad \ldots \quad \text{(iv)}$$

Multiplying (iv) by 5 and subtracting (iii) from the result,

$$40x - 20y = 65 \quad \ldots \quad \ldots \quad \ldots \quad \ldots \quad \text{(v)}$$
$$40x - 36y = 45$$
$$16y = 20$$
$$y = 1\tfrac{1}{4}$$

Substituting $y = 1\tfrac{1}{4}$ into (iv),

$$8x - 4 \times 1\tfrac{1}{4} = 13$$
$$8x = 13 + 5$$
$$8x = 18$$
$$x = 2\tfrac{1}{4}$$

The values of x and y are $2\tfrac{1}{4}$ and $1\tfrac{1}{4}$ respectively.   Ans.

3.
$$a(1 + 2b) = 3$$
$$a(1 - 3b) = 0\cdot5$$

Removing brackets,

$$a + 2ab = 3 \quad \ldots \quad \ldots \quad \ldots \quad \ldots \quad \text{(i)}$$
$$a - 3ab = 0\cdot5 \quad \ldots \quad \ldots \quad \ldots \quad \ldots \quad \text{(ii)}$$

If (ii) is subtracted from (i) to eliminate a, it would still leave a term containing two unknowns, therefore proceed to eliminate the terms containing ab by multiplying (i) by 3, and (ii) by 2,

$$3a + 6ab = 9$$
$$2a - 6ab = 1$$
add $$5a \qquad = 10$$
$$a = 2$$

Substitute $a = 2$ into (i),

$$2 + 2 \times 2 \times b = 3$$
$$4b = 3 - 2$$
$$4b = 1$$
$$b = 0\cdot25$$

The values of a and b are 2 and 0·25 respectively.   Ans.

Alternatively divide the original equations, thus,

$$\frac{a(1 + 2b)}{a(1 - 3b)} = \frac{3}{0\cdot5}$$

a cancels, $$\frac{1 + 2b}{1 - 3b} = 6$$

$$1 + 2b = 6(1 - 3b)$$
$$1 + 2b = 6 - 18b$$
$$20b = 5$$
$$b = 0\cdot25$$

Substituting $b = 0\cdot25$ into the first equation,

$$a(1 + 2 \times 0\cdot25) = 3$$
$$1\cdot5a = 3$$
$$a = 2$$
$$\therefore a = 2 \quad \text{and} \quad b = 0\cdot25 \quad \text{as before.}$$

4. Let $x =$ age of grandson
   and $y =$ age of grand-daughter

$$4x + 3y = 72 \quad \ldots \quad \ldots \quad \ldots \quad \ldots \quad \text{(i)}$$
$$3x + 4y = 68 \quad \ldots \quad \ldots \quad \ldots \quad \ldots \quad \text{(ii)}$$

Multiplying (i) by 4 and (ii) by 3 and subtracting,

$$16x + 12y = 288$$
$$9x + 12y = 204$$
$$\overline{7x \qquad = 84}$$
$$x = 12$$

Substituting $x = 12$ into (ii),

$$3 \times 12 + 4y = 68$$
$$4y = 68 - 36$$
$$4y = 32$$
$$y = 8$$

Their ages are 12 and 8 years respectively.   Ans.

5. Let $x =$ one number
and $y =$ other number,

$$x - y = 2 \quad \ldots \quad \ldots \quad \ldots \quad \ldots \quad \text{(i)}$$
$$x^2 - y^2 = 6 \quad \ldots \quad \ldots \quad \ldots \quad \ldots \quad \text{(ii)}$$

Factorise (ii) and divide by (i),

$$\frac{(x + y)(x - y)}{(x - y)} = \frac{6}{2}$$

$x - y$ cancels,

$$x + y = 3 \quad \ldots \quad \ldots \quad \ldots \quad \ldots \quad \text{(iii)}$$

Add (iii) to (i),

$$x - y = 2$$
$$\underline{x + y = 3}$$
$$2x \quad\;\; = 5$$
$$x = 2\tfrac{1}{2}$$

Substitute $x = 2\tfrac{1}{2}$ into (iii),

$$2\tfrac{1}{2} + y = 3$$
$$y = \tfrac{1}{2}$$

The numbers are $2\tfrac{1}{2}$ and $\tfrac{1}{2}$.   Ans.

6. Inserting the two sets of values of F and m,

$$55 = a + b \times 70 \quad \ldots \quad \ldots \quad \ldots \quad \ldots \quad \text{(i)}$$
$$\text{subtract} \quad \underline{35 = a + b \times 30} \quad \ldots \quad \ldots \quad \ldots \quad \ldots \quad \text{(ii)}$$
$$20 = 40b$$
$$b = 0\cdot5$$

Substituting $b = 0.5$ into (i),

$$55 = a + 0.5 \times 70$$
$$55 = a + 35$$
$$a = 20$$

Constants are, $a = 20$ and $b = 0.5$.   Ans. (a)
Linear law is, $F = 20 + 0.5\ m$.   Ans. (b)
When $m = 60$,

$$F = 20 + 0.5 \times 60$$
$$= 20 + 30$$
$$= 50\ \text{N}\quad \text{Ans. (c)}$$

7. Let $x =$ original speed of A
and $y =$ original speed of B,

Time for A to be overtaken $= 9$ h

Time for B to overtake A $= 8$ h

Distance from port to point of overtaking is the same for each ship,
and distance $=$ speed $\times$ time.

$$\therefore x \times 9 = y \times 8$$
$$y = \frac{9x}{8} \qquad \ldots \quad \ldots \quad \ldots \quad \ldots \quad \text{(i)}$$

If speed had been 4 knot slower,
Speed of A would be $(x - 4)$ knot
Speed of B would be $(y - 4)$ knot,

Time for A to be overtaken $= 7$ h

Time for B to overtake A $= 6$ h

$$\therefore (x - 4) \times 7 = (y - 4) \times 6$$
$$7x - 28 = 6y - 24$$
$$7x - 6y = 4 \qquad \ldots \quad \ldots \quad \ldots \quad \ldots \quad \text{(ii)}$$

Substituting value of y from (i) into (ii),

$$7x - \frac{6 \times 9x}{8} = 4$$
$$7x - 6\tfrac{3}{4}x = 4$$
$$\tfrac{1}{4}x = 4$$
$$x = 16$$

Substituting $x = 16$ into (i),

$$y = \frac{9 \times 16}{8}$$
$$y = 18$$

∴ Original speeds of ships are 16 and 18 knot respectively.   Ans.

8. Let a represent $\dfrac{x}{2 - y}$ and let b represent $\dfrac{1}{x}$:

then the two equations may be written,

$$a + 6b = 4 \quad \ldots \quad \ldots \quad \ldots \quad \ldots \quad \text{(i)}$$
$$2a - 9b = 1 \quad \ldots \quad \ldots \quad \ldots \quad \ldots \quad \text{(ii)}$$

Multiplying (i) by 2 and subtracting (ii) from the result,

$$2a + 12b = 8$$
$$\underline{2a - 9b = 1}$$
$$21b = 7$$
$$b = \tfrac{1}{3}$$

Substituting $b = \tfrac{1}{3}$ into (i),

$$a + 6 \times \tfrac{1}{3} = 4$$
$$a = 4 - 2$$
$$a = 2$$

$$a = 2, \quad \therefore \quad \frac{x}{2 - y} = 2 \quad \text{Ans. (a)}$$

$$b = \frac{1}{3}, \quad \therefore \quad \frac{1}{x} = \frac{1}{3} \quad \text{Ans. (b)}$$

$$\frac{1}{x} = \frac{1}{3}, \quad \therefore \quad x = 3 \quad \text{Ans. (c)}$$

$$\frac{x}{2 - y} = 2, \quad \therefore \quad \frac{3}{2 - y} = 2$$

$$3 = 4 - 2y$$
$$2y = 4 - 3$$
$$2y = 1$$
$$y = \tfrac{1}{2} \quad \text{Ans. (d)}$$

9. From the first equation,

$$2^x = 4^y$$
$$2^x = 2^{2y}$$
$$\therefore \quad x = 2y \qquad \ldots \quad \ldots \quad \ldots \quad \ldots \quad \text{(i)}$$

From the second equation,

$$4^{x-1} = 2^{y+1}$$
$$2^{2x-2} = 2^{y+1}$$
$$\therefore 2x - 2 = y + 1$$
$$2x - y = 3 \qquad \ldots \quad \ldots \quad \ldots \quad \ldots \quad \text{(ii)}$$

Substituting $x = 2y$ from (i) into (ii),

$$2 \times 2y - y = 3$$
$$3y = 3$$
$$y = 1$$

Substituting $y = 1$ into (i),

$$x = 2$$

The values of x and y are 2 and 1 respectively.   Ans.

10.
$$1\cdot259^{x+1} \times 1\cdot175^{y-1} = 2\cdot323$$
$$3\cdot162^x \times 1\cdot778^y = 25\cdot12$$

Expressing the equations in log form,

$$(\lg 1\cdot259)(x + 1) + (\lg 1\cdot175)(y - 1) = \lg 2\cdot323$$
$$(\lg 3\cdot162) \times x + (\lg 1\cdot778) \times y = \lg 25\cdot12$$

Inserting log values,

$$0\cdot1000(x + 1) + 0\cdot0700(y - 1) = 0\cdot3660$$
$$0\cdot5000 \times x + 0\cdot2500 \times y = 1\cdot4000$$

Simplifying the equations,

$$0\cdot1x + 0\cdot07y = 0\cdot336 \quad \ldots \quad \ldots \quad \ldots \quad \ldots \quad \text{(i)}$$
$$0\cdot5x + 0\cdot25y = 1\cdot4 \quad \ldots \quad \ldots \quad \ldots \quad \ldots \quad \text{(ii)}$$

Multiplying (i) by 5, subtracting (ii) from the result, and solving y,

$$0 \cdot 5x + 0 \cdot 35y = 1 \cdot 68$$
$$\underline{0 \cdot 5x + 0 \cdot 25y = 1 \cdot 4}$$
$$0 \cdot 1y = 0 \cdot 28$$
$$y = 2 \cdot 8$$

Substituting $y = 2 \cdot 8$ into (i) and solving x,

$$0 \cdot 1x + 0 \cdot 07 \times 2 \cdot 8 = 0 \cdot 336$$
$$0 \cdot 1x = 0 \cdot 336 - 0 \cdot 196$$
$$0 \cdot 1x = 0 \cdot 14$$
$$x = 1 \cdot 4$$

The values of x and y are $1 \cdot 4$ and $2 \cdot 8$ respectively.   Ans.

11. Taking square root throughout,

$$\frac{d}{x} = \frac{x}{y} = \frac{y}{D}$$

From $\dfrac{d}{x} = \dfrac{y}{D}, \quad y = \dfrac{dD}{x}$ ...   .   (i)

From $\dfrac{d}{x} = \dfrac{x}{y}, \quad x^2 = dy$ ...   .   (ii)

Substituting the value of y in (i) into (ii),

$$x^2 = \frac{d \times dD}{x}$$
$$\therefore \quad x^3 = d^2 D$$
$$x = \sqrt[3]{d^2 D} \quad \text{Ans. (a)}$$

Inserting values of d and D,

$$x = \sqrt[3]{25^2 \times 75} = 36 \cdot 06$$

Inserting values of d, D and x into (i),

$$y = \frac{25 \times 75}{36 \cdot 06} = 52$$

The values of x and y are $36 \cdot 06$ and 52 respectively.   Ans.

12. $3a + 6b - 2c = 7 \cdot 25$ ... ... (i)

                    $2a + 3b + 4c = 26$ ... ... (ii)

                    $4a - 2b + c = 10 \cdot 25$ ... ... (iii)

Multiplying (i) by 2 and adding (ii) to the result,

$$6a + 12b - 4c = 14 \cdot 5$$
$$\underline{2a + 3b + 4c = 26}$$
$$8a + 15b = 40 \cdot 5 \quad \text{... ... ...} \quad \text{(iv)}$$

Multiplying (iii) by 4 and subtracting (ii) from the result,

$$16a - 8b + 4c = 41$$
$$\underline{2a + 3b + 4c = 26}$$
$$14a - 11b = 15 \quad \text{... ... ...} \quad \text{(v)}$$

Multiplying (iv) by 7, multiplying (v) by 4, and subtracting,

$$56a + 105b = 283 \cdot 5$$
$$\underline{56a - 44b = 60}$$
$$149b = 223 \cdot 5$$
$$b = 1 \cdot 5$$

Substituting $b = 1 \cdot 5$ into (iv),

$$8a + 15 \times 1 \cdot 5 = 40 \cdot 5$$
$$8a = 40 \cdot 5 - 22 \cdot 5$$
$$8a = 18$$
$$a = 2 \cdot 25$$

Substituting $a = 2 \cdot 25$ and $b = 1 \cdot 5$ into (iii),

$$4 \times 2 \cdot 25 - 2 \times 1 \cdot 5 + c = 10 \cdot 25$$
$$c = 10 \cdot 25 - 9 + 3$$
$$c = 4 \cdot 25$$

Values of a, b and c are $2 \cdot 25$, $1 \cdot 5$ and $4 \cdot 25$ respectively.   Ans.

SOLUTIONS TO TEST EXAMPLES 5

1. (i) $\qquad (2x + 8)(3x - 5) = 0$

either $\quad 2x + 8 = 0 \qquad$ or $\quad 3x - 5 = 0$

then $\qquad 2x = -8 \qquad$ then $\qquad 3x = 5$

$\qquad\qquad x = -4 \qquad\qquad\qquad x = 1\frac{2}{3}$

$\qquad x = -4 \quad$ or $\quad 1\frac{2}{3} \quad$ Ans. (i)

(ii) $\qquad (0{\cdot}5x - 10)(0{\cdot}25x + 5) = 0$

either $\quad 0{\cdot}5x - 10 = 0 \qquad$ or $\qquad 0{\cdot}25x + 5 = 0$

then $\qquad\qquad 0{\cdot}5x = 10 \qquad$ then $\qquad\qquad 0{\cdot}25x = -5$

$\qquad\qquad x = 20 \qquad\qquad\qquad\qquad x = -20$

$\qquad x = \pm 20 \quad$ Ans. (ii)

(iii) $\qquad (5x + 0{\cdot}5)(4x + 0{\cdot}8) = 0$

either $\quad 5x + 0{\cdot}5 = 0 \qquad$ or $\qquad 4x + 0{\cdot}8 = 0$

then $\qquad\qquad 5x = -0{\cdot}5 \qquad$ then $\qquad\qquad 4x = -0{\cdot}8$

$\qquad\qquad x = -0{\cdot}1 \qquad\qquad\qquad\qquad x = -0{\cdot}2$

$\qquad x = -0{\cdot}1 \quad$ or $\quad -0{\cdot}2 \quad$ Ans. (iii)

2. (i) $\qquad\qquad 3x^2 + 2x - 33 = 0$

$\qquad\qquad (x - 3)(3x + 11) = 0$

either $\quad x - 3 = 0 \qquad$ or $\quad 3x + 11 = 0$

then $\qquad x = 3 \qquad$ then $\qquad\qquad 3x = -11$

$\qquad\qquad\qquad\qquad\qquad\qquad x = -3\frac{2}{3}$

$\qquad x = 3 \quad$ or $\quad -3\frac{2}{3} \quad$ Ans. (i)

(ii) $$4x^2 - 17x + 4 = 0$$
$$(x - 4)(4x - 1) = 0$$

either $x - 4 = 0$ | or $4x - 1 = 0$
then $x = 4$ | then $4x = 1$
                                $x = \frac{1}{4}$

$x = 4$ or $\frac{1}{4}$ Ans. (ii)

(iii) $$12x^2 + 10x - 12 = 0$$
$$2(6x^2 + 5x - 6) = 0$$
$$2(3x - 2)(2x + 3) = 0$$

either $3x - 2 = 0$ | or $2x + 3 = 0$
then $3x = 2$ | then $2x = -3$
                $x = \frac{2}{3}$ | $x = -1\frac{1}{2}$

$x = \frac{2}{3}$ or $-1\frac{1}{2}$ Ans. (iii)

3. (i) $$x^2 - x - 3\frac{3}{4} = 0$$
$$x^2 - x + (\tfrac{1}{2})^2 = 3\tfrac{3}{4} + (\tfrac{1}{2})^2$$
$$x - \tfrac{1}{2} = \pm\sqrt{4}$$
$$x = \pm 2 + \tfrac{1}{2}$$
$$x = 2\tfrac{1}{2} \quad \text{or} \quad -1\tfrac{1}{2} \quad \text{Ans. (i)}$$

(ii) $$3x^2 + 2x - 1 = 0$$
$$x^2 + \tfrac{2}{3}x - \tfrac{1}{3} = 0$$
$$x^2 + \tfrac{2}{3}x + (\tfrac{1}{3})^2 = \tfrac{1}{3} + (\tfrac{1}{3})^2$$
$$x + \tfrac{1}{3} = \pm\sqrt{\tfrac{4}{9}}$$
$$x = \pm\tfrac{2}{3} - \tfrac{1}{3}$$
$$x = \tfrac{1}{3} \quad \text{or} \quad -1 \quad \text{Ans. (ii)}$$

(iii)
$$4x^2 - 9x + 2 = 0$$

$$x^2 - \frac{9}{4}x + \frac{1}{2} = 0$$

$$x^2 - \frac{9x}{4} + \left(\frac{9}{8}\right)^2 = \left(\frac{9}{8}\right)^2 - \frac{1}{2}$$

$$x - \frac{9}{8} = \pm\sqrt{\frac{81 - 32}{64}}$$

$$x - \frac{9}{8} = \pm\sqrt{\frac{49}{64}}$$

$$x = \pm\frac{7}{8} + \frac{9}{8}$$

$$x = 2 \quad \text{or} \quad \tfrac{1}{4} \quad \text{Ans. (iii)}$$

4. (i)
$$3x^2 - 2x + 0{\cdot}25 = 0$$

$$a = 3, \quad b = -2, \quad c = 0{\cdot}25$$

$$x = \frac{2 \pm \sqrt{4 - 3}}{2 \times 3}$$

$$x = \frac{2 \pm 1}{6}$$

$$x = \frac{1}{2} \quad \text{or} \quad \frac{1}{6} \quad \text{Ans. (i)}$$

(ii)
$$5x^2 + 4x - 5{\cdot}52 = 0$$

$$a = 5, \quad b = 4, \quad c = -5{\cdot}52$$

$$x = \frac{-4 \pm \sqrt{16 + 110{\cdot}4}}{2 \times 5}$$

$$x = \frac{-4 \pm 11{\cdot}24}{10}$$

$$x = \frac{7{\cdot}24}{10} \quad \text{or} \quad \frac{-15{\cdot}24}{10}$$

$$x = 0{\cdot}724 \quad \text{or} \quad -1{\cdot}524 \quad \text{Ans. (ii)}$$

(iii) $10x^2 - x - 0\cdot2 = 0$

$$a = 10, \quad b = -1, \quad c = -0\cdot2$$

$$x = \frac{1 \pm \sqrt{1 + 8}}{2 \times 10}$$

$$x = \frac{1 \pm 3}{20}$$

$$x = \frac{4}{20} \quad \text{or} \quad \frac{-2}{20}$$

$$x = 0\cdot2 \quad \text{or} \quad -0\cdot1 \quad \text{Ans. (iii)}$$

5. $\log 0\cdot5x = 2 \times \log(x - 6)$

$$0\cdot5x = (x - 6)^2$$

$$0\cdot5x = x^2 - 12x + 36$$

$$x^2 - 12\cdot5x + 36 = 0$$

Solving this quadratic,

$$x = 8 \quad \text{or} \quad 4\cdot5 \quad \text{Ans.}$$

6. $6b^4 - 2\cdot46b^2 + 0\cdot24 = 0$

Dividing throughout by 6,

$$b^4 - 0\cdot41b^2 + 0\cdot04 = 0$$

Let x represent b^2,

$$x^2 - 0\cdot41x + 0\cdot04 = 0$$

The solution of this quadratic gives,

$$x = 0\cdot25 \quad \text{or} \quad 0\cdot16$$

$$x = b^2, \quad \therefore b = \sqrt{x}$$

$$b = \pm\sqrt{0\cdot25} \quad \text{or} \quad \pm\sqrt{0\cdot16}$$

$$b = \pm0\cdot5 \quad \text{or} \quad \pm0\cdot4 \quad \text{Ans.}$$

7. $V^{2\cdot8} - 5\cdot1V^{1\cdot4} + 5\cdot6 = 0$

Let x represent $V^{1\cdot4}$

$$x^2 - 5\cdot1x + 5\cdot6 = 0$$

The solution of this quadratic gives,

$$x = 3\cdot5 \quad \text{or} \quad 1\cdot6$$
$$x = V^{1\cdot4}, \quad \therefore \quad V = {}^{1\cdot4}\sqrt{x}$$
$$V = {}^{1\cdot4}\sqrt{3\cdot5} \quad \text{or} \quad {}^{1\cdot4}\sqrt{1\cdot6}$$
$$V = 2\cdot446 \quad \text{or} \quad 1\cdot399 \quad \text{Ans.}$$

8.
$$x^2 - xy + 2y^2 = 16 \quad \dots \quad \dots \quad \dots \quad \dots \quad \text{(i)}$$
$$x + 2y = 8 \quad \dots \quad \dots \quad \dots \quad \dots \quad \text{(ii)}$$

From (ii)

$$2y = 8 - x$$
$$y = 4 - 0\cdot5x \quad \dots \quad \dots \quad \dots \quad \dots \quad \text{(iii)}$$

Substitute this value of y into equation (i),

$$x^2 - x(4 - 0\cdot5x) + 2(4 - 0\cdot5x)^2 = 16$$
$$x^2 - 4x + 0\cdot5x^2 + 2(16 - 4x + 0\cdot25x^2) = 16$$
$$x^2 - 4x + 0\cdot5x^2 + 32 - 8x + 0\cdot5x^2 = 16$$
$$x^2 + 0\cdot5x^2 + 0\cdot5x^2 - 4x - 8x + 32 - 16 = 0$$
$$2x^2 - 12x + 16 = 0$$
$$x^2 - 6x + 8 = 0$$

By factors,

$$(x - 2)(x - 4) = 0$$
either $\quad x - 2 = 0,$ $\quad$ then $\quad x = 2$
or $\quad x - 4 = 0,$ $\quad$ then $\quad x = 4$

From (iii)

if $\quad x = 2,$ $\quad y = 4 - 0\cdot5 \times 2 = 3$
if $\quad x = 4,$ $\quad y = 4 - 0\cdot5 \times 4 = 2$

Values are:

$$\left.\begin{array}{l} x = 2 \quad \text{and} \quad y = 3 \\ \text{or} \quad x = 4 \quad \text{and} \quad y = 2 \end{array}\right\} \quad \text{Ans.}$$

9. Let x = speed of slow ship (knot).

$$\text{Time to do 330 naut. miles} = \frac{330}{x} \text{ h} \qquad \ldots \quad \ldots \quad \ldots \qquad (i)$$

$(x + 3\frac{1}{2})$ = speed of fast ship (knot).

$$\text{Time to do 334 naut. miles} = \frac{334}{x + 3\frac{1}{2}} \text{ h} \qquad \ldots \quad \ldots \quad \ldots \qquad (ii)$$

Time (ii) is 5 h less than time (i), therefore,

$$\frac{330}{x} - \frac{334}{x + 3\frac{1}{2}} = 5$$

$$330(x + 3\tfrac{1}{2}) - 334x = 5x(x + 3\tfrac{1}{2})$$

$$330x + 1155 - 334x = 5x^2 + 17 \cdot 5x$$

$$5x^2 + 21 \cdot 5x - 1155 = 0$$

$$x^2 + 4 \cdot 3x - 231 = 0$$

The solution of this quadratic gives $x = 13 \cdot 2$,

$$\left.\begin{array}{l} \therefore \text{ speed of slow ship} = 13 \cdot 2 \text{ knot} \\ \text{speed of fast ship} = 13 \cdot 2 + 3 \cdot 5 = 16 \cdot 7 \text{ knot} \end{array}\right\} \text{ Ans.}$$

10. Working in cm;

Let L = length, and B = breadth,

length × breadth = area,	$\therefore L \times B = 76$	(i)
length + breadth = $\frac{1}{2}$ perimeter,	$\therefore L + B = 17 \cdot 5$	(ii)

Substituting $B = \dfrac{76}{L}$ from (i) into (ii),

$$L + \frac{76}{L} = 17 \cdot 5$$

Multiplying throughout by L,

$$L^2 + 76 = 17 \cdot 5L$$

$$L^2 - 17 \cdot 5L + 76 = 0$$

The solution of this quadratic gives $L = 9 \cdot 5$ or 8,

$$\left.\begin{array}{l} \therefore \text{ length} = 9 \cdot 5 \text{ cm} = 95 \text{ mm} \\ \text{breadth} = 8 \text{ cm} = 80 \text{ mm} \end{array}\right\} \text{ Ans.}$$

11. $2x^3 + 3x^2 - 17x - 30 = 0$

Finding the first root by trial,

Try $x = 1$, $2 \times 1^3 + 3 \times 1^2 - 17 \times 1 - 30$
$$= 2 + 3 - 17 - 30$$
$$= -42$$

Try $x = 2$, $2 \times 2^3 + 3 \times 2^2 - 17 \times 2 - 30$
$$= 16 + 12 - 34 - 30$$
$$= -36$$

Try $x = 3$, $2 \times 3^3 + 3 \times 3^2 - 17 \times 3 - 30$
$$= 54 + 27 - 51 - 30$$
$$= 0$$

$x = 3$ satisfies the equation, this is one root and $x - 3$ must be a factor. Divide the cubic equation by this factor.

$$
\begin{array}{r}
2x^2 + 9x + 10 \\
x - 3 \overline{)\,2x^3 + 3x^2 - 17x - 30} \\
\underline{2x^3 - 6x^2} \\
9x^2 - 17x - 30 \\
\underline{9x^2 - 27x} \\
10x - 30 \\
\underline{10x - 30}
\end{array}
$$

Equating the resulting quadratic to zero and finding its roots by formula,

$$2x^2 + 9x + 10$$

$$x = \frac{-b \pm \sqrt{b^2 - 4ac}}{2a}$$

$$= \frac{-9 \pm \sqrt{9^2 - 4 \times 2 \times 10}}{2 \times 2}$$

$$= \frac{-9 \pm 1}{4}$$

$$= -2 \quad \text{or} \quad -2{\cdot}5$$

The roots of the given equation are:

$$3, \; -2, \text{ and } -2{\cdot}5. \quad \text{Ans.}$$

12.
$$2x - \frac{16}{x}\left\{2 - \frac{3}{x}\right\} = 3$$

Multiplying terms within the brackets by the multiplier outside, to eliminate the brackets,

$$2x - \frac{32}{x} + \frac{48}{x^2} = 3$$

Multiply throughout by the least common denominator, which is x^2, to eliminate fractions,

$$2x^3 - 32x + 48 = 3x^2$$

Arrange all terms on left hand side in order of descending powers of x,

$$2x^3 - 3x^2 - 32x + 48 = 0$$

Proceed to solve this cubic equation by finding the first root by trial,

Try $x = 1$,
$$2 \times 1^3 - 3 \times 1^2 - 32 \times 1 + 48$$
$$= 2 - 3 - 32 + 48$$
$$= 15$$

Try $x = 2$,
$$2 \times 2^3 - 3 \times 2^2 - 32 \times 2 + 48$$
$$= 16 - 12 - 64 + 48$$
$$= -12$$

Try $x = 3$,
$$2 \times 3^3 - 3 \times 3^2 - 32 \times 3 + 48$$
$$= 54 - 27 - 96 + 48$$
$$= -21$$

Try $x = 4$,
$$2 \times 4^3 - 3 \times 4^2 - 32 \times 4 + 48$$
$$= 128 - 48 - 128 + 48$$
$$= 0$$

$x = 4$ is a root and $x - 4$ is a factor. Divide the cubic equation by this factor,

$$x - 4)2x^3 - 3x^2 - 32x + 48(2x^2 + 5x - 12$$
$$\underline{2x^3 - 8x^2}$$
$$5x^2 - 32x + 48$$
$$\underline{5x^2 - 20x}$$
$$-12x + 48$$
$$\underline{-12x + 48}$$

Finding the roots of the resulting quadratic by formula,

$$2x^2 + 5x - 12 = 0$$

$$x = \frac{-b \pm \sqrt{b^2 - 4ac}}{2a}$$

$$= \frac{-5 \pm \sqrt{5^2 - 4 \times 2 \times (-12)}}{2 \times 2}$$

$$= \frac{-5 \pm 11}{4}$$

$$= 1 \cdot 5 \quad \text{or} \quad -4$$

The roots of the given equation are:

$$4, \quad 1 \cdot 5, \quad \text{and} \quad -4 \quad \text{Ans.}$$

SOLUTIONS TO TEST EXAMPLES 6

1. Finding plotting points:

(i) $y = 2 + x$,

$$\text{when} \quad x = 0, \qquad y = 2 + 0 = 2$$
$$\text{when} \quad x = 12, \qquad y = 2 + 12 = 14$$

(ii) $y = 12 - 1 \cdot 5x$,

$$\text{when} \quad x = 0, \qquad y = 12 - 0 = 12$$
$$\text{when} \quad x = 12, \qquad y = 12 - 18 = -6$$

(iii) $y = -1 - 0 \cdot 5x$,

$$\text{when} \quad x = 0, \qquad y = -1 - 0 = -1$$
$$\text{when} \quad x = 12, \qquad y = -1 - 6 = -7$$

(iv) $y = -4 + 1 \cdot 25x$,

$$\text{when} \quad x = 0, \qquad y = -4 + 0 = -4$$
$$\text{when} \quad x = 12, \qquad y = -4 + 15 = 11$$

The four plotted graphs are as shown.

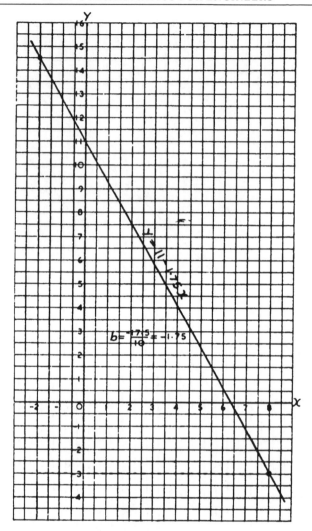

2. From the graph:

$$a = 11$$
$$b = -17{\cdot}5 \div 10 = -1{\cdot}75$$

∴ the equation is $y = 11 - 1{\cdot}75x$.   Ans.

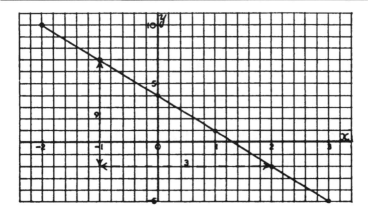

3. From the above graph:

$$a = 4$$
$$b = -9 \div 3 = -3$$

∴ Law is $y = 4 - 3x$.   Ans.

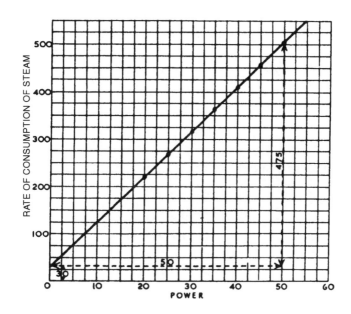

4. Reading the graph rate of consumption and power (previous page):

$$a = 30$$
$$b = 475 \div 50 = 9{\cdot}5$$

$\therefore$ Law is $m = 30 + 9{\cdot}5P$.   Ans.

5. Expressing y in terms of the other quantities,

first equation, $3x + 5y = 23$

$$5y = 23 - 3x$$
$$y = 4{\cdot}6 - 0{\cdot}6x \qquad \ldots \quad \ldots \quad (i)$$

second equation, $5x - 2y = 12{\cdot}5$

$$-2y = 12{\cdot}5 - 5x$$
$$2y = 5x - 12{\cdot}5$$
$$y = -6{\cdot}25 + 2{\cdot}5x \qquad \ldots \quad \ldots \quad (ii)$$

Choosing two plotting points for the graphs of each equation,

equation (i),   when $x = 0$, $y = 4{\cdot}6 - 0 = 4{\cdot}6$

when $x = 5$, $y = 4{\cdot}6 - 3 = 1{\cdot}6$

equation (ii),   when $x = 0$, $y = -6{\cdot}25 + 0 = -6{\cdot}25$

when $x = 4$, $y = -6{\cdot}25 + 10 = 3{\cdot}75$

The two graphs are now drawn from which read the point of intersection,

$$\left. \begin{array}{l} x = 3{\cdot}5 \\ y = 2{\cdot}5 \end{array} \right\} \quad \text{Ans.}$$

6. Expressing p in each equation in terms of the other quantities,

$$5p - 2q = 5{\cdot}6$$
$$5p = 5{\cdot}6 + 2q$$
$$p = 1{\cdot}12 + 0{\cdot}4q \qquad \ldots \quad \ldots \quad (i)$$
$$2p - 3q = -4{\cdot}8$$
$$2p = -4{\cdot}8 + 3q$$
$$p = -2{\cdot}4 + 1{\cdot}5q \qquad \ldots \quad \ldots \quad (ii)$$

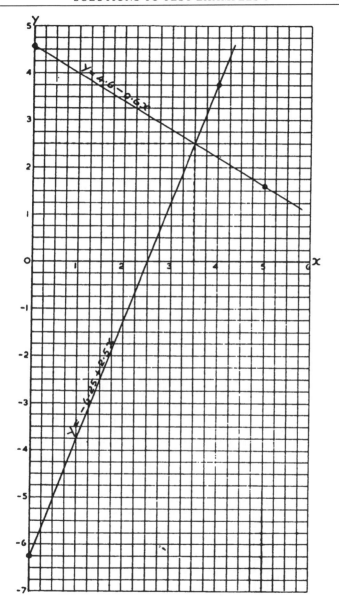

Plotting points for each equation:

(i) when $q = 0$, $p = 1 \cdot 12 + 0 = 1 \cdot 12$
     when $q = 5$, $p = 1 \cdot 12 + 2 = 3 \cdot 12$

(ii) when $q = 0$, $p = -2 \cdot 4 + 0 = -2 \cdot 4$
     when $q = 4$, $p = -2 \cdot 4 + 6 = 3 \cdot 6$

From the graphs:

$$p = 2 \cdot 4 \text{ and } q = 3 \cdot 2. \quad \text{Ans.}$$

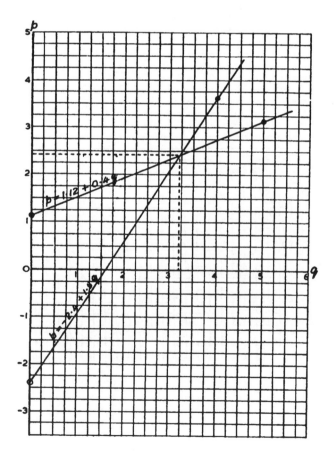

7. $x^2 - 5x + 5\frac{1}{4} = 0$

Let $y = x^2 - 5x + 5\frac{1}{4}$

when $x = 0,$ $y =$ $0 -$ $0 + 5\frac{1}{4} = 5\frac{1}{4}$

when $x = 1,$ $y =$ $1 -$ $5 + 5\frac{1}{4} = 1\frac{1}{4}$

when $x = 2,$ $y =$ $4 - 10 + 5\frac{1}{4} = -\frac{3}{4}$

when $x = 3,$ $y =$ $9 - 15 + 5\frac{1}{4} = -\frac{3}{4}$

when $x = 4,$ $y = 16 - 20 + 5\frac{1}{4} = 1\frac{1}{4}$

From the graph,

$$y = 0 \quad \text{when} \quad x = 1 \cdot 5 \quad \text{and} \quad 3 \cdot 5$$

Therefore the roots of the equation are $1 \cdot 5$ and $3 \cdot 5$.   Ans.

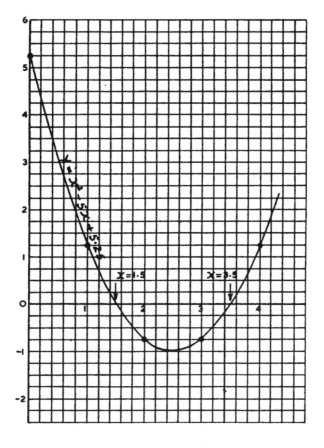

8. Finding plotting points,

$$y = 0\cdot5x^2 - 2x - 6$$

$x = -4, \quad y = 0\cdot5(-4)^2 - 2(-4) - 6 = 10$

$x = -3, \quad y = 0\cdot5(-3)^2 - 2(-3) - 6 = 4\cdot5$

$x = -2, \quad y = 0\cdot5(-2)^2 - 2(-2) - 6 = 0$

$x = -1, \quad y = 0\cdot5(-1)^2 - 2(-1) - 6 = -3\cdot5$

$x = 0, \qquad y = 0 - 0 - 6 \qquad\qquad = -6$

$x = 1, \qquad y = 0\cdot5 - 2 - 6 \qquad\quad = -7\cdot5$

$x = 2, \qquad y = 2 - 4 - 6 \qquad\qquad = -8$

$x = 3, \qquad y = 4\cdot5 - 6 - 6 \qquad\quad = -7\cdot5$

$x = 4, \qquad y = 8 - 8 - 6 \qquad\qquad = -6$

$x = 5, \qquad y = 12\cdot5 - 10 - 6 \qquad = -3\cdot5$

$x = 6, \qquad y = 18 - 12 - 6 \qquad\quad = 0$

$x = 7, \qquad y = 24\cdot5 - 14 - 6 \qquad = 4\cdot5$

$x = 8, \qquad y = 32 - 16 - 6 \qquad\quad = 10$

The points are plotted and the graph drawn as shown.

(i) $0\cdot5x^2 - 2x - 6 = 0$

The roots of this equation are where the graph crosses the base line $y = 0$, thus

$$x = -2 \quad \text{and} \quad +6 \quad \text{Ans. (i)}$$

(ii) The difference between

$$0\cdot5x^2 - 2x - 6$$

and $\quad \underline{0\cdot5x^2 - 2x - 4}$ (subtract)

is $\qquad\qquad -2$

Thus, when $y = -2$ on the graph of $y = 0\cdot5x^2 - 2x - 6$ we read the roots of the equation $0\cdot5x^2 - 2x - 4 = 0$, that is,

$$x = -1\cdot5 \quad \text{and} \quad +5\cdot5 \quad \text{Ans. (ii)}$$

(iii) The difference between

$$0\cdot5x^2 - 2x - 6$$

and $\quad \underline{0\cdot5x^2 - 2x - 1}$ (subtract)

is $\qquad\qquad -5$

Therefore the values of x in this equation are where the graph crosses the line of $y = -5$, thus,

$$x = -0\cdot5 \quad \text{and} \quad +4\cdot5 \quad \text{Ans. (iii)}$$

(iv) The difference between

$$0.5x^2 - 2x - 6$$

and $0.5x^2 - 2x$ (subtract)

is -6

Hence, values of x are read where the graph crosses the line of $y = -6$,

$$x = 0 \quad \text{and} \quad 4 \quad \text{Ans. (iv)}$$

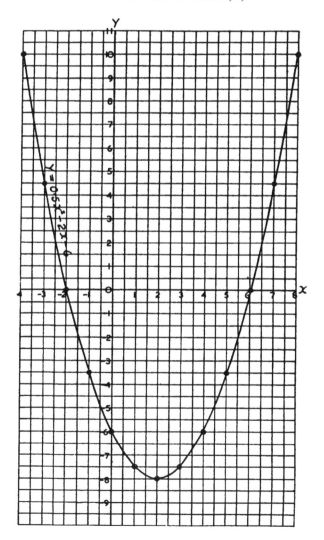

(v) The difference between

$$0.5x^2 - 2x - 6$$

and $0.5x^2 - 2x + 1$ (subtract)

is $\overline{\; -7}$

Then read off the graph values of x when $y = -7$,

$$x = 0.6 \quad \text{and} \quad 3.4 \quad \text{Ans. (v)}$$

9. The plotting points are calculated and the two graphs drawn for each equation.

$$x^2 - 2.5x - 3.5 = 0$$

can be written $x^2 - (2.5x + 3.5) = 0$

and represented by $y_1 - y_2 = 0$

where $y_1 = x^2$,   and $y_2 = 2.5x + 3.5$

Hence, where the graphs intersect gives the value of x where $y_1 - y_2 = 0$ and therefore the roots of the equation $x^2 - 2.5x - 3.5 = 0$.

$$\therefore x = -1 \quad \text{and} \quad +3.5 \quad \text{Ans.}$$

10. The two graphs are plotted (p. 328). The points of intersection produce the values of x and y as:

$$\left.\begin{array}{l} x = 1 \quad \text{and} \quad y = -0.6 \\ x = 10 \quad \text{and} \quad y = 12 \end{array}\right\} \quad \text{Ans.}$$

11. The graphs are as plotted (p. 329). The points of intersection give the values of x and y as:

$$\left.\begin{array}{l} x = 3.65 \quad \text{and} \quad y = 7.6 \\ x = 5.4 \quad \text{and} \quad y = -9.7 \end{array}\right\} \quad \text{Ans.}$$

12. The graphs are as plotted (p. 330). Note that $y = e^{-x}$ is $y = 1/e^x$ where $e = 2.718$. Point of intersection is solution of equation

$$x = 0.71 \quad \text{and} \quad y = 0.5 \quad \text{Ans.}$$

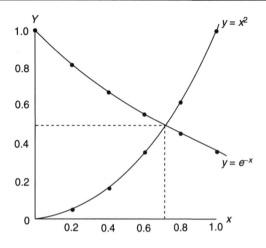

SOLUTIONS TO TEST EXAMPLES 7

1. (i)

$$1 \text{ rad} = 57 \cdot 3^\circ = 57^\circ 18'$$
$$114^\circ 36' = 114 \cdot 6^\circ$$
$$114 \cdot 6 \div 57 \cdot 3 = 2 \text{ rad.} \quad \text{Ans. (i)}$$
$$286^\circ 30' = 286 \cdot 5^\circ$$
$$286 \cdot 5 \div 57 \cdot 3 = 5 \text{ rad.} \quad \text{Ans. (i)}$$

(ii) (a)   Radius of circle = 5 m

$$10 \div 5 = 2 \text{ rad.} \quad \text{Ans. (ii) (a)}$$
$$30 \cdot 4 \div 5 = 6 \cdot 08 \text{ rad.} \quad \text{Ans. (ii) (a)}$$

(ii) (b)

$$\text{Deg} = \text{rad} \times 57 \cdot 3$$
$$2 \times 57 \cdot 3 = 114 \cdot 6^\circ = 114^\circ 36' \quad \text{Ans. (ii) (b)}$$
$$6 \cdot 08 \times 57 \cdot 3 = 348 \cdot 384^\circ = 348^\circ 23' \quad \text{Ans. (ii) (b)}$$

2.

$$v = \omega r$$
$$10 \cdot 52 \times 0 \cdot 1 = 1 \cdot 052 \text{ m/s} \quad \text{Ans. (i)}$$
$$10 \cdot 52 \times 0 \cdot 5 = 5 \cdot 26 \text{ m/s} \quad \text{Ans. (ii)}$$
$$\text{Circumference} = \pi \times \text{diameter}$$

In one revolution, rim travels $\pi \times 2$ m

In one min., rim travels $\pi \times 2 \times 125$ m

In one s, rim travels $\dfrac{\pi \times 2 \times 125}{60}$ m

$$\text{Linear velocity} = 13 \cdot 09 \text{ m/s} \quad \text{Ans. (iii)}$$

3.

$$(AB)^2 = (AC)^2 + (BC)^2$$
$$AB = \sqrt{36^2 + 27^2}$$
$$= \sqrt{2025} = 45 \text{ mm} \quad \text{Ans. (i)}$$

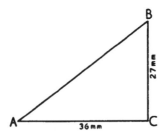

$$\sin B = \frac{\text{opposite}}{\text{hypotenuse}} = \frac{36}{45} = 0{\cdot}8 \quad \text{Ans. (ii)}$$

$$\cos B = \frac{\text{adjacent}}{\text{hypotenuse}} = \frac{27}{45} = 0{\cdot}6 \quad \text{Ans. (iii)}$$

$$\tan B = \frac{\text{opposite}}{\text{adjacent}} = \frac{36}{27} = 1{\cdot}333 \quad \text{Ans. (iv)}$$

4.
$$\sin^2 \theta + \cos^2 \theta = 1$$
$$\sin^2 \theta = 1 - \cos^2 \theta$$
$$\sin \theta = \sqrt{1 - 0{\cdot}4924^2}$$
$$= \sqrt{0{\cdot}7575} = 0{\cdot}8704 \quad \text{Ans. (i)}$$
$$\tan \theta = \frac{\sin \theta}{\cos \theta} = \frac{0{\cdot}8704}{0{\cdot}4924}$$
$$= 1{\cdot}767 \quad \text{Ans. (ii)}$$

5.

ANGLE	SINE	COSINE	TANGENT	
10°33′	0·1831	0·9831	0·1862	
46°55′	0·7304	0·6831	1·0692	Ans.
150°47′	0·4882	−0·8728	−0·5593	
201°21′	−0·3641	−0·9314	0·3909	
287°14′	−0·9551	0·2963	−3·2235	

sine and cosine curves are as shown (p. 333). Ans.

6.

RATIO	VALUE	ANGLE	
sine	0·3783	22°14′ and 157°46′	
sine	−0·7005	224°28′ and 315°32′	
cosine	0.9687	14°22′ and 345°38′	Ans.
cosine	−0·8769	151°16′ and 208°44′	
tangent	0·2010	11°22′ and 191°22′	
tangent	−3·2006	107°21′ and 287°21′	

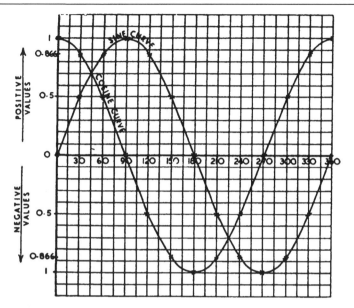

7.
$$\sin 80° = 0.9848$$
$$\cos 80° = 0.1736$$
$$\sin 2\theta = \sin 160° = 0.342$$
$$\cos 2\theta = \cos 160° = -0.9397$$
$$\sin^2 \theta = (0.9848)^2 = 0.9701$$
$$\cos^2 \theta = (0.1736)^2 = 0.03013$$

Ans.

8.
$$\sin^2 \theta + \cos^2 \theta = 1$$
$$\therefore \ \sin^2 \theta = 1 - \cos^2 \theta$$

Substituting this value of $\sin^2 \theta$ into the given equation,

$$\cos \theta - \sin^2 \theta = 0$$
$$\cos \theta - (1 - \cos^2 \theta) = 0$$
$$\cos \theta - 1 + \cos^2 \theta = 0$$

This is a quadratic equation, re-arrange in the usual way in descending powers of the unknown,

$$\cos^2 \theta + \cos \theta - 1 = 0$$

Solve this quadratic equation either by formula or 'completing the square', if preferred, let x stand for $\cos\theta$,

$$x^2 + x - 1 = 0$$

Solution to this quadratic is $0{\cdot}618$ or $-1{\cdot}618$

$$\therefore \ \cos\theta = 0{\cdot}618 \text{ (other value inadmissable)}$$

$$\left.\begin{array}{l}\theta = 51°50' \\ \text{or } (360° - 51°50') = 308°10'\end{array}\right\} \text{ Ans.}$$

9.

$$\frac{a^2}{2} = \frac{2b^2}{5} - 4$$

$$\frac{2^2 \sin^2\theta}{2} = \frac{2 \times 5^2 \cos^2\theta}{5} - 4$$

$$2\sin^2\theta = 10\cos^2\theta - 4$$

$$\sin^2\theta = 5\cos^2\theta - 2$$

$$\sin^2\theta = 5(1 - \sin^2\theta) - 2$$

$$\sin^2\theta = 5 - 5\sin^2\theta - 2$$

$$6\sin^2\theta = 3$$

$$\sin^2\theta = 0{\cdot}5$$

$$\sin\theta = \pm\sqrt{0{\cdot}5} = \pm0{\cdot}7071$$

For angles between $0°$ and $180°$, only the positive value of the sine is applicable.

$$\sin\theta = 0{\cdot}7071$$

$$\therefore \ \theta = 45° \quad \text{or} \quad 135° \quad \text{Ans.}$$

10.
$$\mathrm{cosec}^2 A + \sec^2 A = \mathrm{cosec}^2 A \sec^2 A$$

Simplifying left hand side of equation:

$$\mathrm{cosec}^2 A + \sec^2 A = \frac{1}{\sin^2 A} + \frac{1}{\cos^2 A}$$

$$= \frac{\cos^2 A + \sin^2 A}{\sin^2 A \cos^2 A} = \frac{1}{\sin^2 A \cos^2 A}$$

$$= \mathrm{cosec}^2 A \sec^2 A = \text{right hand side of equation.} \quad \text{Ans.}$$

11.
$$\frac{1 - \sin A}{1 + \sin A} = (\sec A - \tan A)^2$$

Simplifying right hand side of equation:

$$(\sec A - \tan A)^2 = \left\{ \frac{1}{\cos A} - \frac{\sin A}{\cos A} \right\}^2$$

$$= \left\{ \frac{1 - \sin A}{\cos A} \right\}^2 = \frac{(1 - \sin A)^2}{\cos^2 A}$$

$$= \frac{(1 - \sin A)^2}{1 - \sin^2 A} = \frac{(1 - \sin A)(1 - \sin A)}{(1 + \sin A)(1 - \sin A)}$$

$$= \frac{1 - \sin A}{1 + \sin A} = \text{left hand side of equation.} \quad \text{Ans.}$$

12. $$(\sec A - \cos A)(\operatorname{cosec} A - \sin A) = \frac{1}{\tan A + \cot A}$$

Simplifying left hand side of equation:

$$(\sec A - \cos A)(\operatorname{cosec} A - \sin A)$$

$$= \left\{ \frac{1}{\cos A} - \cos A \right\} \left\{ \frac{1}{\sin A} - \sin A \right\}$$

$$= \frac{1 - \cos^2 A}{\cos A} \times \frac{1 - \sin^2 A}{\sin A} = \frac{\sin^2 A}{\cos A} \times \frac{\cos^2 A}{\sin A}$$

$$= \sin A \cos A \quad \dots \quad \dots \quad \dots \quad \dots \quad \dots \quad \dots \quad (i)$$

Simplifying right hand side of equation:

$$\frac{1}{\tan A + \cot A} = \frac{1}{\dfrac{\sin A}{\cos A} + \dfrac{\cos A}{\sin A}}$$

$$= \frac{1}{\dfrac{\sin^2 A + \cos^2 A}{\sin A \cos A}} = \frac{\sin A \cos A}{\sin^2 A + \cos^2 A}$$

$$= \frac{\sin A \cos A}{1} = \sin A \cos A \quad \dots \quad \dots \quad (ii)$$

From (i) and (ii) both sides of the equation are equal to the same quantity, which proves the given identity. Ans.

13. $$\omega = \frac{2\pi \text{ rev/min}}{60} = \frac{2\pi \times 150}{60} = 15\cdot71 \text{ rad/s.}$$

$r = \text{half-stroke} = 0\cdot5 \text{ m}$

$$n = \frac{\text{connecting rod length}}{\text{crank length}} = \frac{2}{0\cdot5} = 4$$

$\theta = 80°$, $\sin 80° = 0\cdot9848$, $\cos 80° = 0\cdot1736$

$2\theta = 160°$, $\sin 160° = 0\cdot342$, $\cos 160° = -0\cdot9397$

$$v = \omega r \left[\sin\theta + \frac{\sin 2\theta}{2n} \right] \text{ m/s}$$

$$= 15\cdot71 \times 0\cdot5 \times \left[0\cdot9848 + \frac{0\cdot342}{2 \times 4} \right]$$

$$= 15\cdot71 \times 0\cdot5 \times 1\cdot02755$$

$$= 8\cdot072 \text{ m/s} \quad \text{Ans. (i)}$$

$$a = \omega^2 r \left[\cos\theta + \frac{\cos 2\theta}{n} \right] \text{ m/s}^2$$

$$= 15\cdot71^2 \times 0\cdot5 \times \left[0\cdot1736 + \frac{-0\cdot9397}{4} \right]$$

$$= 15\cdot71^2 \times 0\cdot5 \times (0\cdot1736 - 0\cdot2349)$$

$$= 15\cdot71^2 \times 0\cdot5 \times (-0\cdot0613)$$

$$= -7\cdot567 \text{ m/s}^2 \quad \text{i.e. deceleration} \quad \text{Ans. (ii)}$$

14. There are two possible triangles which satisfy the conditions given as shown.

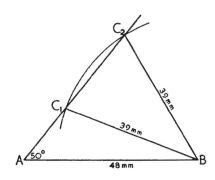

One triangle:

$$\text{Remaining side, } AC_1 = 18 \text{ mm}$$
$$\text{Remaining angles, B and } C_1 = 20\tfrac{1}{2}^\circ \text{ and } 109\tfrac{1}{2}^\circ \Bigg\} \text{ Ans.}$$

Other triangle:

$$\text{Remaining side, } AC_2 = 44 \text{ mm}$$
$$\text{Remaining angles, B and } C_2 = 59\tfrac{1}{2}^\circ \text{ and } 70\tfrac{1}{2}^\circ \Bigg\} \text{ Ans.}$$
$$48 : 60 :: 39 : BC$$
$$BC = 48 \cdot 75 \text{ mm} \quad \text{Ans.}$$

15.

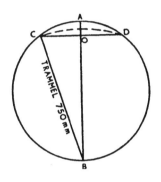

$$\text{Chord } CD = 78 \text{ mm}$$

$$CO = DO = 39 \text{ mm}$$

$$(BO)^2 = (BC)^2 - (CO)^2$$

$$BO = \sqrt{750^2 - 39^2} = 749 \text{ mm}$$

$$AO \times BO = CO \times DO$$

$$AO \times 749 = 39 \times 39$$

$$AO = \frac{39 \times 39}{749} = 2 \cdot 031 \text{ mm}$$

$$\text{Diameter} = AO + BO$$

$$= 2 \cdot 031 + 749 = 751 \cdot 031 \text{ mm}$$

$$\text{Increase} = 751 \cdot 031 - 750$$

$$= 1 \cdot 031 \text{ mm} \quad \text{Ans.}$$

16.

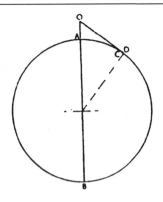

$$AO = 30 \text{ m} = 0.03 \text{ km}$$
$$BO = 12750 + 0.03 = 12750.03 \text{ km}$$

this can be taken as 12750 km

$$CO = DO = \text{observation distance.}$$
$$AO \times BO = CO \times DO$$
$$0.03 \times 12750 = (CO)^2$$
$$CO = 19.55 \text{ km} \quad \text{Ans.}$$

17.

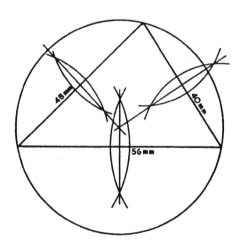

Radius of circumscribing circle $= 28.6$ mm.   Ans.

18.

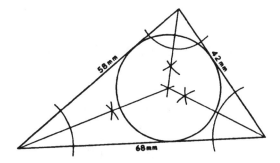

Radius of inscribed circle = 14·4 mm.   Ans.

SOLUTIONS TO TEST EXAMPLES 8

1.

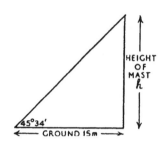

$$\frac{\text{opposite (mast)}}{\text{adjacent (ground)}} = \tan 45°34'$$

$$\therefore h = 15 \times \tan 45°34'$$

$$= 15\cdot3 \text{ m Ans.}$$

2.

$$\frac{\text{opposite (cliff)}}{\text{adjacent (sea)}} = \tan 14°25'$$

$$\text{adjacent} = \frac{\text{opposite}}{\tan 14°25'}$$

$$= \frac{95}{\tan 14°25'} = 369\cdot5 \text{ m} \quad \text{Ans. (i)}$$

$$\frac{\text{opposite}}{\text{hypotenuse}} = \sin 14°25'$$

$$\text{hypotenuse} = \frac{\text{opposite}}{\sin 14°25'}$$

$$= \frac{95}{\sin 14°25'} = 381\cdot5 \text{ m} \quad \text{Ans. (ii)}$$

3.

opposite $= 120 \times \sin 28°37'$

$\qquad = 57.48$ mm   Ans. (i)

adjacent $= 120 \times \cos 28°37'$

$\qquad = 105.3$ mm   Ans. (ii)

area $= \frac{1}{2}$(base $\times$ perp. height)

$\qquad = \dfrac{105.3 \times 57.48}{2}$

$\qquad = 3026$ mm^2 or 30.26 cm^2 Ans. (iii)

4.

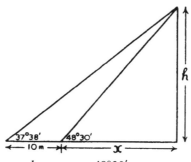

$h = x \times \tan 48°30'$

$\quad = x \times 1.1303$ $\qquad$ ... ... (i)

also, $\quad h = (10 + x) \times \tan 37°38'$

$\qquad = (10 + x) \times 0.7710$

$\qquad = 7.71 + 0.771x$ $\qquad$ ... ... (ii)

From (i) and (ii),

$\quad 1.1303x = 7.71 + 0.771x$

$\quad 0.3593x = 7.71$

$\qquad x = 21.46$ m   Ans. (a)

From (i),

$\quad h = x \times 1.1303$

$\qquad = 21.46 \times 1.1303$

$\qquad = 24.25$ m   Ans. (b)

5.

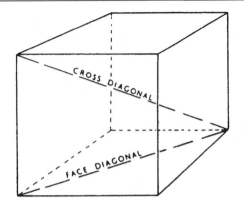

By Pythagoras,

$$\text{diagonal across face} = \sqrt{60^2 + 60^2} = \sqrt{7200}$$
$$= 84\cdot85 \text{ mm}\quad \text{Ans. (i)}$$

Cross diagonal to opposite corners, through centre,

$$= \sqrt{60^2 + 84\cdot85^2}$$
$$= \sqrt{60^2 + 60^2 + 60^2} = \sqrt{10\,800}$$
$$= 103\cdot9 \text{ mm}\quad \text{Ans. (ii)}$$

6.

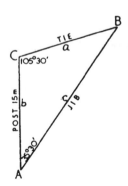

$B = 180° - (105°30' + 35°30') = 39°.$
By sine rule,

$$\frac{a}{\sin A} = \frac{b}{\sin B}$$

$$a = \frac{b \times \sin A}{\sin B}$$

$$= \frac{15 \times \sin 35°30'}{\sin 39°} = 13.84 \text{ m}$$

$$\frac{b}{\sin B} = \frac{c}{\sin C}$$

$$c = \frac{b \times \sin C}{\sin B}$$

$$= \frac{15 \times \sin 105°30'}{\sin 39°} = 22.97 \text{ m}$$

$$\left.\begin{array}{l} \text{Length of jib} = 22.97 \text{ m} \\ \text{Length of tie} = 13.84 \text{ m} \end{array}\right\} \text{ Ans.}$$

7. On the sketch (p. 344) the x is the distance the crosshead has moved from the top of its stroke when the crank is 35° past top centre.

Crank length $= \frac{1}{2}$ stroke $= 400$ mm
When crank is on top dead centre,
distance from shaft centre to crosshead
$= 1600 + 400 = 2000$ mm

When crank is 35° past top dead centre, distance from shaft centre to crosshead is now to be calculated:

$$\frac{a}{\sin A} = \frac{c}{\sin C}$$

$$\sin A = \frac{a \times \sin C}{c}$$

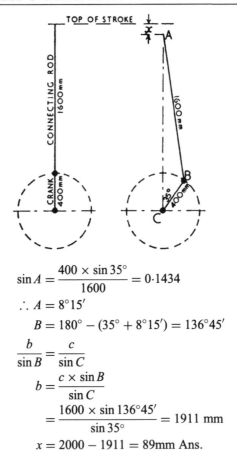

$$\sin A = \frac{400 \times \sin 35°}{1600} = 0·1434$$

$$\therefore A = 8°15'$$

$$B = 180° - (35° + 8°15') = 136°45'$$

$$\frac{b}{\sin B} = \frac{c}{\sin C}$$

$$b = \frac{c \times \sin B}{\sin C}$$

$$= \frac{1600 \times \sin 136°45'}{\sin 35°} = 1911 \text{ mm}$$

$$x = 2000 - 1911 = 89 \text{mm Ans.}$$

8. Let stroke $= 1$, crank length $= 0·5$, conn. rod length $= 2$.
   When crank is on top dead centre, distrance from shaft centre to crosshead $= 0·5 + 2 = 2·5$
   When crosshead has moved down $0·1$ of its stroke, distance from shaft centre to crosshead $= 2·5 - 0·1 = 2·4$,
   By cosine rule,

$$\cos C = \frac{a^2 + b^2 - c^2}{2ab}$$

$$= \frac{0·5^2 + 2·4^2 - 2^2}{2 \times 0·5 \times 2·4} = 0·8375$$

$$\therefore C = 33°7' \text{ Ans.}$$

9.

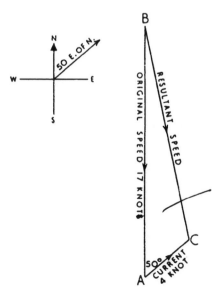

By cosine rule,

$$a^2 = b^2 + c^2 - 2bc\cos A$$
$$= 4^2 + 17^2 - 2 \times 4 \times 17 \times \cos 50°$$
$$= 16 + 289 - 87{\cdot}42$$
$$a = \sqrt{217{\cdot}58} = 14{\cdot}75$$

By sine rule,

$$\frac{a}{\sin A} = \frac{b}{\sin B}$$
$$\sin B = \frac{b \times \sin A}{a}$$
$$= \frac{4 \times \sin 50°}{14{\cdot}75} = 0{\cdot}2078$$
$$\therefore B = 12°$$

$\therefore$ Resultant speed of ship = 14·75 knot
Resultant direction of ship = 12°East of South $\Big\}$ Ans.

10.

Let x = nearest ship's distance from port
then $2x$ = other ship's distance from port.
$$a^2 = b^2 + c^2 - 2bc\cos A$$
$$32^2 = (2x)^2 + x^2 - 2 \times 2x \times x \times \cos 23°$$
$$1024 = 4x^2 + x^2 - 3{\cdot}682x^2$$
$$1024 = 1{\cdot}318x^2$$

$$x = \sqrt{\frac{1024}{1{\cdot}318}} = 27{\cdot}87$$

$\therefore$ distances from port = 27·87 naut. miles
and 27·87 × 2 = 55·74 naut. miles $\Big\}$ Ans.

11.

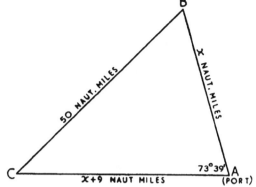

$\frac{1}{2}$ h at 18 knot represents a distance of 9 naut. miles.

Let x naut. miles = distance of first ship from port

then $(x + 9)$ naut. miles = distance of second ship from port

By cosine rule,

$$a^2 = b^2 + c^2 - 2bc \cos A$$
$$50^2 = (x + 9)^2 + x^2 - 2(x + 9) \times x \times \cos 73°39'$$
$$2500 = x^2 + 18x + 81 + x^2 - 2 \times x \times 0{\cdot}2815(x + 9)$$
$$2500 = 2x^2 + 18x + 81 - 0{\cdot}563x^2 - 5{\cdot}067x$$
$$2419 = 1{\cdot}437x^2 + 12{\cdot}933x$$

or, $1{\cdot}437x^2 + 12{\cdot}933x - 2419 = 0$

Solving this quadratic,

$$x = 36{\cdot}8$$

$\therefore$ Distance from port = 36·8 naut. miles $\Big\}$

and $(36·8 + 9) = 45·8$ naut. miles $\Big\}$ Ans.

12.

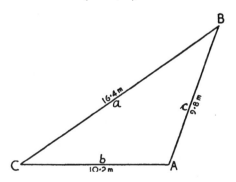

By cosine rule,

$$\cos A = \frac{b^2 + c^2 - a^2}{2bc}$$

$$= \frac{10 \cdot 2^2 + 9 \cdot 8^2 - 16 \cdot 4^2}{2 \times 10 \cdot 2 \times 9 \cdot 8}$$

$$= \frac{104 + 96 \cdot 04 - 268 \cdot 96}{2 \times 10 \cdot 2 \times 9 \cdot 8}$$

$$= \frac{-68.92}{2 \times 10 \cdot 2 \times 9 \cdot 8} = -0 \cdot 3447$$

$\therefore$ Angle $A = 180° - 69°50' = 110°10'$

By sine rule,

$$\frac{a}{\sin A} = \frac{b}{\sin B}$$

$$\sin B = \frac{b \times \sin A}{a}$$

$$= \frac{10 \cdot 2 \times \sin 110°10'}{16 \cdot 4} = 0 \cdot 5838$$

$\therefore$ Angle $B = 35°43'$

Angle $C = 180° - (110°10' + 35°43')$

$$= 34°7'$$

The three angles are,

$$110°10', 35°43' \text{ and } 34°7' \text{ Ans.}$$

13. $$\text{Area} = \frac{ab \sin C}{2}$$

$$= \frac{6 \cdot 5 \times 7 \cdot 5 \times \sin 46°51'}{2}$$

$$= 17 \cdot 78 \text{ m}^2 \text{ Ans.}$$

14.
$$\text{Area} = \sqrt{s(s-a)(s-b)(s-c)}$$
$$s = \frac{7\cdot1 + 4\cdot2 + 5\cdot3}{2} = 8\cdot3$$
$$s - a = 8\cdot3 - 7\cdot1 = 1\cdot2$$
$$s - b = 8\cdot3 - 4\cdot2 = 4\cdot1$$
$$s - c = 8\cdot3 - 5\cdot3 = 3\cdot0$$
$$\text{Area} = \sqrt{8\cdot3 \times 1\cdot2 \times 4\cdot1 \times 3}$$
$$= 11\cdot07 \text{ cm}^2 \quad \text{Ans.}$$

15.
$$\text{Area} = 0\cdot433 \times \text{side}^2$$
$$\text{side} = \sqrt{\frac{\text{area}}{0\cdot433}} = \sqrt{\frac{57\cdot27}{0\cdot433}}$$
$$= 11\cdot5 \text{ cm} \quad \text{Ans.}$$

16.
$$\sin^2 \theta + \cos^2 = 1$$
$$\therefore \cos^2 \theta = 1 - \sin^2 \theta$$

Substituting this value of $\cos^2 \theta$ into the equation:

$$\cos 2\theta = \cos^2 \theta - \sin^2 \theta$$
$$= 1 - \sin^2 \theta - \sin^2 \theta$$
$$\therefore \cos 2\theta = 1 - 2\sin^2 \theta \quad \text{Ans. (i)}$$
$$\sin^2 \theta + \cos^2 \theta = 1$$
$$\therefore \sin^2 \theta = 1 - \cos^2 \theta$$

Substituting this value of $\sin^2 \theta$ into the equation:

$$\cos 2\theta = \cos^2 \theta - \sin^2 \theta$$
$$= \cos^2 \theta - (1 - \cos^2 \theta)$$
$$= \cos^2 \theta - 1 + \cos^2 \theta$$
$$\therefore \cos 2\theta = 2\cos^2 \theta - 1 \quad \text{Ans. (ii)}$$

$$(1 + \cot^2 \theta)(1 - \cos 2\theta)$$

$$= \left\{1 + \frac{\cos^2 \theta}{\sin^2 \theta}\right\} \times \{1 - (1 - 2\sin^2 \theta)\}$$

$$= \left\{\frac{\sin^2 \theta + \cos^2 \theta}{\sin^2 \theta}\right\} \times \{1 - 1 + 2\sin^2 \theta\}$$

$$= \frac{1}{\sin^2 \theta} \times 2\sin^2 \theta = \frac{2\sin^2 \theta}{\sin^2 \theta}$$

$$= 2 \quad \text{Ans. (iii)}$$

17.
$$\sin 2\theta = \frac{2\tan \theta}{1 + \tan^2 \theta}$$

Simplifying right hand side of equation:

$$\frac{2\tan \theta}{1 + \tan^2 \theta} = \frac{2\tan \theta}{\sec^2 \theta} = \frac{2\sin \theta}{\cos \theta} \times \frac{\cos^2 \theta}{1}$$

$$= 2\sin \theta \cos \theta = \sin 2\theta = \text{left hand side of equation.} \quad \text{Ans. (i)}$$

$$\cos 2\theta = \frac{1 - \tan^2 \theta}{1 + \tan^2 \theta}$$

Simplifying right hand side of equation:

$$\frac{1 - \tan^2 \theta}{1 + \tan^2 \theta} = \frac{1 - \dfrac{\sin^2 \theta}{\cos^2 \theta}}{\sec^2 \theta}$$

$$\frac{\cos^2 \theta - \sin^2 \theta}{\cos^2 \theta} \times \frac{\cos^2 \theta}{1} = \cos^2 \theta - \sin^2 \theta$$

$$= \cos 2\theta = \text{left hand side of equation.} \quad \text{Ans. (ii)}$$

$$\sin 2\theta + 2\cos 2\theta = 1$$

$$\frac{2\tan \theta}{1 + \tan^2 \theta} + \frac{2(1 - \tan^2 \theta)}{1 + \tan^2 \theta} = 1$$

$$2\tan \theta + 2 - 2\tan^2 \theta = 1 + \tan^2 \theta$$

$$3\tan^2 \theta - 2\tan \theta - 1 = 0$$

Positive solution of this quadratic for angle between $0°$ and $90°$, $\tan \theta = 1$,

$$\therefore \ \theta = 45° \quad \text{Ans. (iii)}$$

18.　$\sin 3\theta$ may be written as a compound angle,

$$\sin 3\theta = \sin (2\theta + \theta)$$

Using the compound angle formula,

$$\sin (A + B) = \sin A \cos B + \cos A \sin B$$

Let $A = 2\theta$, and $B = \theta$, then,

$$\sin (2\theta + \theta) = \sin 2\theta \cos \theta + \cos 2\theta \sin \theta$$

Substitute for $\sin 2\theta$ and $\cos 2\theta$ from the identities,

$$\sin 2\theta = 2 \sin \theta \cos \theta$$

and　$\cos 2\theta = 1 - 2 \sin^2 \theta$

thus,

$$\sin (2\theta + \theta) = \sin 2\theta \cos \theta + \cos 2\theta \sin \theta$$
$$= (2 \sin \theta \cos \theta) \times \cos \theta + (1 - 2 \sin^2 \theta) \times \sin \theta$$
$$= 2 \sin \theta \cos^2 \theta + \sin \theta - 2 \sin^3 \theta$$

Substitute for $\cos^2 \theta$ from the identity,

$$\cos^2 \theta = 1 - \sin^2 \theta$$

thus,

$$\sin (2\theta + \theta) = 2 \sin \theta \cos^2 \theta + \sin \theta - 2 \sin^3 \theta$$
$$= 2 \sin \theta (1 - \sin^2 \theta) + \sin \theta - 2 \sin^3 \theta$$
$$= 2 \sin \theta - 2 \sin^3 \theta + \sin \theta - 2 \sin^3 \theta$$
$$\sin 3\theta = 3 \sin \theta - 4 \sin^3 \theta \quad \text{Ans.}$$

SOLUTIONS TO TEST EXAMPLES 9

1.

By cosine rule, working in cm:

$$\cos ADC = \frac{(AD)^2 + (CD)^2 - (AC)^2}{2 \times (AD) \times (CD)}$$

$$= \frac{10^2 + 6^2 - 14^2}{2 \times 10 \times 6}$$

$$= -0 \cdot 5$$

$$\therefore \text{ Angle ADC} = 180° - 60° = 120°$$

Obtuse angles are each $120°$
Acute angles $= 180° - 120° = 60°$ $\Big\}$ Ans. (i)

$$(BD)^2 = (AD)^2 + (AB)^2 - 2 \times (AD) \times (AB) \times \cos BAD$$

$$= 10^2 + 6^2 - 2 \times 10 \times 6 \times \cos 60°$$

$$BD = \sqrt{76}$$

short diagonal $= 8 \cdot 718$ cm $= 87 \cdot 18$ mm   Ans. (ii)

Angle CDE $= 60°$

Perpendicular height CE $= 6 \times \sin 60°$

$$= 5 \cdot 196 \text{ cm} = 51 \cdot 96 \text{ mm}$$ Ans. (iii)

Area $=$ base $\times$ perpendicular height

$$= 10 \times 5 \cdot 196$$

$$= 51 \cdot 96 \text{ cm}^2 \text{ or } 5196 \text{ mm}^2$$ Ans. (iv)

2.

$$\sin \alpha = \frac{24}{32} = 0.75$$

$$\therefore \alpha = 48°35'$$

each obtuse angle $= 2 \times 48°35' = 97°10'$
each acute angle $= 180° - 97°10' = 82°50'$ } Ans. (i)

$\frac{1}{2}$ length of short diagonal $= BE = 32 \times \cos 48°35'$

$$= 21.16$$

$\therefore$ short diagonal $= 21.6 \times 2 = 42.32$ mm Ans. (ii)

Area $= \frac{1}{2}$ product of diagonals

$$= \frac{48 \times 42.32}{2}$$

$$= 1016 \text{ mm}^2 \quad \text{Ans. (iii)}$$

3.

Referring to sketch, working in cm:

$$\text{Mean length} = \tfrac{1}{2}(10 + 6) = 8 \text{ cm}$$
$$\text{Area} = \text{mean length} \times \text{perp. height}$$
$$= 8 \times 5$$
$$= 40 \text{ cm}^2 \quad \text{Ans. (i)}$$

Each half area is to be 20 cm^2, let dividing line EF be at x from CD

$$\text{AG} = 10 - 6 = 4 \text{ cm}$$

By similar triangles,

$$\frac{\text{GA}}{\text{DG}} = \frac{\text{HF}}{\text{DH}}$$
$$\frac{4}{5} = \frac{\text{HF}}{x}$$
$$\text{HF} = \frac{4x}{5} = 0\!\cdot\!8x$$
$$\text{EF} = 6 + 0\!\cdot\!8x$$

Mean length of half area FECD

$$= \tfrac{1}{2}(\text{CD} + \text{EF})$$
$$= \tfrac{1}{2}(6 + 6 + 0\!\cdot\!8x)$$
$$= 6 + 0\!\cdot\!4x$$
$$\text{Area} = \text{mean length} \times \text{perp. height}$$
$$20 = (6 + 0\!\cdot\!4x) \times x$$
$$20 = 6x + 0\!\cdot\!4x^2$$
$$0\!\cdot\!4x^2 + 6x - 20 = 0$$
$$x^2 + 15x - 50 = 0$$

Solving this quadratic, $x = 2\!\cdot\!81$

$\therefore$ Dividing line should be at $2\!\cdot\!81$ cm $= 28\!\cdot\!1$ mm from CD

Ans. (ii)

4.

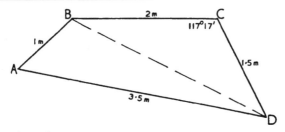

By cosine rule,

$$(BD)^2 = (BC)^2 + (CD)^2 - 2 \times (BC) \times (CD) \times \cos BCD$$
$$= 2^2 + 1 \cdot 5^2 - 2 \times 2 \times 1 \cdot 5 \times \cos 117°17'$$
$$= 4 + 2 \cdot 25 + 2 \cdot 75$$
$$BD = \sqrt{9} = 3 \text{ m}$$

Semi-sum of sides of triangle BCD

$$= \tfrac{1}{2}(2 + 1 \cdot 5 + 3) = 3 \cdot 25 \text{ m}$$
$$\text{Area of BCD} = \sqrt{s(s - a)(s - b)(s - c)}$$
$$= \sqrt{3 \cdot 25 \times 1 \cdot 25 \times 1 \cdot 75 \times 0 \cdot 25}$$
$$= 1 \cdot 333 \text{ m}^2$$

Alternatively the area could be found by $\tfrac{1}{2}(ab \sin C)$.

Semi-sum of sides of triangle ABD

$$= \tfrac{1}{2}(3 + 3 \cdot 5 + 1) = 3 \cdot 75 \text{ m}$$
$$\text{Area ABD} = \sqrt{3.75 \times 0 \cdot 75 \times 0 \cdot 25 \times 2 \cdot 75}$$
$$= 1 \cdot 391 \text{ m}^2$$

Area of quadrilateral = sum of areas of the two triangles

$$= 1 \cdot 333 + 1 \cdot 391$$
$$= 2 \cdot 724 \text{ m}^2 \quad \text{Ans.}$$

5.

Let x mm = thickness of piece cut off. The piece cut off is a trapezium, consisting of a rectangle $80 \times x$ and two equal triangles; the height of each triangle being x, then the side perpendicular to this, marked y in the sketch, is $x \tan 30° = 0.5774x$, hence,

Area of piece cut off,

$$= (80 \times x) + (2 \times \tfrac{1}{2} \times 0.5774x \times x)$$
$$= 80x + 0.5774x^2 \qquad \ldots \quad \ldots \quad \ldots \quad (i)$$

Area of hexagon $= 6 \times 0.433 \text{ side}^2 = 2.598 \text{ side}^2$

Area of piece cut off $= 0.1 \times 2.598 \times 80^2$
$$= 1663 \text{ mm}^2 \qquad \ldots \quad \ldots \quad (ii)$$
$$\therefore \quad 80x + 0.5774x^2 = 1663$$
$$0.5774x^2 + 80x - 1663 = 0$$
or, $\quad x^2 + 138.6x - 2880 = 0$
Solving this quadratic, $\quad x = 18.35$ mm   Ans.

6. Considering one of the eight constituent triangles,

Apex angle $= 360 \div 8 = 45°$
Each base angle $= \tfrac{1}{2}(180 - 45) = 67.5°$
Perpendicular height $= 15 \times \tan 67°30'$
$$= 36.21 \text{ mm}$$
Area of each triangle $= \tfrac{1}{2}(\text{base} \times \text{perp. height})$
$$= \tfrac{1}{2} \times 30 \times 36.21$$
Area of octagon $= 8 \times \tfrac{1}{2} \times 30 \times 36.21$
$$= 4346 \text{ mm}^2$$
Area of hole $= 0.7854 \times 50^2$
$$= 1963 \text{ mm}^2$$
Area of plate $= 4346 - 1963$
$$= 2383 \text{ mm}^2 \quad \text{Ans.}$$

7.

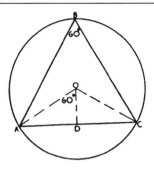

Radius = AO = 60 mm

Being an equilateral triangle, all angles are 60°

Angle at centre AOC is twice the angle at the apex.

$$\therefore \ \text{AOC} = 120°, \text{ and AOD} = 60°$$
$$\text{AD} = \text{AO} \times \sin 60°$$
$$= 60 \times 0.866 = 51.96 \text{ mm}$$
$$\text{length of sides} = \text{AC} = 2 \times \text{AD}$$
$$= 103.92 \text{ mm} \quad \text{Ans. (i)}$$
$$\text{OD} = \text{AO} \times \cos 60°$$
$$= 60 \times 0.5 = 30 \text{ mm}$$
$$\text{BD} = \text{BO} + \text{OD}$$
$$= 60 + 30 = 90 \text{ mm}$$
$$\text{Area} = \tfrac{1}{2}(\text{base} \times \text{perp. height})$$
$$= \tfrac{1}{2} \times 103.92 \times 90$$
$$= 4676 \text{ mm}^2 \quad \text{Ans. (ii)}$$
(or formula, Area = 0.433 × side² could be used)

8.
$$\text{Area of collar} = 0.7854 \ (D^2 - d^2)$$
$$= 0.7854(D + d)(D - d)$$
$$= 0.7854(755 + 415)(755 - 415)$$
$$= 0.7854 \times 1170 \times 340$$

Effective area $= 0.7 \times 0.7854 \times 1170 \times 340 \text{ mm}^2$

$$1 \text{ m}^2 = (10^3)^2 \text{ mm}^2 = 10^6 \text{ mm}^2$$

$\therefore$ Area $= 0.7 \times 0.7854 \times 1170 \times 340 \times 10^{-6} \text{ m}^2$

$$= 0.2187 \text{ m}^2 \quad \text{Ans. (i)}$$

At a pressure of 2000 kN/m^2:

Total force $= 0.2187 \times 2000$

$$= 437.4 \text{ kN} \quad \text{Ans. (ii)}$$

9. Working in cm:

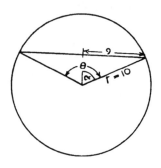

$$\sin \alpha = \frac{9}{10} = 0.9,$$

$$\therefore \quad \alpha = 64°9'$$

$$\theta = 2\alpha = 128°18'$$

$$\sin 128°18' = \sin (180° - 128°18') = \sin 51°42' = 0.7848$$

$$\frac{128.3}{57.3} = 2.239 \text{ rad}$$

Area of segment $= \dfrac{r^2}{2}[\theta - \sin \theta]$

$$= \frac{10^2}{2}(2.239 - 0.7848)$$

$$= 50 \times 1.4542$$

$$= 72.71 \text{ cm}^2 \quad \text{Ans.}$$

10.   Curved surface area of sphere $= \pi d \times d$

Curved surface area of hemisphere $= \dfrac{\pi d^2}{2}$

Surface area of circular base $= \dfrac{\pi d^2}{4}$

Total surface area $= \dfrac{\pi d^2}{2} + \dfrac{\pi d^2}{4}$

$\therefore 58 \cdot 9 = \pi d^2 (\tfrac{1}{2} + \tfrac{1}{4})$

$58 \cdot 9 = \pi d^2 \times \tfrac{3}{4}$

$d = \sqrt{\dfrac{58 \cdot 9 \times 4}{\pi \times 3}} = 4 \cdot 999$

say 5 cm or 50 mm dia.   Ans.

11. By crossed chords,

$$AO \times BO = CO \times DO$$

Let d mm = depth of indentation $= CO$

DO = ball diameter $- CO = 10 - d$

AO = BO $= \tfrac{1}{2}$ surface diameter $= 2 \cdot 5$ mm

$$AO \times BO = CO \times DO$$

$$2 \cdot 5 \times 2 \cdot 5 = d \times (10 - d)$$

$$6 \cdot 25 = 10d - d^2$$

$$d^2 - 10d + 6 \cdot 25 = 0$$

Solving this quadratic, $d = 9 \cdot 33$ or $0 \cdot 67$

$\therefore$ depth $= 0 \cdot 67$ mm Ans. (i)

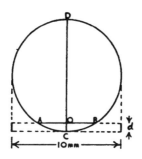

Curved surface area of indentation is equal to the curved surface area of a slice of same depth off a circumscribing cylinder of same diameter as the ball,

$$= \pi \times \text{ball diameter} \times \text{depth of indent}$$
$$= \pi \times 10 \times 0.67$$
$$= 21.05 \text{ mm}^2 \quad \text{Ans. (ii)}$$

12.

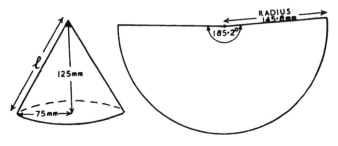

Slant height $= \sqrt{125^2 + 75^2} = 145.8$ mm

this is the radius of the sector.

Arc of sector = circumference of base of cone

$$= \pi \times 150 = 471.3 \text{ mm}$$

Angle of sector $= \dfrac{\text{arc}}{\text{radius}}$

$$= \frac{471.3}{145.8} = 3.232 \text{ rad}$$

$$3.232 \times \frac{360}{2\pi} = 185.2°$$

∴ dimensions of sector are:

$$\left. \begin{array}{l} \text{Radius} = 145.8 \text{ mm} \\ \text{Angle at centre} = 185.2° \end{array} \right\} \quad \text{Ans.}$$

13.

$$l = \sqrt{170^2 + 70^2} = 183 \cdot 8 \text{ mm}$$

By Theorem of Pappus, considering l as the line rotated one revolution about the fixed axis o o

c.g. of line from o o = $\frac{1}{2}(90 + 160) = 125$ mm

Area swept out = length of line × distance c.g. moves

∴ Curved surface area = $183 \cdot 8 \times 2\pi \times 125$

$$= 1 \cdot 444 \times 10^5 \text{ mm}^2 \quad \text{Ans.}$$

14.

Diameter of bar = difference in outer and inner radii

$$= 320 - 220 = 100 \text{ mm}$$

Circumference of bar = $\pi \times 100$ mm
Position of centroid from centre axis o o = $220 + 50 = 270$ mm
By Theorem of Pappus,

Area swept out = length of line × distance centroid moves

∴ Curved surface area = $\pi \times 100 \times 2\pi \times 270$

$$= 5 \cdot 331 \times 10^5 \text{ mm}^2 \quad \text{Ans.}$$

15. Areas of similar figures vary as the square of their corresponding dimensions.

Ratio of corresponding dimensions = 125 : 175

Dividing each by 125,

$$\text{Ratio of dimensions} = 1 \quad : \quad 1\cdot4$$
$$\text{Ratio of areas} = 1^2 \quad : \quad 1\cdot4^2$$
$$= 1 \quad : \quad 1\cdot96$$
$$= 100 : \quad 196$$

∴. Area of larger triangle is 96% greater than smaller Ans.

16.

SEMI-ORDINATES	SIMPSON'S MULTIPLIERS	PRODUCTS
0·1	1	0·1
3·0	4	12·0
5·85	2	11·7
7·2	4	28·8
8·1	2	16·2
8·4	4	33·6
8·4	2	16·8
8·25	4	33·0
8·1	2	16·2
7·5	4	30·0
6·3	2	12·6
3·75	4	15·0
0·5	1	0·5
		sum = 226·5

Number of ordinates = 13

∴   Number of spaces = 12

$$\text{Common interval} = \text{length} \div \text{no. of spaces}$$
$$= 150 \div 12$$
$$= 12\cdot5 \text{ m}$$

Area = sum of products × $\frac{1}{3}$ common interval

$$= \frac{226\cdot5 \times 12\cdot5}{3} = 943\cdot75 \text{ m}^2$$

As *semi*-ordinates have been used then this is the *half*-area of the water-plane.

$$\text{Total area} = 2 \times 943 \cdot 75$$

$$= 1887 \cdot 5 \text{ m}^2 \quad \text{Ans.}$$

17. Plotting points for the two curves:

x	$y = x^2 + 3x + 6$	$y = 2x^2 - x + 1$
0	6	1
1	10	2
2	16	7
3	24	16
4	34	29

The plotted curves are shown (p. 364).

Finding area between curves by Simpson's rule:

ORDINATES BETWEEN CURVES	SIMPSON'S MULTIPLIERS	PRODUCTS
$6 - 1 = 5$	1	5
$10 - 2 = 8$	4	32
$16 - 7 = 9$	2	18
$24 - 16 = 8$	4	32
$34 - 29 = 5$	1	5
		sum = 92

Common interval between ordinates $= 1$

$$\text{Area} = \text{sum of products} \times \tfrac{1}{3} \text{ common interval}$$

$$= 92 \times \tfrac{1}{3} \times 1$$

$$= 30\tfrac{2}{3} \text{ units}^2 \quad \text{Ans.}$$

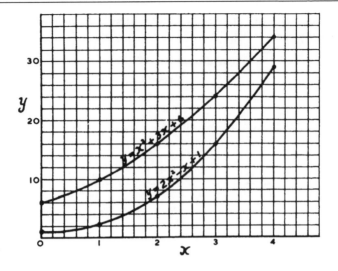

18.   Sum of mid-ordinates $= 82.5$ mm

Mean height $= 82.5 \div 10 = 8.25$ mm   Ans. (i)

Mean effective pressure $= 8.25 \times 160$

$$= 1320 \text{ kN/m}^2 \quad \text{Ans. (ii)}$$

SOLUTIONS TO TEST EXAMPLES 10

1.

Working in cm:

$$\text{Area of top flange} = 10 \times 1\cdot2 = 12 \text{ cm}^2$$
$$\text{Area of bottom flange} = 14 \times 1\cdot4 = 19\cdot6 \text{ cm}^2$$
$$\text{Area of centre web} = 12\cdot4 \times 1 = \underline{12\cdot4 \text{ cm}^2}$$
$$\text{Total area} = 44\cdot0 \text{ cm}^2$$

Volume of 1 m length

$$= \text{area} \times \text{length}$$
$$= 44 \times 100 = 4400 \text{ cm}^3$$
$$\text{Mass (m)} = \text{volume (V)} \times \text{density } (\rho)$$
$$= 4400 \times 7\cdot86$$
$$= 3\cdot458 \times 10^4 \text{g}$$
$$= 34\cdot58 \text{ kg/m run.} \quad \text{Ans.}$$

2. Working in m:

Volume of shaft body $= \text{area of end} \times \text{length}$
$$= 0\cdot7854 \,(0\cdot4^2 - 0\cdot2^2) \times 6$$
$$= 0\cdot5654 \text{ m}^3$$

Volume of two couplings

$$= 0.7854 \, (0.76^2 - 0.4^2) \times 0.075 \times 2$$
$$= 0.0492 \text{ m}^3$$

Total volume $= 0.5654 + 0.0492 = 0.6146 \text{ m}^3$

$$m = V\rho$$
$$= 0.6146 \times 7.86$$

Mass $= 4.831$ t   Ans.

3.

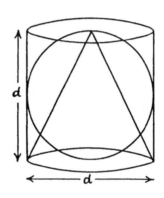

Vol. of cylinder : Vol. of sphere : Vol. of cone

$$= \frac{\pi}{4}d^2 \times d \; : \; \frac{\pi}{6}d^3 \qquad\qquad : \frac{1}{3} \times \frac{\pi}{4}d^2 \times d$$

dividing throughout by $\dfrac{\pi}{12}d^3$

$$= 3 \; : \; 2 \; : \; 1 \quad \text{Ans.}$$

4. Working in m:

$$\text{Area of sector} = \frac{240}{360} \times \text{area of full circle}$$
$$= \tfrac{2}{3} \times \pi \times 0.18^2 \text{ m}^2$$
$$\text{Mass of material} = \tfrac{2}{3} \times \pi \times 0.18^2 \times 6.5$$
$$= 0.4412 \text{ kg} \quad \text{Ans. (i)}$$

Working in mm:

Circumference of cone base = arc of sector

$$\pi \times d = \frac{240}{360} \times 2\pi \times 180$$

$$d = \tfrac{2}{3} \times 2 \times 180$$

$$\therefore \text{ diameter} = 240 \text{ mm} \quad \text{Ans. (ii)}$$

Slant height of cone = radius of sector = 180 mm

Radius of cone base = 120 mm

$$\therefore \text{ Perp. height of cone} = \sqrt{180^2 - 120^2}$$

$$= 134 \cdot 2 \text{ mm} \quad \text{Ans. (iii)}$$

Volume of cone $= \tfrac{1}{3} \times$ area of base $\times$ perp. ht.

$$= \tfrac{1}{3} \times \pi r^2 \times h$$

$$= \tfrac{1}{3} \times \pi \times 120^2 \times 134 \cdot 2$$

$$= 2 \cdot 024 \times 10^6 \text{ mm}^3$$

$$1 \text{ litre} = 10^6 \text{ mm}^3$$

$$\therefore \text{ Capacity} = 2 \cdot 024 \text{ l} \quad \text{Ans. (iv)}$$

5.   Volume of hemisphere $= \dfrac{1}{2} \times \dfrac{\pi}{6} d^3$

$$= \dfrac{\pi}{12} \times 6^3 \text{ cm}^3$$

Volume of cone $= \dfrac{1}{3} \times \dfrac{\pi}{4} d^2 \times h$

$$= \dfrac{\pi}{12} \times 6^2 \times 5 \text{ cm}^3$$

Total Volume $= \dfrac{\pi}{12} \times 6^3 + \dfrac{\pi}{12} \times 6^2 \times 5$

$$= \dfrac{\pi}{12} \times 6^2(6 + 5)$$

$$= \dfrac{\pi}{12} \times 36 \times 11 \text{ cm}^3$$

Mass $= \dfrac{\pi}{12} \times 36 \times 11 \times 8 \cdot 4$

$$= 871 \text{ g} \quad \text{Ans.}$$

6.   Volume of lead in hollow sphere $= \dfrac{3000}{11\cdot4}$ cm^3

Let $D =$ outside diameter, in cm, then inside diameter $= (D - 2)$ cm

$$\frac{\pi}{6}(D^3 - d^3) = \frac{3000}{11\cdot4}$$

$$D^3 - (D - 2)^3 = \frac{3000 \times 6}{11\cdot4 \times \pi}$$

$$D^3 - (D^3 - 6D^2 + 12D - 8) = 502\cdot5$$

$$6D^2 - 12D + 8 = 502\cdot5$$

$$6D^2 - 12D - 494\cdot5 = 0$$

$$\text{or,} \quad D^2 - 2D - 82\cdot41 = 0$$

Solving this quadratic equation,

$$D = 10\cdot135 \text{ cm} \quad \text{or} \quad 101\cdot35 \text{ mm Ans.}$$

7.

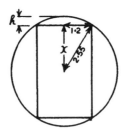

radius of sphere $= \frac{1}{2} \times 5\cdot1 = 2\cdot55$ cm

radius of hole $= \frac{1}{2} \times 2\cdot4 = 1\cdot2$ cm

half depth of hole $= x$ cm

$$x = \sqrt{2\cdot55^2 - 1\cdot2^2} = \sqrt{5\cdot0625} = 2\cdot25 \text{ cm}$$

Thickness of spherical segments at top and bottom of hole

$$= h \text{ cm}$$

$$h = \frac{1}{2}d - x = 2\cdot55 - 2\cdot25 = 0\cdot3 \text{ cm}$$

$$\text{Vol. of sphere} = \frac{\pi}{6}d^3$$

$$= \frac{\pi}{6} \times 5\cdot1^3 = 69\cdot465 \text{ cm}^3$$

$$\text{Vol. of cylindrical hole} = \frac{\pi}{4}d^2 l$$

$$= \frac{\pi}{4} \times 2 \cdot 4^2 \times (2 \times 2 \cdot 25) = 20 \cdot 36 \text{ cm}^3$$

$$\text{Volume of segment} = \frac{\pi}{6}h^2(3d - 2h)$$

Volume of the two end segments

$$= 2 \times \frac{\pi}{6} \times 0 \cdot 3^2 (3 \times 5 \cdot 1 - 2 \times 0 \cdot 3)$$

$$= 2 \times \frac{\pi}{6} \times 0 \cdot 09 \times 14 \cdot 7$$

$$= 1 \cdot 386 \text{ cm}^3$$

Net vol. = vols. (sphere − cyl. hole − 2 end segments)

$$= 69 \cdot 465 - 20 \cdot 36 - 1 \cdot 386$$

$$= 47 \cdot 72 \text{ cm}^3 \quad \text{Ans. (i)}$$

Density = 7·86 g/cm^3

Mass = volume × density

$$= 47 \cdot 72 \times 7 \cdot 86$$

Mass = 375·1 g   Ans. (ii)

8.

By similar triangles, from sketch,

$$\frac{h}{16} = \frac{60}{64} \qquad h = 15 \text{ mm}$$

height of hole $= 60 - 15 = 45$ mm

Volume of complete cone

$$= \tfrac{1}{3} \times \text{area of base} \times \text{perp. height}$$
$$= \tfrac{1}{3} \times 0{\cdot}7854 \times 64^2 \times 60 = 64\,340 \text{ mm}^3$$

Volume of top cone cut off

$$= \tfrac{1}{3} \times 0{\cdot}7854 \times 16^2 \times 15 = 1006 \text{ mm}^3$$

Volume of bored hole, this is a frustum of a cone,

$$= \tfrac{1}{12} \pi h (D^2 + Dd + d^2)$$
$$= \tfrac{1}{12} \times \pi \times 45(28^2 + 28 \times 16 + 16^2) = 17\,530 \text{ mm}^2$$

Net volume

$$= 64\,340 - 1006 - 17\,530$$
$$= 45\,804 \text{ mm}^3 \text{ or } 45{\cdot}804 \text{ cm}^3 \quad \text{Ans. (i)}$$
$$\text{m} = \text{V}\rho$$
$$= 45{\cdot}804 \times 8{\cdot}4$$
$$\text{Mass} = 384{\cdot}8 \text{ g} \quad \text{Ans. (ii)}$$

Alternatively, the volume can be obtained by the Theorem of Pappus. Volume remaining after boring is equal to the volume swept out when triangular area ABD is swept through one complete revolution about the centre axis of the cone. This can be found by the difference between the volumes swept out by triangles ACD and BCD, the volumes in each case being area × distance moved by centroid (see sketch).

Area of ACD $= \tfrac{1}{2} \times 24 \times 45 = 540$ mm^2

Distance of its centroid from centre axis

$$= \tfrac{1}{3} \times 24 + 8 = 16 \text{ mm}$$
$$\text{Area of BCD} = \tfrac{1}{2} \times 6 \times 45 = 135 \text{ mm}^2$$

Distance of its centroid from centre axis

$$= \tfrac{1}{3} \times 6 + 8 = 10 \text{ mm}$$
$$\text{Net volume} = 540 \times 2\pi \times 16 - 135 \times 2\pi \times 10$$
$$= 2\pi(8640 - 1350)$$
$$= 45\,810 \text{ mm}^3 \quad \text{or} \quad 45 \cdot 81 \text{ cm}^3 \text{ (as before)}$$

9.   Area of hexagonal base = six equilateral triangles

$$= 6 \times 0 \cdot 433 \times \text{side}^2$$
$$= 2 \cdot 598 \times 2 \cdot 5^2$$
$$\text{Volume of pyramid} = \tfrac{1}{3} \times \text{area of base} \times \text{perp. ht.}$$
$$= \tfrac{1}{3} \times 2 \cdot 598 \times 2 \cdot 5^2 \times 6$$
$$= 32 \cdot 48 \text{ cm}^3 \quad \text{Ans. (i)}$$

Volumes of similar objects vary as the cube of their corresponding dimensions, therefore,

$$\frac{\text{vol. of top pyramid cut off}}{\text{vol. of whole pyramid}} = \frac{3^3}{6^3} = \frac{1}{8}$$

$\therefore$ vol. of top pyramid cut off = $\tfrac{1}{8}$ of whole pyramid

Volume of frustum = the remaining $\tfrac{7}{8}$ of the whole pyramid
$$= \tfrac{7}{8} \times 32 \cdot 48$$
$$= 28 \cdot 42 \text{ cm}^3 \quad \text{Ans. (ii)}$$

10. Volumes of similar objects vary as the cube of their corresponding dimensions, therefore volume varies as depth^3.

Let V = volume when depth is 7 cm

$$\frac{V}{200} = \frac{7^3}{5^3}$$

$$V = \frac{200 \times 7^3}{5^3} = 548 \cdot 8 \text{ cm}^3$$

Additional volume required = $548 \cdot 8 - 200$

$$= 348 \cdot 8 \text{ cm}^3 \text{ i.e. } 348 \cdot 8 \text{ ml} \quad \text{Ans.}$$

11.

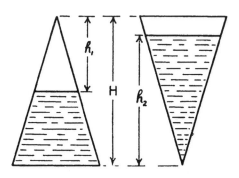

Volumes of similar objects vary as the cube of their corresponding dimensions. Comparing similar cones (before inversion):

Let V = volume of whole cone

H = height of whole cone

v = volume of conical empty space

h_1 = height of conical empty space

$$\frac{V}{v} = \frac{H^3}{h_1^3} = \frac{500^3}{250^3} = \left\{\frac{500}{250}\right\}^3 = 2^3 = 8$$

$$\therefore V = 8 \times v \quad \text{or} \quad v = \tfrac{1}{8}V$$

thus, the volume of the empty space is one-eighth of the whole volume, and the volume of the water is seven-eighths ($= 0 \cdot 875$) of the whole volume.

Comparing similar cones (after inversion):

$$\frac{V}{0 \cdot 875\, V} = \frac{H^3}{h_2{}^3}$$

$$h_2 = 500 \times \sqrt[3]{0 \cdot 875} = 478 \cdot 3 \text{ mm} \quad \text{Ans.}$$

12.   Ratio of surface areas $= 1 \cdot 5 \quad : 1$

Ratio of diameters $= \sqrt{1 \cdot 5} \ : \sqrt{1}$

$= 1 \cdot 225 : 1$

Ratio of volumes $= 1 \cdot 225^3 \ : 1^3$

$= 1 \cdot 8375 : 1$

Let $v =$ volume of smaller sphere, in cm^3,
then volume of larger sphere $= (v + 10)\,\text{cm}^3$

$$\frac{v + 10}{v} = \frac{1 \cdot 8375}{1}$$

$$1 \cdot 8375 v = v + 10$$

$$0 \cdot 8375 v = 10$$

$$v = 11 \cdot 94 \text{ cm}^3 \quad \text{Ans. (i)}$$

$$\text{volume} = \frac{\pi}{6} d^3$$

$$\text{diameter} = \sqrt[3]{\frac{11 \cdot 94 \times 6}{\pi}}$$

$$= 2 \cdot 836 \text{ cm} \quad \text{Ans. (ii)}$$

13. Working in decimetres,

SECTIONAL AREAS	SIMPSON'S MULTIPLIERS	PRODUCTS
$0 \cdot 7854 \times 3 \cdot 95^2$	1	$0 \cdot 7854 \times 15 \cdot 6$
$0 \cdot 7854 \times 4 \cdot 77^2$	4	$0 \cdot 7854 \times 91 \cdot 0$
$0 \cdot 7854 \times 5 \cdot 00^2$	2	$0 \cdot 7854 \times 50 \cdot 0$
$0 \cdot 7854 \times 4 \cdot 77^2$	4	$0 \cdot 7854 \times 91 \cdot 0$
$0 \cdot 7854 \times 3 \cdot 95^2$	1	$0 \cdot 7854 \times 15 \cdot 6$
		sum $= 0 \cdot 7854 \times 263 \cdot 2$

There are 5 ordinates therefore 4 spaces

Common interval

$$= 5 \cdot 81 \div 4$$

Volume = sum of products $\times \frac{1}{3}$ common interval

$$= \frac{0 \cdot 7854 \times 263 \cdot 2 \times 5 \cdot 81}{3 \times 4}$$

$$= 100 \cdot 1 \ \text{dm}^3 = 100 \cdot 1 \ \text{l} \quad \text{Ans.}$$

14. Finding plotting points, $y = 5 + 4x - x^2$,

x	-1	0	1	2	3	4	5
y	0	5	8	9	8	5	0

The graph of these values is shown. Sweeping the area bounded by this graph through one revolution, the y ordinates of the graph become the radii at regular intervals along the length of the solid generated. Putting the cross-sectional areas of the solid through Simpson's rule to find the volume:

RADII	CROSS-SECT. AREAS	SIMPSON'S	
r	πr^2	MULTIPLIERS	PRODUCTS
0	0	1	0
5	$\pi \times 25$	4	$\pi \times 100$
8	$\pi \times 64$	2	$\pi \times 128$
9	$\pi \times 81$	4	$\pi \times 324$
8	$\pi \times 64$	2	$\pi \times 128$
5	$\pi \times 25$	4	$\pi \times 100$
0	0	1	0
			sum $= \pi \times 780$

Common interval between ordinates $= 1$

$$\text{Volume} = \pi \times 780 \times \tfrac{1}{3} \times 1$$

$$= 816 \cdot 9 \ \text{units}^3 \quad \text{Ans.}$$

15.

Half-breadth of water level $= 0.18 \times \tan 40° = 0.151$ m

Area of cross-section $= \frac{1}{2}$ (breadth $\times$ perp. ht.)

$$= 0.151 \times 0.18 \text{ m}^2$$

Volume flow $=$ area $\times$ velocity

$$= 0.151 \times 0.18 \times 0.5 \times 3600$$

$$= 48.94 \text{ m}^3/\text{h} \quad \text{Ans.}$$

16.

By similar triangles, $\dfrac{h}{6} = \dfrac{h+4}{8}$

$$\therefore h = 12 \text{ cm}$$

$$H = 12 + 4 = 16 \text{ cm}$$

c.g. of a cone is at $\frac{1}{4}$ height from base.

Volume of whole cone $= \frac{1}{3} \times \pi \times 4^2 \times 16 \text{ cm}^3$

c.g. from base $= \frac{1}{4}$ of $16 = 4 \text{ cm}$

Volume of top cone cut off $= \frac{1}{3} \times \pi \times 3^2 \times 12 \text{ cm}^3$

c.g. from base $= 4 + \frac{1}{4}$ of $12 = 7 \text{ cm}$

Moments about base:

$$\bar{y} = \frac{\Sigma \text{ moments of volumes}}{\Sigma \text{ volumes}}$$

$$= \frac{\text{moment of whole cone} - \text{moment of top cone}}{\text{volume of whole cone} - \text{volume of top cone}}$$

$$= \frac{\frac{1}{3} \times \pi \times 4^2 \times 16 \times 4 - \frac{1}{3} \times \pi \times 3^2 \times 12 \times 7}{\frac{1}{3} \times \pi \times 4^2 \times 16 - \frac{1}{3} \times \pi \times 3^2 \times 12}$$

$\frac{1}{3}$, π and 4 cancel from every term,

$$\bar{y} = \frac{4^2 \times 16 - 3^2 \times 3 \times 7}{4^2 \times 4 - 3^2 \times 3} = \frac{67}{37}$$

$$= 1 \cdot 811 \text{ cm} = 18 \cdot 11 \text{ mm from base.} \quad \text{Ans.}$$

17. Considering the plate as a rectangle 300 mm by 375 mm with a triangle 225 mm by 300 mm cut off one corner (as in Fig. 123),

Area of rectangle $= 30 \times 37 \cdot 5 = 1125$ cm^2

Distance of its centroid from 375 mm side $= 15$ cm

Distance of its centroid from 300 mm side $= 18 \cdot 75$ cm

Area of triangle $= \frac{1}{2}(22 \cdot 5 \times 30) = 337 \cdot 5$ cm^2

Distance of its centroid from 375 mm side
$$= 30 - \frac{1}{3} \times 22 \cdot 5 = 22 \cdot 5 \text{ cm}$$

Distance of its centroid from 300 mm side
$$= 37 \cdot 5 - \frac{1}{3} \times 30 = 27 \cdot 5 \text{ cm}$$

(centroid of triangle is at $\frac{1}{3}$ height from its base)

Moments about 375 mm side:

$$\bar{x} = \frac{\Sigma \text{ moments of areas}}{\Sigma \text{ areas}}$$

$$= \frac{1125 \times 15 - 337 \cdot 5 \times 22 \cdot 5}{1125 - 337 \cdot 5} = 11 \cdot 79 \text{ cm}$$

Moments about 300 mm side:

$$\bar{y} = \frac{1125 \times 18 \cdot 75 - 337 \cdot 5 \times 27 \cdot 5}{1125 - 337 \cdot 5} = 15 \text{ cm}$$

$$\bar{x} = 117 \cdot 9 \text{ mm}, \bar{y} = 150 \text{ mm.} \quad \text{Ans.}$$

18.

Taking moments about end of shank (p. 377):

$$\text{c.g.} = \frac{\Sigma \text{ moments of volumes}}{\Sigma \text{ volumes}}$$

All parts being cylindrical of volume $0.7854 \times d^2 \times l$, the multiplier 0.7854 is common to all terms and therefore cancels out.

$$\text{c.g.} = \frac{(6^2 \times 4 \times 25) + (4^2 \times 23 \times 11.5) + (6^2 - 4^2) \times 4 \times 13.1}{(6^2 \times 4) + (4^2 \times 23) + (6^2 - 4^2) \times 4}$$

$$= \frac{3600 + 4232 + 1048}{144 + 368 + 80} = \frac{8880}{592}$$

$$= 15 \text{ cm or } 150 \text{ mm.} \quad \text{Ans.}$$

SOLUTIONS TO TEST EXAMPLES 11

1. (a) $\qquad y = x^3 + 3x^2 - 9x + 4$

$$\frac{dy}{dx} = 3x^2 + 6x - 9 \quad \text{Ans. (a).}$$

(b) $\qquad y = \frac{2x^3}{3} - \frac{7}{x^2} + x$

i.e. $\quad y = \frac{2x^3}{3} - 7x^{-2} + x$

$$\frac{dy}{dx} = 2x^2 + 14x^{-3} + 1$$

$$= 2x^2 + \frac{14}{x^3} + 1 \quad \text{Ans. (b)}$$

(c) $\qquad y = \sqrt[5]{x^3} + 1$

$$y = x^{\frac{3}{5}} + 1$$

$$\frac{dy}{dx} = \frac{3x^{-\frac{2}{5}}}{5}$$

$$= \frac{3}{5x^{\frac{2}{5}}} \quad \text{Ans. (c).}$$

(d) $\qquad y = 5\cos x - 7\cos x + 2\sin x$

$$\frac{dy}{dx} = -5\sin x + 7\sin x + 2\cos x \quad \text{Ans. (d).}$$

2.

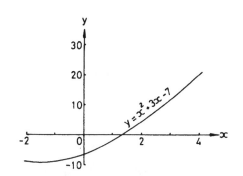

$$y = x^2 + 3x - 7 \text{ (see sketch)}$$

$$\frac{dy}{dx} = 2x + 3$$

when $x = 3$,

$$\frac{dy}{dx} = 6 + 3$$

i.e. gradient $= 9$

when $x = -2$

$$\frac{dy}{dx} = -4 + 3$$

i.e. gradient $= -1$ Ans.

3. (a) $$s = 20t - 5t^2 + 4$$

$$v = \frac{ds}{dt} = 20 - 10t \quad \ldots \quad \ldots \quad \ldots \quad \ldots \quad (i)$$

when $t = 1$,

$$v = 20 - 10$$

$$= 10 \text{ m/s}   \text{ Ans. (a)}$$

(b)   when $v = 0$,

$$20 - 10t = 0$$

$$t = \frac{20}{10}$$

$$\therefore t = 2 \text{ s}   \text{ Ans. (b)}$$

(c) From equation (i),

$$v = 20 - 10t$$

$$a = \frac{dv}{dt}$$

$$\therefore a = -10 \text{ m/s}^2.   \text{ Ans. (c)}$$

4. $$y = 4x + \frac{1}{x}$$

i.e. $y = 4x + x^{-1}$

$$\text{Gradient} = \frac{dy}{dx} = 4 - x^{-2}$$

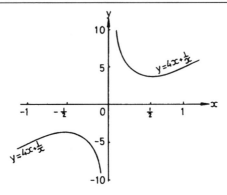

$\therefore$ At any point on the curve,

$$\text{gradient} = 4 - \frac{1}{x^2}$$

When the gradient is zero,

$$\frac{dy}{dx} = 0$$

$$4 - \frac{1}{x^2} = 0$$

$$\frac{1}{x^2} = 4$$

$$x = \sqrt{\tfrac{1}{4}}$$

$\therefore x = \pm\tfrac{1}{2}$ (see above sketch)

Gradient is zero when $x = \tfrac{1}{2}$ and $x = -\tfrac{1}{2}$ Ans.

5. $y = 3x^2 - x + 2$ (see sketch, p. 382)

$$\text{Gradient} = \frac{dy}{dx} = 6x - 1$$

When the gradient is -7,

$$6x - 1 = -7$$

$$6x = -6$$

$$\therefore x = -1$$

Substituting $x = -1$ in equation (i),

$$y = 3 + 1 + 2$$

$$= 6$$

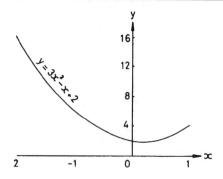

The gradient is -7 at the point $x = -1, y = 6$.   Ans.

6.
$$\theta = 2 + 16t - \frac{t^2}{2}$$

$$\omega = \frac{d\theta}{dt} = 16 - t$$

when $t = 2$,

$$\omega = 16 - 2$$
$$= 14 \text{ rad/s}$$

when angular velocity $= 0$,

$$16 - t = 0$$
$$\therefore t = 16$$

i.e. shaft comes to rest after 16 s.   Ans.

7. (a)
$$y = x^3 + 3x + \ln x$$
$$\frac{dy}{dx} = 3x^2 + 3 + \frac{1}{x}$$
$$= 3x^2 + 3 + x^{-1}$$
$$\frac{d^2y}{dx^2} = 6x - x^{-2}$$
$$= 6x - \frac{1}{x^2}$$ Ans. (a)

(b) $$y = 3\cos\theta - 7\cos\theta + \theta$$

$$\frac{dy}{d\theta} = -3\sin\theta + 7\sin\theta + 1$$

$$\frac{d^2y}{d\theta^2} = -3\cos\theta + 7\cos\theta \quad \text{Ans. (b)}$$

8. $$y = 12x + 3x^2 - 2x^3 \quad \ldots \quad \ldots \quad \ldots \quad \text{(i)}$$

$$\frac{dy}{dx} = 12 + 6x - 6x^2$$

$$\frac{d^2y}{dx^2} = 6 - 12x \ \ldots \quad \ldots \quad \ldots \quad \ldots \quad \ldots \quad \text{(ii)}$$

For maximum or minimum values,

$$\frac{dy}{dx} = 0$$

i.e. $12 + 6x - 6x^2 = 0$

$$2 + x - x^2 = 0$$

$$x^2 - x - 2 = 0$$

Solve for x:

$$(x - 2)(x + 1) = 0$$

$$\therefore \quad x = 2 \quad \text{or} \quad x = -1$$

Substituting in equation (ii):

when $x = 2$,

$$\frac{d^2y}{dx^2} = 6 - 24 \text{ (i.e. negative)}$$

when $x = -1$,

$$\frac{d^2y}{dx^2} = 6 + 12 \text{ (positive)}$$

$\therefore$ A maximum value occurs when $x = 2$.

Substituting in equation (i):

$$\text{Maximum value of } y = 24 + 12 - 16$$

$$= 20 \quad \text{Ans.}$$

9.

$$M = \frac{wlx}{2} - \frac{wx^2}{2}$$

Differentiating with respect to x:

$$\frac{dM}{dx} = \frac{wl}{2} - wx \quad \ldots \quad \ldots \quad \ldots \quad \ldots \quad \ldots \quad \text{(i)}$$

$$\frac{d^2M}{dx^2} = -w \text{ (i.e. negative)}$$

For maximum or minimum value,

$$\frac{dM}{dx} = 0$$

From equation (i):

$$\frac{wl}{2} - wx = 0$$

$$\frac{wl}{2} = wx$$

$$x = \frac{l}{2}$$

$\therefore$ Maximum bending moment occurs when

$$x = \frac{l}{2}$$

i.e. At the centre of the beam.   Ans.

10. (a)

$$t = 2{\cdot}1\,\sqrt[3]{\frac{1}{\theta^2}} - \frac{4}{\sqrt[5]{\theta}}$$

$$= 2{\cdot}1\theta^{-\frac{2}{3}} - 4\theta^{-\frac{1}{5}}$$

$$\frac{dt}{d\theta} = -1{\cdot}4\theta^{-\frac{5}{3}} + 0{\cdot}8\theta^{-\frac{6}{5}}$$

$$= \frac{-0{\cdot}8}{\sqrt[5]{\theta^6}} - \frac{1{\cdot}4}{\sqrt[3]{\theta^5}} \quad \text{Ans. (a)}$$

(b)

$$z = \frac{au^n - 1}{C}$$

$$\frac{dz}{du} = \frac{anu^{n-1}}{C} \quad \text{Ans. (b)}$$

(c)
$$y = 3x(x^2 - 4)$$
$$= 3x^3 - 12x$$
$$\frac{dy}{dx} = 9x^2 - 12$$
$$= 3(3x^2 - 4) \quad \text{Ans. (c)}$$

(d)
$$y = 2\cos\theta + 5$$
$$\frac{dy}{d\theta} = -2\sin\theta \quad \text{Ans. (d)}$$

11.
$$f(x) = \frac{x^3}{3} - 2x^2 + 3x + 1 \qquad \dots \quad \dots \quad \dots \quad \text{(i)}$$
$$f'(x) = x^2 - 4x + 3 \qquad \dots \quad \dots \quad \dots \quad \dots \quad \text{(ii)}$$
$$f''(x) = 2x - 4 \qquad \dots \quad \dots \quad \dots \quad \dots \quad \text{(iii)}$$
$$f'(x) = 0 \text{ for a maximum or a minimum}$$
$$0 = x^2 - 4x + 3 \text{ from (ii)}$$
$$= (x - 1)(x - 3)$$
$$\therefore x = 1 \quad \text{or} \quad x = 3$$
when $x = 1$ in (iii)
$$f''(x) = -2 \text{ i.e. a maximum}$$
when $x = 3$ in (iii)
$$f''(x) = 2 \text{ i.e. a minimum}$$
when $x = 3$ in (i)
$$f(x) = 9 - 18 + 9 + 1$$
$$= 1 \text{ for a minimum} \quad \text{Ans.}$$

12.
$$P = aV^b$$
$$\frac{dP}{dV} = abV^{b-1} \quad \text{Ans. (a)}$$
$$= 0{\cdot}5 \times 10^{-10} \times 6 \times 100^5$$
$$= 0{\cdot}5 \times 10^{-10} \times 6 \times 10^{10}$$
$$\therefore \text{Power/Volt} = 3 \text{ units at } 100 \text{ V} \quad \text{Ans. (b)}$$

13. Let each of two sides be x long

Remaining two sides are $\frac{l}{2} - x$ long

$$\text{Length} = 2\left(\frac{l}{2} - x\right) + 2x$$

$$\text{Area A} = x\left(\frac{l}{2} - x\right) \qquad \ldots \quad \ldots \quad \ldots \quad \text{(i)}$$

$$= \frac{xl}{2} - x^2$$

$$f'(A) = \frac{l}{2} - 2x \qquad \ldots \quad \ldots \quad \ldots \quad \text{(ii)}$$

$$f''(A) = -2 \text{ i.e. a maximum}$$

$$0 = \frac{l}{2} - 2x \text{ from (ii)}$$

$$x = \frac{l}{4} \quad \text{Ans.}$$

14. (a)
$$f(\theta) = \cos\theta - \ln\theta$$

$$f'(\theta) = -\sin\theta - \frac{1}{\theta}$$

$$f''(\theta) = \frac{1}{\theta^2} - \cos\theta \quad \text{Ans. (a)}$$

(b)
$$f(t) = at^2 + 2\ln t$$

$$f'(t) = 2at + \frac{2}{t}$$

$$f''(t) = 2a - \frac{2}{t^2}$$

$$= 2\left(a - \frac{1}{t^2}\right) \quad \text{Ans. (b)}$$

(c)
$$f(x) = 5e^x$$

$$f''(x) = 5e^x \quad \text{Ans. (c)}$$

15. $x = 0.2t^2 + 10.4$ ...   .   (i)

         $f'(x) = 0.4t$ ...   .   (ii)

            $= 2$ m/s i.e. velocity at t = 5 s   ⎫

                                                        ⎬ Ans. (a)

         $f''(x) = 0.4$ m/s^2 i.e. (constant) acceleration ⎭

            $100 = 0.2t^2 + 10.4$ i.e. $x = 100$ in (i)

            $500 = t^2 + 52$

               $t = 21.17$ s

         $f'(x) = 0.4 \times 21.17$ i.e. $t = 21.17$ in (ii)

            $= 8.468$ m/s i.e. velocity   ⎫

                                                  ⎬ Ans. (b)

         $f''(x) = 0.4$ m/s^2 i.e. acceleration ⎭

16. $\theta = 2.1 - 3.2t + 4.8t^2$

       $f'(t) = 9.6t - 3.2$

          $= 9.6 \times 1.5 - 3.2$ at $t = 1.5$ s

          $= 11.2$ rad/s angular velocity   ⎫

                                                              ⎬ Ans.

       $f''(t) = 9.6$ rad/s^2 (constant) angular acceleration ⎭

17. $f(x) = x^5 - 5x$ ...   .   (i)

      $f'(x) = 5x^4 - 5$ ...   .   (ii)

         $0 = 5x^4 - 5$ for maximum/minimum

         $x^4 = 1$

         $x = 1$ or $x = -1$

         $x = 1$ in (i) gives $f(x) = -4$

         $x = -1$ in (i) gives $f(x) = 4$

      $f''(x) = 20x^3$ ...   .   (iii)

           $= 20$ i.e. a minimum when $x = 1$ ⎫

                                                     ⎬ Ans.

           $= -20$ i.e. a maximum when $x = -1$ ⎭

         $\therefore x = 1, f(x) = -4$,   minimum   ⎫

                                                ⎬ Ans.

    and $x = -1, f(x) = 4$, maximum ⎭

18.

$$y = ax^2 + bx + c$$

$$\frac{dy}{dx} = 2ax + b$$

$$= 4x + 2$$

$$\therefore a = b = 2$$

$$\frac{d^2y}{dx^2} = 4 \text{ i.e. positive, so minimum}$$

$$0 = 4x + 2 \text{ for minimum}$$

$$\therefore x = -\tfrac{1}{2}$$

$$y = ax^2 + bx + c$$

$$l = 2x^2 + 2x + c \text{ at minimum}$$

$$l = 2\left(-\tfrac{1}{2}\right)^2 + 2\left(-\tfrac{1}{2}\right) + c$$

$$\therefore c = \tfrac{3}{2}$$

$$a = b = 2 \text{ and } c = \tfrac{3}{2} \quad \text{Ans.}$$

SOLUTIONS TO TEST EXAMPLES 12

1. (a) $\int (x^4 + x^2 - 8x + 5)\, dx = \dfrac{x^5}{5} + \dfrac{x^3}{3} - 4x^2 + 5x + C$ Ans. (a)

(b) $$\int \left(\dfrac{4}{x^2} + \dfrac{1}{x} \right) dx$$

The expression above is re-arranged as:

$$\int (4x^{-2} + x^{-1})\, dx = -4x^{-1} + \ln x + C$$

$$= -\dfrac{4}{x} + \ln x + C \quad \text{Ans. (b)}$$

(c) $\displaystyle\int_1^3 (2x - 3x^2 - 1)\, dx = [x^2 - x^3 - x]_1^3$

$$= [9 - 27 - 3] - [1 - 1 - 1]$$
$$= [-21] - [-1]$$
$$= -21 + 1$$
$$= -20 \quad \text{Ans. (c)}$$

2.   Gradient $= \dfrac{dy}{dx} = x^2 + x - 2$

$$y = \int \dfrac{dy}{dx}\, dx$$

$$\therefore y = \int (x^2 + x - 2)\, dx$$

$$y = \dfrac{x^3}{3} + \dfrac{x^2}{2} - 2x + C \qquad \dots \quad \dots \quad \text{(i)}$$

when $y = 5, x = 2$.

$$\therefore 5 = \dfrac{(2)^3}{3} + \dfrac{(2)^3}{2} - 2 \times (2) + C$$

$$5 = \dfrac{8}{3} + 2 - 4 + C$$

$$\therefore C = 4\tfrac{1}{3} \qquad \dots \quad \dots \quad \dots \quad \dots \quad \text{(ii)}$$

From (i) and (ii):

$$y = \frac{x^3}{3} + \frac{x^2}{2} - 2x + 4\tfrac{1}{3} \quad \text{Ans.}$$

3. (a) $\displaystyle\int (3 \cos x - 2 \sin x + 4) \, dx = 3 \sin x + 2 \cos x + 4x + C$

Ans. (a)

(b) $\displaystyle\int (4 \cos x - \cos x + x) \, dx = 4 \sin x - \sin x + \frac{x^2}{2} + C$

Ans. (b)

(c)
$$\int_0^{\frac{\pi}{2}} \cos x \, dx = [\sin x]_0^{\frac{\pi}{2}}$$

$$= \left[\sin \frac{\pi}{2}\right] - [\sin 0]$$

$$= 1 - 0$$

$$= 1 \qquad \text{Ans. (c)}$$

4.
$$y = x^3 - 4x^2 + 3x$$

$$\therefore \text{Area} = \int_1^3 (x^3 - 4x^2 + 3x) \, dx$$

$$= \left[\frac{x^4}{4} - \frac{4x^3}{3} + \frac{3x^2}{2}\right]_1^3$$

$$= \left[-\frac{27}{12}\right] - \left[\frac{5}{12}\right]$$

$$= -2\tfrac{2}{3}$$

Note: the negative sign indicates that the area is below the x-axis. This is confirmed by the sketch.

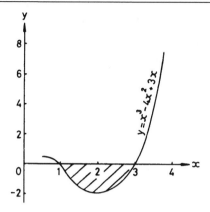

$\therefore$ Area $= 2\frac{2}{3}$ units^2 Ans.

5.

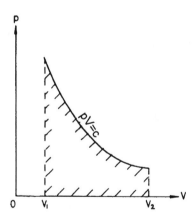

The law of expansion is $pV = C$ $\ldots$ $\ldots$ $\ldots$ $\ldots$ (i)

$$\text{i.e. } p = \frac{C}{V}$$

The standard equation

$$\text{Area} = \int_a^b y \, dx$$

must be amended to suit the symbols in this problem:

$$\text{Area under curve} = \int_{V_1}^{V_2} p \, dV$$

$$= \int_{V_1}^{V_2} \frac{C}{V} dV$$

$$= C \int_{V_1}^{V_2} \frac{1}{V} dV$$

$$= C[\ln V]_{V_1}^{V_2}$$

$$= C\{[\ln V_2] - [\ln V_1]\}$$

$$= C \times \ln \frac{V_2}{V_1} \qquad \ldots \quad \ldots \quad \ldots \quad \text{(ii)}$$

$$\left(\text{Note: } \ln V_2 - \ln V_1 \text{ is numerically equal to } \ln \frac{V_2}{V_1} \right)$$

From equations (i) and (ii),

$$\text{Area under curve} = pV \ln \frac{V_2}{V_1} \quad \text{Ans.}$$

6. (a) $$a = 6t$$

$$\therefore v = \int 6t \, dt$$

$$v = 3t^2 + C \qquad \ldots \quad \ldots \quad \ldots \quad \text{(i)}$$

Substitute $v = 0, t = 0$ in equation (i),

$$0 = 0 + C$$
$$\therefore C = 0$$

Hence $v = 3t^2$ Ans. (a)

(b) when $t = 2$, $v = 3(2)^2$

$= 12$

when $t = 3$, $v = 3(3)^2$

$= 27$

∴ Average velocity $= \dfrac{12 + 27}{2}$

$= 19.5$ m/s   Ans. (b)

(c)   when $t = 2.5$, $v = 3(2.5)^2$

i.e. Instantaneous velocity $= 18.75$ m/s   Ans. (c)

7. $s = \displaystyle\int v\, dt$

$= \displaystyle\int (3t^2 + 8t + 12)\, dt$

∴ $s = t^3 + 4t^2 + 12t + C$ ... ... (i)

Substitute $s = 10$, $t = 0$ in equation (i),

$10 = 0 + 0 + 0 + C$

∴ $C = 10$ ... ... (ii)

From equations (i) and (ii),

$s = t^3 + 4t^2 + 12t + 10$

when $t = 10$,

$s = 1000 + 400 + 120 + 10$

Displacement $= 1530$ m   Ans.

8.

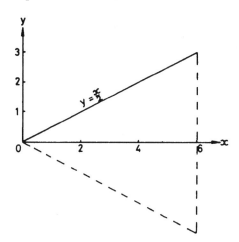

Volume of solid of revolution $= \pi \int_a^b y^2 dx$ (see previous sketch)

$$= \pi \int_0^6 \left(\frac{x}{2}\right)^2 dx$$

$$= \pi \int_0^6 \frac{x^2}{4} dx$$

$$= \pi \left[\frac{x^3}{12}\right]_0^6$$

$$= \pi \left[\frac{6^3}{12}\right] - \pi[0]$$

$$= 56 \cdot 55 \text{ units}^3 \quad \text{Ans.}$$

9. At the points where the curve intersects the x-axis, x has zero value.

$$\text{i.e. } x^2 - x = 0$$

hence, $x = 0$ or $x = 1$.

$\therefore$ The curve intersects the x-axis at $x = 0$ and $x = 1$.

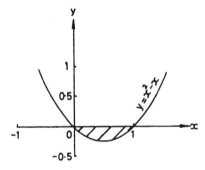

Volume of solid of revolution $= \pi \int_0^1 (x^2 - x)^2 dx$

$$= \pi \int_0^1 (x^4 - 2x^3 + x^2) \, dx$$

$$= \pi \left[\frac{x^5}{5} - \frac{x^4}{2} + \frac{x^3}{3}\right]_0^1$$

$$= \pi \left[\frac{1}{5} - \frac{1}{2} + \frac{1}{3}\right] - 0$$

$$= 0 \cdot 105 \text{ units}^3 \quad \text{Ans.}$$

10. (a) $\int (x+1)(x+2)\,dx = \int (x^2+3x+2)\,dx$

$$= \frac{x^3}{3} + \frac{3x^2}{2} + 2x + C \quad \text{Ans. (a)}$$

(b) $\int \left(\frac{1}{x} - \frac{1}{x^2}\right) dx = \ln x + \frac{1}{x} + C \quad \text{Ans. (b)}$

(c) $\int_1^2 (a+2b)(x+1)\,dx = a + 2b \int_1^2 (x+1)dx$

$$= a + 2b\left[\frac{x^2}{2} + x\right]_1^2$$

$$= a + 2b[(2+2) - (\tfrac{1}{2}+1)]$$

$$= \tfrac{5}{2}(a+2b) \quad \text{Ans. (c)}$$

(d) $\int 3e^{3x}\,dx = 3\int e^x\,dx$

$$= 3e^x + C \quad \text{Ans. (d)}$$

11. $\text{Area} = \int_6^8 (0.06x^2 + 10)\,dx = \left[\frac{0.06x^3}{3} + 10x\right]_6^8$

$$= \left[\frac{8^3 \times 0.06}{3} + 80\right] - \left[\frac{6^3 \times 0.06}{3} + 60\right]$$

$$= (0.02 \times 512) + 80 - (0.02 \times 216) - 60$$

$$= 0.02 \times 296 + 20 = 5.92 + 20$$

$$= 25.92 \text{ units}^2 \quad \text{Ans.}$$

12. $\text{Area} = \int_{V_1}^{V_2} p\,dV = \int_{V_1}^{V_2} \frac{C}{V^n}\,dV$

$$= C \int_{V_1}^{V_2} V^{-n}\,dV$$

$$= C\left[\frac{1}{1-n} V^{1-n}\right]_{V_1}^{V_2}$$

$$= C\frac{1}{1-n}(V_2^{1-n} - V_1^{1-n})$$

$$= \frac{-C}{n-1}\left(\frac{1}{V_2^{n-1}} - \frac{1}{V_1^{n-1}}\right) \quad \text{Ans.}$$

13. (a) $$\int \left(\sin\theta - \frac{1}{2}\right)\frac{d\theta}{3} = \frac{1}{3}\int \sin d\theta - \frac{1}{3}\int \frac{d\theta}{2}$$

$$= -\frac{1}{3}\left(\cos\theta + \frac{\theta}{2}\right) + C \qquad \text{Ans. (a)}$$

(b) $$\int_0^\pi \sin x \, dx = [-\cos x]_0^\pi$$

$$= (-\cos\pi) - (-\cos 0)$$

$$= 1 + 1$$

$$= 2 \quad \text{Ans. (b)}$$

(c) $$\int_0^{\frac{\pi}{2}} (5\cos x + 3\sin x - x)\, dx = \left[5\sin x - 3\cos x - \frac{x^2}{2}\right]_0^{\frac{\pi}{2}}$$

$$= \left(5\sin\frac{\pi}{2} - 3\cos\frac{\pi}{2} - \frac{\pi^2}{8}\right)$$

$$- (5\sin 0 - 3\cos 0 - 0)$$

$$= \left(5 - 0 - \frac{\pi^2}{8}\right) - (0 - 3 - 0)$$

$$= 8 - \frac{\pi^2}{8} \quad \text{Ans. (c)}$$

14.

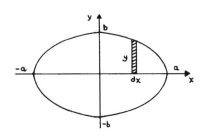

$$V = \pi \int_{-a}^{a} y^2 dx$$

$$y^2 = b^2\left(1 - \frac{x^2}{a^2}\right)$$

$$V = \pi b^2 \int_{-a}^{a} \left(1 - \frac{x^2}{a^2}\right) dx$$

$$= \pi b^2 \left[x - \frac{x^3}{3a^2}\right]_{-a}^{a}$$

$$= \pi b^2 \left[\left(a - \frac{a^3}{3a^2}\right)\right]$$

$$- \pi b^2 \left[\left(-a - \frac{(-a)^3}{3(-a)^2}\right)\right]$$

$$= \pi b^2 \left(a - \frac{a}{3} + a - \frac{a}{3}\right)$$

Volume $V = \dfrac{4}{3} ab^2 \pi$ Ans.

15.

$$\frac{dv}{dt} = -kv$$

$$\frac{dv}{v} = -kt$$

$$\ln v = -kt + C$$

when $t = 0$ $v = u$ so $C = \ln u$

$$\ln v - \ln u = -kt$$

$$\ln \frac{v}{u} = -kt$$ Ans.

16.

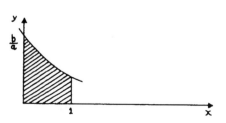

$$\text{Area} = \int_0^1 y\, dx = \int_0^1 \frac{b}{x+a}\, dx \quad \text{(see sketch)}$$

$$= b\int \frac{dx}{x+a} = b[\ln(x+a)]_0^1$$

$$= b[\ln(1+a) - \ln(0+a)]$$

$$= b[\ln(1+a) - \ln a]$$

$$= b\ln \frac{1+a}{a}$$

$$= 2\ln 2$$

$$= 1{\cdot}385 \text{ units}^2 \quad \text{Ans.}$$

17. (a)
$$\int \frac{3}{x}\, dx = 3\int \frac{dx}{x}$$

$$= 3\ln x + C \quad \text{Ans. (a)}$$

(b)
$$\int \frac{1}{a} x^3\, dx = \frac{1}{a} \int x^3\, dx$$

$$= \frac{x^4}{4a} + C \quad \text{Ans. (b)}$$

(c) $\displaystyle \int (4z^3 + 3z^2 + 2z + 1)\, dz = z^4 + z^3 + z^2 + z + C \quad \text{Ans. (c)}$

(d) $\displaystyle \int (2\cos\theta - 5\sin\theta)\, d\theta = 2\sin\theta + 5\cos\theta + C \quad \text{Ans. (d)}$

18.
$$a = \frac{dv}{dt} = -2t^2$$

$$v = -\int 2t^2\, dt$$

$$= -\tfrac{2}{3}t^3 + k_1$$

but $\quad v = 5$ when $t = 0$

$$\therefore \quad k_1 = 5$$

$$v = \frac{ds}{dt} = -\tfrac{2}{3}t^3 + 5$$

$$s = -\int (\tfrac{2}{3}t^3 - 5)dt$$

$$= -\tfrac{1}{6}t^4 + 5t + k_2$$

but $s = 0$ when $t = 0$

$\therefore$ $k_2 = 0$

$$\left.\begin{array}{l} a = -2t^2 \\ v = 5 - \frac{2}{3}t^3 \\ s = 5t - \frac{1}{6}t^4 \end{array}\right\} \quad \text{at } t \text{ seconds}$$

$$\left.\begin{array}{l} a = -18 \text{ m/s}^2 \\ v = -13 \text{ m/s} \\ s = 1\frac{1}{2} \text{ m} \end{array}\right\} \quad \text{at 3 s}$$

$\therefore$ Particle is $1\frac{1}{2}$ m along OX moving in the direction XO at 13 m/s, decelerating at 18 m/s². Ans.

SELECTION OF EXAMINATION QUESTIONS

1. Determine the second differential coefficients of:

   (a) $y = x^4 - \dfrac{2}{x^2} + 7x - 9$

   (b) $y = \ln x + \sin x$

2. (a) Prove that x can have any value to satisfy the equation:

   $$\left(x + \frac{1}{x}\right)^2 - \left(x - \frac{1}{x}\right)^2 = 4$$

   (b) Find the values of (i) $x^2 + \dfrac{1}{x^2}$, (ii) $x^4 + \dfrac{1}{x^4}$, and (iii) x, in the equation

   $$\left\{x + \frac{1}{x}\right\}^2 = 9$$

3. Water flows along a horizontal pipe of 100 mm internal diameter, the depth of water in the pipe is 75 mm. Calculate the hydraulic mean depth d of the water from the formula:

   $$d = \frac{\text{cross-sectional area of water stream}}{\text{perimeter of wetted pipe surface}}$$

4. Given $p = 120/V$, where p and V represent the pressure (N/m^2) and volume (m^3) of a given mass of gas at constant temperature, calculate by integration the work done when the gas expands from

   $$V = 0\cdot5 \text{ m}^3 \text{ to } V = 6\cdot5 \text{ m}^3$$

5. The volumetric analysis of a certain mixture is 68% water, 18% alcohol and the remainder solids. Calculate (a) how much water should be added to each 1 of this mixture to reduce the alcohol content to 15%, (b) the percentage analysis of the new mixture.

6. Differentiate the following with respect to x.

(a) $Rgx - \dfrac{Cx^3}{64L}$ (b) $ax^3 + \dfrac{b}{x^2}$

Integrate the following.

(c) $\displaystyle\int_{+1}^{+2} (k^{2\cdot6} - 1)\, dk$ with respect to k, and

(d) $\displaystyle\int [(2v^2 - 4)v]\, dv$ with respect to v.

7. Sketch the graph of $y = 11 + 7x - 2x^2$ and use differential calculus to determine the maximum value of y.

8. A component consists of a cone of base diameter 52·5 mm and perpendicular height 45 mm, standing concentrically on the top of a solid cylinder 60 mm diameter and 40 mm high. The base of this component is firmly fixed on to a flat base-plate. Calculate the total surface area of the component exposed above the base-plate.

9. (a) The distance s metres travelled by a body in time t seconds is given by:

$$s = t^3 - 5\cdot5t^2 - 4t + 68\cdot5$$

Determine the time, distance travelled and acceleration of the body when its velocity becomes zero.

(b) Integrate with respect to x:

(i) $3\sqrt{x} - 3x^2$

(ii) $\dfrac{2}{x^3} + 2$

10. A roof has the form of a square pyramid, the base is 24 m square and the length of the ridge from corner of base to apex is 18 m. Find (i) the perpendicular height from base to apex, (ii) the total surface area of the roof.

11. (i) Multiply $2x^3 - 3x^2 + 2x + 4$ by $x^2 - 3x + 5$
    (ii) Divide $6x^5 + x^4 + 2x^3 - 4x^2 - 7x + 4$
        by $3x^3 - x^2 + 3x - 4$
    (iii) Multiply $(2a^2b)^3$ by $(3ab^2)^2$
    (iv) Divide $(3ab^2)^3$ by $(ab^3)^2$

12. Find the values of angle θ between $0°$ and $360°$ which will satisfy the equation:

$$\tan \theta = \cos \theta$$

13. (a) Determine the second differential coefficients of:

   (i) $4 \cos x + \ln x$

   (ii) $3x^3 + \dfrac{4}{x^2} + 6x - 2$

   (b) The expression $T = 1700 + 16000/x^2 + 0 \cdot 6x^2$ is used to calculate the hoop tensile strength T of certain rotating discs. If x is the disc radius, use calculus to determine the value of x for which T is a minimum and the corresponding value of T at that radius.

14. The following table gives corresponding values of x and y. Plot y against x and, assuming they are connected by a straight line law, find the values of the constants and state the law.

x	$-3 \cdot 8$	-2	$+2 \cdot 1$	$+4 \cdot 1$	$+5 \cdot 9$	$+8$
y	-18	$-13 \cdot 7$	$-5 \cdot 9$	-2	$+1 \cdot 7$	$+6$

15. A sector of a circle is cut out of a piece of sheet metal, the radius of the sector being 102 mm and the angle at the centre $150°$. The sector is then rolled into the shape of a cone. Find the surface area of the metal used, the diameter of the base of the cone and its perpendicular height.

16. Find the values of x and y in the simultaneous linear equations:

$$10y + 4b = -2x$$
$$3a + x = y$$

given that the same values of a and b in the above also satisfy the equations:

$$19a + 27b = 43$$
$$7a + 4b = -2$$

17. The rim of a flywheel is elliptical in cross-section with the major axis in the radial direction. The major and minor axes of the rim section measures 300 and 200 mm respectively, and the overall

diameter of the wheel is 3·6 m. If the material is cast iron of density $7·21 \times 10^3$ kg/m^3, find the mass of the rim.

18. Determine the gradient of a tangent to any point in the curve

$$y = \frac{x^3}{4} - \frac{x^2}{2}$$

and show that there are two points where the gradient is zero. Determine the point on the curve where y is a minimum.

19. Factorise completely:
   (i) $2x^2 - 2$
   (ii) $7x^2 + 9xy - 10y^2$
   (iii) $14x^3y^2 + 22x^2y^3 - 12xy^4$
   (iv) $3x^3 + 8x^2y - xy^2 - 10y^3$ given that $(x - y)$ is one of the factors.

20. Using integral calculus determine the difference in area bounded by the curves $y = 10x^2 + x + 4$ and $y = x^2/2 - 1/x - 1/2$ and the x axis between the ordinates $x = 1$ and $x = 5$.

21. (a) Using integral calculus, determine the area bounded by the curve $y = 2\cos x$ and the x-axis between the ordinates at $x = 0$ and $x = \pi/4$.
   (b) A curve which passes through the point $(x = 1, y = -2)$ has a gradient of $3x^2 - 4$. Determine the equation of the curve.

22. (i) Prove that the solution of a quadratic equation of the form,

$$ax^2 + bx + c = 0$$

can be obtained from,

$$x = \frac{-b \pm \sqrt{b^2 - 4ac}}{2a}$$

   (ii) Solve the following quadratic equation by the method of 'completing the square',

$$x^2 + 5x = 84$$

   (iii) Find the value of x in the following quadratic equation by factorising,

$$2x^2 - 3ax - bx = 0$$

23. Determine the second differential coefficient of:

(a) $y = x^2 - 5x + 7 - \dfrac{1}{x}$

(b) $y = 2\cos x - 3\sin x$

24. A block of brass is 80 mm long and has a varying cross-section throughout its length. Commencing at one end the cross-sectional areas, at regular distances apart, are 0, 2·9, 3·8, 4·1, 3·7, 2·7 and 1·1 cm^2 respectively. Find the volume by Simpson's rule and the mass taking the density of brass as 8·4 g/cm^3.

25. On a certain production machine, the cost C of manufacturing N articles is given by $C = a + bN$ where a and b are constants. If it costs £8·50 for 300 articles, and £7·50 for 200 (a) produce an equation to give the cost in pounds to manufacture any number of articles, (b) find the cost to make 150, (c) what is the minimum cost of running the machine?

26. Using integral calculus, determine the area bounded by the curve.

$$y = \sin x + \tfrac{1}{2}\cos x$$

and the values $x = 60°$ and $x = 30°$

27. A piece of wire 1 m long is cut into two pieces and each is bent into a form of a square.

Using differential calculus, determine the least possible sum of the two areas.

28. A flat mild steel plate of elliptical shape measuring 420 mm across the major axis and 370 mm across the minor axis is 45 mm thick. There is a groove around the whole of the perimeter, 13 mm wide by 13 mm deep. Taking the density of steel as 7·86 g/cm^3, find the mass of the plate.

29. Two chords, 60 and 80 mm long respectively, are drawn parallel to each other inside a circle. If the chords are 10 mm apart, find the radius of the circle.

30. A railway cutting, in the form of a trapezium, is 10 m wide at the bottom, 15 m wide at the top, and 14 m deep. The cutting sweeps around on a circular arc, the radius of the arc to the centre of the

cutting is 805 m, and the angle subtended is 6°. Calculate the volume of earth removed, in m³, in the making of the cutting.

31. In a triangle ABC the lengths of the sides AB and AC are 50 and 30 mm respectively and the angle BAC is 20°. Calculate the length of the other side, the two remaining angles, and the area.

32. Draw graphs of the following simultaneous equations between the limits $x = -2$ and $x = +3$ and find the values of x and y,

$$x^2 - y = 1$$
$$2y - 3x = 4$$

33. Determine the area contained between the curves
$p = \dfrac{78}{V^{1.2}}, p = \dfrac{7}{V^{1.15}}$ and the ordinates at $V = 2$ and $V = 5$.

34. A body moves s metres in t seconds according to the relationship

$$s = t^3 - 6t^2 + 9t + 3$$

Given that velocity $v = ds/dt$ and acceleration $a = dv/dt$, calculate

(i) the values of t at which the body is stationary
(ii) the values of the acceleration corresponding to the values of t determined in (i).

35. Find the value of x in the following equation:

$$\frac{x+2}{x-1} - \frac{x-1}{3x-4} = \frac{7}{2}$$

36. Calculate the area of the largest isoceles triangular plate with base angles of 75° that can be cut out of a circular plate having an area of 804·2 cm².

37. (a) Differentiate the following equations,

   (i) $y = (Ei - Ri^2)$ with respect to i

   (ii) $y = \left[\dfrac{C}{1-n}\right]\left[v^{1-n} - p^{1-n}\right]$ with respect to v

   (b) evaluate the following integrals,

   (i) $\displaystyle\int_0^1 12x^7 dx$

(ii) $\dfrac{3}{2\pi r^3} \displaystyle\int_0^r \pi(r^2 - x^2)dx$

38. (i) Prove that $\sin^2 \theta + \cos^2 \theta = 1$

(ii) Find the values of θ between $0°$ and $360°$ which will satisfy the equation:

$$2\sin^2 \theta - 2\cos^2 \theta - 2 = 0$$

39. Prove that the radius of a circle inscribed in a triangle is given by:

$$R = \frac{2 \times \text{area of triangle}}{\text{perimeter of triangle}}$$

and calculate the radius of the circle inscribed in a triangle of sides 50, 60 and 70 mm respectively.

40. Determine the value of x for which expression

$$y = 4x^3 - 3x^2 - 18x$$

is a maximum or minimum, and calculate the corresponding values of y stating whether it is a maximum or minimum.

41. A solid consists of a right circular cone of 100 mm base diameter mounted concentrically on the flat surface of a hemisphere of equal diameter, the perpendicular height of the conical part being also 100 mm.

Calculate the volume of the solid in cm^3 and the curved surface area in cm^2.

If another similar solid was made with all linear dimensions double those of the original, what would be its volume and curved surface area?

42. Plot the graph of the equation $y = x^2 - 8x + 7$ between $x = 0$ and $x = 9$, using intervals of unity. From the graph solve for x in each of the following equations:

(a) $x^2 - 7x + 6 = 0$

(b) $x^2 - 9x + 8 = 0$

Suggested scales: x axis   2 cm $= 1$

y axis   2 cm $= 5$

43. For a certain ship at deadweight displacement, an expression connecting the power of the main engines and the speed of the ship is given by:

$$P = V(a + bV^2)$$

where, P = power of the engines in kW.

V = speed of the ship in knot.

a and b = constants.

If the powers are 6024 and 13408 kW when the speeds are 12 and 16 knot respectively, calculate the probable power when the speed is 14 knot.

44. Obtain the second differential coefficients of:

(i) $y = \dfrac{x^3}{3} - \dfrac{3}{x^3} + 3x^2 - 2x$

(ii) $y = 3\sin x + 4\cos x$

45. A buoy is constructed by welding the base of a hollow cone to the flat base rim of a hollow hemisphere, the common diameter of their bases being 2·44 m. The greatest length of the buoy is 4·27 m. Calculate (i) the curved surface area of the cone, (ii) the angle subtended at the centre of the sector of a circle when the cone is developed, (iii) the curved surface area of the hemisphere, (iv) the external volume of the buoy.

46. Solve for a, b, c and d in the following four simultaneous equations:

$$3a + 7b + 2c = 25$$
$$2a + 6b + c = 18$$
$$a + b + c + d = 14$$
$$2a + d = 9$$

47. A lens is flat on one side and convex on the other side, the convex surface being part of a sphere. The diameter of the flat surface is 60 mm. The maximum thickness of the lens is 4 mm and the minimum thickness is nil. Calculate the curved surface area of the lens in cm^2.

48. (a) If $dy/dx = -\cos x - 2\sin x$, determine an expression for y in terms of x, given that $y = 3$ when $x = 0$.

(b) The area bounded by the curve

$$y = \frac{x^2}{4}$$

the ordinate $x = 4$ and the x-axis between 0 and 4 is rotated once around the x-axis. Use integral calculus to determine the volume of the solid generated.

49. Transpose the terms in the following equation to make K the subject:

$$p = \left[\frac{wu^2}{g\left\{ \dfrac{K+a}{K(2a+K)+a^2} + \dfrac{D}{Et} \right\}} \right]^{\frac{1}{2}}$$

50. (i) If x varies directly as z and inversely as y^2, calculate the percentage change in x when z is increased by 12% and y is decreased by 20%.

(ii) The time for one beat of a pendulum varies as the square root of its length. If a pendulum 174·4 mm long makes 105 beats in 44 s, calculate the length of a similar pendulum to beat exactly once every second.

51. Solve the following simultaneous equations to give the smallest values of the angles x and y:

$$3\cos x + 4\sin y = 2\sqrt{2} - 1\cdot5$$
$$5\cos x - \sqrt{2}\sin y = -3\cdot5$$

52. Show the height of a frustum of a right circular cone is one-third the height of the complete cone when the volume of the frustum is 19/27 that of the complete cone.

53. (a) Determine the area bounded by the curve $y = 2\sin\theta$ and the θ axis between the ordinates $\theta = \pi/6$ rad and $\theta = 5\pi/6$ rad.

(b) Evaluate:

(i) $\displaystyle\int_{\frac{\pi}{2}}^{\pi} (3\cos\theta)\, d\theta$

(ii) $\displaystyle\int_1^2 (x^2 - 6x)\, dx$

(iii) $\displaystyle\int_1^3 (x^4 - 7x + 8)\, dx$

54. Express V in terms of v, f_1 and f_2 in the following expression where $K = f_1/f_2$ and find the values of V when $f_1 = 12, f_2 = 18$ and $v = 20$,

$$K = \left\{\frac{V + v}{V - v}\right\}^2$$

55. Plot the graph $y = x^2 + 2x - 8$ between the limits $x = -4$ and $x = +2$. If the area bounded by this curve and the x-axis is rotated through one revolution about the x-axis, calculate the volume generated, using Simpson's rule.

56. The total area of metal A needed to make a box of stated volume is given by the expression

$$A = x^2 + \frac{16000}{x}$$

where x is the side of the square base. Use calculus to find:

(i) the value of x for which A is a minimum.

(ii) the minimum value of A.

57. Three steel ball bearings, each 2 cm diameter, are placed inside a cylinder 6 cm diameter, equally spaced around the bottom, then another ball bearing 4 cm diameter is placed on top of these. Calculate the volume of water, in ml, required to pour into the cylinder so that the top ball is just submerged.

If all linear dimensions were half of those given above, what would be the volume of water required?

58. The distance from the centre to a corner of a regular pentagon is 3 cm, find the area of the pentagon. If a piece is sliced off by a straight cut from one corner at an angle of 30° to a side, find the ratio of the areas of the two pieces so formed.

59. (a) Find the angles between $0°$ and $360°$ that will satisfy the equation:

$$2 \sin^2 \theta - \cos \theta = 1$$

(b) Find the angles between $0°$ and $360°$ that will satisfy the equation:

$$3 \cos 2\theta + 2 \cos \theta = 0$$

60. The resistance R (newton) to motion of a body and its velocity V (m/s) is tabulated below:

V	5	10	15	20	25
R	10	25	50	85	130

Show that these values are connected by the law $R = k + cV^2$, find the values of the constants k and c and calculate the probable resistance to motion when the velocity is 40 m/s.

61. Transpose the following to express k in terms of p and V, and find the value of k when $p = 9.2$ and $V = 0.42$,

$$p = V + \frac{k(p + V)}{k + p + V}$$

62. (a) Calculate the area of a trapezium inscribed in a semi-circle of radius 10 cm if the length of each non-parallel side of the trapezium is equal to the radius of the semi-circle.

(b) If this trapezium is rotated through one complete revolution about an axis passing through the centre of, and perpendicular to, its long side, calculate the volume of the solid frustum of a cone thus generated.

63. (a) Find the values of a, b and w in the simultaneous equations:

$$4a + 3b + 2w = 2$$
$$2a + 8b + 3w = 11$$
$$3a + 5b - 6w = -36$$

(b) Find the values of x and y in the simultaneous equations:

$$x^2 + y^2 = 18.5$$
$$x - y = 1$$

64. (a) Prove, $\dfrac{1 - \tan^2 \theta}{1 + \tan^2 \theta} = \cos^2 \theta - \sin^2 \theta$

(b) Prove, $\sin \theta + \sin \theta \cot^2 \theta + \dfrac{\tan \theta}{\cos \theta} = \dfrac{1}{\sin \theta \cos^2 \theta}$

65. Draw the graphs of the following equations between the limits $x = -2$ and $x = +8$ and find the area of the triangle enclosed by the graphs,

$$4y - x - 20 = 0$$
$$y - x + 1 = 0$$
$$2y + x - 7 = 0$$

66. A hexagon of unit side is to have its area reduced by 20% by cutting it parallel to one side. Calculate the thickness of the piece cut off and the distance from the centre of the original hexagon to the corner of the new face.

67. Using Simpson's rule, with eleven ordinates, calculate the area between the curve $y = e^{-2x}$ and the x axis between the limits $x = 0$ and $x = +2$ and hence determine the length of the mean ordinate for this section of the curve.

68. The metal from the melting down of a solid cone 60 cm base diameter and 50 cm slant height is to be cast into the form of a hollow sphere of $1 \cdot 5$ cm uniform thickness. Calculate the outer and inner diameters.

69. Transpose for h in the following expression and use the result to evaluate h when $a = 1 \cdot 5, c = 15, s = 16$ and $d = 17$

$$a = \frac{c}{2s} \left\{ \frac{h^2}{d - h} \right\}$$

70. Three points A, B and C lie on a horizontal ground. C is due North of A, and B is due East of a point W which lies on the line joining A and C. A vertical mast stands on point B and the angle of elevation to the top of the mast from A is 20°, AB = 60 m, BC = 32 m, and AC = 68 m.

(a) Prove that the angle at B is a right angle.

(b) Find the angles at A and C.

SELECTION OF EXAMINATION QUESTIONS 413

(c) Calculate the height of the mast.

(d) Find the angle of elevation from point W to the top of the mast.

71. Draw the graph $y = x^2 + 1$ between the limits $x = -2$ and $x = +3$ and use this to solve the equation $x^2 - x = 2$.

72. (a) Prove that the area of a segment of a circle is equal to

$$\frac{r^2}{2}(\theta - \sin\theta)$$

where r = radius of circle
θ = angle subtended (rad).

(b) A horizontal pipe is more than half full of water. The breadth of the water-level is 60 cm and the height from water-level to crown of pipe is 15 cm. Calculate (i) the diameter of the pipe, (ii) the cross-sectional area of the water, (iii) l of water contained over a length of 2 m.

73. (a) Find the values of WZ, W^2Z, W^2/Z and Z^3/W when $W = x^{a+b}$ and $Z = x^{a-b}$

(b) Find the values of x and y in the simultaneous linear equations:

$$4x + y = 10$$
$$\frac{2}{x} + \frac{7}{y} = 3$$

74. In each of the following formulae, transpose and re-write in terms of k:

(a) $Q = \sqrt{\dfrac{2ghDk^2}{d(s^2 - k^2)}}$

(b) $F = \dfrac{1}{2\pi}\sqrt{\dfrac{1}{Lk}}$

(c) $L = \dfrac{\pi}{2}(k + b) + \dfrac{(k - b)}{4c} + 2C$

75. The equation $7x^2 - 28 + 7y^2 = 0$ represents the law of a circle. Use integral calculus to determine the volume of revolution generated by the middle part of the circle about its x axis between the limits $x = +1$ and $x = -1$.

Take each unit of x and y as representing 1 cm.

76. Show that, if x is numerically less than 1,

$$\frac{1}{\sqrt{1-x}} = 1 + \frac{1 \times 3}{2 \times 4}x^2 + \frac{1 \times 3 \times 5}{2 \times 4 \times 6}x^3 \text{ approx.}$$

Evaluate such an approximation for $x = 0.1$.

77. Due to bad weather a ship's speed is decreased by 20% for 8 h. The ship then runs at normal speed for 10 h. In order to catch a tide the speed is then increased for 6 h. Over the 24 h period the fuel consumption was found to be unchanged from the normal consumption. Given that the fuel consumption C is directly proportional to the cube of the ship's speed V determine the percentage increase in the ship's speed in the last 6 h.

78. (a) Simplify the expression $\dfrac{x^{n+4}\sqrt{x^{6n-7}}}{x^{3n}\sqrt{x^{2n-1}}}$

   (b) Solve for x in the equation: $10^x = 20^{x-4}$

79. (a) (i) Determine the square root of $64^{-1}a^8 b^{12}$
       (ii) Determine the cube root of $216a^{-12}b^{0.6}$

   (b) Solve for a, b and c in the following simultaneous equations:

   $$a - b + c = 3$$
   $$2a + 8b - 3c = 56$$
   $$7a + 3b + 3c = 69$$

80. The co-ordinates for two points on each of two straight line graphs are as follows:
   first graph: $x_1 = -4, y_1 = 6$ and $x_2 = 2, y_2 = -10$
   second graph: $x_3 = -5, y_3 = -10$ and $x_4 = 2, y_4 = 4$

   (a) Draw the two straight line graphs using the same axes.
   (b) Using the graphs determine:
       (i) the algebraic expression for each straight line in the form $y = ax + b$;
       (ii) the values of x and y which satisfy both expressions when considered as simultaneous equations.
          Suggested scales x axis   1 unit $= 2$ cm
                              y axis   1 unit $= 1$ cm

81. A tower 50 m high stands on the top of a hill which has a 20° incline. The angle of depression from the horizontal from the top of

the tower to a marker A on the hill is 55°. At a point further down the slope in the same vertical plane is another marker B at an angle of depression of 40° from the horizontal from the top of the tower. Determine the distance between A and B.

82. A ship's fuel consumption varies inversely as the calorific value of the fuel and varies directly as the (ship speed in knot).³ The ship burns 60 t/day of fuel of calorific value 40 MJ/kg when travelling at 20 knot. Determine the daily consumption when using fuel of calorific value 42 MJ/kg and steaming at 16 knot.

83. By plotting two graphs for unit values between $x = 2$ and $x = 10$ on the same axis solve the equation

$$0 \cdot 5 \lg x = \frac{5}{2x}$$

Suggested scales x axis 1 unit $= 2$ cm
               y axis 1 unit $= 10$ cm

84. Two chords are drawn from a common point on the circumference of a circle such that both lie on the same side of the centre of the circle. One chord is 20 cm long and the other is 27·5 cm long. The straight line distance between the remote ends of the chords is 12·5 cm. Given that for a circumscribed circle

$$\frac{a}{\text{Sin A}} = \frac{b}{\text{Sin B}} = \frac{c}{\text{Sin C}} = D$$

where D is the diameter of the circle, calculate the diameter of the circle.

85. The sketch (overleaf) shows a diesel engine unit which has a stroke of 300 mm and a connecting rod AB of length 550 mm. Between the vertical and the position of the connecting rod is an angle CAB.

Twice during the downward movement of the piston angle CAB equals 10°. Determine the piston travel between these piston positions.

86. (a) For the function $y = \dfrac{x^3}{4} - \dfrac{x^2}{2}$:

    (i) show that there are two points on the curve where the gradient is zero;

    (ii) determine the values of x and y at the point where the curve is a minimum.

  (b) Determine the second differential coefficient of
$y = 4\cos x - 3\sin x$.

87. (a) Using integral calculus determine the area bounded by the curve $y = 4\cos x$ and the x axis between the ordinates

$$x = \frac{\pi}{9} \text{ and } x = \frac{\pi}{2}$$

  (b) A curve passes through the point $x = 3$ $y = -2$ and has a gradient of $2x^2 - 2$.

    Determine the equation of the curve.

88. (a) Determine the mass of the frustum of a cone made of wood of density $0 \cdot 9$ g/cm^3 given that the diameters of the two paralleled surfaces are 20 cm and 40 cm and the vertical height of the frustum is 16 cm.

  (b) The frustum was made by removing a smaller top cone base diameter 20 cm from the large original cone, base diameter 40 cm.

Determine the ratio by mass of the smaller cone which was removed to the mass of the remaining frustum.

89. A glass vessel has a uniform circular bore and a hemispherical end of the same radius. With the hemispherical end at the bottom the container is filled to 0·7 of its overall height. When the container is inverted the level of the liquid drops down to 0·6 of the vessel's height and is below the hemispherical section.

The vessel contains 100 ml of water. Determine:

(a) the bore;
(b) the overall height.

90. Determine the volume of the solid of revolution formed when the shaded area shown is rotated about the x axis.

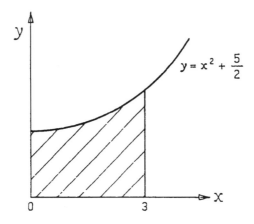

Note: Volume of revolution $= \int \pi y^2 dx$

SOLUTIONS TO EXAMINATION QUESTIONS

1. (a)
$$y = f(x) = x^4 - \frac{2}{x^2} + 7x - 9$$
$$f(x) = x^4 - 2x^{-2} + 7x - 9$$
$$f'(x) = 4x^3 + 4x^{-3} + 7$$
$$f''(x) = 12x^2 - 12x^{-4}$$
$$f''(x) = 12\left(x^2 - \frac{1}{x^4}\right) \quad \text{Ans. (a)}$$

(b)
$$y = f(x) = \ln x + \sin x$$
$$f'(x) = \frac{1}{x} + \cos x$$
$$f'(x) = x^{-1} + \cos x$$
$$f''(x) = -x^{-2} - \sin x$$
$$f''(x) = -\left(\sin x + \frac{1}{x^2}\right) \quad \text{Ans. (b)}$$

2.
$$\left\{x + \frac{1}{x}\right\}^2 - \left\{x - \frac{1}{x}\right\}^2 = 4$$

This is the 'difference between two squares', similar to $a^2 - b^2$.

Factorising $a^2 - b^2$ gives $(a + b)(a - b)$

Factorising the given expression:

$$\left[\left(x + \frac{1}{x}\right) + \left(x - \frac{1}{x}\right)\right] \times \left[\left(x + \frac{1}{x}\right) - \left(x - \frac{1}{x}\right)\right] = 4$$
$$\left[x + \frac{1}{x} + x - \frac{1}{x}\right] \times \left[x + \frac{1}{x} - x + \frac{1}{x}\right] = 4$$
$$2x \times \frac{2}{x} = 4$$
$$4 = 4$$

x cancels therefore it can have any value.   Ans. (a)

$$\left\{x + \frac{1}{x}\right\}^2 = 9$$

$$x^2 + 2 + \frac{1}{x^2} = 9$$

$$\therefore x^2 + \frac{1}{x^2} = 7 \quad \text{Ans. (b) (i)}$$

Squaring both sides,

$$x^4 + 2 + \frac{1}{x^4} = 49$$

$$x^4 + \frac{1}{x^4} = 47 \quad \text{Ans. (b) (ii)}$$

$$\left\{x + \frac{1}{x}\right\}^2 = 9$$

Taking square root of both sides,

$$x + \frac{1}{x} = 3$$

Multiplying throughout by x,

$$x^2 + 1 = 3x$$
$$\text{or, } x^2 - 3x + 1 = 0$$

Solving this quadratic,

$$x = 2 \cdot 618 \quad \text{or} \quad 0 \cdot 382 \quad \text{Ans. (b) (iii)}$$

3.

Working in cm:

$$\cos \alpha = \frac{2 \cdot 5}{5} = 0 \cdot 5 \quad \alpha = 60°$$

$$\theta = 360° - (2 \times \alpha) = 240°$$

θ in rad

$$= \frac{240}{360} \times 2\pi = 4 \cdot 19$$

$$\sin \theta = -\sin (240° - 180°) = -\sin 60° = -0 \cdot 866$$

Area of segment of angle θ,

$$= 0 \cdot 5 r^2 (\theta - \sin \theta)$$
$$= 0 \cdot 5 \times 5^2 [4 \cdot 19 - (-0 \cdot 866)]$$
$$= 12 \cdot 5 \times 5 \cdot 056 = 63 \cdot 2 \text{ cm}^2$$

Wetted perimeter of pipe surface

$$= \frac{240}{360} \times \pi \times 10 = 20 \cdot 94 \text{ cm}$$

Hydraulic mean depth

$$= \frac{63 \cdot 2}{20 \cdot 94} = 3 \cdot 017 \text{ cm or } 30 \cdot 17 \text{ mm} \quad \text{Ans.}$$

4. $$W = \int_{V_1}^{V_2} p \, dV \text{ where } W \text{ is work done}$$

$$= \int_{0 \cdot 5}^{6 \cdot 5} \frac{120 \, dV}{V}$$
$$= 120 [\ln V]_{0 \cdot 5}^{6 \cdot 5}$$
$$120 [\ln 6 \cdot 5 - \ln 0 \cdot 5]$$
$$= 120 \ln \frac{6 \cdot 5}{0 \cdot 5}$$
$$= 120 \ln 13$$
$$= 120 \times 2 \cdot 565$$
$$W = 307 \cdot 8 \text{ Nm} \quad \text{Ans.}$$

5. By adding x l of water, the original 1 l of the mixture is increased to $(1 + x)$ l; the original amount of alcohol was 18% of 1 l $= 0 \cdot 18$ l, and this is to be 15% of the new mixture.

$$\frac{15}{100}(1 + x) = 0.18$$

$$15(1 + x) = 0.18 \times 100$$

$$15 + 15x = 18$$

$$15x = 3$$

$$x = 0.21 \quad \text{or} \quad 200 \text{ ml} \quad \text{Ans. (i)}$$

$$\% \text{ water in new mixture} = \frac{0.68 + 0.2}{1 + 0.2} \times 100$$

$$= \frac{0.88 \times 100}{1.2}$$

$$= 73\tfrac{1}{3}$$

$$\% \text{ solids} = \text{remainder} = 100 - (73\tfrac{1}{3} + 15)$$

$$= 11\tfrac{2}{3}$$

$\therefore$ New anlaysis is : Water $= 73\tfrac{1}{3}\%$ ⎫
⎬ Ans.

Alcohol $= 15\%$

Solids $= 11\tfrac{2}{3}\%$ ⎭

6. (a) $$y = Rgx - \frac{Cx^3}{64L}$$

$$\frac{dy}{dx} = Rg - \frac{3Cx^2}{64L} \quad \text{Ans. (a)}$$

(b)
$$y = ax^3 + \frac{b}{x^2}$$
$$y = ax^3 + bx^{-2}$$
$$\frac{dy}{dx} = 3ax^2 - 2bx^{-3}$$
$$= 3ax^2 - \frac{2b}{x^3} \quad \text{Ans. (b)}$$

(c)
$$\int_{+1}^{+2} (k^{2 \cdot 6} - 1)dk$$

$$= \left[\frac{k^{3 \cdot 6}}{3 \cdot 6} - k \right]_1^2$$

$$= \left[\frac{2^{3 \cdot 6}}{3 \cdot 6} - 2 \right] - \left[\frac{1^{3 \cdot 6}}{3 \cdot 6} - 1 \right]$$

$$= \left[\frac{12 \cdot 13}{3 \cdot 6} - 2 \right] - \left[\frac{1}{3 \cdot 6} - 1 \right]$$

$$= [3 \cdot 369 - 2] - [0 \cdot 2778 - 1]$$

$$= 1 \cdot 169 + 0 \cdot 7222$$

$$= 1 \cdot 891 \quad \text{Ans. (c)}$$

(d)
$$= \int [(2v^2 - 4)v]dv$$

$$= \int (2v^3 - 4v)dv$$

$$= \frac{v^4}{2} - 2v^2 + C \quad \text{Ans. (d)}$$

7.

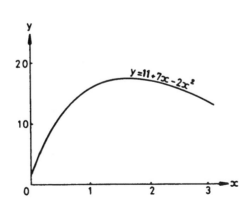

$y = 11 \cdot 7x - 2x^2$

$$y = 11 + 7x - 2x^2 \text{ (see sketch)}$$
$$\frac{dy}{dx} = 7 - 4x$$

For turning points,

$$7 - 4x = 0$$
$$\therefore x = \frac{7}{4}$$

From the graph, it is obvious that $x = 1\frac{3}{4}$ gives a *maximum* value of y.

$$\therefore \quad y = 11 + 7(\tfrac{7}{4}) - 2(\tfrac{7}{4})^2$$
$$= 11 + \frac{49}{4} - \frac{98}{16}$$
$$= 17\tfrac{1}{8} \quad \text{Ans.}$$

8.   Radius of cone base $= \frac{1}{2} \times 5\cdot25 = 2\cdot625$ cm

Slant height of cone $= \sqrt{4\cdot5^2 + 2\cdot625^2} = 5\cdot21$ cm

Curved surface area of cone $= \pi r l$
$$= \pi \times 2\cdot625 \times 5\cdot21$$
$$= 42\cdot96 \text{ cm}^2 \qquad \dots \quad \dots \quad \text{(i)}$$

Area of annulus between top of cylinder and base of cone,

$$= 0.7854 \times (D^2 - d^2)$$

$$= 0.7854(6 + 5.25)(6 - 5.25)$$

$$= 6.628 \text{ cm}^2 \qquad \ldots \quad \ldots \quad \text{(ii)}$$

Curved surface area of cylinder

$$= \pi dh$$

$$= \pi \times 6 \times 4$$

$$= 75.41 \text{ cm}^2 \qquad \ldots \quad \ldots \quad \text{(iii)}$$

Total surface area exposed $= 42.96 + 6.628 + 75.41$

$$= 124.998$$

say $125 \text{ cm}^2 = 12\,500 \text{ mm}^2$ Ans.

9. (a) $\qquad\qquad s = t^3 - 5.5t^2 - 4t + 68.5$

$$v = \frac{ds}{dt} = 3t^2 - 11t - 4 = 0$$

$$0 = (3t + 1)(t - 4)$$

$t = 4s$ i.e. minus time inadmissable

$$s = 4^3 - 5.5 \times 4^2 - 4 \times 4 + 68.5$$

$$= 64 - 88 - 16 + 68.5$$

$$= 28.5 \, m$$

$$a = \frac{dv}{dt} = 6t - 11$$

$$= 24 - 11$$

$$= 13 \text{ m/s}^2$$

Time $= 4$ s ⎫
Distance travelled $= 28.5$ m ⎬ when velocity is zero.   Ans. (a)
Acceleration $= 13$ m/s^2 ⎭

(b) (i)

$$\int (3\sqrt{x} - 3x^2)\, dx$$

$$= \int (3x^{1/2} - 3x^2)\, dx$$

$$= 2x^{3/2} - x^3 + C$$

$$= 2\sqrt{x^3} - x^3 + C \quad \text{Ans. (b) (i)}$$

(b) (ii)

$$\int \left(\frac{2}{x^3} + 2\right) dx$$

$$= \int (2x^{-3} + 2)\, dx$$

$$= -x^{-2} + 2x + C$$

$$= 2x - \frac{1}{x^2} + C \quad \text{Ans. (b) (ii)}$$

10.

$$AB = 18, BD = 12, DC = 12$$

$$(AD)^2 = (AB)^2 - (BD)^2$$

$$= 18^2 - 12^2$$

$$AD = \sqrt{180} = 13 \cdot 42$$

$$(AC)^2 = (AD)^2 - (DC)^2$$

$$AC = \sqrt{18^2 - 12^2 - 12^2}$$

$$= 6\,\text{m} \quad \text{Ans. (i)}$$

Area of one sloping triangular flat surface,

$$= \tfrac{1}{2} \times BE \times AD$$

Total surface area of roof $\quad = 4 \times \tfrac{1}{2} \times 24 \times 13 \cdot 42$

$$= 644 \cdot 2\,\text{m}^2 \quad \text{Ans. (ii)}$$

11.
$$2x^3 - 3x^2 + 2x + 4$$
$$x^2 - 3x + 5$$
$$+ 10x^3 - 15x^2 + 10x + 20$$
$$- 6x^4 + 9x^3 - 6x^2 - 12x$$
$$+ 2x^5 - 3x^4 + 2x^3 + 4x^2$$
$$2x^5 - 9x^4 + 21x^3 - 17x^2 - 2x + 20 \quad \text{Ans. (i)}$$

$$3x^3 - x^2 + 3x - 4)6x^5 + x^4 + 2x^3 - 4x^2 - 7x + 4(2x^2 + x - 1 \quad \text{Ans. (ii)}$$
$$6x^5 - 2x^4 + 6x^3 - 8x^2$$
$$3x^4 - 4x^3 + 4x^2 - 7x$$
$$3x^4 - x^3 + 3x^2 - 4x$$
$$- 3x^3 + x^2 - 3x + 4$$
$$- 3x^3 + x^2 - 3x + 4$$

$$(2a^2b)^3 \times (3ab^2)^2 = 8a^6b^3 \times 9a^2b^4$$
$$= 72a^8b^7 \quad \text{Ans. (iii)}$$

$$(3ab^2)^3 \div (ab^3)^2 = 27a^3b^6 \div a^2b^6$$
$$= \frac{27a^3b^6}{a^2b^6}$$
$$= 27a \quad \text{Ans. (iv)}$$

12.
$$\tan\theta = \cos\theta$$
$$\frac{\sin\theta}{\cos\theta} = \cos\theta$$
$$\sin\theta = \cos^2\theta$$

From the standard identity,
$$\sin^2\theta + \cos^2\theta = 1$$
$$\cos^2\theta = 1 - \sin^2\theta$$

Substituting for $\cos^2\theta$ and simplifying:
$$\sin\theta = 1 - \sin^2\theta$$
$$\sin^2\theta + \sin\theta - 1 = 0$$

Solving this quadratic of sin θ,

$$\sin \theta = 0.6180 \quad \text{or} \quad -1.618$$

$$\sin \theta = 0.6180 \text{ (other value is inadmissable)}$$

$$\left. \begin{array}{c} \theta = 38°10' \\ \text{and } 180° - 38°10' = 141°50' \end{array} \right\} \quad \text{Ans.}$$

13. (a) (i)

$$f(x) = 4\cos + \ln x$$

$$f'(x) = -4\sin x + \frac{1}{x}$$

$$= -4\sin x + x^{-1}$$

$$f''(x) = -4\cos x - \frac{1}{x^2}$$

$$= -\left(4\cos x + \frac{1}{x^2}\right) \quad \text{Ans. (a) (i)}$$

(a) (ii)

$$f(x) = 3x^3 + \frac{4}{x^2} + 6x - 2$$

$$= 3x^3 + 4x^{-2} + 6x - 2$$

$$f'(x) = 9x^2 - 8x^{-3} + 6$$

$$f''(x) = 18x + 24x^{-4}$$

$$= 6\left(\frac{4}{x^4} + 3x\right) \quad \text{Ans. (a) (ii)}$$

(b)

$$T = 1700 + \frac{16\,000}{x^2} + 0.6x^2$$

$$= 1700 + 16\,000x^{-2} + 0.6x^2$$

$$\frac{dT}{dx} = -16\,000 \times 2x^{-3} + 0.6 \times 2x$$

$$= 1.2x - \frac{32\,000}{x^3}$$

$$1.2x = \frac{32\,000}{x^3} \quad \text{for maximum or minimum}$$

$$1.2 = \frac{32\,000}{x^4}$$

$$x = \sqrt[4]{\frac{32\,000}{1.2}}$$

$$= \sqrt[4]{\frac{26667}{1}}$$

$$x = 12.77 \text{ for T minimum} \quad \text{Ans. (b) (i)}$$

$$\frac{dT}{dx} = 1{\cdot}2x - \frac{32\,000}{x^3}$$

$$= 1{\cdot}2x - 32\,000x^{-3}$$

$$\frac{d^2T}{dx^2} = 1{\cdot}2 + 96\,000x^{-4}$$

$$= 1{\cdot}2 + \frac{96\,000}{x^4} \text{ positive when } x = 12{\cdot}77 \text{ i.e. a minimum}$$

$$T = 1700 + \frac{16\,000}{x^2} + 0{\cdot}6x^2$$

$$= 1700 + \frac{16\,000}{12{\cdot}77^2} + 0{\cdot}6 \times 12{\cdot}77^2$$

$$= 1700 + \frac{16\,000}{163{\cdot}07} + 0{\cdot}6 \times 163{\cdot}07$$

$$= 1700 + 98{\cdot}12 + 97{\cdot}84$$

$$T = 1896 \text{ for a minimum} \quad \text{Ans. (b) (ii)}$$

14. Representing the straight line graph by the equation,

$$y = a + bx$$

where a and b are constants,

the graph is drawn as shown in Chapter 6 from which measure:

$$\left.\begin{array}{l} \text{constant } a = -10 \\ \text{constant } b = 2 \end{array}\right\} \quad \text{Ans. (i)}$$

The equation for this graph is therefore:

$$y = -10 + 2x$$
$$\text{or} \quad y = 2x - 10 \quad \text{Ans. (ii)}$$

15.   Area of sector $= \dfrac{150}{360} \times \pi \times 10{\cdot}2^2$

$$= 136{\cdot}2 \text{ cm}^2 \quad \text{Ans. (i)}$$

Length of arc $= \dfrac{150}{360} \times 2\pi \times 10{\cdot}2$

this is the circumference of the cone base, let its diameter $=d$,

$$\pi d = \frac{150}{360} \times 2\pi \times 10\cdot2$$

$$d = \frac{150 \times 2 \times \pi \times 10\cdot2}{360 \times \pi}$$

$$= 8\cdot5 \text{ cm} = 85 \text{ mm} \quad \text{Ans. (ii)}$$

slant height of cone = radius of sector = $10\cdot2$ cm

radius of cone base = $\frac{1}{2} \times 8\cdot5 = 4\cdot25$ cm

perpendicular height = $\sqrt{10\cdot2^2 - 4\cdot25^2}$

$$= 9\cdot27 \text{ cm} = 92\cdot7 \text{ mm} \quad \text{Ans. (iii)}$$

16.
$$19a + 27b = 43 \quad \ldots \quad \ldots \quad \ldots \quad \ldots \quad \text{(i)}$$
$$7a + 4b = -2 \quad \ldots \quad \ldots \quad \ldots \quad \ldots \quad \text{(ii)}$$

Multiplying (i) by 7 and (ii) by 19,

$$133a + 189b = 301 \quad \ldots \quad \ldots \quad \ldots \quad \ldots \quad \text{(iii)}$$
$$133a + 76b = -38 \quad \ldots \quad \ldots \quad \ldots \quad \ldots \quad \text{(iv)}$$

Subtracting (iv) from (iii),

$$113b = 339$$
$$b = 3$$

Substituting value of b into (ii),

$$7a + 12 = -2$$
$$7a = -14$$
$$a = -2$$
$$10y + 4b = -2x$$
$$3a + x = y$$

Substituting values of a and b,

$$10y + 12 = -2x$$
$$-6 + x = y$$

Re-arranging,

$$2x + 10y = -12 \quad \ldots \quad \ldots \quad \ldots \quad \ldots \quad \text{(v)}$$
$$x - y = 6 \quad \ldots \quad \ldots \quad \ldots \quad \ldots \quad \text{(vi)}$$

Multiplying (vi) by 2 and then subtracting from (v),

$$2x + 10y = -12$$
$$2x - 2y = 12$$
$$\overline{12y = -24}$$
$$y = -2$$

Substituting value of y into (vi),

$$x + 2 = 6$$
$$x = 4$$
$$x = 4, \text{ and } y = -2 \quad \text{Ans.}$$

17.   Area of elliptical section $= 0.7854Dd$

$$= 0.7854 \times 0.3 \times 0.2 \text{ m}^2$$

Centre of ellipse from centre of wheel

$$= 1.8 - 0.15 = 1.65 \text{ m}$$

By Theorem (Pappus), in one revolution of the elliptical sectional area about centre of wheel:

Volume swept out $=$ area $\times$ distance its centroid moves

Volume of rim $= 0.7854 \times 0.3 \times 0.2 \times 2\pi \times 1.65$

$$= 0.4887 \text{ m}^3$$

Mass $= V\rho = 0.4887 \times 7.21 \times 10^3$

$$\text{m} = 3523 \text{ kg} \quad \text{Ans.}$$

18. $y = \dfrac{x^3}{4} - \dfrac{x^2}{2}$ (see sketch).

$$\text{Gradient} = \frac{dy}{dx} = \frac{3x^2}{4} - x \quad \text{Ans. (i)}$$

$$\frac{d^2y}{dx^2} = \frac{6x}{4} - 1$$

For zero gradient,

$$\frac{3x^2}{4} - x = 0$$

$$\frac{3x^2}{4} = x$$

$$x^2 = \tfrac{4}{3}x$$

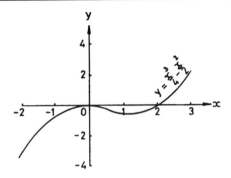

$\therefore$ $x = 0$ or $x = \frac{4}{3}$

i.e. Gradient is zero at $x = 0$ and $x = \frac{4}{3}$ Ans. (ii)

When $x = 0$,

$$\frac{d^2y}{dx^2} = -1 \text{ (i.e. negative)}$$

When $x = \frac{4}{3}$,

$$\frac{d^2y}{dx^2} = 2 - 1 \text{ (positive)}$$

$\therefore$ y is a minimum at the point $x = 1\frac{1}{3}$.   Ans. (iii)

The solution is confirmed by the sketch of the graph.

19.   (i) $2x^2 - 2 = 2(x^2 - 1) = 2(x + 1)(x - 1)$ Ans. (i)

    (ii) $7x^2 + 9xy - 10y^2 = (7x - 5y)(x + 2y)$ Ans. (ii)

    (iii) $14x^3y^2 + 22x^2y^3 - 12xy^4$

$$= 2xy^2(7x^2 + 11xy - 6y^2)$$
$$= 2xy^2(7x - 3y)(x + 2y) \quad \text{Ans. (iii)}$$

    (iv) Dividing first by the given factor:

$$x - y)3x^3 + 8x^2y - xy^2 - 10y^3(3x^2 + 11xy + 10y^2$$
$$\underline{3x^3 - 3x^2y}$$
$$11x^2y - xy^2$$
$$\underline{11x^2y - 11xy^2}$$
$$10xy^2 - 10y^3$$
$$\underline{10xy^2 - 10y^3}$$

Factors are: $(x - y)(3x^2 + 11xy + 10y^2)$

$$= (x - y)(3x + 5y)(x + 2y) \quad \text{Ans. (iv)}$$

20.

$$A_1 = \int_1^5 (10x^2 + x + 4) \, dx$$

$$= \left[\frac{10x^3}{3} + \frac{x^2}{2} + 4x \right]_1^5$$

$$= \left(\frac{1250}{3} + \frac{25}{2} + 20 \right) - \left(\frac{10}{3} + \frac{1}{2} + 4 \right)$$

$$= 449 \cdot 2 - 7 \cdot 833$$

$$= 441 \cdot 37 \text{ units}^2$$

$$A_2 = \int_1^5 \left(\frac{1}{2}x^2 - \frac{1}{x} - \frac{1}{2} \right) dx$$

$$= \int_1^5 \left(\frac{x^2}{2} - \frac{1}{x} - \frac{1}{2} \right) dx$$

$$= \left[\frac{x^3}{6} - \ln x - \frac{x}{2} \right]_1^5$$

$$= \left(\frac{125}{6} - \ln 5 - \frac{5}{2} \right) - \left(\frac{1}{6} - 0 - \frac{1}{2} \right)$$

$$= (20 \cdot 83 - 1 \cdot 608 - 2 \cdot 5) - (0 \cdot 167 - 0 \cdot 5)$$

$$= 16 \cdot 73 + 0 \cdot 33$$

$$= 17 \cdot 06 \text{ units}^2$$

$$\text{Area} = A_1 - A_2 = 441 \cdot 37$$

$$= 424 \cdot 31 \text{ units}^2 \quad \text{Ans.}$$

21. (a)

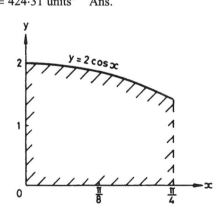

$$A = \int_a^b y \, dx$$

$$= \int_0^{\frac{\pi}{4}} (2\cos x) \, dx \quad \text{(see sketch)}$$

$$= [2\sin x]_0^{\frac{\pi}{4}}$$

$$= [2\sin 45°] - [2\sin 0°]$$

$$A = 1{\cdot}414 \text{ units}^2. \quad \text{Ans. (a)}$$

(b) $$\frac{dy}{dx} = 3x^2 - 4$$

$$\therefore \quad y = \int (3x^2 - 4) \, dx$$

$$y = x^3 - 4x + C$$

when $x = 1, y = -2$,

$$-2 = (1)^3 - 4 \times (1) + C$$

$$C = 1$$

$\therefore$ The equation is $y = x^3 - 4x + 1$ Ans. (b)

22. (i) See Chapter 5 for proof of formula. Ans. (i)

$$x^2 + 5x = 84$$

$$x^2 + 5x + 2{\cdot}5^2 = 84 + 2{\cdot}5^2$$

$$x + 2{\cdot}5 = \pm\sqrt{84 + 6{\cdot}25}$$

$$x + 2{\cdot}5 = \pm\sqrt{90{\cdot}25}$$

$$x = \pm 9{\cdot}5 - 2{\cdot}5$$

$$x = +7 \text{ or } -12 \quad \text{Ans. (ii)}$$

$$2x^2 - 3ax - bx = 0$$

$$x(2x - 3a - b) = 0$$

$$\text{Either} \quad x = 0$$

$$\text{or,} \quad 2x - 3a - b = 0$$

$$2x = 3a + b$$

$$x = \tfrac{1}{2}(3a + b)$$

$$\therefore \quad x = 0 \quad \text{or} \quad \tfrac{1}{2}(3a + b) \quad \text{Ans. (iii)}$$

23. (a)
$$y = x^2 - 5x + 7 - \frac{1}{x}$$

i.e. $y = x^2 - 5x + 7 - x^{-1}$

$$\therefore \quad \frac{dy}{dx} = 2x - 5 + x^{-2}$$

$$\frac{d^2y}{dx^2} = 2 - 2x^{-3}$$

i.e. $\dfrac{d^2y}{dx^2} = 2 - \dfrac{2}{x^3}$ Ans. (a)

(b)
$$y = 2\cos x - 3\sin x$$

$$\therefore \quad \frac{dy}{dx} = -2\sin x - 3\cos x$$

$$\frac{d^2y}{dx^2} = -2\cos x + 3\sin x \quad \text{Ans. (b)}$$

There are 7 cross-sectional areas, therefore 6 spaces.

24.

SECTIONAL AREAS	SIMPSON'S MULTIPLIERS	PRODUCTS
0	1	0
2·9	4	11·6
3·8	2	7·6
4·1	4	16·4
3·7	2	7·4
2·7	4	10·8
1.1	1	1·1
		sum = 54·9

Common interval = length ÷ no. of spaces

= 8 cm ÷ 6

Volume = sum of products × $\frac{1}{3}$ common interval

$$= \frac{54\cdot9 \times 8}{3 \times 6} = 24\cdot4 \text{ cm}^3 \quad \text{Ans. (i)}$$

m = Vρ

= 24·4 × 8·4

Mass = 205 g   Ans. (ii)

25. $C = a + bN$

Inserting given values,

$$8\cdot5 = a + b \times 300 \qquad \ldots \quad \ldots \quad \ldots \quad \text{(i)}$$
$$7\cdot5 = a + b \times 200 \qquad \ldots \quad \ldots \quad \ldots \quad \text{(ii)}$$
$$\overline{1\cdot0 = \qquad\qquad 100b \text{ by subtraction}}$$
$$b = 0\cdot01$$

Substituting value of b into (i),

$$8\cdot5 = a + 0\cdot01 \times 300$$
$$a = 8\cdot5 - 3$$
$$a = 5\cdot5$$

∴ cost equation is:

$$C = 5\cdot5 + 0\cdot01 \, N \text{ pounds} \quad \text{Ans. (a)}$$

When $N = 150$,

$$C = 5\cdot5 + 0\cdot01 \times 150$$
$$= £7\cdot00 \quad \text{Ans. (b)}$$

Minimum cost is when machine is running idly and no articles are being manufactured,

When $N = 0$, $C = 5\cdot5 + 0\cdot01 \times 0$
$$C = 5\cdot5$$

∴ minimum cost = £5·50   Ans. (c)

26. $$y = \sin x + \frac{1}{2}\cos x$$

$$\text{Area} = \int_{\pi/6}^{\pi/3} y \, dx$$
$$= \int_{\pi/6}^{\pi/3} \left(\sin x + \frac{1}{2}\cos x \right) dx$$
$$= \left[-\cos x + \frac{1}{2}\sin x \right]_{\pi/6}^{\pi/3}$$
$$= \left(-\cos\frac{\pi}{3} + \frac{1}{2}\sin\frac{\pi}{3} \right) - \left(-\cos\frac{\pi}{6} + \frac{1}{2}\sin\frac{\pi}{6} \right)$$
$$= (-0\cdot5 + 0\cdot433) - (-0\cdot866 + 0\cdot25)$$
$$= -0\cdot0067 + 0\cdot616$$
$$\text{Area} = 0\cdot549 \text{ units}^2 \quad \text{Ans.}$$

27. Let pieces be x and $(1 - x)$ long

First area $= \left(\dfrac{x}{4}\right)^2 = \dfrac{x^2}{16}$

Second area $= \left(\dfrac{1-x}{4}\right)^2 = \dfrac{1}{16}(1 - 2x + x^2)$

Sum of areas $A = \dfrac{1}{16}(1 - 2x + 2x^2)$

$\dfrac{dA}{dx} = -\dfrac{1}{8} + \dfrac{x}{4}$

$0 = -1 + 2x$ for maximum or minimum

$x = \dfrac{1}{2}$

$\dfrac{d^2 A}{dx^2} = \dfrac{1}{4}$ i.e. positive, as a minimum

$A = \dfrac{1}{16}\left(1 - 1 + \dfrac{1}{2}\right)$ when $x = \dfrac{1}{2}$

$A = \dfrac{1}{32} m^2$, least possible sum of the two areas   Ans.

28. Solid plate without groove:

Area $= 0{\cdot}7854 Dd$

$= 0{\cdot}7854 \times 42 \times 37 = 1220$ cm^2

Volume $= 1220 \times 4{\cdot}5 = 5490$ cm^3

At bottom of groove:

Major axis $= 42 - (2 \times 1{\cdot}3) = 39{\cdot}4$ cm

Minor axis $= 37 - (2 \times 1{\cdot}3) = 34{\cdot}4$ cm

Cross-sect. area of plate at bottom of groove

$= 0{\cdot}7854 \times 39{\cdot}4 \times 34{\cdot}4 = 1064$ cm^2

Volume of groove

$= (1220 - 1064) \times 1{\cdot}3 = 202{\cdot}8$ cm^3

Net volume of grooved plate

$$= 5490 - 202 \cdot 8 = 5287 \cdot 2 \text{ cm}^3$$

$$\text{Mass} = 5287 \cdot 2 \times 7 \cdot 86 \times 10^{-3}$$

$$= 41 \cdot 56 \text{ kg}   \text{Ans.}$$

29.

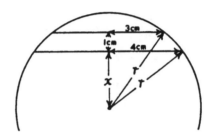

Referring to sketch, working in cm:

$$r^2 = 4^2 + x^2$$
$$= 16 + x^2 \qquad \ldots \quad \ldots \quad \ldots \quad \text{(i)}$$
$$r^2 = 3^2 + (x+1)^2$$
$$= 9 + x^2 + 2x + 1$$
$$= 10 + x^2 + 2x \qquad \ldots \quad \ldots \quad \ldots \quad \text{(ii)}$$
$$\therefore \ 10 + x^2 + 2x = 16 + x^2$$
$$2x = 6$$
$$x = 3$$

From (i), $r^2 = 4^2 + x^2$

$$r = \sqrt{(16 + 9)}$$
$$r = 5 \text{ cm} = 50 \text{ mm}   \text{Ans.}$$

30.

Area of cross section = average width × depth

$$= \tfrac{1}{2}(15 + 10) \times 14$$

$$= 175 \text{ m}^2$$

Length of arc $= \dfrac{6}{360} \times$ full circumference

$$= \dfrac{1}{60} \times 2\pi \times 805 \text{ m}$$

By Theorem of Pappus,

Volume swept out = area of section × distance centroid moves

$$= 175 \times \dfrac{1}{60} \times 2\pi \times 805$$

$$= 14\,750 \text{ m}^3 \quad \text{Ans.}$$

31.

$$a^2 = b^2 + c^2 - 2bc \cos A$$

$$= 3^2 + 5^2 - 2 \times 3 \times 5 \times \cos 20°$$

$$= 9 + 25 - 28{\cdot}191$$

$$a = \sqrt{5{\cdot}809}$$

$$= 2{\cdot}41 \text{ cm} = 24{\cdot}1 \text{ mm}$$

$$\dfrac{a}{\sin A} = \dfrac{b}{\sin B}$$

$$\dfrac{2{\cdot}41}{\sin 20°} = \dfrac{3}{\sin B}$$

$$\sin B = \dfrac{3 \times 0{\cdot}342}{2{\cdot}41} = 0{\cdot}4257$$

∴   Angle $B = 25°12'$

Angle $C = 180° - (20° + 25°12')$

$$= 134°48'$$

$$\text{Area} = \dfrac{bc \sin A}{2}$$

$$= \dfrac{3 \times 5 \times \sin 20°}{2} = 2{\cdot}565 \text{ cm}^2$$

Remaining side = 24·1 mm

Remaining angles = 25°12′ and 134°48′ } Ans.

Area = 2·565 cm²

32.

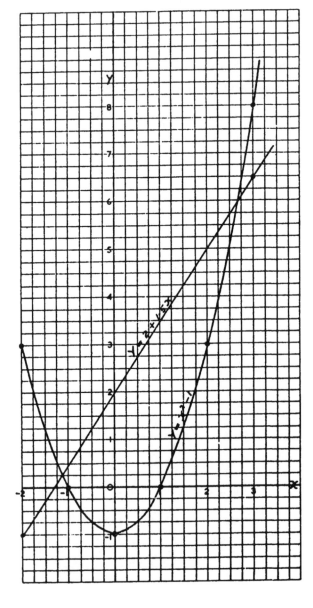

$$x^2 - y = 1 \qquad \therefore y = x^2 - 1$$

Calculating plotting points for this curve:

$$
\begin{array}{rccccccc}
x & = -2 & -1 & 0 & +1 & +2 & +3 \\
y & = +3 & 0 & -1 & 0 & +3 & +8
\end{array}
$$

$$2y - 3x = 4 \qquad \therefore y = 2 + 1{\cdot}5x$$

Being a straight line, two values only are required to plot this graph:

$$
\begin{array}{cc}
x = -2 & x = +3 \\
y = -1 & y = +6{\cdot}5
\end{array}
$$

The graphs are now plotted as shown from which values of x and y are read thus:

$$
\left. \begin{array}{l}
x = 2{\cdot}64 \quad \text{and } y = 5{\cdot}96 \\
\text{or} \quad x = -1{\cdot}14 \quad \text{and } y = 0{\cdot}3
\end{array} \right\} \quad \text{Ans.}
$$

33. $$\text{Area } A_1 = \int_2^5 \frac{78 \, dV}{V^{1\cdot2}}$$

$$= 78 \int_2^5 V^{-1\cdot2} dV$$

$$= 78 \left[-\frac{V^{-0\cdot2}}{0\cdot2} \right]_2^5$$

$$= -390 \left[\left(\frac{1}{5^{0\cdot2}} \right) - \left(\frac{1}{2^{0\cdot2}} \right) \right]$$

$$= -390 \left(\frac{1}{0\cdot138} - \frac{1}{0\cdot1149} \right)$$

$$= -390(7{\cdot}276 - 8{\cdot}703)$$

$$= -390 \times -1{\cdot}427$$

$$A_1 = 556 \cdot 5 \text{ units}^2$$

$$A_2 = \int_2^5 \frac{7dV}{V^{1 \cdot 15}}$$

$$= \frac{-7}{0 \cdot 15}\left[\left(\frac{1}{5^{0 \cdot 15}}\right) - \left(\frac{1}{2^{0 \cdot 15}}\right)\right]$$

$$= -46 \cdot 67\left(\frac{1}{0 \cdot 1279} - \frac{1}{0 \cdot 1110}\right)$$

$$= -46 \cdot 67(7 \cdot 843 - 9 \cdot 009)$$

$$= -46 \cdot 67 \times -1 \cdot 166$$

$$A_2 = 54 \cdot 42 \text{ units}^2$$

$A = A_1 - A_2$ is area between the two curves

$$= 556 \cdot 5 - 54 \cdot 42$$

$$= 502 \cdot 08 \text{ units}^2 \quad \text{Ans.}$$

34.
$$s = t^3 - 6t^2 + 9t + 3$$

$$v = \frac{ds}{dt} = 3t^2 - 12t + 9$$

$$a = \frac{dv}{dt} = 6t - 12$$

(i) When the body is stationary, velocity $=$ zero,

$$\therefore \quad 3t^2 - 12t + 9 = 0$$

$$t^2 - 4t + 3 = 0$$

$$(t - 1)(t - 3) = 0$$

$$t = 1 \quad \text{or} \quad t = 3$$

The body is stationary when $t = 1$ and $t = 3s$ Ans. (i)

(ii) when $t = 1$,

$$\text{acceleration} = 6 - 12$$

$$= -6 \text{ m/s}^2 \quad \text{Ans. (ii)}$$

when $t = 3$,

$$\text{acceleration} = 18 - 12$$

$$= 6 \text{ m/s}^2 \quad \text{Ans. (ii)}$$

35.
$$\frac{x + 2}{x - 1} - \frac{x - 1}{3x - 4} = \frac{7}{2}$$

Common denominator is $2(x - 1)(3x - 4)$,

Multiplying throughout by this:

$$2(3x - 4)(x + 2) - 2(x - 1)(x - 1) = 7(x - 1)(3x - 4)$$
$$2(3x^2 + 2x - 8) - 2(x^2 - 2x + 1) = 7(3x^2 - 7x + 4)$$
$$6x^2 + 4x - 16 - 2x^2 + 4x - 2 = 21x^2 - 49x + 28$$
$$6x^2 - 2x^2 - 21x^2 + 4x + 4x + 49x - 16 - 2 - 28$$
$$= 0$$
$$-17x^2 + 57x - 46 = 0$$
$$17x^2 - 57x + 46 = 0$$

Solving by formula,

$$x = \frac{-b \pm \sqrt{b^2 - 4ac}}{2a}$$

$$= \frac{57 \pm \sqrt{57^2 - 4 \times 17 \times 46}}{2 \times 17}$$

$$= \frac{57 \pm \sqrt{121}}{34} = \frac{57 \pm 11}{34}$$

$$= \frac{68}{34} \text{ or } \frac{46}{34}$$

$$= 2 \quad \text{or} \quad 1 \cdot 353 \quad \text{Ans.}$$

36.

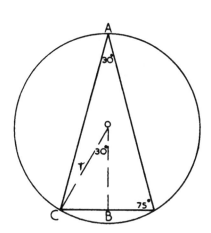

$$\text{Area of circle} = \pi r^2$$

$$\therefore r = \sqrt{\frac{804\cdot2}{\pi}} = 16 \text{ cm}$$

$$\text{Angle at apex of triangle} = 180° - (2 \times 75°) = 30°$$

Angle at centre of circle for a triangle on the same base is twice angle at apex,

$$= 2 \times 30° = 60°$$

Referring to sketch,

$$\text{Angle COB} = 30°$$
$$\text{CB} = r\sin 30° = 16 \times 0\cdot5 = 8 \text{ cm}$$
$$\text{Base of triangle} = 2 \times 8 = 16 \text{ cm}$$
$$\text{OB} = r\cos 30° = 16 \times 0\cdot866 = 13\cdot856 \text{ cm}$$
$$\text{AB} = \text{AO} + \text{OB} = 16 + 13\cdot856 = 29\cdot856 \text{ cm}$$
$$\text{Area of triangle} = \tfrac{1}{2}(\text{base} \times \text{perp. height})$$
$$= \tfrac{1}{2} \times 16 \times 29\cdot856$$
$$= 238\cdot8 \text{ cm}^2 \quad \text{Ans.}$$

37. (a) (i)

$$y = Ei - Ri^2$$

$$\frac{dy}{di} = E - 2Ri \quad \text{Ans. (a) (i)}$$

(a) (ii)

$$y = \left[\frac{C}{1-n}\right]\left[v^{1-n} - p^{1-n}\right]$$

$$\frac{dy}{dv} = \frac{C(1-n)}{1-n}v^{-n}$$

$$= \frac{C}{v^n} \quad \text{Ans. (a) (ii)}$$

(b) (i)

$$\int_0^1 12x^7 dx$$

$$= \left[1\cdot5x^8\right]_0^1$$

$$= 1\cdot5 \quad \text{Ans. (b) (i)}$$

(b) (ii)

$$\frac{3}{2\pi r^3} \int_0^r \pi(r^2 - x^2)\, dx$$

$$= \frac{3}{2r^3} \left[r^2 x - \frac{x^3}{3} \right]_0^r$$

$$= \frac{3}{2r^3} \left[\left(r^3 - \frac{r^3}{3} \right) - 0 \right]$$

$$= 1 \cdot 0 \quad \text{Ans. (b) (ii)}$$

38. See Chapter 7 for proof of $\sin^2 \theta + \cos^2 \theta = 1$ Ans. (i)

$$2 \sin^2 \theta - 2 \cos^2 \theta - 2 = 0$$

$$\sin^2 \theta - \cos^2 \theta - 1 = 0$$

substituting, $\cos^2 \theta = 1 - \sin^2 \theta$,

$$\sin^2 \theta - (1 - \sin^2 \theta) - 1 = 0$$

$$\sin^2 \theta - 1 + \sin^2 \theta - 1 = 0$$

$$2 \sin^2 \theta - 2 = 0$$

$$2 \sin^2 \theta = 2$$

$$\sin^2 \theta = 1$$

$$\sin \theta = \sqrt{1} = \pm 1$$

$\therefore \quad \theta = 90°$ and $270°$ Ans. (ii)

39. See Chapter 8 for proof of formula.   Ans.

Sum of sides $= 5 + 6 + 7 = 18$ cm

Semi-sum $= 9$ cm

Area of triangle $= \sqrt{s(s-a)(s-b)(s-c)}$

$$= \sqrt{9 \times 4 \times 3 \times 2}$$

$$= 14 \cdot 7 \text{ cm}^2$$

Radius of circle $= \dfrac{2 \times \text{area of triangle}}{\text{perimeter of triangle}}$

$$= \frac{2 \times 14 \cdot 7}{18}$$

$$= 1 \cdot 633 \text{ cm} = 16 \cdot 33 \text{ mm}   \text{Ans.}$$

40. $y = 4x^3 - 3x^2 - 18x$

$$\frac{dy}{dx} = 12x^2 - 6x - 18$$

$$0 = 12x^2 - 6x - 18$$

$$0 = (4x - 6)(3x + 3)$$

$$4x = 6 \quad \text{i.e. } x = 1.5$$

or $3x = -3 \quad \text{i.e. } x = -1.0$

$$\frac{d^2y}{dx^2} = 24x - 6$$

$x = 1.5, \dfrac{d^2y}{dx^2}$ is positive i.e. minimum

$x = -1.0, \dfrac{d^2y}{dx^2}$ is negative i.e. maximum

$x = 1.5, y = 13.50 - 6.75 - 27 = -20.25$

$x = -1.0, y = -4 - 3 + 18 = 11.0$

$\left.\begin{array}{l} y = -20.25, (x = 1.5), \text{minimum} \\ y = 11.00, (x = -1.0), \text{maximum} \end{array}\right\}$ Ans.

41.   Volume of cone $= \frac{1}{3}$(area of base $\times$ perp. height)

$$= \frac{1}{3} \times \frac{\pi}{4} \times 10^2 \times 10 = 261.8 \text{ cm}^3$$

Volume of hemisphere $= \dfrac{1}{2}$ of $\dfrac{\pi}{6} d^3$

$$= \frac{1}{2} \times \frac{\pi}{6} \times 10^3 = 261.8 \text{cm}^3$$

Total volume $= 261.8 + 261.8 = 523.6 \text{ cm}^3$ Ans. (i)

Curved surface area of cone

$$= \pi r \times \text{slant height}$$

$$= \pi \times 5 \times \sqrt{10^2 + 5^2} = 175.6 \text{ cm}^2$$

Curved surface area of hemisphere

$$= \text{surface area of circumscribing cylinder}$$
$$= \pi \times \text{diameter} \times \text{height}$$
$$= \pi \times 10 \times 5 = 157 \cdot 1 \text{ cm}^2$$

Total surface area $= 175 \cdot 6 + 157 \cdot 1 = 332 \cdot 7 \text{ cm}^2$ Ans. (ii)

Volumes of similar objects vary as the cube of their corresponding dimensions. As the large object has linear dimensions twice that of the smaller, then:

$$\text{Volume of larger solid} = 523 \cdot 6 \times 2^3$$
$$= 4188 \cdot 8 \text{ cm}^3 \quad \text{Ans. (iii)}$$

Areas of similar figures vary as the square of their corresponding dimensions, therefore:

$$\text{Surface area of larger solid} = 332 \cdot 7 \times 2^2$$
$$= 1330 \cdot 8 \text{ cm}^2 \quad \text{Ans. (iv)}$$

42. $$y = x^2 - 8x + 7 \qquad \ldots \quad \ldots \quad \ldots \quad \text{(i)}$$

Calculate plotting points for this equation:

x:	0	1	2	3	4	5	6	7	8	9
y:	7	0	−5	−8	−9	−8	−5	0	7	16

A sketch of the graph is as shown.

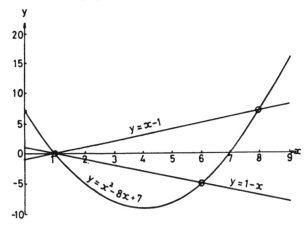

(a) To solve the equation $x^2 - 7x + 6 = 0$:
From equation (i), by adding $x - 1$,

$$x^2 - 8x + 7 + x - 1 = x^2 - 7x + 6$$
$$\therefore \quad x^2 - 8x + 7 + x - 1 = 0$$
$$x^2 - 8x + 7 = 1 - x$$
$$\therefore \quad y = 1 - x$$

Calculate plotting points for $y = 1 - x$

$$x = 0, y = 1$$
$$x = 9, y = -8$$

The straight-line graph for this equation is also shown.

At the points of intersection, $x = 1$, and $x = 6$.   Ans. (a)
(b) To solve the equation $x^2 - 9x + 8 = 0$
Adding $-x + 1$ to equation (i):

$$\text{i.e.} \quad x^2 - 8x + 7 - x + 1 = x^2 - 9x + 8$$
$$x^2 - 8x + 7 - x + 1 = 0$$
$$x^2 - 8x + 7 = x - 1$$
$$\therefore \quad y = x - 1$$

Calculate plotting points,

$$x = 0, \quad y = -1$$
$$x = 9, \quad y = 8$$

The graph is shown. At the points of intersection between the graph and the curve $y = x^2 - 8x + 7$.

$$x = 1 \text{ and } x = 8 \quad \text{Ans. (b)}$$

43.
$$P = V(a + bV^2)$$
$$\text{or,} \quad P = aV + bV^3$$

Inserting given values to form simultaneous equations:

$$13\,408 = a \times 16 + b \times 16^3 \qquad \ldots \quad \ldots \quad \text{(i)}$$
$$6024 = a \times 12 + b \times 12^3 \qquad \ldots \quad \ldots \quad \text{(ii)}$$

Multiplying (i) by 3, and (ii) by 4,

$$40\,224 = 48a + 12\,288b \qquad \ldots \quad \ldots \quad \text{(iii)}$$
$$24\,096 = 48a + 6912b \qquad \ldots \quad \ldots \quad \text{(iv)}$$

Subtracting (iv) from (iii),

$$16\,128 = 5376b$$
$$b = 3$$

Substituting, $b = 3$ into (ii),

$$6024 = 12a + 5184$$
$$12a = 840$$
$$a = 70$$
$$\therefore \quad \text{Law is, } P = 70V + 3V^3$$

inserting $V = 14$ knot and evaluating,

$$P = 70 \times 14 + 3 \times 14^3$$
$$= 980 + 8232$$
$$P = 9212 \text{ kW} \quad \text{Ans.}$$

44.
$$y = \frac{x^3}{3} - \frac{3}{x^3} + 3x^2 - 2x$$

rearranging : $y = \dfrac{x^3}{3} - 3x^{-3} + 3x^2 - 2x$

$$\frac{dy}{dx} = x^2 + 9x^{-4} + 6x - 2$$

$$\frac{d^2y}{dx^2} = 2x - 36x^{-5} + 6$$

$$= 2x - \frac{36}{x^5} + 6 \quad \text{Ans. (i)}$$

(ii)
$$y = 3\sin x + 4\cos x$$

$$\frac{dy}{dx} = 3\cos x - 4\sin x$$

$$\frac{d^2y}{dx^2} = -3\sin x - 4\cos x \quad \text{Ans. (ii)}$$

45. Referring to the cone (see Fig. 85):

$$\text{Radius of base} = 1{\cdot}22 \text{ m}$$

Perp. height = total height − height of hemisphere

$$= 4{\cdot}27 - 1{\cdot}22$$
$$= 3{\cdot}05 \text{ m}$$

$$\text{Slant height} = \sqrt{3{\cdot}05^2 + 1{\cdot}22^2} = 3{\cdot}285 \text{ m}$$

Curved surface area $= \pi r l$

$$= \pi \times 1{\cdot}22 \times 3{\cdot}285$$
$$= 12{\cdot}6 \text{ m}^2 \quad \text{Ans. (i)}$$

The slant height is the radius of the developed sector, angle subtended at centre

$$= \frac{\text{arc of sector}}{\text{circum. of whole circle}} \times 360°$$
$$= \frac{\pi \times 2{\cdot}44}{2\pi \times 3{\cdot}285} \times 360°$$
$$= 133{\cdot}7° \quad \text{Ans. (ii)}$$

Curved surface area of hemisphere

$$= \text{curved surface of circumscribing half cylinder}$$
$$= \tfrac{1}{2}\pi d^2$$
$$= \tfrac{1}{2} \times \pi \times 2{\cdot}44^2$$
$$= 9{\cdot}354 \text{ m}^2 \quad \text{Ans. (iii)}$$

Total volume = vol. of cone + vol. of hemisphere

$$= \tfrac{1}{3}(\text{area of base} \times \text{perp. ht.}) + \frac{1}{2} \times \frac{\pi}{6} d^3$$
$$= \frac{1}{3} \times \pi \times 1{\cdot}22^2 \times 3{\cdot}05 + \frac{\pi}{12} \times 2{\cdot}44^3$$
$$= 4{\cdot}755 + 3{\cdot}804$$
$$= 8{\cdot}559 \text{ m}^3 \quad \text{Ans. (iv)}$$

46.
$$3a + 7b + 2c = 25 \quad \dots \quad \dots \quad \dots \quad \dots \quad \text{(i)}$$
$$2a + 6b + c = 18 \quad \dots \quad \dots \quad \dots \quad \dots \quad \text{(ii)}$$
$$a + b + c + d = 14 \quad \dots \quad \dots \quad \dots \quad \dots \quad \text{(iii)}$$
$$2a + d = 9 \quad \dots \quad \dots \quad \dots \quad \dots \quad \text{(iv)}$$

From equation (iv),

$$d = 9 - 2a$$

Substitute $d = 9 - 2a$ in equation (iii),

$$a + b + c + 9 - 2a = 14$$
$$\therefore -a + b + c = 5 \quad \ldots \quad \ldots \quad \ldots \quad \ldots \quad (v)$$

To eliminate c, subtract (v) from (ii),

$$2a + 6b + c = 18$$
$$\underline{-a + \; b + c = 5}$$
$$3a + 5b \quad\;\; = 13 \quad \ldots \quad \ldots \quad \ldots \quad \ldots \quad (vi)$$

Multiply (v) by 2 and subtract from (i),

$$3a + 7b + 2c = 25$$
$$\underline{-2a + 2b + 2c = 10}$$
$$5a + 5b \quad\;\;\; = 15 \quad \ldots \quad \ldots \quad \ldots \quad \ldots \quad (vii)$$

To solve: subtract (vii) from (vi),

$$3a + 5b = 13$$
$$\underline{5a + 5b = 15}$$
$$-2a \quad\quad = -2$$
$$\therefore \;\; a = 1$$

Substitute $a = 1$ in (vii),

$$5 + 5b = 15$$
$$\therefore \;\; b = 2$$

Substitute $a = 1, b = 2$ in (v),

$$-1 + 2 + c = 5$$
$$\therefore \;\; c = 4$$

Substitute $a = 1$ in (iv),

$$2 + d = 9$$
$$\therefore \;\; d = 7$$
$$\therefore \;\; a = 1, b = 2, c = 4, d = 7 \quad \text{Ans.}$$

47.

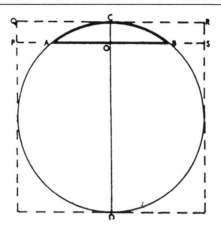

$$\text{AO} \times \text{BO} = \text{CO} \times \text{DO}$$
$$30 \times 30 = 4 \times \text{DO}$$
$$\text{DO} = 225 \text{ mm}$$
$$\text{Dia. of circle} = \text{CO} + \text{DO}$$
$$= 4 + 225 = 229 \text{ mm}$$

Curved surface of lens = curved surface area of slice of sphere of 22·9 cm dia. and 0·4 cm thick

= curved surface area of slice PQRS of circumscribing cylinder

$$- \pi \times 22\text{·}9 \times 0\text{·}4$$
$$= 28\text{·}78 \text{ cm}^2 \quad \text{Ans.}$$

48. (a)

$$\frac{dy}{dx} = -\cos x - 2 \sin x$$

$$\therefore y = \int (-\cos x - 2 \sin x) dx$$

$$y = -\sin x + 2 \cos x + C$$

when $y = 3, x = 0$
(Note: $\sin 0° = 0, \cos 0° = 1$)

$$3 = 0 + 2 + C$$
$$\therefore C = 1$$
$$y = -\sin x + 2 \cos x + 1 \quad \text{Ans. (a).}$$

(b)

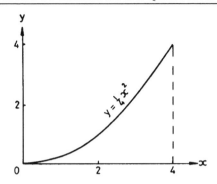

$$\text{Vol.} = \pi \int_0^4 y^2\,dx$$

$$= \pi \int_0^4 \left(\frac{x^2}{4}\right)^2 dx$$

$$= \pi \int_0^4 \frac{x^4}{16}\,dx$$

$$= \pi \left[\frac{x^5}{80}\right]_0^4$$

$$= \pi \left[\frac{1024}{80}\right] - 0$$

$$\therefore \text{Volume} = 40{\cdot}212 \text{ units}^3 \quad \text{Ans. (b)}$$

49.
$$p = \left[\frac{wu^2}{g\left\{\dfrac{K+a}{K(2a+K)+a^2} + \dfrac{D}{Et}\right\}}\right]^{\frac{1}{2}}$$

$$\therefore p^2 g = \frac{wu^2}{\dfrac{K+a}{K(2a+K)+a^2}} + \frac{D}{Et}$$

$$\therefore \frac{K+a}{2aK+K^2+a^2} + \frac{D}{Et} = \frac{wu^2}{p^2g}$$

$$\frac{K+a}{(K+a)^2} = \frac{wu^2}{p^2g} - \frac{D}{Et}$$

$$\frac{1}{K+a} = \frac{wu^2Et - Dp^2g}{p^2gEt}$$

$$K+a = \frac{p^2gEt}{wu^2Et - Dp^2g}$$

$$\therefore K = \frac{p^2gEt}{wu^2Et - Dp^2g} - a \quad \text{Ans.}$$

50.

$$x \propto \frac{z}{y^2} \qquad \therefore \frac{xy^2}{z} = \text{constant}$$

$$\frac{x_1y_1^2}{z_1} = \frac{x_2y_2^2}{z_2}$$

Let each of the original values of x, y and z be represented by unity, then:

$$\text{new value of } y = 1 - 0\cdot2 = 0\cdot8$$

$$\text{new value of } z = 1 + 0\cdot12 = 1\cdot12$$

$$x_2 = \frac{1 \times 1\cdot12}{0\cdot8^2} = 1\cdot75$$

Fractional increase in $x = 1\cdot75 - 1 = 0\cdot75$

Percentage increase $= 0\cdot75 \times 100 = 75$ Ans. (i)

$$\text{time} \propto \sqrt{\text{length}} \quad \therefore \frac{\text{time}}{\sqrt{\text{length}}} = \text{constant}$$

$$\frac{t_1}{\sqrt{l_1}} = \frac{t_2}{\sqrt{l_2}}$$

$$\text{time for one beat of 1st pendulum} = \frac{44}{105} \text{ s}$$

$$\text{time for one beat of 2nd pendulum} = 1 \text{ s}$$

$$\frac{44}{105 \times \sqrt{174 \cdot 4}} = \frac{1}{\sqrt{l_2}}$$

$$\sqrt{l_2} = \frac{105 \times \sqrt{174 \cdot 4}}{44}$$

$$l_2 = \frac{105^2 \times 174 \cdot 4}{44^2}$$

$$= 993 \text{ mm}\quad\text{Ans.}$$

51.
$$3\cos x + 4\sin y = 2\sqrt{2} - 1\cdot 5 \quad \ldots \quad \ldots \quad \text{(i)}$$

$$5\cos x - \sqrt{2}\sin y = -3\cdot 5 \quad \ldots \quad \ldots \quad \ldots \quad \text{(ii)}$$

$$15\cos x + 20\sin y = 6\cdot 64 \quad \ldots \quad \ldots \quad \ldots \quad \text{(iii)}$$

$$15\cos x - 4\cdot 242\sin y = -10\cdot 5 \quad \ldots \quad \ldots \quad \ldots \quad \text{(iv)}$$

Multiplying (i) by 5, Muliplying (ii) by 3.
Subtracting (iv) from (iii).

$$24\cdot 242\sin y = 17\cdot 14$$

$$\sin y = 0\cdot 7071$$

$$y = 45°$$

Substituting $\sin y = 0\cdot 7071$ into (i)

$$3\cos x + 2\cdot 828 = 1\cdot 328$$

$$3\cos x = -1\cdot 5$$

$$\cos x = -0\cdot 5$$

$$x = 180° - 60° = 120°$$

$$x = 120°, y = 45°\quad\text{Ans.}$$

52.

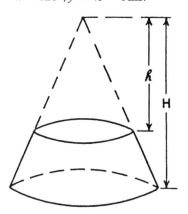

$$\text{Vol. of frustum} = \frac{19}{27} \times \text{vol. of complete cone}$$

Let volume of complete cone = 27

Let volume of complete frustum = 19

then volume of top cut off $= 27 - 19 = 8$

Volumes of similar objects vary as the cube of their corresponding dimensions

$$\therefore \frac{\text{Vol. of complete cone}}{\text{Vol. of top cut off}} = \frac{\text{Height}^3 \text{ of complete cone}}{\text{height}^3 \text{ of top cut off}}$$

$$\frac{27}{8} = \frac{H^3}{h^3}$$

$$h = H \times \frac{\sqrt[3]{8}}{\sqrt[3]{27}}$$

$$h = \frac{2}{3}H$$

$\therefore$ Height of frustum $= \frac{1}{3}H$ Ans.

53. (a)

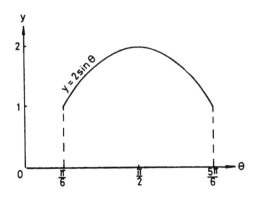

$$\text{Area} = \int_{\frac{\pi}{6}}^{\frac{5\pi}{6}} (2\sin\theta)\, d\theta$$

$$= [-2\cos\theta]_{\frac{\pi}{6}}^{\frac{5\pi}{6}}$$

$$= [-2 \times \cos 150°] - [-2\cos 30°]$$

$$= 1{\cdot}732 + 1{\cdot}732$$

$$\text{Area} = 3{\cdot}464 \text{ units}^2 \quad \text{Ans. (a)}$$

(b) (i) $\displaystyle\int_{\frac{\pi}{2}}^{\pi} (3\cos\theta)d\theta = [3\sin\theta]_{\frac{\pi}{2}}^{\pi}$

$$= [3\sin 180°] - [3\sin 90°]$$
$$= -3 \quad \text{Ans. (b)(i)}$$

(ii) $\displaystyle\int_{1}^{2}(x^2-6x)dx = \left[\frac{x^3}{3} - 3x^2\right]_{1}^{2}$

$$= \left[\frac{8}{3} - 12\right] - \left[\frac{1}{3} - 3\right]$$
$$= [-9\tfrac{1}{3}] - [-2\tfrac{2}{3}]$$
$$= -6\tfrac{2}{3} \quad \text{Ans. (b)(ii)}$$

(iii) $\displaystyle\int_{1}^{3}(x^4 - 7x + 8)dx = \left[\frac{x^5}{5} - \frac{7x^2}{2} + 8x\right]_{1}^{3}$

$$= \left[\frac{243}{5} - \frac{63}{2} + 24\right] - \left[\frac{1}{5} - \frac{7}{2} + 8\right]$$
$$= 41{\cdot}1 - 4{\cdot}7$$
$$= 36{\cdot}4 \quad \text{Ans. (b)(iii)}$$

54. $$K = \left\{\frac{V+v}{V-v}\right\}^2$$

Firstly, take square root of both sides to get rid of the power.
Secondly, multiply both sides by the least common denominator to
eliminate fractions. Then simplify and proceed to get terms
containing V on one side with all other terms on other side of
equation.

$$\sqrt{K} = \frac{V+v}{V-v}$$
$$\sqrt{K}(V-v) = V+v$$
$$\sqrt{K}V - \sqrt{K}v = V+v$$
$$\sqrt{K}V - V = \sqrt{K}v + v$$
$$V(\sqrt{K} - 1) = v(\sqrt{K} + 1)$$
$$V = v\frac{\sqrt{K}+1}{\sqrt{K}-1}$$

$$= v\left\{\frac{\sqrt{\dfrac{f_1}{f_2}} + 1}{\sqrt{\dfrac{f_1}{f_2}} - 1}\right\} \quad \text{Ans.}$$

Inserting values,

$$\sqrt{\frac{f_1}{f_2}} = \sqrt{\frac{12}{18}} = \pm 0 \cdot 8165$$

$$V = 20 \times \frac{\pm 0 \cdot 8165 + 1}{\pm 0 \cdot 8165 - 1}$$

$$= \frac{20 \times 1 \cdot 8165}{-0 \cdot 1835} = -198$$

$$\text{or } \frac{20 \times 0 \cdot 1835}{-1 \cdot 8165} = -2 \cdot 02$$

Values of V are,

$$-198 \text{ and } -2 \cdot 02 \quad \text{Ans.}$$

55. Plotting points for $y = x^2 + 2x - 8$:

x	-4	-3	-2	-1	0	$+1$	$+2$
y	0	-5	-8	-9	-8	-5	0

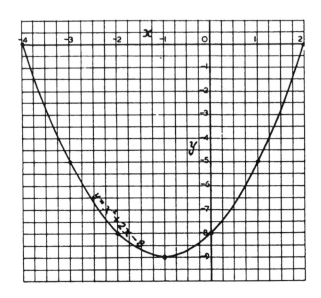

When the area bounded by the graph is swept one complete revolution about the x-axis, the y ordinates of the graph become the radii at regular intervals along the length of the solid swept out. Putting the cross-sectional areas of these radii through Simpson's rule:

RADII	CROSS-SECT. AREAS	SIMPSON'S MULTIPLIERS	PRODUCTS
r	πr^2		
0	$\pi \times 0$	1	0
5	$\pi \times 25$	4	$\pi \times 100$
8	$\pi \times 64$	2	$\pi \times 128$
9	$\pi \times 81$	4	$\pi \times 324$
8	$\pi \times 64$	2	$\pi \times 128$
5	$\pi \times 25$	4	$\pi \times 100$
0	$\pi \times 0$	1	0
			sum $= \pi \times 780$

Common intervals between ordinates

$$= 1$$
$$\text{Volume generated} = \pi \times 780 \times \tfrac{1}{3} \times 1$$
$$= 816 \cdot 9 \text{ units}^3 \quad \text{Ans.}$$

56. (i)
$$A = x^2 + \frac{16000}{x}$$
$$\therefore A = x^2 + 16000x^{-1}$$
$$\frac{dA}{dx} = 2x - \frac{16000}{x^2}$$

for max.^{m} or min.^{m} values,

$$\frac{dA}{dx} = 0$$
$$\text{i.e. } 2x - \frac{16000}{x^2} = 0$$
$$2x = \frac{16000}{x^2}$$
$$x^3 = 8000$$

∴ For a max.^{m} or min.^{m} value of A,

$$x = 20$$

Differentiating again, $\dfrac{d^2A}{dx^2} = 2 + \dfrac{16000}{x^3}$

$$= 2 + \dfrac{16000}{20^3} \text{ (i.e. positive)}$$

hence, when $x = 20$, A has a minimum value. Ans. (i).

(ii) For minimum value,

$$A = 20^2 + \dfrac{16000}{20}$$

∴ Minimum area = 1200 units^2 Ans. (ii).

57.

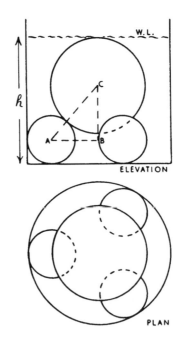

Referring to triangle ABC in elevation of sketch 1,

AC = radius of 2 cm ball + radius of 4 cm ball

= 1 + 2 = 3 cm

AB = radius of cyl. − radius of 2 cm ball

= 3 − 1 = 2 cm

$$\text{BC} = \sqrt{(\text{AC})^2 - (\text{AB})^2} = \sqrt{3^2 - 2^2}$$

$$= \sqrt{5} = 2\cdot236 \text{ cm}$$

$$h = \text{radius of 2 cm ball} + \text{BC} + \text{radius of 4 cm ball}$$

$$= 1 + 2\cdot236 + 2 = 5\cdot236 \text{ cm}$$

Internal vol. of cylinder up to height h

$$= 0\cdot7854 \times d^2 \times h$$

$$= 0\cdot7854 \times 6^2 \times 5\cdot236 = 148 \text{ cm}^3$$

$$\text{Volume of sphere} = \frac{\pi}{6}d^3$$

$$\text{Volume of 3 small balls} = 3 \times \frac{\pi}{6} \times 2^3$$

$$\text{Volume of the large ball} = \frac{\pi}{6} \times 4^3$$

$$\text{Total volume of balls} = \frac{\pi}{6}(3 \times 2^3 + 4^3)$$

$$= \frac{\pi}{6} \times 88 = 46\cdot08 \text{ cm}^3$$

Volume of space for water to fill

$$= \text{vol. of cyl.} - \text{vol. of balls}$$

$$= 148 - 46\cdot08$$

$$= 101\cdot92 \text{ cm}^3$$

$$\text{Volume of water} = 101\cdot92 \text{ ml} \quad \text{Ans. (i)}$$

If all linear dimensions were half of those above,

$$\text{Volume required} = (\tfrac{1}{2})^3 = \tfrac{1}{8} \text{ of above}$$

because similar volumes vary as the cube of their corresponding linear dimensions.

$$\text{Volume} = \tfrac{1}{8} \times 101\cdot92 = 12\cdot74 \text{ ml} \quad \text{Ans. (ii)}$$

58.

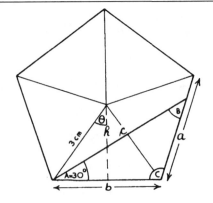

Pentagon is composed of 5 isosceles triangles,

$$\text{Angles at centre} = 360° \div 5 = 72°$$
$$\theta = \tfrac{1}{2} \text{ of } 72° = 36°$$
$$h = 3 \times \cos 36° = 2\cdot427$$
$$b = 2 \times 3 \sin 36° = 3\cdot527$$

Areas of isosceles triangle

$$= \tfrac{1}{2}bh$$
$$= \tfrac{1}{2} \times 3\cdot527 \times 2\cdot427$$
$$= 4\cdot28 \text{ cm}^2$$

$$\text{Area of pentagon} = 5 \times 4\cdot28$$
$$= 21\cdot4 \text{ cm}^2 \quad \text{Ans. (a)}$$
$$\text{Angle C} = 2 \times (90° - \theta) = 108°$$
$$\text{Angle B} = 180° - A - C = 42°$$

$$\frac{a}{\sin A} = \frac{b}{\sin B}$$
$$a = \frac{3\cdot527 \times \sin 30°}{\sin 42°} = 2\cdot636 \text{ cm}$$

$$\text{Area of triangle } abc = \tfrac{1}{2}ab \sin C$$
$$= \tfrac{1}{2} \times 2\cdot636 \times 3\cdot527 \times \sin 108°$$
$$= 4\cdot421 \text{ cm} \quad \ldots \quad \ldots \quad \ldots \quad \ldots \quad (i)$$

Remaining piece of pentagon

$$= 21 \cdot 4 - 4 \cdot 421 = 16 \cdot 979 \text{ cm} \qquad \text{(ii)}$$

Ratio of (i) and (ii)

$$= 4 \cdot 421 \; : \; 16 \cdot 979$$

Dividing both by 4·421

$$\text{Ratio} = 1 \; : \; 3 \cdot 84 \quad \text{Ans. (b)}$$

59. (a) $\qquad\qquad 2\sin^2\theta - \cos\theta = 1$

From the identity,

$$\sin^2\theta + \cos^2\theta = 1$$
$$\sin^2\theta = 1 - \cos^2\theta$$

Substitute for $\sin^2\theta$ into original equations and simplify,

$$2\sin^2\theta - \cos\theta = 1$$
$$2(1 - \cos^2\theta) - \cos\theta = 1$$
$$2 - 2\cos^2\theta - \cos\theta = 1$$
$$-2\cos^2\theta - \cos\theta + 1 = 0$$
$$2\cos^2\theta + \cos\theta - 1 = 0$$

Factorising,

$$(2\cos\theta - 1)(\cos\theta + 1) = 0$$

Either $\qquad 2\cos\theta - 1 = 0$, then $\cos\theta = 0\cdot5$

or $\qquad\qquad \cos\theta + 1 = 0$, then $\cos\theta = -1$

When $\cos\theta = 0\cdot5$, $\theta = 60°$ and $(360° - 60°) = 300°$
When $\cos\theta = -1$, $\theta = 180°$

$\therefore$ Angles are $60°$, $180°$ and $300°$ Ans. (a)

(b) $\qquad\qquad\qquad 3\cos 2\theta + 2\cos\theta = 0$

$$3(2\cos^2\theta - 1) + 2\cos\theta = 0$$
$$6\cos^2\theta - 3 + 2\cos\theta = 0$$
$$6\cos^2\theta + 2\cos\theta - 3 = 0$$

Solving by quadratic formula,

$$\cos \theta = \frac{-b \pm \sqrt{b^2 - 4ac}}{2a}$$

$$= \frac{-2 \pm \sqrt{4 + 72}}{12}$$

$$= \frac{-2 \pm 8{\cdot}718}{12}$$

$$= 0{\cdot}5598 \text{ or } -0.8932$$

When $\cos \theta = 0{\cdot}5598$, $\theta = 55° \, 57'$ and $360° - 55° \, 57' = 304° \, 3'$
When $\cos \theta = -0{\cdot}8932$, $\theta = 180° - 26° \, 44' = 153°16'$
and $180° + 26° \, 44' = 206° \, 44'$

Angles are,

$55°57'$, $153°16'$, $206°44'$ and $304°3'$ Ans. (b)

60.
V	5	10	15	20	25
V^2	25	100	225	400	625
R	10	25	50	85	130

By plotting the points of R and V^2, they lie on a straight line, therefore the equation is of the form $y = a + bx$ where x represents V^2.

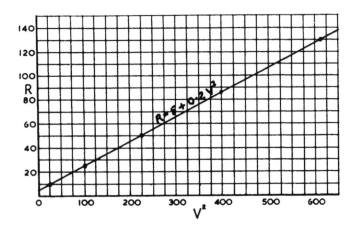

Taking two points on the line such as:

$$\text{when } V^2 = 400, R = 85$$
$$\text{when } V^2 = 100, R = 25$$

Inserting these into $R = k + cV^2$,

$$85 = k + c \times 400 \qquad \dots \quad \dots \quad \dots \quad \text{(i)}$$
$$25 = k + c \times 100 \qquad \dots \quad \dots \quad \dots \quad \text{(ii)}$$
$$60 = c \times 300 \text{ by subtraction}$$
$$c = \frac{60}{300} = 0\cdot2$$

From (i)
$$85 = k + 0\cdot2 \times 400$$
$$k = 85 - 80 = 5$$

Constants are,

$$k = 5 \text{ and } c = 0\cdot2 \quad \text{Ans. (i)}$$
$$\text{when } V = 40,$$
$$R = k + cV^2$$
$$= 5 + 0\cdot2 \times 40^2$$
$$= 325 \text{ N} \quad \text{Ans. (ii)}$$

61.
$$p = V + \frac{k(p + V)}{k + p + V}$$

$$p - V = \frac{k(p + V)}{k + p + V}$$

$$(p - V)(k + p + V) = k(p + V)$$
$$kp + p^2 - kV - V^2 = kp + kV$$
$$p^2 - V^2 = kp - kp + kV + kV$$
$$p^2 - V^2 = 2kV$$
$$\frac{p^2 - V^2}{2V} = k$$
$$\text{or, } k = \frac{p^2 - V^2}{2V} \quad \text{Ans. (i)}$$

When $p = 9.2$ and $V = 0.42$,

$$k = \frac{p^2 - V^2}{2V} = \frac{(p + V)(p - V)}{2V}$$
$$= \frac{(9.2 + 0.42)(9.2 - 0.42)}{2 \times 0.42}$$
$$= \frac{9.62 \times 8.78}{0.84}$$
$$= 100.55 \quad \text{Ans. (ii)}$$

62.

 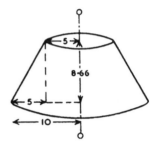

The length of each non-parallel side being equal to the radius, the trapezium is composed of three equilateral triangles, therefore angle at the base is 60°, length of short side of trapezium = 10 cm, length of long side = $2 \times 10 = 20$ cm, and $h = 10 \sin 60° = 8.66$ cm.

$$\text{Area of trapezium} = \tfrac{1}{2}(a + b) \times \text{perp. ht.}$$
$$= \tfrac{1}{2}(10 + 20) \times 8.66$$
$$= 129.9 \text{ cm}^2 \quad \text{Ans. (a)}$$

Alternatively, area of this trapezium

$$= \text{area of 3 equilateral triangles}$$
$$= 3 \times 0.433 \times \text{side}^2$$
$$= 3 \times 0.433 \times 10^2$$
$$= 129.9 \text{ cm}^2 \text{ as above}$$
$$\text{Volume of frustum} = \tfrac{1}{3}\pi h(R^2 + Rr + r^2)$$
$$= \tfrac{1}{3} \times \pi \times 8.66(10^2 + 10 \times 5 + 5^2)$$
$$= \tfrac{1}{3} \times \pi \times 8.66 \times 175$$
$$= 1587 \text{ cm}^3 \quad \text{Ans. (b)}$$

As an alternative to the latter part, the volume can be found by the Theorem of Pappus:

$$\text{Area of triangle} = \tfrac{1}{2} \times 5 \times 8{\cdot}66 = 21{\cdot}65 \text{ cm}^2$$
$$\text{Centroid from axis} = 5 + \tfrac{1}{3} \times 5 = \tfrac{4}{3} \times 5 \text{ cm}$$
$$\text{Area of rectangle} = 5 \times 8{\cdot}66 = 43{\cdot}3 \text{ cm}^2$$
$$\text{Centroid from axis} = \tfrac{1}{2} \times 5 = 2{\cdot}5 \text{ cm}$$
$$\text{Volume swept out} = \text{area} \times \text{distance centroid moves}$$
$$\text{Volume swept out by triangle} = 21{\cdot}65 \times 2\pi \times \tfrac{4}{3} \times 5 = 907 \text{ cm}^3$$
$$\text{Volume swept out by rectangle} = 43{\cdot}3 \times 2\pi \times 2{\cdot}5 = 680 \text{ cm}^3$$
$$\text{Total volume} = 907 + 680 = 1587 \text{ cm}^3$$
$$\text{(as previous)}$$

As a further alternative, volume of frustum may be calculated from volume of whole cone minus volume of top cone removed. All these methods are explained in the text.

63. (a)
$$4a + 3b + 2w = 2 \quad \dots \quad \dots \quad \dots \quad \dots \quad \text{(i)}$$
$$2a + 8b + 3w = 11 \quad \dots \quad \dots \quad \dots \quad \dots \quad \text{(ii)}$$
$$3a + 5b - 6w = -36 \dots \quad \dots \quad \dots \quad \dots \quad \text{(iii)}$$

Proceeding to eliminate w:
Multiply (i) by 3 and (ii) by 2 and subtract,

$$12a + 9b + 6w = 6$$
$$\underline{4a + 16b + 6w = 22}$$
$$8a - 7b = -16 \dots \quad \dots \quad \dots \quad \dots \quad \text{(iv)}$$

Multiply (i) by 3 and add (iii),

$$12a + 9b + 6w = 6$$
$$\underline{3a + 5b - 6w = -36}$$
$$15a + 14b = -30 \quad \dots \quad \dots \quad \dots \quad \dots \quad \text{(v)}$$

Proceeding to eliminate b and find the value of a:
Multiply (iv) by 2 and add (v),

$$16a - 14b = -32$$
$$\underline{15a + 14b = -30}$$
$$31a = -62$$
$$a = -2$$

Substitute value of a into (iv) to find b,

$$8 \times (-2) - 7b = -16$$
$$-16 - 7b = -16$$
$$-7b = 0$$
$$b = 0$$

Substitute values of a and b into (i) to find w,

$$4 \times (-2) + 3 \times 0 + 2w = 2$$
$$-8 + 0 + 2w = 2$$
$$2w = 10$$
$$w = 5$$

Values of a, b and w are, respectively,

$$-2, 0 \text{ and } 5 \quad \text{Ans. (a)}$$

(b) $$x^2 + y^2 = 18 \cdot 5 \quad \ldots \quad \ldots \quad \ldots \quad \ldots \quad \text{(i)}$$
$$x - y = 1 \quad \ldots \quad \ldots \quad \ldots \quad \ldots \quad \text{(ii)}$$

From (ii), $y = x - 1$, substitute this into (i),

$$x^2 + (x - 1)^2 = 18 \cdot 5$$
$$x^2 + x^2 - 2x + 1 = 18 \cdot 5$$
$$2x^2 - 2x - 17 \cdot 5 = 0$$
$$x^2 - x - 8 \cdot 75 = 0$$

Solving this by quadratic formula,

$$x = \frac{-b \pm \sqrt{b^2 - 4ac}}{2a}$$
$$= \frac{1 \pm \sqrt{1 + 35}}{2} = \frac{1 \pm 6}{2}$$
$$= 3 \cdot 5 \text{ or } -2 \cdot 5$$

From (i), $y = x - 1$
If $x = 3 \cdot 5, y = 3 \cdot 5 - 1 = 2 \cdot 5$
If $x = -2 \cdot 5, y = -2 \cdot 5 - 1 = -3 \cdot 5$

Therefore, $x = 3 \cdot 5$ and $y = 2 \cdot 5$ $\left.\begin{array}{l} \\ \\ \end{array}\right\}$ Ans. (b)
or, $x = -2 \cdot 5$ and $y = -3 \cdot 5$

64. (a) Simplifying left hand side:

$$\frac{1 - \tan^2\theta}{1 + \tan^2\theta} = \frac{1 - \dfrac{\sin^2\theta}{\cos^2\theta}}{1 + \dfrac{\sin^2\theta}{\cos^2\theta}}$$

$$= \frac{\dfrac{\cos^2\theta - \sin^2\theta}{\cos^2\theta}}{\dfrac{\cos^2\theta + \sin^2\theta}{\cos^2\theta}} = \frac{\cos^2\theta - \sin^2\theta}{\cos^2\theta + \sin^2\theta}$$

$$= \frac{\cos^2\theta - \sin^2\theta}{1} = \cos^2\theta - \sin^2\theta = \text{r.h.s.} \quad \text{Ans. (a)}$$

(b) Simplifying left hand side:

$$\sin\theta + \sin\theta\cot^2\theta + \frac{\tan\theta}{\cos\theta}$$

$$= \sin\theta + \sin\theta \times \frac{1}{\tan^2\theta} + \frac{\sin\theta}{\cos\theta \times \cos\theta}$$

$$\text{l.h.s.} = \sin\theta + \frac{\sin\theta \times \cos^2\theta}{\sin^2\theta} + \frac{\sin\theta}{\cos^2\theta}$$

$$= \sin\theta + \frac{\cos^2\theta}{\sin\theta} + \frac{\sin\theta}{\cos^2\theta}$$

$$= \frac{\sin^2\theta\cos^2\theta + \cos^4\theta + \sin^2\theta}{\sin\theta\cos^2\theta}$$

$$= \frac{\cos^2\theta(\sin^2\theta + \cos^2\theta) + \sin^2\theta}{\sin\theta\cos^2\theta}$$

$$= \frac{\cos^2\theta \times 1 + \sin^2\theta}{\sin\theta\cos^2\theta}$$

$$\text{l.h.s.} = \frac{1}{\sin\theta\cos^2\theta} = \text{r.h.s.} \quad \text{Ans. (b)}$$

65.
$$4y - x - 20 = 0, \therefore \quad y = 5 + 0.25x$$
When $x = -2, y = 5 - 0.5 = 4.5$
When $x = +8, y = 5 + 2 = 7$
$$y - x + 1 = 0, \therefore \quad y = -1 + x$$
When $x = -2, y = -1 - 2 = -3$
When $x = +8, y = -1 + 8 = 7$
$$2y + x - 7 = 0, \therefore y = 3.5 - 0.5x$$
When $x = -2, y = 3.5 + 1 = 4.5$
When $x = +8, y = 3.5 - 4 = -0.5$

The graphs are shown plotted and enclose a triangle. Let the lengths of the sides of the triangle be a, b and c.

Graph forming side a rises 2·5 over a horizontal length of 10, therefore

$$a = \sqrt{2.5^2 + 10^2} = 10.31$$

Graph forming side b rises 5 over a horizontal length of 5, therefore,

$$b = \sqrt{5^2 + 5^2} = 7.071$$

Graph forming side c drops 2·5 over a horizontal length of 5, therefore,

$$c = \sqrt{2.5^2 + 5^2} = 5.59$$

$$\text{Area of triangle} = \sqrt{s(s - a)(s - b)(s - c)}$$

where a, b and c are the lengths of the three sides and s is their semi-sum

$$s = \tfrac{1}{2}(10.31 + 7.071 + 5.59)$$
$$= 11.486$$
$$\text{Area} = \sqrt{11.486 \times 1.176 \times 4.415 \times 5.896}$$
$$= \sqrt{351.6}$$
$$= 18.75 \text{ units}^2 \quad \text{Ans.}$$

66.

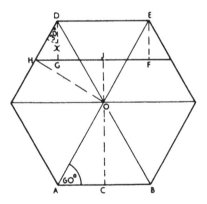

Hexagon is composed of 6 equilateral triangles with all angles of 60°, each side equal to unity.

$$OC = OA \sin 60° = 1 \times 0 \cdot 866 = 0 \cdot 866$$
$$\text{Area of triangle OAB} = \tfrac{1}{2} \times 1 \times 0 \cdot 866 = 0 \cdot 433$$

(or obtain this from the formula, area of equilateral triangle

$$= 0.433 \text{ side}^2)$$

$$\text{Area of hexagon} = 6 \times \text{area of triangle}$$

$$= 6 \times 0.433 = 2.598$$

Area to be cut off is the shape of a trapezium consisting of a central rectangle and a triangle at each end.

Let thickness DG be represented by x

$$\text{Area cut off} = \text{area of rect.} + \text{two triangles}$$

$$= \text{DE} \times x + 2 \times \tfrac{1}{2} \times \text{HG} \times x$$

$$= 1 \times x + 1 \times (x \tan 30°) \times x$$

$$= x + 0.5774 x^2$$

and this is to be equal to 20% of the area of the hexagon,

$$x + 0.5774 x^2 = 0.2 \times 2.598$$

$$0.5774 x^2 + x - 0.5196 = 0$$

a quadratic equation, divide by coefficient of x^2,

$$x^2 + 1.732 x - 0.9 = 0$$

Apply the formula

$$x = \frac{-b \pm \sqrt{b^2 - 4ac}}{2a}$$

$$= \frac{-1.732 \pm \sqrt{3 + 3.6}}{2}$$

$$= \frac{-1.732 \pm 2.569}{2}$$

$$= 0.4185 \quad \text{Ans. (i)}$$

(negative answer inadmissible)

$$\text{OJ} = \text{OC} - x$$

$$= 0.866 - 0.4185 = 0.4475$$

$$\text{HJ} = \text{HG} + \text{GJ}$$

$$= x \tan 30° + \tfrac{1}{2} \text{ side}$$

$$= 0.4185 \times 0.5774 + 0.5 = 0.7416$$

$$\text{OH} = \sqrt{(\text{HJ})^2 + (\text{OJ})^2}$$

$$= \sqrt{0.7416^2 + 0.4475^2}$$

$$= 0.8662 \quad \text{Ans. (ii)}$$

67.

$$y = e^{-2x}$$

$$\text{i.e. } y = \frac{1}{e^{2x}}$$

when	$x = 0$	$y = 1\cdot0$
	$x = 0\cdot2$	$y = 0\cdot67$
	$x = 0\cdot4$	$y = 0\cdot449$
	$x = 0\cdot6$	$y = 0\cdot301$
	$x = 0\cdot8$	$y = 0\cdot202$
	$x = 1\cdot0$	$y = 0\cdot135$
	$x = 1\cdot2$	$y = 0\cdot091$
	$x = 1\cdot4$	$y = 0\cdot061$
	$x = 1\cdot6$	$y = 0\cdot041$
	$x = 1\cdot8$	$y = 0\cdot027$
	$x = 2\cdot0$	$y = 0\cdot018$

ORDINATES	SIMPSON'S MULTIPLIERS	PRODUCTS
1·0	1	1·0
0·67	4	2·68
0·449	2	0·898
0·301	4	1·204
0·202	2	0·404
0·135	4	0·54
0·091	2	0·182
0·061	4	0·244
0·041	2	0·082
0·027	4	0·108
0·018	1	0·018
		Sum = 7·39

$$\text{Area} = \tfrac{1}{3} \times \text{common interval} \times \text{sum of products}$$
$$= \tfrac{1}{3} \times 0\cdot2 \times 7\cdot36$$
$$= 0\cdot4907 \text{ units}^2$$

$$\text{Mean ordinate} = \frac{\text{area}}{\text{length of base}} \quad \text{(see sketch overleaf)}$$
$$= \frac{0\cdot4907}{2}$$
$$= 0\cdot245 \text{ units.} \quad \text{Ans.}$$

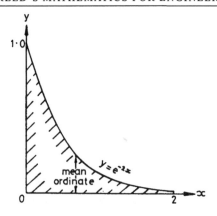

68. By Pythagoras, referring to section of cone,

$$\text{Perp. height} = \sqrt{(\text{slant ht.})^2 - (\text{radius})^2}$$

$$= \sqrt{50^2 - 30^2}$$

$$= 40 \text{ cm}$$

$$\text{Volume of cone} = \tfrac{1}{3} \text{ area of base} \times \text{perp. height}$$

$$= \tfrac{1}{3} \times \pi \times 30^2 \times 40 \text{ cm}^3 \tag{i}$$

$$\text{Volume of hollow sphere} = \frac{\pi}{6}(D^3 - d^3)$$

Substituting $D = d + (2 \times \text{thickness}) = d + 3$,

$$\text{Volume} = \frac{\pi}{6}\left\{(d+3)^3 - d^3\right\}$$

$$= \frac{\pi}{6}\left\{d^3 + 9d^2 + 27d + 27 - d^3\right\}$$

$$= \frac{\pi}{6}\left\{9d^2 + 27d + 27\right\}$$

$$V = \frac{\pi \times 9}{6}(d^2 + 3d + 3) \tag{ii}$$

Equating (i) and (ii),

$$\frac{\pi \times 9}{6}(d^2 + 3d + 3) = \tfrac{1}{3} \times \pi \times 30^2 \times 40$$

$$d^2 + 3d + 3 = \frac{\pi \times 30^2 \times 40 \times 6}{3 \times \pi \times 9}$$

$$d^2 + 3d = 8000 - 3$$

$$d^2 + 3d - 7997 = 0$$

Solving this quadratic by formula,

$$d = \frac{-b \pm \sqrt{b^2 - 4ac}}{2a}$$

$$= \frac{-3 \pm \sqrt{9 + 31988}}{2}$$

$$\left. \begin{array}{l} d = \dfrac{-3 \pm 178 \cdot 9}{2} = 87 \cdot 95 \text{ cm} \\[2mm] D = 87 \cdot 95 + 3 \quad = 90 \cdot 95 \text{ cm} \end{array} \right\} \quad \text{Ans.}$$

(negative answer is inadmissible).

69.
$$a = \frac{c \times h^2}{2s \times (d - h)}$$

$$2as(d - h) = ch^2$$

$$2asd - 2ash = ch^2$$

This is a quadratic equation. Set down in the usual way and solve by quadratic formula:

$$ch^2 + 2ash - 2asd = 0$$

$$h = \frac{-b \pm \sqrt{b^2 - 4ac}}{2a}$$

where, $a = c, b = 2as, c = -2asd$

$$h = \frac{-2as \pm \sqrt{4a^2s^2 - 4 \times c \times (-2asd)}}{2c}$$

$$= \frac{-2as \pm \sqrt{4a^2s^2 + 8casd}}{2c}$$

$$= \frac{-2as \pm \sqrt{4as(as + 2cd)}}{2c}$$

$$= \frac{-as \pm \sqrt{as(as + 2cd)}}{c} \quad \text{Ans. (i)}$$

Substituting numerical values:

$$h = \frac{-1\cdot5 \times 16 \pm \sqrt{1\cdot5 \times 16(1\cdot5 \times 16 + 2 \times 15 \times 17)}}{15}$$

$$= \frac{-24 \pm \sqrt{12816}}{15}$$

$$= \frac{89\cdot2}{15} \text{ or } \frac{-137\cdot2}{15}$$

$$= 5\cdot947 \text{ or } -9\cdot147 \quad \text{Ans. (ii)}$$

70.

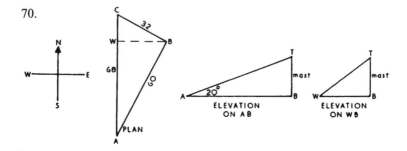

Referring to plan view, if the angle opposite the longest side is a right angle, then by Pythagoras, the longest side is the hypotenuse and the square of this side will be equal to the sum of the squares of the other two sides.

$$(\text{AC})^2 = 68^2 = 4624 \qquad \ldots \quad \ldots \quad \text{(i)}$$

$$(\text{AB})^2 + (\text{BC})^2 = 60^2 + 32^2$$

$$= 3600 + 1024 = 4624 \ldots \quad \ldots \quad \text{(ii)}$$

(i) and (ii) are equal, therefore angle B is a right angle. Ans. (a)

$$\tan A = \frac{32}{60} = 0\cdot5333$$

$$\left. \begin{array}{l} \text{Angle A} = 28^\circ\ 4' \\ \text{Angle C} = 90^\circ - 28^\circ\ 4' = 61^\circ\ 56' \end{array} \right\} \quad \text{Ans. (b)}$$

Referring to elevation on AB,

$$\text{Height of mast TB} = \text{AB} \tan A$$

$$= 60 \tan 20^\circ = 21\cdot84 \text{ m} \quad \text{Ans. (c)}$$

Referring to plan view,

$$WB = AB \sin A$$
$$= 60 \sin 28°4' = 28 \cdot 23 \text{ m}$$

Referring to elevation on WB,

$$\tan W = \frac{TB}{WB}$$
$$= \frac{21 \cdot 84}{28 \cdot 23} = 0 \cdot 7736$$

Angle $W = 37° \ 44'$ Ans. (d)

71. Plotting points for $y = x^2 + 1$:

x	−2	−1	0	1	2	3
y	5	2	1	2	5	10

The graph is shown.
Difference between equations

$$y = x^2 + 1$$
$$\text{and } 0 = x^2 - x - 2$$
$$\overline{\text{is } y = x + 3}$$

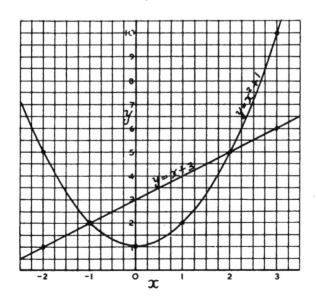

Drawing this straight line graph on the same axes using the plotting points:

$$\text{When } x = -2, \quad y = -2 + 3 = 1$$
$$\text{When } x = +3, \quad y = +3 + 3 = 6$$

The straight line cuts the curve at $x = -1$ and $x = +2$, therefore $x = -1$ and $+2$ Ans.

72. (a) See Chapter 9 for Area of Segment. Ans. (a)

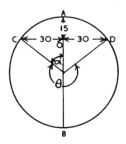

By crossed chords:

$$AO \times BO = CO \times DO$$
$$15 \times BO = 30 \times 30$$
$$BO = 60 \text{ cm}$$
$$\text{Diameter of pipe} = AO + BO$$
$$= 15 + 60 = 75 \text{ cm} \quad \text{Ans. (i)}$$
$$\sin \alpha = \frac{CO}{\text{radius}} = \frac{30}{37.5} = 0.8$$
$$\alpha = 53° \, 8'$$
$$\theta = 360° - 2 \times 53° \, 8' = 253° \, 44'$$
$$\sin \theta = \sin 253° \, 44'$$
$$= -\sin (253° \, 44' - 180°)$$
$$= -\sin 73° \, 44' = -0.96$$
$$\theta \text{ rad} = 253° \, 44' \times \frac{2\pi}{360} \text{ or } \frac{253.73°}{57.3}$$
$$\theta = 4.428 \text{ rad}$$

$$\text{Area of segment} = \tfrac{1}{2}r^2(\theta - \sin\theta)$$
$$= \tfrac{1}{2} \times 37\cdot5^2\{4\cdot428 - (-0\cdot96)\}$$
$$= \tfrac{1}{2} \times 37\cdot5^2 \times 5\cdot388$$
$$= 3788 \text{ cm}^2 \quad \text{Ans. (ii)}$$
$$\text{Volume} = \text{area} \times \text{length}$$
$$V = 3788 \times 2 \times 100 \text{ cm}^3$$
$$= 757\cdot6\,1 \quad \text{Ans. (iii)}$$

73. (a) $\qquad\qquad WZ = x^{a+b} \times x^{a-b}$

Adding the indices,

$$a + b + a - b = 2a$$
$$\therefore WZ = x^{2a} \quad \text{Ans. (a)}$$
$$W^2Z = x^{2(a+b)} \times x^{a-b}$$

Adding the indices,

$$2a + 2b + a - b = 3a + b$$
$$\therefore W^2Z = x^{3a+b} \quad \text{Ans. (a)}$$
$$\frac{W^2}{Z} = \frac{x^{2(a+b)}}{x^{a-b}}$$

Subtracting the indices,

$$2a + 2b - (a - b) = a + 3b$$
$$\therefore \frac{W^2}{Z} = x^{a+3b} \quad \text{Ans. (a)}$$
$$\frac{Z^3}{W} = \frac{x^{3(a-b)}}{x^{a+b}}$$

Subtracting the indices,

$$3a - 3b - (a + b) = 2a - 4b = 2(a - 2b)$$
$$\therefore \frac{Z^3}{W} = x^{2(a-2b)} \quad \text{Ans. (a)}$$

(b) $\qquad\qquad 4x + y = 10 \quad \cdots \quad \cdots \quad \cdots \quad \cdots \quad \text{(i)}$

$$\frac{2}{x} + \frac{7}{y} = 3 \quad \cdots \quad \cdots \quad \cdots \quad \cdots \quad \text{(ii)}$$

From (i), $y = 10 - 4x$, substitute into (ii),

$$\frac{2}{x} + \frac{7}{10 - 4x} = 3$$

Multiply every term by least common denominator, which is $x(10 - 4x)$,

$$2(10 - 4x) + 7x = 3x(10 - 4x)$$
$$20 - 8x + 7x = 30x - 12x^2$$
$$12x^2 - 31x + 20 = 0$$

By quadratic formula,

$$x = \frac{-b \pm \sqrt{b^2 - 4ac}}{2a}$$
$$= \frac{31 \pm \sqrt{961 - 960}}{24}$$
$$= 1\tfrac{1}{3} \text{ or } 1\tfrac{1}{4}$$

From (i),

When $x = 1\tfrac{1}{3}, y = 10 - 4 \times 1\tfrac{1}{3} = 4\tfrac{2}{3}$
When $x = 1\tfrac{1}{4}, y = 10 - 4 \times 1\tfrac{1}{4} = 5$

$$\left. \begin{array}{l} x = 1\tfrac{1}{3} \text{ and } y = 4\tfrac{2}{3} \\ \text{or,} \quad x = 1\tfrac{1}{4} \text{ and } y = 5 \end{array} \right\} \quad \text{Ans. (b)}$$

74. (a)

$$Q = \sqrt{\frac{2ghDk^2}{d(s^2 - k^2)}}$$

$$Q^2 = \frac{2ghDk^2}{d(s^2 - k^2)}$$

$$\therefore Q^2 d(s^2 - k^2) = 2ghDk^2$$

$$Q^2 ds^2 - Q^2 dk^2 = 2ghDk^2$$

$$2ghDk^2 + Q^2 dk^2 = Q^2 ds^2$$

$$k^2(2ghD + Q^2 d) = Q^2 ds^2$$

$$\therefore k^2 = \frac{Q^2 ds^2}{2ghD + Q^2 d}$$

$$k = \sqrt{\frac{Q^2 ds^2}{2ghD + Q^2 d}}$$

$$\therefore k = Qs\sqrt{\frac{d}{2ghD - Q^2 d}} \quad \text{Ans. (a)}$$

(b)
$$F = \frac{1}{2\pi}\sqrt{\frac{1}{Lk}}$$

$$\therefore 2\pi F = \sqrt{\frac{1}{Lk}}$$

$$4\pi^2 F^2 = \frac{1}{Lk}$$

$$4\pi^2 F^2 Lk = 1$$

$$\therefore k = \frac{1}{4\pi^2 F^2 L} \quad \text{Ans. (b)}$$

(c)
$$L = \frac{\pi}{2}(k + b) + \frac{(k - b)}{4c} + 2c$$

$$\therefore \frac{\pi}{2}(k + b) + \frac{(k - b)}{4c} = L - 2c$$

$$\frac{4c\pi}{2}(k + b) + (k - b) = 4c(L - 2c)$$

$$2c\pi(k + b) + (k - b) = 4cL - 8c^2$$

$$2c\pi k + 2c\pi b + k - b = 4cL - 8c^2$$

$$2c\pi k + k = 4cL - 8c^2 + b - 2c\pi b$$

$$k(2\pi c + 1) = 4cL - 8c^2 + b - 2c\pi b$$

$$\therefore k = \frac{4cL - 8c^2 + b - 2c\pi b}{2c\pi + 1} \quad \text{Ans. (c)}$$

75.

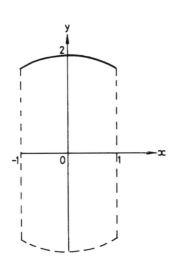

$$7x^2 - 28 + 7y^2 = 0$$
$$\therefore x^2 - 4 + y^2 = 0$$
$$\therefore y = \sqrt{4 - x^2} \quad \text{(see sketch)}$$

$$\text{Volume of revolution} = \pi \int_a^b y^2 dx$$

$$= \pi \int_{-1}^{+1} \left(\sqrt{4 - x^2}\right)^2 dx$$

$$= \pi \int_{-1}^{+1} (4 - x^2) dx$$

$$= \pi \left[4x - \frac{x^3}{3}\right]_{-1}^{+1}$$

$$= \pi[4 - \tfrac{1}{3}] - \pi[-4 + \tfrac{1}{3}]$$

$$= 4\pi - \frac{\pi}{3} + 4\pi - \frac{\pi}{3}$$

$$= 7\tfrac{1}{3}\pi$$

$$V = 23 \cdot 04 \text{ cm}^3 \quad \text{Ans.}$$

76. $$(1 + x)^n = 1 + nx + \frac{n(n-1)}{2 \times 1}x^2 + \frac{n(n-1)(n-2)}{3 \times 2 \times 1}x^3 \quad \text{approx.}$$

$$\frac{1}{\sqrt{1-x}} = (1 - x)^{-1/2}$$

$$= 1 + \frac{1}{2}x + \frac{(-\frac{1}{2})(-\frac{3}{2})}{2 \times 1}x^2 + \frac{(-\frac{1}{2})(-\frac{3}{2})(-\frac{5}{2})}{3 \times 2 \times 1}x^3 \quad \text{approx.}$$

$$= 1 + \frac{1}{2}x + \frac{1 \times 3}{2 \times 4}x^2 + \frac{1 \times 3 \times 5}{2 \times 4 \times 6}x^3 \quad \text{approx. Ans.}$$

$$(1 - 0 \cdot 1)^{-1/2} = 1 + 0 \cdot 05 + 0 \cdot 00375 + 0 \cdot 0003125$$

$$= 1 \cdot 0540625 \quad \text{Ans.}$$

77. $$C \propto V^3$$
$$C = kV^3$$

For the first 8 h,

$$C_1 = k(0 \cdot 8V)^3 \text{ per hour}$$

For the next 10 h,

$$C_2 = k(V)^3 \text{ per hour}$$

For the last 6 h, with a speed increase from V to xV:

$$C_3 = k(xV)^3 \text{ per hour}$$

For the 24 h,

$$8C_1 + 10C_2 + 6C_3 = 24C_2$$
$$8C_1 + 6C_3 = 14C_2$$
$$8k(0\cdot8V)^3 + 6k(xV)^3 = 14k(V)^3$$
$$4\cdot096 + 6x^3 = 14$$

$$x = \sqrt[3]{\frac{9.904}{6}}$$

$$x = 1\cdot182$$

% Increase in speed in the last 6 h is 18·2. Ans.

78. (a) $\dfrac{x^{n+4}\sqrt{x^{6n-7}}}{x^{3n}\sqrt{x^{2n-1}}}$ squaring gives :

$\dfrac{x^{2n+8}x^{6n-7}}{x^{6n}x^{2n-1}}$ simplifying gives;

$\dfrac{x^{8n+1}}{x^{8n-1}}$ simplifying gives

$x^{8n+1}x^{-8n+1}$ giving x^2 Ans. (a)

(b) $$10^x = 20^{x-4}$$

by taking logarithms then:

$$x \log 10 = (x-4)\log 20$$
$$x \lg 10 = (x-4)\lg 20 \quad \text{to base 10}$$
$$x \times 1\cdot000 = (x-4) \times 1\cdot3012$$
$$x = 1\cdot3012x - 5\cdot2048$$
$$x = 17\cdot29 \quad \text{Ans. (b)}$$

79. (a) (i) $\sqrt{64^{-1}a^8b^{12}}$

$$= \sqrt{\frac{a^8b^{12}}{64}}$$

$$= \frac{a^4b^6}{8} \quad \text{Ans. (a) (i)}$$

(a) (ii)
$$\sqrt[3]{216a^{-12}b^{0.6}}$$
$$= 6a^{-4}b^{0.2}$$
$$= \frac{6 \times \sqrt[5]{b}}{a^4} \quad \text{Ans. (a) (ii)}$$

(b)
$$a - b + c = 3 \qquad \ldots \quad \ldots \quad \ldots \quad \text{(i)}$$
$$2a + 8b - 3c = 56 \qquad \ldots \quad \ldots \quad \ldots \quad \text{(ii)}$$
$$7a + 3b + 3c = 69 \qquad \ldots \quad \ldots \quad \ldots \quad \text{(iii)}$$

add 3 times (i) to (ii) $5a + 5b = 65 \qquad \ldots \quad \ldots \quad$ (iv)

add (ii) to (iii) $9a + 11b = 125 \qquad \ldots \quad \ldots \quad$ (v)

9 times (iv) is $45a + 45b = 585$

5 times (v) is $\underline{45a + 55b = 625}$

$$\qquad\qquad\qquad 10b = 40 \quad \therefore b = 4$$

sub. in (i) times 2 $\quad 2a + 2c = 14$

sub. in (ii) $\quad \underline{2a - 3c = 24}$

$$\qquad\qquad 5c = -10 \quad \therefore c = -2$$

sub. for b and c in (i) $\qquad\qquad \therefore a = 9$

$$a = 9, b = 4, c = -2 \quad \text{Ans. (b)}$$

80. (a) As plotted. Ans. (a)

(b) (i) Graph 2.

$$\text{Slope, } a = \frac{4}{2} = 2$$

Intercept, $b = 0$

Equation $y = 2x$ Ans. (b) (i)

Graph 1.

$$\text{slope, } a = \frac{-4}{1.5} = -2.67$$

Intercept, $b = -4.65$

Equation $y = -2.67x - 4.65$ Ans. (b) (i)

(b) (ii) Solution of both as simultaneous equations i.e. intersection of graphs is

$$x = -1, y = -2 \quad \text{Ans. (b) (ii)}$$

81.

$$\text{Angle } D\hat{C}A = 35°$$

$$D\hat{A}C = 55° - 20° = 35°$$

∴ Triangle ADC is isosceles

$$CD = 50 \text{ m} = DA$$

$$A\hat{B}C = 40° - 20° = 20°$$

$$D\hat{C}B = 50°$$

$$\frac{50}{\sin A\hat{B}C} = \frac{DB}{\sin D\hat{C}B}$$

$$DB = \frac{50 \times 0·766}{0·342}$$

$$DB = 112 \text{ m}$$
$$AB = DB - DA$$
$$= 112 - 50$$

Distance AB is 62 m   Ans.

82. Let fuel consumption be F
Let fuel calorific value be C
Let ship speed in knots be S

$$F \propto \frac{S^3}{C}$$
$$F = \frac{kS^3}{C}$$
$$60 = \frac{k \times 20^3}{40}$$
$$k = 0\cdot3$$
$$F = \frac{0\cdot3 \times 16^3}{42}$$
$$= 29\cdot26$$

Daily fuel consumption is 29·26 t.   Ans.

83.

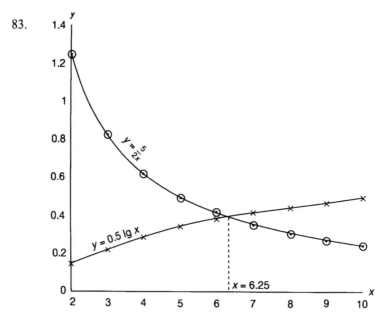

Let y_1 values be for $y = 0.5 \lg x$

Let y_2 values be for $y = \dfrac{5}{2x}$

x	2	3	4	5	6	7	8	9	10
y_1	·1505	·2386	·3011	·3495	·3891	·4226	·4516	·4771	0·5
y_2	1·25	·8333	·625	0·5	·4167	·3571	·3125	·2777	0·25

The two curves, as plotted, and they intersect at $x = 6.25$ which is the solution of the equation $0.5 \lg x = \dfrac{5}{2x}$ Ans.

84.

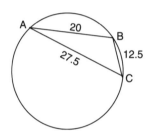

$$12 \cdot 5^2 = 27 \cdot 5^2 + 20^2 - 2 \times 27 \cdot 5 \times 20 \times \cos A$$
$$-1000 = -1100 \cos A$$
$$A = 24°37'$$
$$\frac{a}{\sin A} = D \text{ the diameter}$$
$$\frac{12 \cdot 5}{0 \cdot 4166} = D$$

Diameter is 30 cm.   Ans.

85.
$$\frac{CB}{\sin A} = \frac{AB}{\sin C}$$
$$\sin C = \frac{550 \times \sin 10°}{150} = 0 \cdot 637$$
$$\text{Angle } C = 39 \cdot 53° \text{ or } 140 \cdot 47°$$

(two positive values of sine in 360°)

$$\text{Angle B} = 130.47° \text{ or } 29.53°$$

$$\frac{AC}{\sin 130.47°} = \frac{CB}{\sin 10°}$$

$$AC = \frac{150 \times \sin 130.47°}{\sin 10°}$$

$$= \frac{150 \times 0.7608}{0.1737}$$

$$AC = 657 \text{ mm}$$

$$\frac{A'C}{\sin 29.53°} = \frac{150}{\sin 10°}$$

$$A'C = \frac{150 \times 0.4929}{0.1737}$$

$$A'C = 425.6 \text{ mm}$$

Piston Travel is A to A′

Piston Travel is AC − A′C

Piston Travel is 657 − 425.6

Piston Travel is 231.4 mm   Ans.

86. (a) (i) $y = \dfrac{x^3}{4} - \dfrac{x^2}{2}$

$\dfrac{dy}{dx} - \dfrac{3x^2}{4} - \dfrac{2x}{2}$ is the gradient

$0 = \dfrac{3x^2}{4} - \dfrac{2x}{2}$ so $x = 0, y = 0$

or $0 = 3x - 4$ so $x = \dfrac{4}{3}, y = -\dfrac{8}{27}$ } Ans. (a) (i)

(a) (ii) $\dfrac{d^2y}{dx^2} = \dfrac{3}{2}x - 1$

when $x = 0$ $\dfrac{d^2y}{dx^2} = -1$ i.e. maximum

when $x = \dfrac{4}{3}$ $\dfrac{d^2y}{dx^2} = +1$ i.e. minimum

Curve is minimum at $x = \frac{4}{3}, y = -\frac{8}{27}$ Ans. (a) (ii)

(b)
$$y = 4\cos x - 3\sin x$$
$$\frac{dy}{dx} = -4\sin x - 3\cos x$$
$$\frac{d^2y}{dx^2} = -4\cos x + 3\sin x \quad \text{Ans. (b)}$$

87. (a)
$$\text{Area} = \int y \, dx$$
$$= \int_{\frac{\pi}{9}}^{\frac{\pi}{2}} 4\cos x \, dx$$
$$= 4[\sin x]_{\frac{\pi}{9}}^{\frac{\pi}{2}}$$
$$= 4(1 - 0.342)$$
$$\text{Area} = 2.632 \text{ units}^2 \quad \text{Ans. (a)}$$

(b)
$$\frac{dy}{dx} = 2x^2 - 2$$
$$y = \int 2x^2 - 2 \, dx$$
$$= \frac{2x^3}{3} - 2x + C$$
$$\text{when } x = 3 \qquad y = -2$$
$$-2 = 18 - 6 + C$$
$$C = -14$$

Equation is:
$$y = \frac{2x^3}{3} - 2x - 14 \quad \text{Ans. (b)}$$

88. (a) Let h be height of small cone
$$\frac{h}{10} = \frac{h + 16}{20} \quad \text{by similar figures}$$
$$h = 16 \text{ cm}$$

Volume of large cone
$$= \tfrac{1}{3}\pi(20^2 \times 32)$$
$$= \frac{\pi}{3} \times 12800$$

Volume of small cone

$$= \tfrac{1}{3}\pi(10^2 \times 16)$$
$$= \frac{\pi}{3} \times 1600$$

Mass of frustum

$$= \frac{\pi}{3}(12800 - 1600) \times 0.9$$
$$= 10560 \text{ g}$$
$$= 10.56 \text{ kg} \quad \text{Ans. (a)}$$

(b) Ratio mass of frustum to mass of small cone (as removed)

$$= (12800 - 1600) \text{ to } 1600$$

Ratio is 112 : 16
Ratio is 1 : $\tfrac{1}{7}$ Ans. (b)

89.

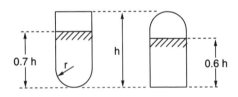

$$100 = \pi r^2(0{\cdot}7h - r) + \tfrac{2}{3}\pi r^3 \qquad \dots \quad \dots \quad \dots \quad \text{(i)}$$
$$100 = \pi r^2(0{\cdot}6h) \qquad\qquad\qquad \dots \quad \dots \quad \dots \quad \text{(ii)}$$

Equating (i) and (ii) and simplifying:

$$0{\cdot}6h = 0{\cdot}7h - r + \tfrac{2}{3}r$$
$$h = \tfrac{10}{3}r$$

Substitute into (ii)

$$100 = \pi r^2(2r)$$
$$r = \sqrt[3]{\frac{100}{6{\cdot}284}} = 2{\cdot}512$$

Bore $= 5{\cdot}024$ cm   Ans. (a)

Overall height $= \dfrac{10}{3} \times 2{\cdot}512 = 8{\cdot}37$ cm   Ans. (b)

90.
$$y = x^2 + \frac{5}{2}$$
$$y^2 = x^4 + 5x^2 + \frac{25}{4}$$

Volume of solid of revolution so:

$$V = \pi \int_0^3 x^4 + 5x^2 + \frac{25}{4} \, dx$$

$$= \pi \left[\frac{x^5}{5} + \frac{5x^3}{3} + \frac{25x}{4} \right]_0^3$$

$$= \pi \left[\frac{243}{5} + \frac{135}{3} + \frac{75}{4} \right]$$

$$= \pi \times 112 \cdot 35$$

$$V = 353 \text{ units}^3 \quad \text{Ans.}$$

INDEX

A

Algebra			23
Angles, acute			109
„ double			161
„ complementary ...			114
„ compound			159
„ obtuse			109
„ over 90°			120
„ reflex			109
„ right		109, 112
„ supplementary ...			115
Area, annulus			171
„ circle			170
„ circular ring surface ...			179
„ cone surface			177
„ cylinder surface... ...			175
„ ellipse			175
„ frustum surface			178
„ hexagon			169
„ octagon			169
„ parallelogram			165
„ polygon			167
„ rhombus			166
„ ring surface			179
„ sector			172
„ segment		173, 176
„ sphere surface			176
„ trapezium			166
„ triangle		154, 167
Areas, by integration			258
„ by Simpson's rule ...			182
„ surface			176
Averages			15

B

Binomial			23
Binomial theorem			41
Brackets			31

C

Calculator		17, 19
Centre of gravity (mass) ...		202, 215
Centroid			203
Characteristic			17
Chords		131, 170
Circle			170
„ circumscribed		136, 156
„ inscribed		137, 158
Circular measure		109, 170
Circumference			170
Common logarithms			18
Compass bearings			128
Complementary angles ...			114
Compound angles			159

Cone, surface area			177
„ volume		194, 206
Congruent triangles			139
Constant of integration ...		253, 256
Constituent parts			13
Construction of triangles			129
Cosecant...			113
Cosine		112, 143
„ rule			150
Cotangent			113
Crossed chords			131
Cubic equations		69, 81
Curve sketching			104
Cyclic quadrilaterals			134
Cyclic triangles			134
Cylinder, surface area			175

D

Degree			109
Density			191
Differential calculus...			227
Differentiation, first principles ...			231
„ by general rule ...			235
„ of sin x, cos x ...			246
„ of ln x and e^x ...			248
„ distance, velocity, acceleration ...			238
Division, algebraic			26
„ by logs			17
„ of powers			1
Double angles...			161

E

Ellipse			175
Equations, logarithmic			55
„ quadratic		69, 95
„ reducible to quadratios			74
„ simple			45
„ simultaneous linear		59, 94
„ simultaneous quadratic		76, 95
Equilateral triangle			156
Evaluation		36, 51
Examination questions, selection			401
„ „ solution			419

F

Factorisation			32
Factor theorem			38
First moments		215, 217
Flow of liquid			213
Force			202
Formulae, selection			273
„ tranposition			51
Fractions...			35

Frustum, surface area 178
„ volume 194, 207
Function 38
Functional notation 249

G
Geometry 130
Geometrical construction of triangles 129
Geometrical facts 130
Gradient 227
Gramme (Gram) 191
Graphs 87
„ sin, cos, tan 124
Gravitational acceleration 202
Gravity, centre of 202, 215
Greenwich mean time 127
Guldinus, theorem of 176, 201

H
Hemisphere 206
Hexagon 168, 169
Hyperbolic logarithms 19

I
Identities 118
Indicator card 186
Indices 1
Inscribed circle 137, 158
Integral calculus... 253
Integration, general rule 254
„ definite integral ... 258
„ sin x, cos x 257
„ of $\frac{1}{x}$ and e^x 257
„ distance and velocity 267
International knot 128
Inverse proportion 7
Irregular figures 182
„ objects... 210
Isosceles triangle 156

K
Kilogramme (Kilogram) 191
Knot 128

L
Latitude 126
Laws, determination of 103
Lifebuoy 180, 202
Lift of valve 214
Litre 191
Logarithmic equations 55
Logarithms, common 18
„ Naperian 19
„ Natural 19
„ to different bases ... 18
Longitude 126
Lowest common multiple 35

M
Mantissa 17

Mass 191
„ flow 213
Maxima and minima 241
Measurement of angles 109
Megagramme (Megagram) ... 191
Mensuration of areas 165
„ of volumes 191
Meridians 127
Method of unity 8
Mid-ordinate rule 185
Millilitre... 191
Minus number 18
Moments 215, 217
Multiplication algebraic 26
„ by logs 17
„ of powers 1

N
Naperian logarithms 19
Natural logarithms 19
Nautical mile 128
Negative indices 2
Newton 202
None right angled triangles ... 146

O
Obtuse angle 109
Octagon 168, 169

P
Pappus, theorem 176, 201
Parallelogram 165, 203
Percentage 11
Polygons 167
Polynomial 38
Powers 1, 4, 17, 25
Prisms 191
Problems involving equations-simple 48
„ „ „ -quadratic 79
Proportion, direct 6
„ inverse 7
Pyramids 193, 204
Pythagoras, theorem 115

Q
Quadratic equations... ... 69, 95

R
Radian 108
Ratios 5
„ trigonometric 112, 143
Reflex angle 109
Relative density 191
Remainder theorem 38
Rhombus 166
Right angle 109
„ „ triangles 143
Ring, surface area 179
Roots 3, 4, 17, 25

S

Secant	113
Second differential coefficient	238
Second moments	217
Sector	170, 172
Segment	170, 173, 197
Semi-circular area, centroid ...	205
Shift of centre of gravity ...	221
Similar figures	181
,, solids	208
,, triangles	137
Simple equations	45
Simpson's rule	182, 210
Simultaneous linear equations	59, 94
Simultaneous quadratic equations	76, 95
Sine	112, 143
,, rule	148
Sketching of curves	104
Specific gravity	191
Sphere, surface area	176
Sphere, volume	196
Spherical segment	197
Supplementary angles	115
Surds	4

T

Tables, trigonometric	120
Tangent	112
Tonne	191
Transposition of formulae ...	51
Trapezium	166, 203
Triangles, area	154, 167
,, centroid	204
,, congruent	139
,, construction ...	129
,, cyclic	134
,, equilateral	156

,, isosceles	156
,, right angled	143
,, similar	137
,, solution of	143
Trigonometric ratios	112, 120
,, tables	120
Trinomial	23

U

Unity, method of	8
Unity, power of	2

V

Variation	9
Volume flow	213
Volume, cone	194, 206
,, frustums	194, 207
,, lifebuoy	202
,, prisms	192
,, pyramid	193
,, ring	201
,, similar solids	208
,, similar sphere	208
,, sphere	196
,, spherical segment ...	197
Volumes	191
,, by Simpson's rule	210
,, by integration	263
,, of solids of revolution ...	263

W

Weight	202

Z

Zero gradient	230
Zero power	2

REED'S MARINE ENGINEERING SERIES

Vol 1 Mathematics
Vol 2 Applied Mechanics
Vol 3 Applied Heat
Vol 4 Naval Architecture
Vol 5 Ship Construction
Vol 6 Basic Electrotechnology
Vol 7 Advanced Electrotechnology
Vol 8 General Engineering Knowledge
Vol 9 Steam Engineering Knowledge
Vol 10 Instrumentation and Control Systems
Vol 11 Engineering Drawing
Vol 12 Motor Engineering Knowledge

Reed's Engineering Knowledge for Deck Officers
Reed's Maths Tables and Engineering Formulae
Reed's Marine Distance Tables
Reed's Sextant Simplified
Reed's Skippers Handbook
Reed's Maritime Meteorology
Sea Transport – Operation and Economics

These books are obtainable from all good nautical
booksellers or direct from:

**Adlard Coles Nautical
A & C Black
P O Box 19
St Neots
Cambs PE19 8SF**

**Tel: 01480 212666
Fax: 01480 405014**

Email: sales@acblack.com